Practical IoT Edge Computing with Python

Develop End-to-End IoT Solutions with Python, Edge Computing, and Containerization for Fast and Reliable Decision-Making

Dr. Rajasi Tushar Athawale

www.orangeava.com

First Published: September 2025

Published By: Orange Education Pvt Ltd, AVA®

Address: 9, Daryaganj, Delhi, 110002, India

275 New North Road Islington Suite 1314 London,
N1 7AA, United Kingdom

ISBN (PBK): 978-93-49888-96-8
ISBN (E-BOOK): 978-93-49888-25-8

Scan the QR code to explore our entire catalogue

www.orangeava.com

Dedicated To

My Husband,

Dr. Tushar Athawale

And

Our Lovely Daughter,

Hridya Tushar Athawale.

About the Author

Dr. Rajasi Tushar Athawale is a voluntary research associate in Mobile Sensing and Intelligence Security (MoSIS Lab), University of Tennessee, Knoxville, USA, working under Dr. Jian Liu. She also conducts independent research on IoT systems integrating ML/AI and edge computing. Her current research focuses on wearable and contactless gait analysis using multi-task transformer architectures to predict running gait parameters from low-cost IMU data. These models are optimized for real-time deployment on edge devices such as Raspberry Pi 4 and Jetson Nano.

Rajasi completed her Ph.D. in Computer Science and Engineering from Motilal Nehru National Institute of Technology (MNNIT) Allahabad in 2024. Her doctoral dissertation, "*Design and Implementation of Edge-based Framework for Smart Monitoring of Public Restrooms in Developing Countries*," presents a Python-based system that adaptively fuses heterogeneous data and user feedback while handling network constraints and power outages. The framework was deployed on Raspberry Pi-based setups and tested using real-world sensor data.

She holds a Master's degree in Advance Networks from ABV-IIITM Gwalior, where her thesis involved designing a MATLAB-based path re-planning algorithm for Autonomous Underwater Vehicles (AUVs), improving navigation by accounting for environmental drift and obstacle avoidance.

Rajasi's technical skillset spans Python, C, C++, TensorFlow, PyTorch, Docker, Kubernetes, Apache Spark, and MATLAB. She is also proficient with networking protocols such as MQTT, CoAP, and HTTP, and has hands-on experience with embedded platforms such as Raspberry Pi, Arduino Uno, and Jetson Nano.

She has co-authored peer-reviewed publications in intelligent systems for public health and continues to contribute to interdisciplinary solutions combining AI, IoT, and sustainable technology.

Her research interests include edge AI, embedded systems, IoT, and smart infrastructure.

About the Technical Reviewers

Dhiraj Singh Rathod is a seasoned technology leader with over 12 years of experience in designing and developing IoT and IIoT enterprise solutions, with expertise in both on-premises and cloud platforms like AWS and Microsoft Azure. His career spans various industries, including steel, power, and manufacturing, where he has delivered robust systems for applications such as smart milking and water management.

Currently serving as a Project Lead at IntraEdge, he focuses on creating scalable, secure, and reliable IoT platforms for Fluidra's connected robotic systems. Dhiraj is passionate about connected product ecosystems and is committed to driving innovation at the intersection of IoT, AI, and industrial digitalization.

Shashank is a seasoned IIoT Engineer with over 8 years of comprehensive experience in industrial automation, IoT system design, and edge computing implementations. Currently serving as Deputy Manager - Research & Development, he brings a unique blend of theoretical knowledge and practical expertise to the field of Industrial Internet of Things (IIoT) and edge computing.

With a Bachelor of Engineering in Electrical and Electronics, Shashank is an expert in the IoT ecosystem, from hardware and firmware to data analytics and machine learning. He is proficient in Python and has hands-on experience with AI algorithms and ML models for industrial asset monitoring. His skills include using industrial communication protocols like OPC-UA/DA and MQTT, along with tools like Docker and AWS IoT services. His portfolio includes successful work in anomaly detection and engine sound classification.

As a technical reviewer for "*Practical IoT Edge Computing with Python*," his extensive experience ensures the book is technically accurate and grounded in real-world applications.

Acknowledgments

I would like to express my sincere gratitude to everyone who supported and contributed to the successful completion and publication of this work. With the blessings of God, my parents and Tushar's parents, this book has finally come to fruition.

First and foremost, I extend my heartfelt thanks to my husband Tushar, whose encouragement, and support were invaluable throughout the writing of this book. Next, I would like to thank my daughter, Hridya, who motivated me every day to keep going in this book writing process.

I would also like to thank Dr. Jian Liu from the University of Tennessee, Knoxville, for the opportunity to work on his research projects. Through this experience, I gained valuable insights into smart IoT technologies, edge computing, AI models and embedded devices.

I also wish to thank my advisors from MNNIT, Allahabad and ABV IIITM, Gwalior, for introducing me to the field of IoT, encouraging my curiosity, and helping me overcome numerous challenges along the way. My heartfelt thanks go to my colleagues and friends for their valuable suggestions and constant motivation, especially during difficult times.

Finally, I extend my sincere thanks to the team at Orange Education Pvt Ltd for their dedicated efforts in reviewing and editing my work . Their constant support and belief in my capabilities played a vital role in shaping this book into what it is today.

Preface

The rapid evolution of connected devices, real-time analytics, and decentralized computing has brought edge computing to the forefront of modern technological innovation. This book is an effort to bridge foundational concepts with practical implementations in the realm of edge-cloud systems, IoT applications, and data-driven intelligence.

The journey begins with a clear distinction between edge and cloud computing, establishing the foundational differences and complementarity between the two in Chapter 1. Chapter 2 mainly focuses on cloud computing, its architecture and services, and it also provides a walkthrough over IoT application use-cases that utilizes popular cloud platforms such as Amazon, AWS and Microsoft Azure. At the end, certain disadvantages of the cloud are also presented followed by the comparison of cloud vs edge. In Chapter 3, details on IoT data and its characteristics are elaborately discussed, along with how it is analyzed by IoT applications. Further, Chapter 3 discusses data storage models, and how data interoperability is provided, and data quality is maintained, while analyzing the data.

Chapter 4 describes the general architecture that utilizes edge computing and cloud computing in an IoT application as well as provides information on different types of edge computing architectures being widely used in detail. In Chapter 5, open-source edge platforms are listed, and popular edge devices used in smart applications are studied. Further, Chapter 5 highlights deployment of computation on mobile edge devices, embedded devices, and smartwatch, being used as an edge device. In Chapter 6, application layer protocols are discussed in detail that are widely used such as CoAP, MQTT and AMQP with their implementations. Later, popular networking technologies being used in edge computing are discussed such as SDN, ICN and CDN.

A significant portion of this book is dedicated to preparing edge devices for real-time computation, networking, and sensor data handling. Chapter 7 discusses pre-processing steps that are performed on edge devices in an edge-cloud architecture. Chapter 8 implements models in python used for information fusion to provide edge intelligence, like ML/DL, and Evidence-based, fuzzy logic. Python implementation of deep learning models, using tensor lite, and advantages of tensor lite are also included in this chapter. Further, Chapter 9 presents processing frameworks that handle data streams, and provide implementations of some popular processing frameworks that are being widely used on edge devices for data stream preprocessing, storage and analysis.

In the concluding Chapters 10, 11, and 12, the focus is shifts to the crucial aspect of security—highlighting how blockchain can be integrated into edge environments—and discuss the future trends that are shaping the edge computing landscape.

Thus, whether you are a student, researcher, or practitioner, this book aims to serve as a comprehensive guide, offering a balance of theory, practical insights, and real-world applications.

Get a Free eBook

We hope you are enjoying your recently purchased book! Your feedback is incredibly valuable to us, and to all other readers looking for great books.

If you found this book helpful or enjoyable, we would truly appreciate it, if you could take a moment to leave a short review with a 5 star rating on Amazon. It helps us grow, and lets other readers discover our books.

As a thank you, we would love to send you a free digital copy of this book, and a **30%** discount code on your next cart value on our official websites:

www.orangeava.com

www.orangeava.in (For Indian Subcontinent)

☑ **Here's how:**

Leave a review for the book on Amazon.

Take a screenshot of your review, and send an email to **info@orangeava.com** (it can be just the confirmation screen).

Once, we receive your screenshot, we will send you the digital file, within 24 hours.

Thank you so much for your support – it means a lot to us!

Downloading the code bundles and colored images

Please follow the links or scan the QR codes to download the **_Code Bundles and Images_** of the book:

https://github.com/ava-orange-education/Practical-IoT-Edge-Computing-with-Python

The code bundles and images of the book are also hosted on **_https://rebrand.ly/b142d8_**

In case there's an update to the code, it will be updated on the existing GitHub repository.

Errata

We take immense pride in our work at **Orange Education Pvt Ltd,** and follow best practices to ensure the accuracy of our content to provide an indulging reading experience to our subscribers. Our readers are our mirrors, and we use their inputs to reflect and improve upon human errors, if any, that may have occurred during the publishing processes involved. To let us maintain the quality and help us reach out to any readers who might be having difficulties due to any unforeseen errors, please write to us at :

errata@orangeava.com

Your support, suggestions, and feedback are highly appreciated.

DID YOU KNOW

Did you know that Orange Education Pvt Ltd offers eBook versions of every book published, with PDF and ePub files available? You can upgrade to the eBook version at **www.orangeava.com** and as a print book customer, you are entitled to a discount on the eBook copy. Get in touch with us at: **info@orangeava.com** for more details.

At **www.orangeava.com**, you can also read a collection of free technical articles, sign up for a range of free newsletters, and receive exclusive discounts and offers on Print Books and eBooks.

PIRACY

If you come across any illegal copies of our works in any form on the internet, we would be grateful if you would provide us with the location address or website name. Please contact us at **info@orangeava.com** with a link to the material.

ARE YOU INTERESTED IN AUTHORING WITH US?

If there is a topic that you have expertise in, and you are interested in either writing or contributing to a book, please write to us at **business@orangeava.com**. We are on a journey to help developers and tech professionals to gain insights on the present technological advancements and innovations happening across the globe and build a community that believes Knowledge is best acquired by sharing and learning with others. Please reach out to us to learn what our audience demands and how you can be part of this educational reform. We also welcome ideas from tech experts and help them build learning and development content for their domains.

REVIEWS

Please leave a review. Once you have read and used this book, why not leave a review on the site that you purchased it from? Potential readers can then see and use your unbiased opinion to make purchase decisions. We at Orange Education would love to know what you think about our products, and our authors can learn from your feedback. Thank you!

For more information about Orange Education, please visit **www.orangeava.com**.

Table of Contents

Chapter 1
Introduction to IoT and Edge

Introduction

The Internet of Things (IoT) has changed the mindset of people, and it is impacting daily lives positively. Earlier, the internet was connecting all digital devices such as laptops, mobile phones, and each had an IP address to exchange data via the internet. With IoT, the internet is able to connect all the things (living/non-living), we can think of around us. Further, with the concept of ubiquitous computing, an IoT can connect any two objects from anywhere in the world, and also make them smart. An object/thing is smart if it has the intelligence to make decisions autonomously. The computations to be performed for thinking intelligently are mostly done in the cloud. However, with multiple IoT devices, the internet is overburdened with lots of data. To reduce data over network, edge computing is a new field that supports Cloud computations.

In this chapter, we will discuss what is IoT, and how ubiquitous computing impacts IoT. Further, we will discuss some IoT applications that are popular in today's world. Discussions on these applications will confirm how important is IoT in our daily lives, and what is its future scope. Next, we will briefly discuss each of the components of IoT applications. Later, we will discuss the communication and computation models used in IoT. One of the computation models is edge computing (the main focus of this book), and we will see its advantages and disadvantages in the IoT technology.

Structure

In this chapter, we will cover the following topics:

- IoT and Ubiquitous Computing
- IoT Components
- Communication Models
- Computing Models

- Edge Computing Benefits
- Challenges in Edge Computing

IoT and Ubiquitous Computing

The term, 'Internet of Things' was coined in 1999 by the computer scientist, Kevin Ashton. The Internet of Things (IoT) technology refers to a network of physical objects, or "things". **Things** are embedded with software, sensors, and connectivity, enabling them to collect and exchange data, facilitating communication and automation. Applications based on the Internet of Things (IoT) are able to provide smart service with the concept of **ubiquitous computing**.

Ubiquitous computing is a type of computing which combines **hardware engineering, software engineering, and networking** to provide smartness to devices anywhere around the globe. Hardware engineering is required to understand how things have to work. The things either sense or perform actions. Software engineering is used to write applications that provide smart solutions. The networking concept is used to connect things and applications by routing data between them. A device is smart if it possesses the ability to learn, adapt, and make decisions based on data, enabling intelligent and responsive interactions. However, ubiquitous computing is only possible, if the devices are connected with each other around the globe, and thus, IoT is a key enabler of ubiquitous computing. *Figure* 1.1 shows the power of ubiquitous computing and IoT.

Figure 1.1: *Ubiquitous Computing with Internet of Things*

The smart things can be anywhere (ubiquitous) in the world, and they communicate with each other through the IoT application to provide smart services to the user. Thus, capabilities of IoT are not limited to geographical boundaries, when combined with ubiquitous computing. IoT technology is being widely used in some popular applications such as smart home, smart healthcare, smart agriculture, smart transport, smart grid and smart cities. Each of these popular applications are discussed in the next subsection to have a clear picture of IoT.

IoT Use-Case Applications for Smart Living

Smart Home

A home consists of different rooms like living rooms, bedrooms and bathrooms with specific appliances such as lights/fans/microwave/trash bins/cabinets/showers, and so on. These appliances can be made smart using IoT technology. The appliances are attached with **embedded devices** so that they can connect to the home network. An embedded device is a special device that is designed to perform a specific task. The appliances with embedded devices are called things. These things coordinate with each other using a hub. A hub is a place that enables data exchange between things. These hubs are known as smart home central hubs, and some popular central hubs are Amazon Echo and Google Home. Further, these appliances can be remotely controlled by the owner with his smartphone. Collectively, with smart things and hubs, the home is called a smart home. *Figure 1.2* illustrates smart home application.

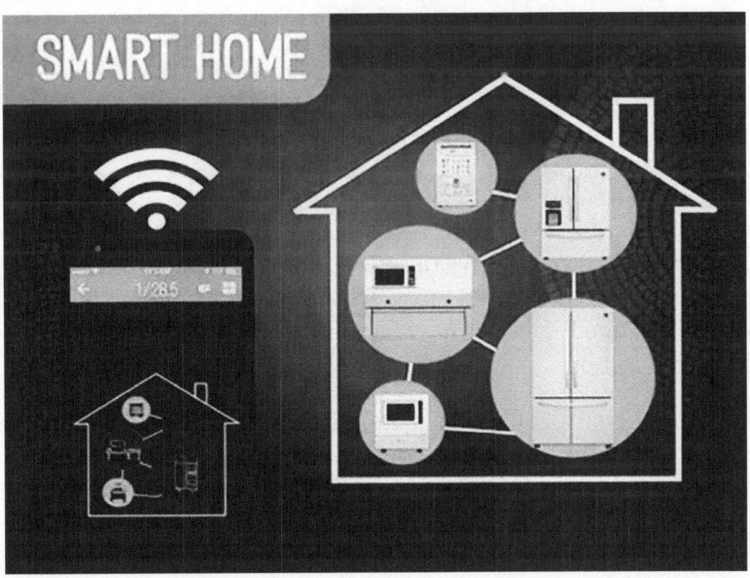

Figure 1.2: *Smart Home Appliances Monitored via Smartphone Using IoT Technology*

Multiple applications connected on a common smart home Wi-Fi network may provide different smart services. Some smart home applications are smart refrigerator, security, automatic ambience adjustment and smart thermostat. Smart refrigerator detects the items, quantifies them, and if any item is missing, it tells the owner via notifications on smartphones. Smart thermostat adjusts its temperature according to the outside weather, and as per the owner's need.

Smart Healthcare

Before IoT, the patients used to take appointments at the hospital, and arrange an ambulance during an emergency. However, long waiting time to have appointments and delayed ambulance service was a common problem. With smart healthcare, the patients are remotely monitored by the doctors. The patients have wearable devices attached to their bodies that continuously monitor their health. The data is communicated to the doctor via internet for keeping a continuous check.

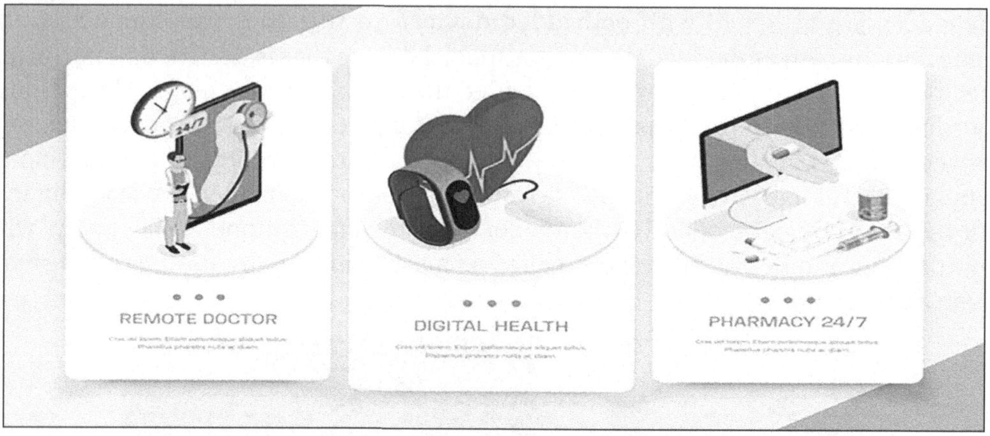

Figure 1.3: *Smart Healthcare Applications*

In case of emergency situations, the wearable device itself contacts the ambulance, and the nearby hospital for fast care. Wearable devices are also made intelligent, and they can detect emergency health concerns, provide diet and health tips, and can also prescribe medicines just as a doctor. *Figure* 1.3 shows how smart healthcare IoT applications have changed lives with everything online. Recently, a patient's life was saved with an Apple watch.

We will study one scenario of a smart healthcare system. Assume, there is an old patient staying all alone in the house, and he falls. With no IoT, there is no way the hospitals can get to know that some accident has happened, unless the patient himself can make a call. For old people, fall injuries are life-threatening, and getting up after a fall is a huge problem. With smart healthcare, the old person has a smart watch that detects fall, and contacts the nearby hospital and ambulance, without delay. The Smart Healthcare Application Model for supporting old people is shown in *Figure* 1.4.

Thus, with smart healthcare, the patients are being cared for, visited, and treated remotely as well as it provides fast response during emergency situations.

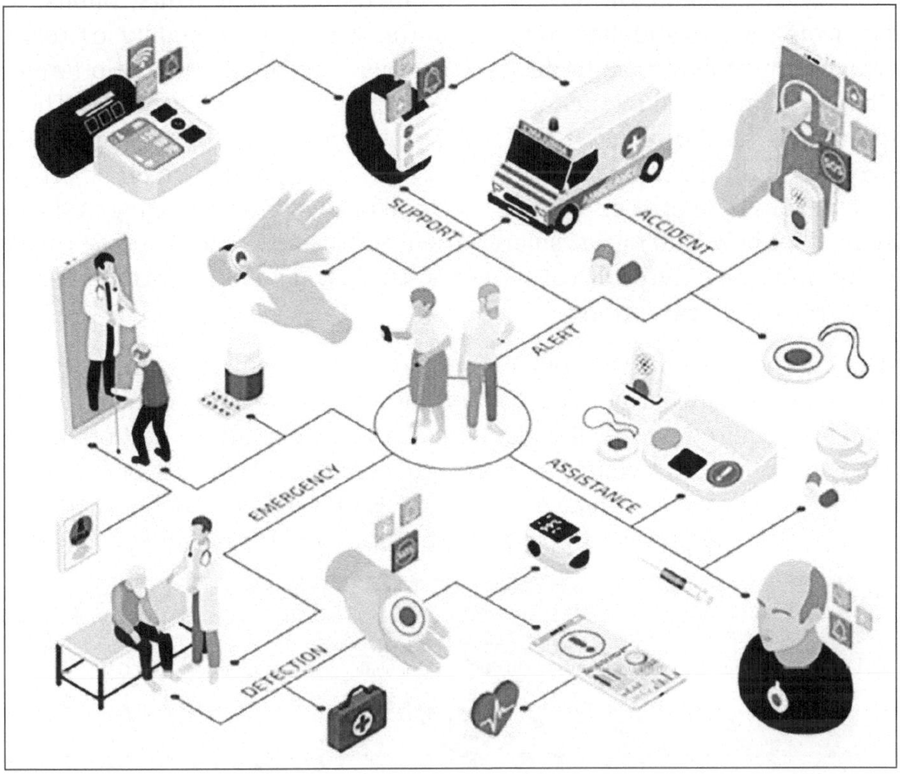

Figure 1.4: *Support for Elderly with IoT*

Smart Agriculture

The food we eat comes from the agriculture sector that has huge farming lands, a variety of vegetation and machines to sow, water and plough. To reduce the workload of the farmers, as well as to have proper food production, the farming is made smart with the help of IoT technology. Smart agriculture connects plants, soil, irrigation systems, farmers on a network, and all of these are known as things of IoT. Sensors are embedded to plants, soil, drones and water sprinklers to detect the health status of a plant, soil, and the water level. There are different sensors available in the market for detecting any specific conditions. For understanding this in a better way, we will see a small-scale example. An IoT application that can be used to monitor home grown plants is "Flora Pod". Flora Pod has specific sensors for monitoring essential environmental factors such as soil moisture (moisture sensor), temperature (temperature sensor), light intensity (light sensor), and nutrient levels (nutrient sensor). A soil moisture sensor is put into the soil to test how much water the soil has to identify, and when to water the plants again. A nutrient sensor works by detecting and measuring the concentration of specific nutrients in a sample, using specialized techniques.

Flora Pod also provides insights to gardeners through a smartphone. Flora pod is a small scale IoT application, and we can relatively think about how complex an IoT application will be to monitor huge fields having thousands of plants. Similar to Flora Pod, data from sensors attached to things of the farms is collected by IoT technology to autonomously monitor the farms, take actions accordingly, and help farmers. All these things are managed by the farmer with the help of his smartphone. The farmer gets the details on the plant's health, soil status, watering timing and the overall farm's condition on his smartphone. Further, the smartphone is made intelligent, to notify techniques to improvise farming and food production, according to the current conditions. Not only land farms, smart agriculture also provides support to livestock farming by monitoring the health of animals, using IoT. *Figure 1.5* illustrates the services of smart agriculture applications.

Precision farming is one of the popular technologies in the smart agriculture system. In this type of farming, the farmer gets to know how much watering of plants, fertilizers, and so on are required by specific plants in a specific climatic condition. In fact, the main motive of precision farming is to provide intelligent utilization of resources over huge farms, saving cost and wastage. Thus, Precision Farming is being used in climate monitoring, cattle monitoring, soil monitoring, crop monitoring and green houses.

Figure 1.5: *Smart Agriculture Applications*

Smart Transport

IoT has aided in efficient management of traffic on road, and in the parking areas with smart transportation systems. The system controls the speed of vehicles as per the traffic, and keeps safe distance to avoid accidents. A smart vehicle automatically notifies the police in case of accidents. Further, the system quickly adjusts the route to the destination as per the current road and weather conditions. The system also helps in controlling pollution by keeping a check on fuel emissions. *Figure* 1.6 shows the application model for smart transportation.

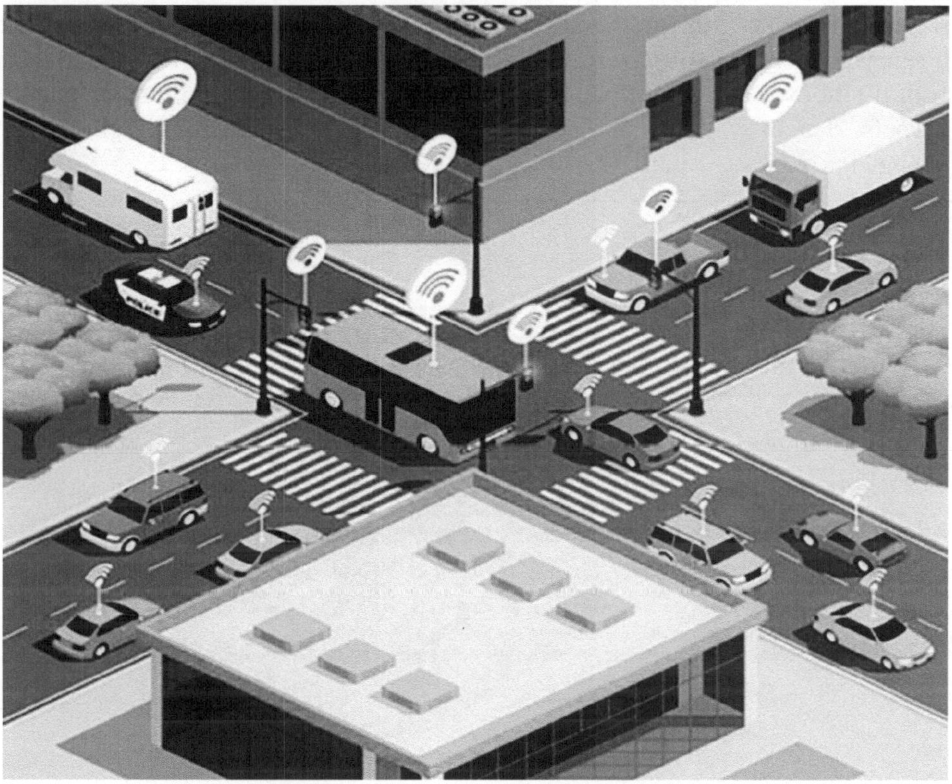

Figure 1.6: *Smart Transport Applications*

Smart parking is one of the IoT applications that has sensors on each parking lot, and users can detect if any lot in a parking space is free, instantly. This application saves a lot of time for the driver in search of parking, and also helps greatly during emergency situations, especially around hospitals.

Another application is smart traffic lights where the lights are made intelligent to sense the number of vehicles at the cross section, and accordingly, manage the timing of the signals. Further, they are able to detect speeding vehicles, and inform the police.

The goals of the smart transportation system are to reduce time to reach destination, reduce time to park, avoid collisions, avoid road congestion, regulate traffic, and provide first aid during emergencies.

Smart Grid

As the population is increasing and digital devices are also increasing, electricity is being consumed more. Smart grid is a solution to provide electricity to consumers in an efficient way, while having minimal resource utilization and a green environment. The idea behind smart grid is to share energy with interconnected grid systems, rather than having specific grid for specific location. The electric grids are also combined with renewable energy sources to produce more electricity as per the demand. Even each of the houses can participate in generating electricity through solar panels on their roofs. The distribution of electricity in smart grid applications is shown in the following *Figure* 1.7.

Figure 1.7: *Smart Grid Application*

All these electric suppliers are controlled and monitored with the help of IoT, and the power is efficiently distributed to consumers as per the demand. Smart grid helps in blackouts by providing saved energy from other locations to the affected location. Even a smart grid can prevent blackouts with the help of a smart meter that captures real-time demand, and provides more electricity, either within the location's grid or outsourcing. Further with smart meters, consumers pay for what they get, rather than having a fixed bill. Hence, in the near future, power will be distributed wirelessly, replacing long cable constructions for routing.

Smart City

A city with automation of various tasks for sustainable and better living is a smart city. Automation is possible with the help of IoT. Everything in the city is connected to the internet, and operates intelligently without manual interventions. Smart homes, smart transportation, and smart grid, together contribute to a smart city. A wide area network connects all the smart applications contributing to a smart city. *Figure* 1.8 shows how different IoT applications get combined to create a smart city application.

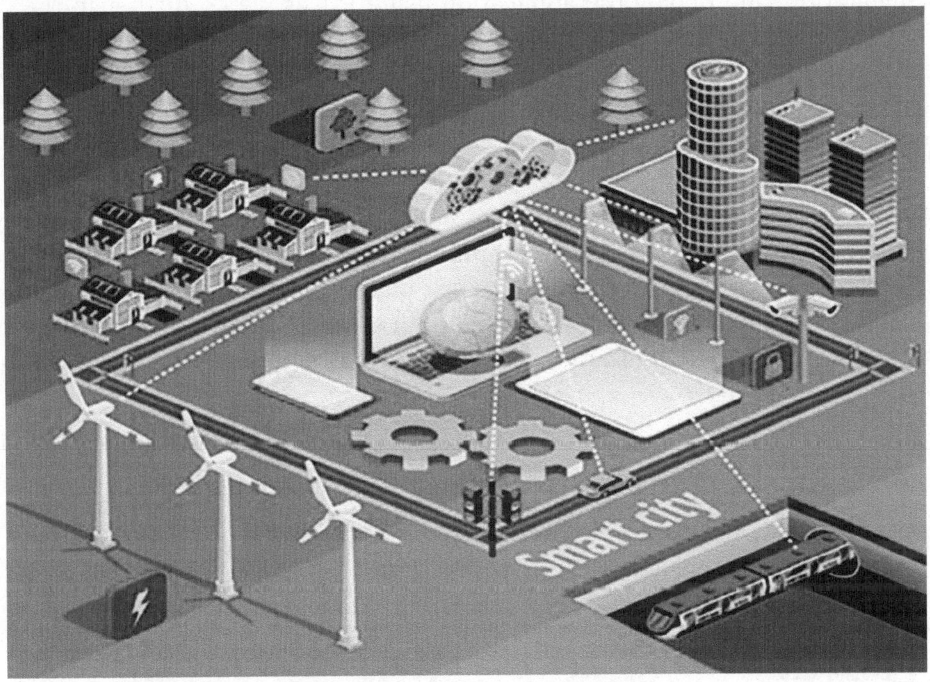

Figure 1.8: *Smart City Application*

One scenario of a smart city is explained as follows. Suppose a person is living in a smart city. In the morning, his smart fridge tells that the milk is over through notification on smartphone. On a smartphone, he is given a choice of whether to go out and buy, or have a home-delivery. The smartphone app can provide suggestions as per the person's schedule or weather conditions. In case of home delivery, the phone application will contact the nearest store that is open, guaranteeing that the store definitely has milk. For finding which store has what products currently available, each of the items in the store will have sensors on each of the items, for easy tracking. In case of buying, the car will automatically set the route of the nearest milk store with milk availability. Thus, the car knows that the milk is over, and the person needs one. Further, the car checks the fuel, and accordingly, directs to the petrol pump or the store. If fuel is required, the map directs to the petrol pump that has space as well as lowest price, and shows the nearest parking to the store. Thus, the fridge, vehicle, maps, store items, parking spaces, petrol pumps, all are made smart using IoT, so that the person buys milk in the morning in an efficient way.

Thus, we discussed the fundamental IoT applications in detail, but more IoT applications are being proposed in research, and are being deployed daily as business. IoT provides comfort to the users, and also helps the environment. Using IoT, we can think intelligently, communicate and act smartly, enabling autonomous monitoring and control. IoT technology is easy to use for application deployment, and in this book, we will see how to deploy applications using IoT. We will consider a small at-home implementation, and deploy the application using IoT as we go further in the book. For deployment, we need to know the components of IoT that are discussed next in this chapter.

IoT Components

An IoT application comprises mainly six components that are sensors/actuators, IoT data, networking, Cloud/Edge computing, analytics and user interface. *Figure 1.9* illustrates the connectivity between each of the IoT components. To deploy an application, you should be comfortable in all these components. We will go through each of these briefly here, but more details on each are discussed in later chapters.

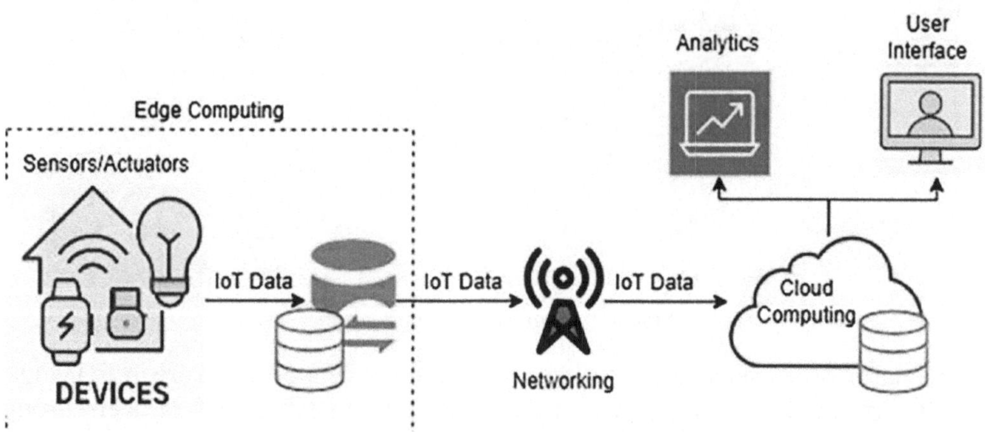

Figure 1.9: *Components of IoT Applications*

- **Sensors/Actuators**

  Sensors are devices that sense the environment, generate electric signals, and convert it into data. There are different sensors for measuring different environment parameters. However, the most popularly used sensors in IoT are motion sensors, air quality sensors, level sensors, proximity sensors, humidity sensors, accelerometers, camera, sound sensor, temperature sensor, and smoke sensors. These sensors continuously sense the specific environment condition, and then represent it in the form of data for evaluation. For instance, a humidity sensor senses the moisture in air, and produces output in RH. Motion sensor senses movement, and produces output 1, when motion happens, and output 0 for no motion. Sensors are selected as per the data requirement of the application. Actuators are opposite of sensors. They take an electric signal as input, and perform action accordingly. Some of the popular actuators are motors, speakers, and displays. Therefore, sensors provide data to the IoT application, and actuators provide the service to the user, as per the decision made by the application.

- **IoT Data**

  IoT Data is collected as application input from IoT sensors for ubiquitous computing, and providing smart service. IoT data size depends on the scale of IoT application. Thus, IoT data may be very small, and can be easily computed at the Cloud, but some of the IoT data is Big Data.

  Big IoT Data needs different processing compared to the small scale IoT data. Big IoT data coming from the sensor has a **value** attached. The data coming from different sensors is huge, in billions, so it is **voluminous**. The data speed is high as sensors are continuously sensing, thus, having **velocity**. The data coming from different sensors will have different values, and thus, the data has **variety**. Lastly, the sensors accurately sense the data, and hence, the data has **veracity**. Computation of Big IoT data is tough compared to normal IoT data as the incoming data requires fast communication, needs a lot of storage, and fast computation.

  Further, IoT data consists of three data types: Structured (csv, txt), Semi-structured (xml, Json), and Unstructured (audio, video). Generally, IoT applications have a combination of data in these three data types, to get the current environment context. Thus, understanding the big data, and modeling is a vital part in developing an IoT application.

- **Networking**

  IoT data from sensors has to be communicated to an application for analysis and decision-making, and the decision is forwarded to actuators. In traditional networking, application data is communicated wirelessly, using HTTP protocol. However, IoT data is communicated using lightweight communication protocols and application protocols. This is because the sensors are very small units, and do not have enough power to communicate data to long distances, using wireless communication protocol and HTTP application protocol. The sensors communicate data to a nearby device that may be a hub, popularly known as an edge device, using lightweight communication protocols such as Bluetooth, ZigBee, and LoraWan. From the hub or edge device, the data is communicated to the application back-end, using specific IoT application protocols.

Some of the popular application protocols in IoT are **Constrained Application Protocol (CoAP), Message Queuing Telemetry Transport (MQTT), and Advanced Message Queuing Protocol (AMQP).** These protocols have very light-weight headers, and thus, help to communicate big or a large volume of data faster over the network with minimal data loss. Moreover, they consume very less energy than resource-constrained devices such as sensors and edge devices.

- **Cloud/Edge Computing**

    The data from sensors is stored and processed at the application back-end server. If IoT data is voluminous, the cloud is used to deploy application servers. The application server stores and retrieves data from the storage, and performs computation using processing frameworks. Cloud has huge capacity to store data, as well as it is fast to process a lot of data in a second. Thus, cloud computing is widely used in IoT applications to store and process huge IoT data.

    Relational databases for storing/retrieving structured data as well as NoSQL databases for managing semi-structured and unstructured data can be deployed on the cloud, depending on the data of the IoT application.

    Processing of data is either done on a batch of data or on a data stream. Apache Hadoop is the most used processing framework for batch processing, whereas Apache Spark and Apache Flink are popular frameworks for stream processing. There are various public clouds available in the market such as Amazon AWS, Microsoft Azure, IBM Cloud, and Google Cloud. They are widely used by currently available IoT applications for processing and storage. To manage data from multiple IoT applications, and provide fast storage and processing, cloud utilizes the concept of virtualization, in which each application has its own virtual environment on the cloud. When the processing and storage of a cloud is shifted closer to the sensors over a nearby device at the edge of the network, it is termed as edge computing. Edge computing may pre-process the data (removing noisy data, or filling missing data), or process critical data for fast response, reducing data on network as well as supporting cloud in managing multiple application data. With the increasing applications and devices on the network, and causing network bottlenecks, edge computing is an emerging solution used by new IoT applications. For instance, cloud service providers like Amazon and Google now provide edge computing services with their cloud. Therefore, both cloud and edge computing are a major component in an IoT application.

- **Analytics**

    The IoT sensor data has to be processed to take actions at the application's back-end server. The processing involves data fusion and information fusion of data from multiple sources. Data fusion extracts relevant features from the incoming data, and then the information fusion model analyzes features to make a decision. The decision is either instantaneous or predictive. Therefore, to better understand the scenario, we take an example of traffic management, using IoT technology. The IoT application acquires input of the current road map, congestions in the map, number of vehicles on a junction, and speed of the vehicles in real-time. On this data, the application decides to change the traffic signal timings on each junction in the roadmap to resolve congestion (instantaneous), and avoid congestion (predictive). For this, the application has to analyze the input data intelligently to make decisions.

For analysis, the information fusion models used are statistical, probabilistic, and fuzzy logic, Machine Learning (ML), Deep Learning (DL) and evidence-based. The choice of the model depends on the data sources, decision complexity, and accuracy in prediction and time constraints for decision-making. IoT data analysis are mainly of four types: **descriptive, predictive, prescriptive and diagnostic**. Descriptive analytics is to analyze the data for having answers to questions such as what, how, where and when, and uses business intelligence tools to generate the reports. Predictive analytics determine trends and co-relations in the data for predicting future actions beforehand. Prescriptive analytics detects problems as well as determines actions for the problem. Diagnostic analytics is used to determine the reason for an event occurrence with the help of the data. For the majority of the IoT applications, commonly used analytics is predictive analytics, and the most used tool for information fusion model is Artificial Intelligence (AI) that comprises ML and DL.

- **User Interface**

  To customize or manage the application, and see the current statistics, applications' front-end interface is required. The user interface at the front-end allows the user to get notifications, see the data acquired, and generate visualizations to determine the best actions. The user interface is either on smartphones as android application, or IOS application, or on system as a web application. The user interface should be developed such that it is easy to use, clearly lists the connected devices, the stored data, the past decisions, quick notifications, and a way to visualize the data history as well as decision history. The two popular tools to develop IoT application's UI and back-end are .NET framework and Node.js.

Communication Models

A machine is considered as a hardware device that senses and communicates the IoT data. This IoT data is communicated from machine to either another machine, or nearby device or cloud. Thus, IoT applications have three communication models:

Machine to Machine (M2M), Machine to Cloud (M2C), and Machine to Gateway (M2G), and these models are illustrated in the following *Figure 1.10*.

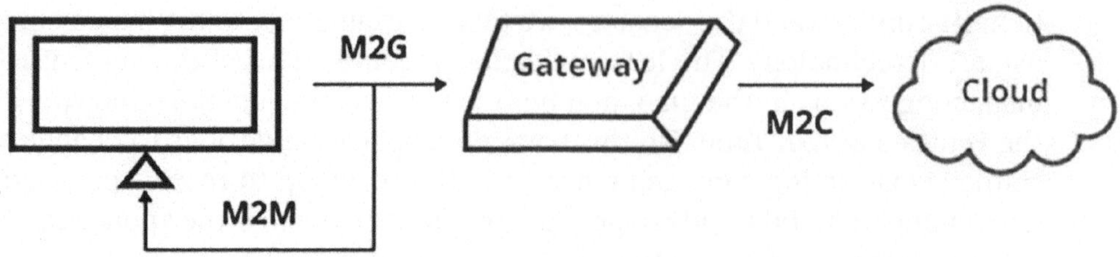

Figure 1.10: *Communication Models*

M2M Model

- The machine sends data directly to another machine, either through wired or wireless channels.
- Machines that need to exchange data have to follow the same communication protocol for direct communication.
- Machines are connected to the same network, and within the same location.
- The number of data packets transmitted are very low.
- The communication range is also low.
- Smart light, smart fridge, and smart watch are examples of machines that can communicate with each other directly.
- The communication protocols for M2M communication are cellular, Bluetooth, Zigbee, LoRaWAN, MQTT, COAP, and AMQP.

M2C Model

- The machine continuously sends data to the cloud for processing, and to get services.
- This communication uses traditional IP network or cellular data, and requires high bandwidth.
- A huge amount of data is communicated for a long distance.
- Cloud provides remote monitoring of the machines by continuously storing and analyzing data.
- Data communication to cloud suffers from high packet loss and network congestions, as the network resources are limited.
- This model is widely used among IoT applications as location of devices, and the cloud are abstracted, as well as services are fast.
- Example of the M2C model is an internet-enabled smartwatch directly communicating to the cloud.

M2G Model

- Data from the machine is communicated indirectly to the cloud via gateway, a network edge device.
- Gateway is a device that acts as mediator, provides security or interoperability between the device and the cloud.
- This communication model suits the devices that have very low power, and are not capable of transferring data directly to the cloud.
- The device communicates data to the gateway using Bluetooth, Zigbee, LoRaWan for nearby gateways, and CoAP, MQTT and AMQP protocols for far away gateways.
- An example of the M2G Model is smartwatches connected to a smartphone via Bluetooth, and the smartphone sends the data to the cloud.

Computing Models

The data communicated by machines to Cloud or Gateway (Edge) requires computation. IoT has three different computation scenarios: Cloud only, Edge-Cloud and Edge only. We will discuss these models through IoT application illustrations to get a better understanding of when to use which model.

Assume, there is an IoT application that takes bank accounts data for analysis to check if there is a fraud transaction. As a huge number of people have accounts in the banks, detecting fraud in the transaction requires huge storage and fast processing with a graph database. Thus, **only a cloud computing model** is suitable for such a scenario, when there is a lot of data to analyze and data has relationships/dependencies on other data.

When an IoT application is monitoring geographically distributed locations, and IoT data from each location is independent of each other, **an edge-cloud computing model** is suitable. For example, there is an IoT application that monitors grids of different locations. It would need data from all the grids at the cloud when the application needs to share electricity amongst locations. However, if, within locality, the energy has to be shared optimally, data can be processed at the gateway/edge.

Some applications that are location-specific, maybe monitoring a remote location and have to handle highly-critical situations accurately and fast, in such case **only edge computing model** is suitable. Suppose, there is an IoT application of forest fire detection. The smoke sensors, temperature sensors, CO2 sensors, humidity sensors are spread across the forest, forming a wireless sensor network. The sensors communicate data to the gateway and analyze the data and detect fire. The gateway fetches data in real-time and makes decisions instantly. The decision-making is highly critical; it requires fast detection of fire. Hence, edge only computing models are utilized in this application scenario.

Thus, according to the application's data and service requirements, the computing model is suitable. Further, not all IoT applications can leverage edge computing. Thus, to deploy IoT applications with edge computing, we should be very sure as to why it is being required in the first place.

Edge Computing Benefits

Edge computing is growing in popularity among multiple IoT applications as it provides multiple advantages over conventional cloud systems.

- The cloud is centralized and hence it is a single point of failure for all the stored data. On the other hand, edge devices can be utilized as distributed data storage.
- Cloud is handling multiple IoT applications and responses may get delayed. However, the edge device has close proximity and provides fast response.
- For remote locations with limited networks, data communication to the cloud takes more time with data loss compared to edge devices.
- If the cloud is hacked, all data is gone and can be misused by third-party, whereas in edge computing the data is stored in a distributed manner. Therefore, in edge computing, all data is not at one place, increasing data security.
- The data generated for cloud communication is voluminous, causing network bottlenecks. With edge computing, network resources are saved as most of the data is reduced at edge itself.
- Edge computing provides data privacy, as the data does not cross the country borders (cloud location can be anywhere) and is processed locally.
- Edge computing offers intelligence for data processing known as edge AI or edge intelligence, significantly reducing data to be communicated to the cloud for analysis.
- Using resources and services in the cloud is very costly, when an application handles big IoT data. But, with edge computing, the data is stored and processed locally. This reduces network cost as well as computation cost.
- Edge computing provides reliable and guaranteed communication of data for processing whereas connection with the cloud is unreliable as it depends on the data traffic over the network.
- Scaling edge devices for processing faster or handling more data is easier over a local network rather than scaling cloud services on global level.
- To analyze the data as per location's context, the cloud has to group data with respect to each location and process them separately. In case of monitoring multiple locations across the country, processing at cloud will take more time

for processing as well as storage. Contrary, edge computing does location-specific analysis only, with respect to location's context, increasing accuracy in decision-making.

Challenges in Edge Computing

Edge computing has benefits, but not all IoT applications can implement edge computing due to following challenges:

- Edge devices for computing have very limited storage compared to the cloud.
- They have very low computational power compared to cloud, and therefore, take more processing time.
- They increase the number of devices over the network, consuming more bandwidth.
- Edge devices are from different manufacturers, and communication between them for doing a task is challenging.
- If the number of edge devices in a specific location increases to a higher number, the local network may also face congestion and delay.

Figure 1.11 shows advantages as well as disadvantages of implementing edge computing in IoT applications. Thus, when to implement edge computing in our application depends on the application's requirement like what type of data it is, what kind of service is expected, what intelligence is required, whether it is a large-scale application or whether data security is a priority.

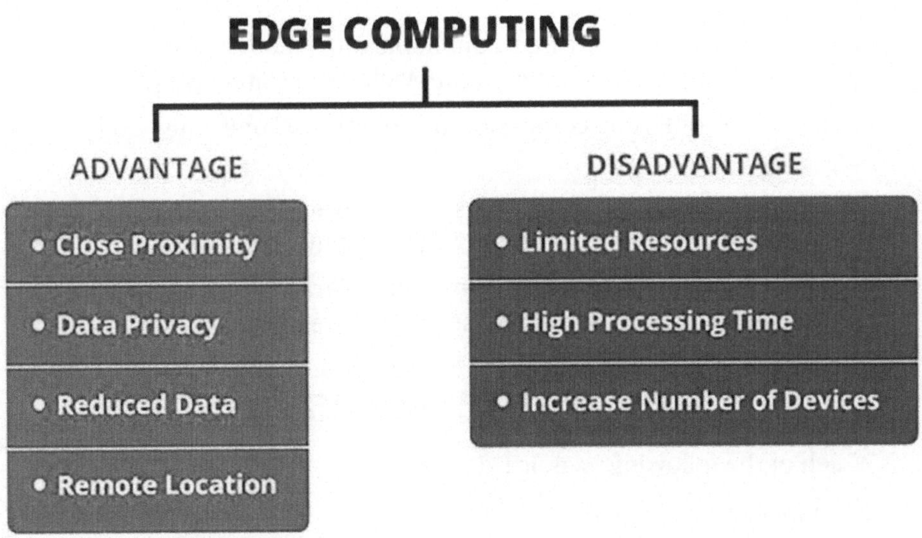

Figure 1.11: *Benefits and Challenges of Edge Computing*

Conclusion

We have covered the fundamentals of IoT, its components, communication and computing models as well as the chapter has a variety of application scenarios to get familiar with the use of IoT technology to build smart applications. We now know how IoT works, and different types of IoT applications. We now have an idea of different components of IoT applications that need to be understood properly to be able to deploy IoT applications by self. We are now familiar with all basics associated with servers and server applications. This chapter is for enabling thinking of new IoT application ideas, and what are the service requirements of the application. Then, once an idea is finalized, and requirements are listed, the reader can think of a computation and communication model for his application. Finally, the reader can decide if the IoT application really requires edge computing, with respect to its pros and cons, and application's requirements.

In the next chapter, we will get into the start of the deployment phase, knowing more about cloud computing and cloud services.

Points to Remember

- Technology that connects all the things and applications, with the help of a network, to provide smart services is termed as IoT.
- An IoT application comprises mainly six components that are sensors/ actuators, IoT Data, Networking, Cloud/Edge computing, Analytics and User interface.
- The IoT application has three communication models: Machine to Machine (M2M), Machine to Cloud (M2C), and Machine to Gateway (M2G).
- IoT has three different computation scenarios: Cloud only, Edge-Cloud and Edge only.
- Edge computing in IoT provides several advantages over cloud computing; however, not all applications need edge computing.
- If edge computing drawbacks are not tolerable for application's service requirement, then it is better to use cloud instead.

Multiple-Choice Questions

1. Which of the following is an IoT device?

    a. Human

    b. Sensors

   c. Plant
   d. Toaster

2. How to make a physical object an IoT device?
   a. By attaching sensors
   b. By attaching embedded device
   c. By attaching both sensors and embedded device separately
   d. By attaching sensors to embedded devices, and embedded devices to physical objects

3. Which is not a M2M IoT protocol?
   a. CoAP
   b. HTTP
   c. MQTT
   d. Bluetooth

4. What does an embedded device do?
   a. Sense the data
   b. Communicates the data
   c. Performs action
   d. None of the above

5. Which of the following is the property of the cloud?
   a. Limited storage
   b. High computation time
   c. Virtualization
   d. Free services

6. What is the concern of edge computing?
   a. Limited resources
   b. Close proximity
   c. Network congestion
   d. Low cost

Answers

1. b
2. d
3. b
4. b
5. c
6. a

Questions

1. Why do we need smart applications?
2. What are the major application domains that IoT technology is supporting?
3. In smart healthcare applications, how IoT technology helps in an emergency?
4. What is IoT data, and how is it managed by IoT applications?
5. How is intelligence provided in IoT applications for decision-making?
6. What are the issues with the M2C communication model?
7. What is the difference between M2M and M2G communication?
8. When to use an edge only computing model?
9. Why do IoT applications use cloud computing?
10. Why is edge computing currently popular in IoT?
11. How does edge computing positively and negatively impact a network?

CHAPTER 2
Conventional Cloud versus Edge

Introduction

Cloud is being used by multiple applications, business models and personal storage from the last decade due to its enormous benefits. Some of the known cloud services that are being generally used over smartphones are Google drive, iCloud and Dropbox for backing up mobile data. Social networking sites such as Facebook and LinkedIn have their own cloud, where huge data from large-scale world population is being stored and managed seamlessly.

IoT applications use cloud computing for specific services, and as per application's requirements. In this chapter, we will discuss cloud architecture and the services. Later, we will go through Cloud-only IoT applications through multiple examples. These examples will help think of how to use cloud in the application given the input specifications and desired services. Two popular clouds used in IoT applications are Amazon AWS and Microsoft Azure. Thus, next we will see how to deploy an application, using both clouds as a case study.

At the end of the chapter, we will go through the drawbacks of using cloud. Further, we will study how edge-cloud applications can be more beneficial than cloud-only applications. Not all IoT applications require cloud computing or edge computing, or both. Hence, this chapter helps to understand when to use cloud computing or edge computing, depending on application's requirements.

Structure

In this chapter, we will cover the following topics:

- Cloud Architecture
    - Components
    - Layered Architecture

    - Types
- Cloud Services
    - Infrastructure as a Service
    - Platform as a Service
    - Software as a Service
- IoT Application Use-cases with Cloud
- Implementation with AWS and Azure
- Disadvantages with Cloud
- Edge with Cloud

Cloud Architecture

Cloud is a large-scale cluster of machines that form a datacenter. It has different components, and has an architecture of its own with varied types.

Components

An application is deployed on the cloud, and it provides service to the application users. The cloud has a designed architecture for managing the application, and providing a good user experience. There are three main components in the cloud: Front-end platform, back-end platform, and network.

- **Front-end platform**: The cloud provides a user-interface as front-end through which users can access application services deployed on cloud. The front-end is developed by HTML, CSS and JavaScript languages. The platform consists of a menu bar, tools, images, buttons, and lists for selection. The design of the front-end platform is very crucial for easy-to-use services for the client without much assistance and time. Front-end platforms of popular clouds have user authorization to preserve data, and keep the account of user's history for personalized experience. The front-end platform has application-specific search tools, and selection tools for collecting user actions, text boxes for collecting user data, and the data is stored at the front-end machine, or communicated to the application's back-end at the cloud. Further, the front-end platform does not require machines with high computational and storage power for deployment. It can be a web application or a mobile application on a one-click download. It can be accessed by user/client from anywhere on any hardware machine. Therefore, in short, the front end comprises a client-side software, a user interface for interacting with the software, and a client device with a network having deployed software. This front-end software is visible to users for accessing service of the application deployed on the cloud. Some of the popular front-end platforms are Netflix, Zoom, and Gmail.

- **Back-end platform**: Cloud hardware having computing and storage resources comprises the back-end of the cloud. Popular Cloud platforms are Amazon AWS, Microsoft Azure, Google Cloud, and IBM Cloud. The back-end is abstracted from the user, and is controlled via the front-end platform. Cloud service provider develops as well as manages back-end platform components. The back-end platform is a network of multiple machines either at the same location, or having different geographic locations and creates a pool of computing and storage resources. Further, the platform is accessed by a high number of front-end users and applications and requires continuous as well as fast access. Amazon AWS and Microsoft Azure are examples of back-end cloud platforms that help manage user data coming from the front-end platform.

  Back-end platform comprises an application, service, cloud runtime environment, infrastructure, storage, management and security. **Application** is deployed at the back-end to provide service to the user upon requests. **Service** means to execute multiple tasks on cloud runtime, and tasks can be application environment setup, data storage, security, and so on. **Cloud runtime** is an operating system that has virtualization technology to provide resources to every running service. It creates a virtual space for applications running in parallel, abstracting hardware availability, and assigning resources as per service requests. Application data is stored in the cloud at suitable **storage**. The storage is different for each cloud provider. Most used storage devices are hard drives, solid state drives, and persistent storage. The application has an allocated partition on the cloud storage drive to run services. The application and services running on the cloud are supported by CPU, GPU, network cards, motherboard, and these form an **infrastructure** of the cloud.

  Infrastructure is the building block of the cloud on which OS, application and services run smoothly and efficiently. Resource allocation and communication between front-end and back-end platforms for providing services is coordinated by the **management software**. This software controls the functioning of the cloud, and running applications in a smooth manner. Lastly, **security** of the infrastructure and application data is crucial for the cloud. Critical tasks are given priority, and data is virtually duplicated to have redundancy. A virtual firewall is deployed on infrastructure to prevent data loss and attacks by keeping check on network traffic during application data communication from front-end to back-end.

  Cloud provides services that make applications easy to deploy and use. One of the popular cloud services is lambda. Lambda is a computing service that scales the computing resources up, and brings them back to zero, depending on the current demand. Amazon AWS has AWS lambda, Azure has Azure function, and Google Cloud has Google cloud function to provide lambda service. Another popular service that cloud provides is secure, and reliable storage. AWS provides S3, Azure provides Blob, and Object Storage of IBM cloud provides storage service. An important service is API gateway (AWS API gateway, AZURE API Management, and IBM API Connect) that connects the user requests with appropriate services, and provides a secure route.

- **Network**: Data and user's request from within front-end services, front-end to back-end, and within back-end services is communicated through networks. Communication within front-end services is handled via **intranet**. Intranet is a type of network, where a group of users within the same organization can share data, collaborate, and request for services. Communication from front-end to back-end is handled via **internet** network as both the platforms are mostly at geographically different locations. Communication within the back-end platform is done with the help of an intracloud network. As the application services run on different virtual machines, the **intracloud network** connects these virtual machines for sharing information. If a cloud needs to share data with another cloud, it will use an intercloud network for communication. End-users of different applications need to exchange data or services, and these applications run on different cloud service providers. Then they communicate via intracloud network. Therefore, cloud networks are a collective form of intranet, internet, intracloud and intercloud to connect multiple users with multiple applications deployed on multiple clouds for getting fast services.

Layered Architecture

The components of the cloud discussed in the preceding paragraph can be viewed as multiple layers for better understanding of how cloud architecture works. The architecture is divided into four layers: Data center layer, infrastructure layer, platform layer and application layer. The first three layers form the back-end platform, and the last layer forms the front-end platform.

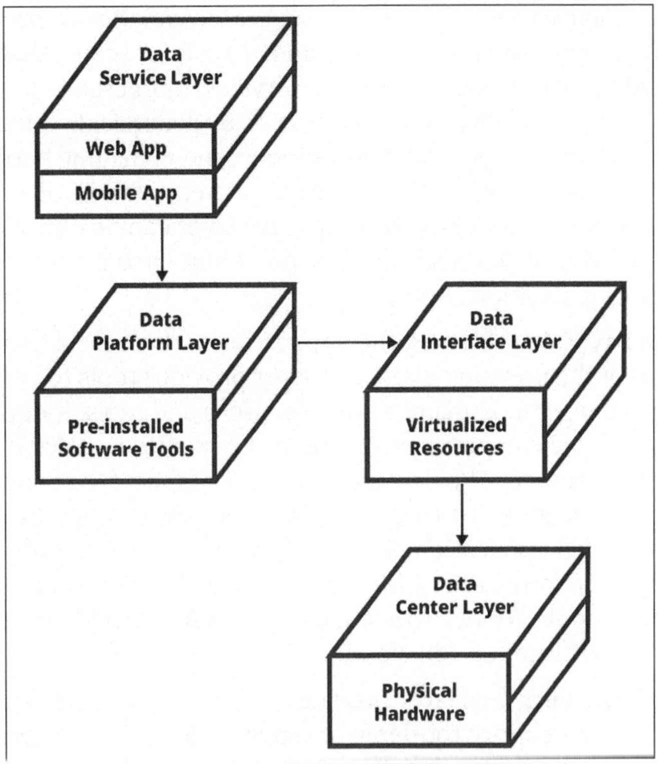

Figure 2.1: *Layered Architecture of Cloud*

Each of these layers are shown in *Figure* 2.1, and is discussed in detail as follows:

- **Datacenter Layer:** Datacenter is a physical hardware layer, consisting of a network of large numbers of powerful machines that collectively provides computing and storage resources. To handle multiple applications on the cloud with a large number of user requests, the cloud requires a huge amount of storage and computational power. Cloud consisting of a single or few machine servers is not sufficient to handle millions of users accessing applications at the same time. To handle such a huge number of user requests, the data center comprises a high number of powerful servers (minimum 5000, and maximum as per applications on the cloud), switches, routers, power supplies, and a cooling system. With such a datacenter for the cloud, the resources are available in plenty for all the end users of different applications deployed over cloud.
- **Infrastructure Layer:** This layer provides physical devices of the datacenter layer as virtual resources, using virtualization technology. It forms a virtual network of virtual machines with virtual storage. With the help of virtualization technology, the physical resources are then used efficiently. The hardware is not directly accessed by the developers to have a fixed number of resources

for their applications. The resources are automatically provisioned to the application as per the requirement, and virtually, it seems that the application has abundant resources for running services, but actually it is not. Thus, this layer provides scalability to the application by dynamically allocating resources virtually for running an application service, and managing hardware resources of the datacenter layer efficiently to prevent underutilization as well as overutilization. To understand better, this layer can be considered as a virtual network of virtual physical devices, providing virtual resources dynamically for running application services.

- **Platform Layer:** In this layer, the application software is deployed onto virtual resources of the previous layer. This layer provides tools to create applications on cloud from scratch, using cloud resources and tools. It deploys application services, assigns computing and storage as required, scales it as per demand, and keeps it secured. The developer has API support for various cloud services to deploy applications with ease. It also provides testing, running, and hosting of the deployed application. This has provision for integrating with services of other cloud providers. Moreover, it provides different virtual platforms to different applications. Thus, this layer is for developers to actually build application software on the cloud.
- **Application Layer:** This layer provides users with access to the cloud through the web or mobile app of the deployed application in the previous layer. Through this layer, users can request services from the cloud as per their need. User authorization is part of this layer. Data from apps is communicated to and from the platform layer, and hence, this layer also manages network connectivity between apps and the cloud. Therefore, to summarize, this layer has clients having multiple mobile apps and web apps to use application services, and it is also responsible for selecting networking protocols for data communication. For example, our phones have Gmail and Facebook apps, and each of these apps communicate as well as store personalized mails of Gmail and chats, and feeds of Facebook over cloud. Further, these apps provide user interface to access services of Gmail and Facebook applications that are deployed over cloud. Thus, these mobile apps, providing user interface to cloud deployed applications, and the network for data communication, form the application layer.

Types

Cloud are of three types: Private cloud, public cloud and hybrid cloud, as shown in *Figure* 2.2. Depending on the application to be deployed, it is very necessary for clients to understand what cloud type they want.

- **Public Cloud:** This type of cloud has a third-party provider, and is open for the public that can be easily accessed via the internet. It consists of a network of multiple data centers located anywhere in the world. The organization that needs to deploy applications, or have services of the cloud need to select the nearest datacenter or the cheapest datacenter, based on application's requirements. The public cloud shares its infrastructure amongst multiple organizations, and deploys as well as manages multiple applications of multiple organizations over the same hardware resources efficiently. Thus, this cloud is a multi-tenant providing different virtual machines for different applications. Further, to use services of the cloud, the organization has to be pay-per-usage, but some resources and services are free to use. Therefore, it saves a lot of cost and work as well as abstracts infrastructure from the organizations with the help of virtualization technology.

Moreover, scalability of applications is easy, and organizations do not require to add machines by themselves. The public cloud has an abundance of resources and they add machines or data centers at another location as they see a rise in the number of applications. Thus, public cloud services are easy to use, and application deployment is quick without worrying about how to manage resources to make it cheap in terms of price. Another advantage of public cloud is that they get updated with new technologies and updated versions of the software, and have better AI capabilities. As public cloud is used by multiple organizations at the same time, there may be a chance of slow service or cloud shutdowns for some time. Additionally, the data is kept secured by the cloud, but can be attacked easily by other organizations, using the same cloud. Applications that work on highly critical data or sensitive data, need to think of ways in such cases, while using public cloud. Examples of Public Cloud are Amazon AWS, Microsoft Azure, Google Cloud Platform, IBM Cloud. Adafruit IO, and ThingSpeak are specific Cloud designed for managing IoT devices.

- **Private Cloud:** This type of cloud is owned by a company (on-premise) or a third party and supports applications of only one client (single tenant). The client is able to customize the cloud resources and the application's data is highly secured. The private cloud needs to be managed by the organization and thus, is more costly. It consists of a datacenter having a high number of hardware and pool of resources under one roof, that need to be managed and maintained by the organization that is deploying applications or the third-party company. This cloud is also known as an internal or corporate cloud. This cloud is dedicated to only one organization and thus has resources limited to application's requirements. Further, the datacenter can be increased by more resources as per the increasing number of applications of the organization. Therefore, in a private cloud, the organization deploying the application has all the control on resources, security, virtualization, infrastructure and services. If the private cloud is managed by a third-party organization, they can only let their cloud to be used by only one organization as a contract and manage the organization's applications. Even if a private cloud is managed by a third-party, the application deployment is more of a self-service. Most of the time, public cloud is beneficial as a lot of work and expenses are saved. However, if the organization's data is highly sensitive or resources are inadequate, or application always requires uptime, then in that case, a private cloud is an appropriate choice.

- **Hybrid Cloud:** It is a cloud formed by private cloud (on-premise), and public cloud. The workloads that run on sensitive information, or are time sensitive are run on a private cloud, and big data tasks run on a public cloud. This cloud is popular, when an application user base is very high, and data is huge as well as the decision has to be made in real-time. Hybrid cloud provides scalability, flexibility, seamless migration and reduced costs. During disasters, hybrid cloud works well as the data from private cloud is backed up at public cloud and vice versa. Thus, data recovery is easy. Further, during huge incoming information like in applications on e-business, the public cloud can come in support of handling tasks running at private cloud.

  Further, if some error of operation occurs at a private cloud, the operation can be migrated to public clouds via containerization technology. Thus, this cloud has benefits of both the clouds as well as its own disadvantages. It is not easy to handle task distribution between private cloud and public cloud. Further, the working of both the clouds need to be coordinated well for handling applications having big data. The organization has to put in more effort in deploying applications to the private cloud, and scheduling tasks of the private cloud onto public clouds. Hybrid clouds have cloud operating systems to provide management and orchestration, among the private clouds and public clouds. VMware cloud and Kubernetes are examples of cloud OS, and it is the first decision to be made for deploying applications on hybrid cloud. Next, depending on the selected cloud OS, application's requirements and requirement for modern technologies in future, the public cloud is chosen. At the end, the on-premise private cloud needs to be connected with the public cloud. Having a private cloud with a public cloud is costly. Moreover, integration of both the clouds is challenging as they are heterogeneous in nature.

- **Multi-Cloud**: This type of cloud consists of either multiple public clouds, or multiple private clouds, or multiple private clouds with public clouds. This type of cloud is for applications that are accessed, and used by users all over the world. Therefore, the application generates big data all across the globe, every second. To manage heavy loads, multiple clouds are required for efficient services. Additionally, multi-cloud can distribute workloads to on-premise edge devices for having more resources to handle huge streaming data (cloud burst). The advantages of multi-cloud are that they are geographically distributed and provide flexibility to use any cloud depending on the application, reducing vendor lock-in. The major issue with using multi-cloud is that a team of experts is required to have experience in working on different cloud providers. However, current IT professionals are mostly proficient in only one cloud. Deployment and management of multi-cloud requires a huge skill set for efficient utilization for application deployment.

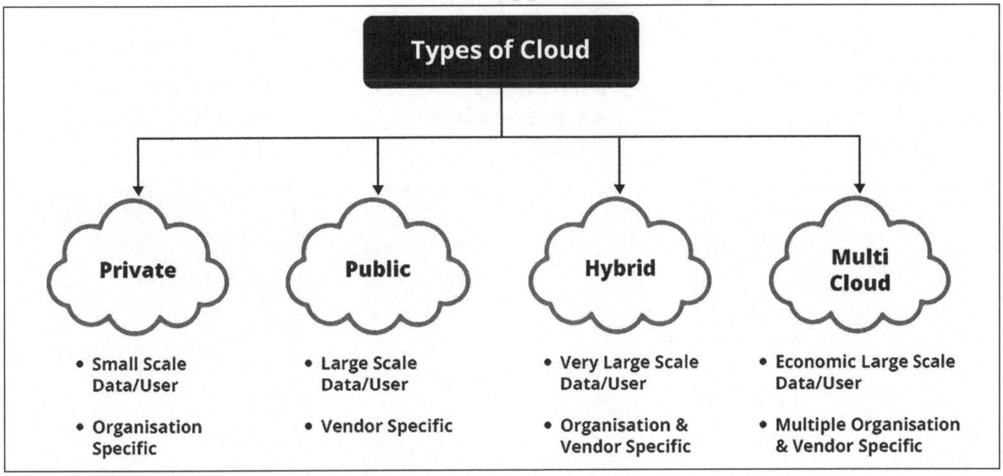

***Figure* 2.2:** *Types of Clouds*

Cloud Service

There are three popular cloud services: Sensing as a service, platform as a service, and infrastructure as a service. To understand them, we will start with an IoT application example to be deployed on the cloud. Suppose, there is a smart healthcare application. The application will have an app to communicate with patients, where the patient needs to register, login, put information, schedule appointments, and get updates. Thus, the app is **cloud-based software** and is front-end. The data from the app gets stored in the cloud and processed using an analytical model at the cloud and information produced from the analysis is communicated back to the app. For handling information from a huge number of users, hardware resources and networking resources of the cloud are used to communicate, store, and process the incoming data in parallel. The hardware and network resources of the cloud is known as **infrastructure**. Further, the appropriate storage model, and the analytical model based on what type of data and analysis is required, are running on the cloud as back-end software over infrastructure. Therefore, infrastructure (hardware resources and networking devices) with installed tools (storage models, analytical models, programming interface, and network protocols) to deploy software (the app) on the cloud is known as a platform.

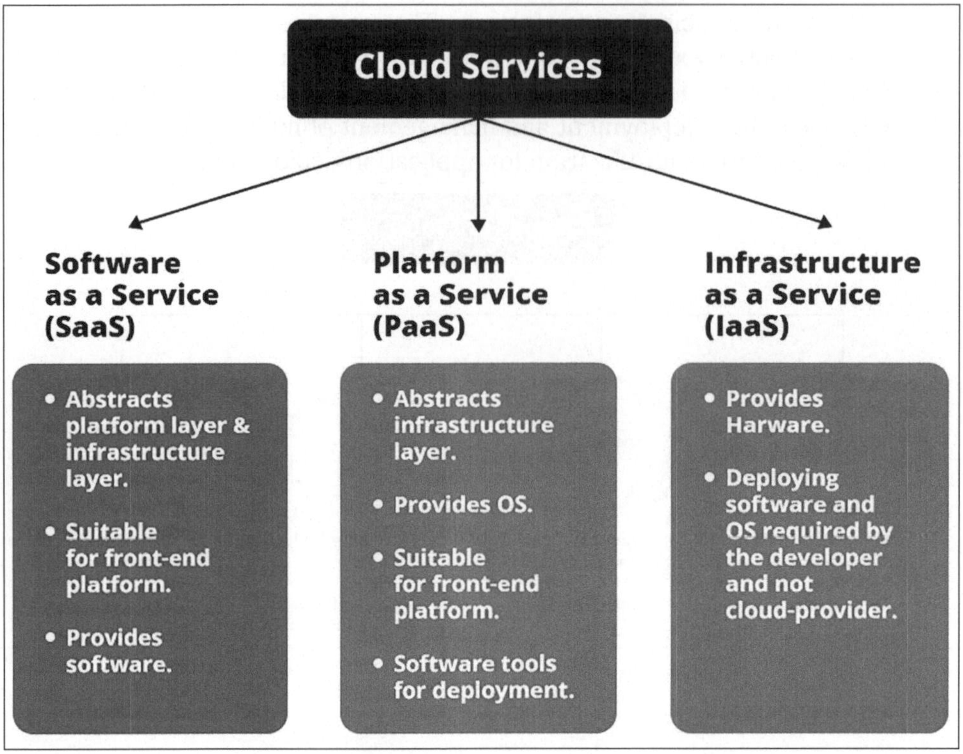

Figure 2.3: *Different Types of Cloud Services*

In this healthcare application, assume the app is pre-deployed on the cloud by the provider over cloud platform, using cloud infrastructure. We are the user, and we download the app from the web on our device. In this scenario, we are using a cloud-based application (software) as a service, and we are not bothered about how many machines and networking devices are used to deploy the application over cloud, and what has been used as a tool for storing and analyzing the data. This is a use-case of **Software-as-a-Service (SaaS)**.

In this healthcare application, if we need to deploy the back-end of the application, where we assume, we need to have a MongoDB (NoSQL) database for storage and Random Forest (ML Model) for analysis. To deploy our storage and analytical model, we use a pre-built OS on the cloud with installed software tools. Further, the pre-built cloud OS has installed networking tools like MQTT that we use for data communication between MongoDB, Random Forest and with the Front-end app. Therefore, in this scenario, we are using a cloud platform to deploy the back-end of the application, and that too with pre-installed tools. This is a use-case of **Platform-as-a-Service (PaaS)**.

Further, assume, the application is deployed with front-end, back-end on a local machine, and for a single user. The application is hosted on a local machine to test how it is working. Once the test is successful, we think of increasing scalability of the application with the help of cloud. Now, we have a whole application ready and the application requires more machines for more storage and computing resources to manage a huge number of users and their data in parallel. Cloud hardware is used to deploy the local machine application using virtualization technology and we can tell the cloud how many resources are required and how much to scale. In this, only cloud infrastructure is being utilized to deploy the pre-built application on the cloud. This is the use-case of **Infrastructure-as-a-Service (IaaS)**.

With this example, it is clear in what situation which cloud service is used. Now, we will go through these services one by one, discussing their advantages and disadvantages, and their comparison is shown in *Figure* 2.3.

- **Software as a Service (SaaS)**: Cloud provides software, developed by third-party, to be used directly on the internet enabled devices. This cloud service is known as software as a service. To use the basic version of software, it may be free. However, to use more features of software, there is monthly or yearly subscription, and you get service lock-in. Further, there is full abstraction of back-end and hardware. There is no need to pay for deployment tools or hardware used and no control over maintenance issues or customization of the application. This software can be used as a full application, or as part of any new application for your own organization. Thus, it is easy to use and affordable; however, privacy and security of the information are not guaranteed.
- **Platform as a Service (PaaS)**: To deploy software on the cloud, rather than using a pre-built version, the cloud provides OS and installed tools as a platform. In other words, it is a cloud framework that is designed for software creation and deployment. It has its own operating system, storage, infrastructure, network, libraries, tools and automatic updates. The applications built on cloud using PaaS are available as well as scalable, as infrastructure is adjusted by the cloud. It is a good option, when an application has to be quickly deployed or an application is being developed by multiple developers, sharing the same space online. The tools that are already available to build the application are standardized; however, they may increase the risk of vendor lock-in. Vendor lock-in means the application cannot use a better, or another version of a tool that is not available in the cloud. It would be very expensive to switch to different tool vendors as the code is tightly coupled and interdependent on different tools from specific clouds.
- **Infrastructure as a Service (IaaS):** Cloud has a huge infrastructure of hardware and networking resources, and they are available for deployment of applications as a service. To deploy an application, having its own OS and software avoiding risk of vendor-lock-in and service lock-in infrastructure as a service is the best option. The resources are provisioned by the application

developer as per the requirements, and then the developed application is deployed over the infrastructure with the help of virtualization. The developer has no control over cloud infrastructure as it is managed by the cloud provider. However, the developer has full control over the type of OS, storage, networking, virtualization and software tools. The infrastructure is shared by multiple organizations, which may lead to security risk. Further, outages in the infrastructure will impact application services. More infrastructure during high peaks would require more cost. IaaS helps manage such a big infrastructure for the deployed application with high access rate in less cost, rather than deploying infrastructure of its own, and maintaining it on-premise. Additionally, it enables dynamic scaling with respect to usage rate.

IoT Application Use-Cases with Cloud

Until now, we know the concept of IoT from the previous chapter, and the concept of cloud from this chapter. Both of these technologies, IoT and Cloud, are being integrated in recent years. Both technologies, when working together, enable large-scale applications with time and resource-efficient services. In general, IoT applications on cloud, the IoT data from devices are communicated to the cloud where the data is stored and analyzed. We will see some use cases of IoT applications in our daily lives that use the cloud for processing of data.

Thus, smart home security is one of the popular IoT applications that is currently being used all over the world. A popular home security system is Vivint. Vivint home security system has sensors attached to doors, and windows. Additionally, it has camera inside the house as well as outside the house for 24*7 monitoring and surveillance. The homeowner gets an app on which notifications are communicated in case the door or window is opened or any suspicious activity is seen. Further, the owner can set security over the house when he is away and can have a full view of the house even in a far-off region. The application uses a space monkey cloud, a private cloud, to store sensor data, video data from each user. The storage is within the home itself and the storage is accessed from anywhere in the world. Thus, space monkey is a cloud having a network of hard drives in each of the homes that is secured by Vivint and it does not have a huge data center in a remote location to sync up all the data. This IoT application uses the cloud to back-up user data and to provide access to data from anywhere. ADT is also a smart home security provider. It uses google cloud platform with on-premise data storage for storing the data for back-up and recovery. In these applications, the cloud is used as they have a large customer base to manage.

Another IoT application that intensively uses the cloud is autonomous self-driving vehicles or driverless cars. These cars require appropriate sensors, communication, real-time decision-making, and cloud for storage as well as processing of data. A popular company that provides driverless cars for renting is Waymo. The company was founded by Google. Waymo cars have four sensors: camera, LiDAR, ultrasonic sensors and radar. With these the car detects other cars on the road ahead for safe driving and avoiding collision. The data from these sensors coming in different formats is stored in the cloud. The decision has to be made really fast in high traffic. Thus, these cars have strong AI in the cloud.

Deep Learning is used as AI for analysis. The decision from the cloud has to be communicated back to the car in real-time as the application is time-critical. The cloud used for storage and analysis is google cloud. One more company provides driverless car rides known as ZOOX. It is developed by amazon company. ZOOX has an on-premises private cloud for computation and they run simulations to have safe drive. However, simulations required more computations and eventually the company had a cloud burst. With that, ZOOX now runs on a hybrid cloud where the private supercomputer is supported by high performance computing AWS cloud, a public cloud. The database used in ZOOX is Amazon S3. Thus, with the help of cloud service, the driverless cars from Waymo and ZOOX are able to successfully run on roads of the USA.

The next very popular IoT application that is successful all over the world, especially in the workout/gym domain, is smart wearable devices. Amongst smart wearable devices, the most used is smart watches that track step counts, heart rate and calories burnt. Smart watches without connecting with the cloud will provide the values without the need of the internet. However, to utilize the maximum out of the smart watch, the IoT plays its role. The smartwatch is connected to the smartphone of the user, from where it is calibrated. The app in the phone of the user collects the smartwatch data, and stores it in the cloud. The app shows timeline performance based on data stored at the cloud, when the user requests about it.

This data is mostly numerical, and is not huge as well as the analytical model is light, in contrast to previous two applications. Fitbit and Garmin watches are smart watches used for fitness tracking by the public. Fitbit is acquired by Google in 2021. It provides daily activity tracking, real-time monitoring, sleep monitoring, stress management, wellness report and many more services. Fitbit uses a 3-level accelerometer for having the readings. The data from Fitbit is stored at google cloud for having better personalized experience on healthcare of the user. Google Cloud BigQuery is utilized for advanced analytics of the data. The Fitbit, with the help of Google Cloud can also monitor chronic conditions, pre and post surgeries, and may also provide clinical analysis using patient's data. For instance, Garmin watches provide more than just fitness tracking. It is a great option for big adventures and long duration sports. These watches have Wrist Heart Rate, Pulse Oximeter, Compass, Altimeter and Barometer sensors. Garmin has their own Garmin servers to store data locally. They do not use public cloud data storage and analysis.

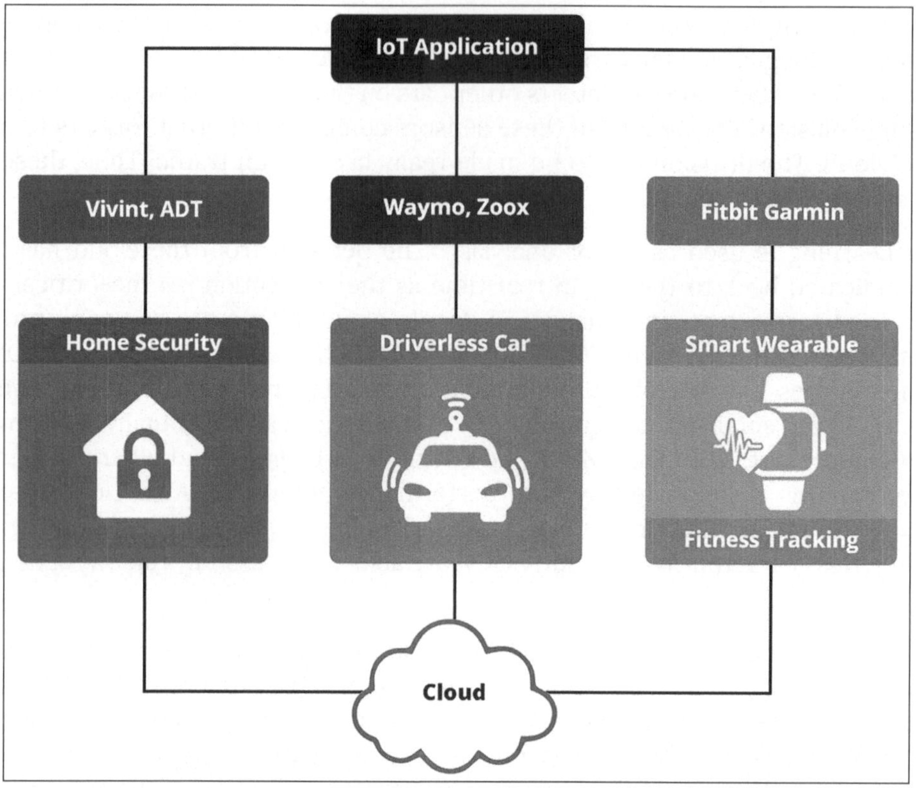

Figure 2.4: *IoT Applications that are Extensively Using Cloud Technologies*

These use-case applications consider Cloud for data processing, and are shown in brief in *Figure 2.4*. However, the cloud considered by each application depends on services required. The cloud may be public, private or hybrid. There are two most common Cloud platforms among IoT applications to process big data. These are Amazon AWS and Microsoft Azure. In the next section, we will learn how to work with these two Clouds with illustrations.

Implementation with AWS and Azure

As we have gone through a lot of theoretical concepts of the cloud, now, we will see a simple IoT web application implementation on two popular cloud platforms. We will not deploy a full-fledged IoT application on Cloud, as it is out of the scope of the book. This exercise is to showcase how applications are deployed at Cloud, and to illustrate advantages and disadvantages of the cloud with respect to edge computing.

During implementation, we will go through each step, and also discuss the challenges faced during deployment of web applications. For implementation, a web application is developed using Flask and Python 3.9. To run Flask on Windows, use visual studio code and install python. Create and activate a virtual environment, and then install flask using pip. For running flask on an Ubuntu machine, install python, and then install flask using sudo apt-get python-flask. The web application is a simple smart lighting application which currently takes input from the user, and not sensors.

In the smart lighting application coded using Python Flask, there is a form "first.html" that takes input about the number of people in the room, outside weather, current light status and activity of the person. Depending on all the four parameter values, a decision is made on switching of lights on and off smartly. For example, if there is dark outside and people are sleeping, lights go off. Otherwise, if there is light outside and people are eating, both lights are on. Multiple such combinations are derived and the flask app makes the decision and the result is shown on webpage result.html.

The local machine used for implementation has Windows 11 OS. To run the code, the command on the terminal is **flask - -app <file> run,** and the web page will open on localhost web browser. The code with all other supporting files is zipped and saved as CloudCode.zip. The zipped folder is then deployed on the cloud from a local machine.

Amazon AWS

The first step is to create a user account on amazon AWS. During sign up, the cloud will ask for email id, credit card details and address. After signing up, the cloud will take a few minutes to a few days to authenticate new user and card credentials. Once sign up is successful, sign in on AWS portal. After signing in, select the payment option as free tier. Steps to deploy application on AWS portal are as follows:

1. Select EC2 (Elastic Compute Cloud) from services, and create a new EC2 instance. EC2 is a virtual machine that provides hardware from the cloud with no need of managing the hardware resources. A virtual machine provides functionality of physical hardware and abstracts the hardware resources from the user. EC2 instances support Microsoft Windows and Linux based distributions like Amazon Linux, Ubuntu, Red Hat.

2. During creation, choose a name for instance and select Ubuntu as OS. For implementation, we choose the name as **`cloud_with_python`**. Select number of instances as 1 and instance type as **t2.micro** (it is free). Only choose free tier selections during learning on the cloud, and start with lightweight applications.

3. Create a key pair, and save it on the localhost machine as a .pem file. We chose **`edge computing.pem`** as the name for the key file. *Figure* 2.5 shows a screenshot of the page, where we need to create a key pair.

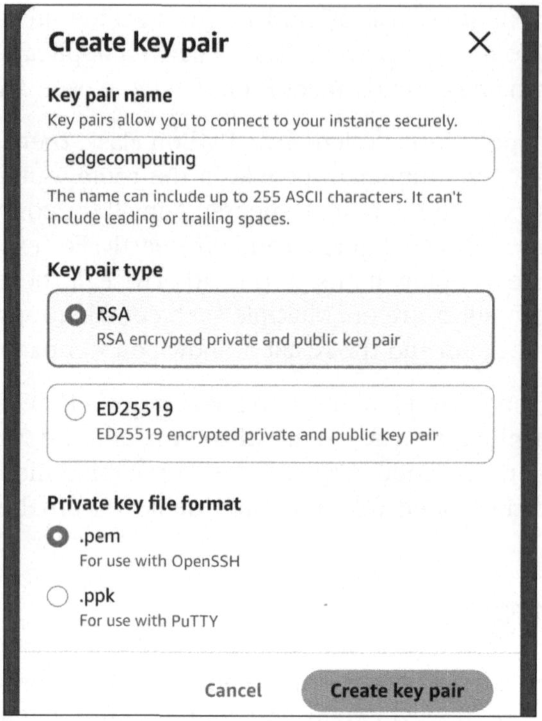

Figure 2.5: *Creation of a Key Pair*

4. Select 8GB memory, while configuring storage, and a maximum of 30 GB is available for free.
5. Select the boxes in the security group allowing all traffic, and then click on '**`launch instance`**'. *Figure* 2.6 shows a screenshot of the security page.

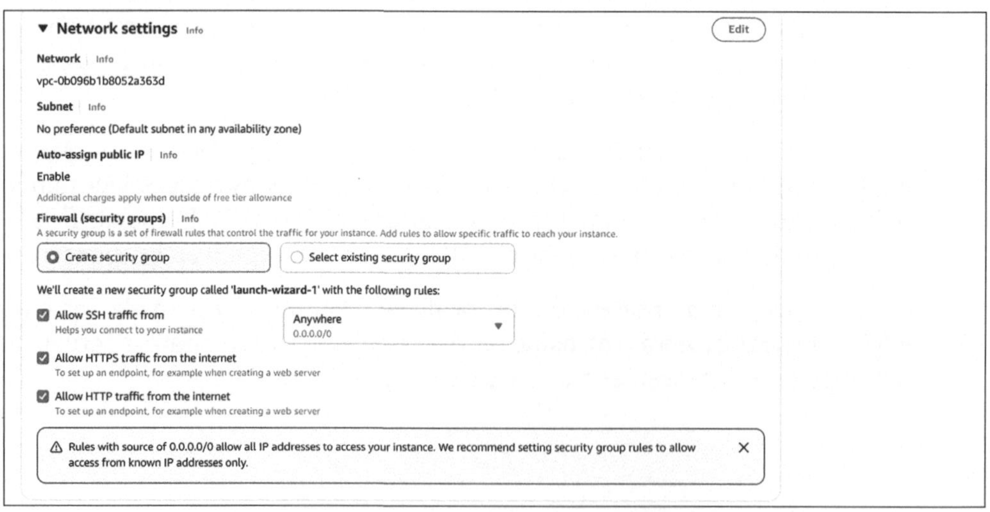

Figure 2.6: A *Screenshot Showing Security Settings of EC2*

6. Now, we can see the created instance in *Figure 2.7*. Select the instance, and click connect.

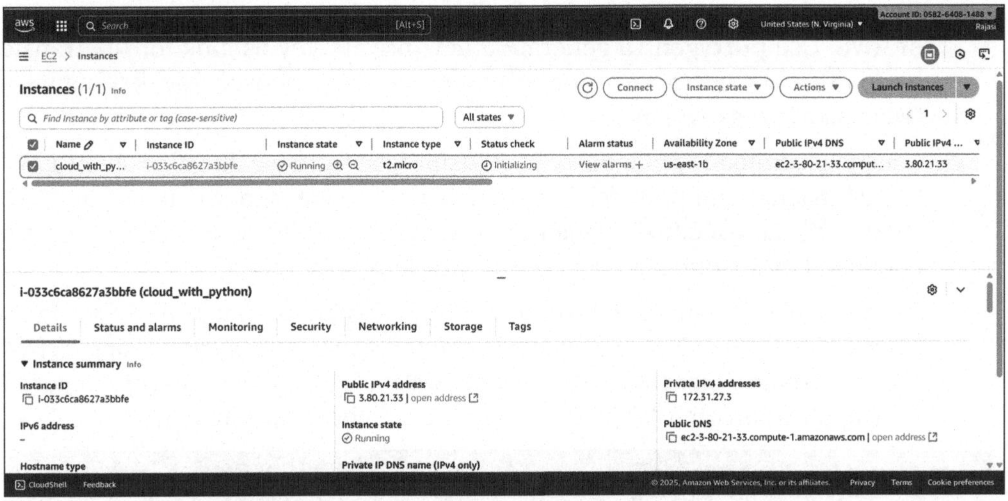

Figure 2.7: *A Screenshot Showing EC2 Instance Created*

7. A page will open having details on doing ssh from a local machine to connect with ubuntu. In our case, we run the **ssh** command on localhost as "**ssh -i "edgecomputing.pem" ubuntu@ec2-18-222-92-12.us-east-2.compute.amazonaws.com**". The following *Figure* 2.8 shows a screenshot of an EC2 instance running on windows terminal.

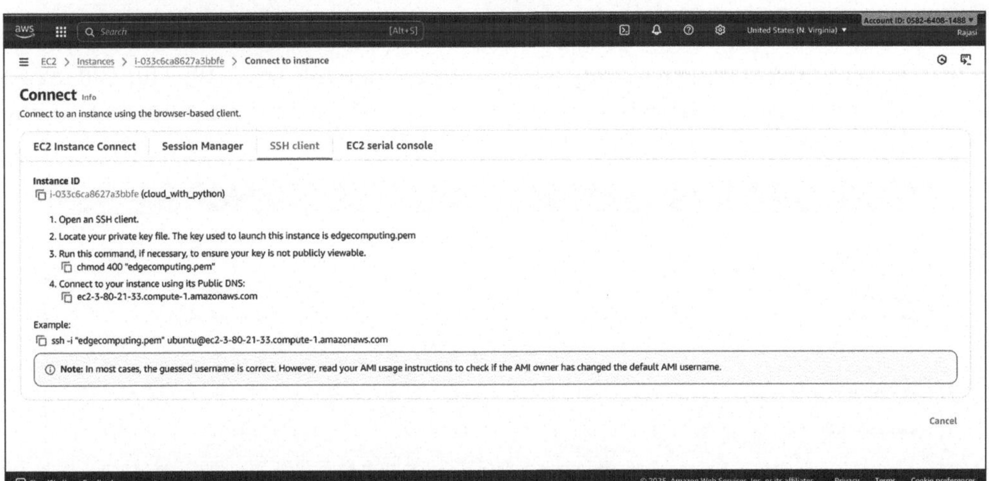

Figure 2.8: *A Screenshot Showing EC2 Instance Accessed through Windows Terminal*

8. An ubuntu terminal will open as a virtual machine on AWS cloud for deploying our localhost files. Do '**sudo apt-get update**' in the ubuntu terminal, and then download python with command '**sudo apt install python3-pip**'. After

python is installed, download flask with the command, '**`sudo apt install python3-flask`**'.

9. Download putty to do file transfer from the local host to ubuntu machine of AWS. Use **puttygen** to generate a new private key as .ppk for file transfer by loading the .pem key. For example, we have chosen the key name as "**`edgecomputingkey.ppk`**".
10. Use **`pscp`** command from putty to transfer files from localhost to ubuntu AWS virtual machine. In powershell type: **`pscp -i edgecomputingkey.ppk "<file path to CloudCode>" ubuntu@dnsservername:/home/ubuntu/.`** Run this command in the directory where the .ppk key is generated.
11. The file will get transferred to the AWS EC2 instance. Unzip the folder in the Ubuntu terminal of EC2 instance and run the command "**`flask -- app app.py run -- debug --host=0.0.0.0 –port=5001`**". Figure 2.9 shows running of the flask application on AWS EC2 through the localhost terminal.

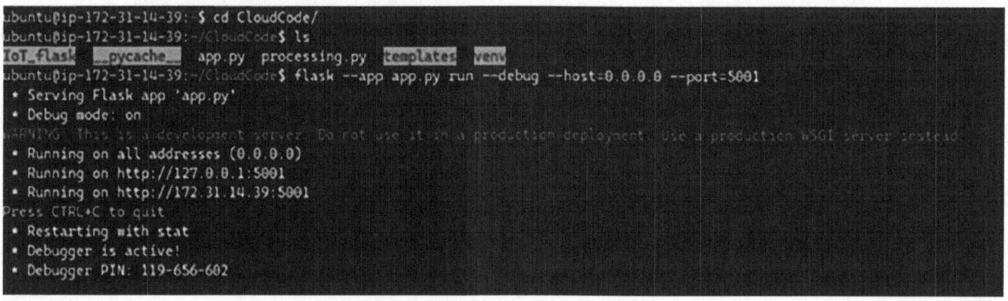

Figure 2.9: *Running Flask Application on EC2 Instance*

12. To see the webpage running, we have to change inbound rules for the created EC2 instances, as shown in *Figure* 2.10. Go to the security group, and add new inbound rules, allowing port 5001` and UDP packets.

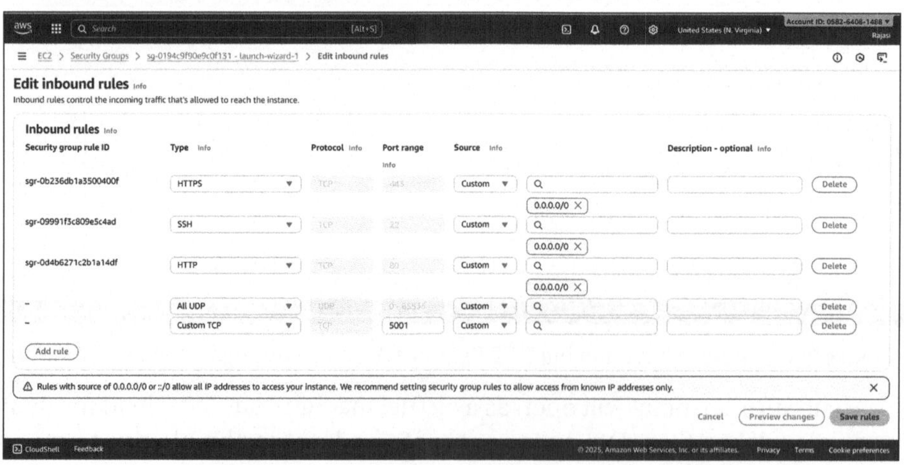

Figure 2.10: *Inbound Rules for Allowing UDP Packets*

13. We have successfully deployed our web application on Amazon AWS, using EC2 instance. The following *Figure* 2.11 takes input from the user, and *Figure* 2.12 displays the decision showing the webpage view on Amazon EC2 instance.

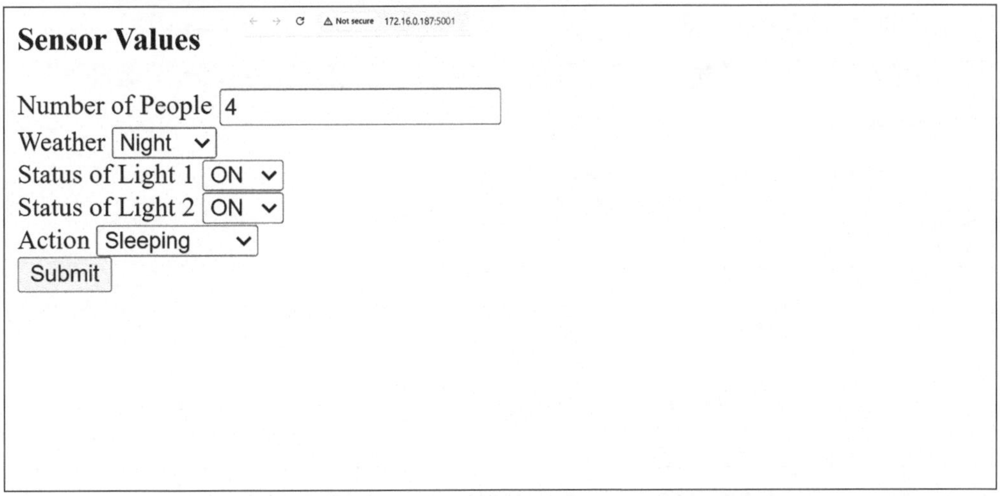

Figure 2.11: *Flask Web App First Page Running on Amazon EC2 Instance*

Figure 2.12: *Flask Web App Result Page Running on Amazon EC2 Instance*

Thus, ECS (Elastic Container Service) is being widely used currently to deploy IoT applications, and is replacing EC2 because ECS is based on containerization technology, and EC2 on virtualization. We will see the benefits of containerization over virtualization in *Chapter 10, Containerization Technology for Edge Intelligence.*

Microsoft Azure

Before deploying, we need to create a Microsoft Azure account. The sign up requires details as name, phone number, address, and credit card. After signing up, we sign into Microsoft Azure portal. The steps for deploying web app onto azure cloud is as follows:

1. Search for app service in the search box, and create a new app as shown in the following *Figure 2.13*.

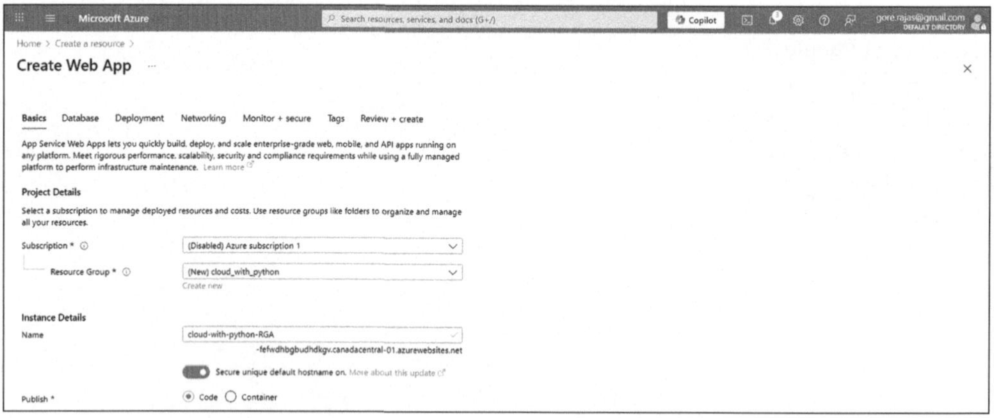

Figure 2.13: *Web App Creation Page on Azure Cloud*

2. Choose a resource name. We are choosing a name as **`Cloud_with_python`** for our example.

3. Choose a service name. We choose cloud-with-python-RGA for implementation purposes.

4. Choose OS as Linux, memory as 1GB, and runtime stack as python 3.9 for environment deployment. Choose a pricing plan as a free tier. For a better experience, it is recommended by the cloud to choose the basic tier.

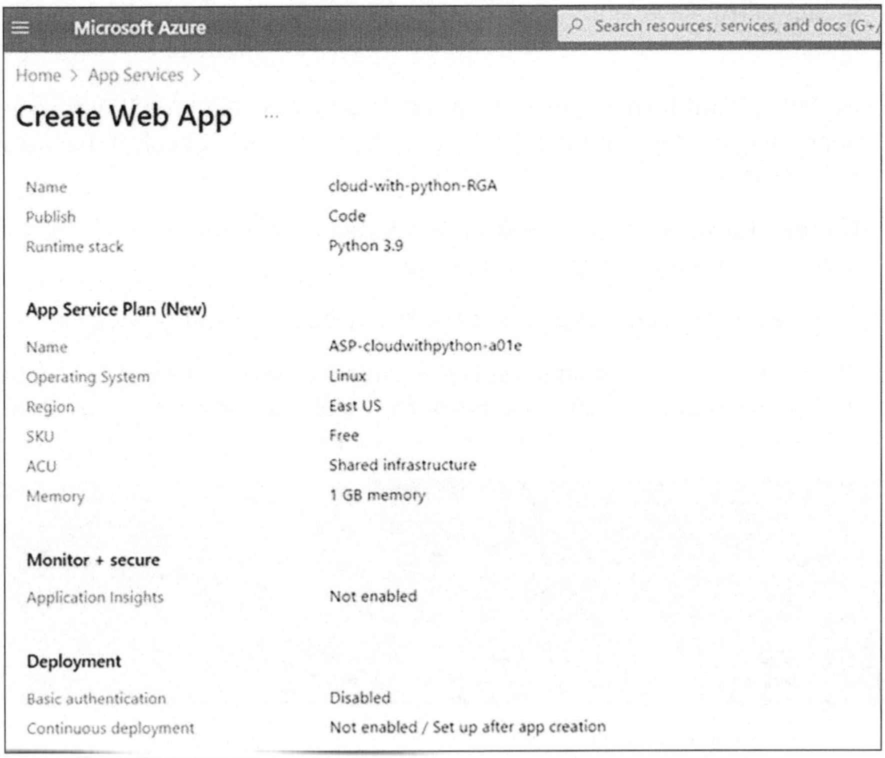

***Figure 2.14**: Summary of the Created Web App on Azure*

5. Click on "**`Review+create`**", and you will see a page shown in *Figure 2.14*.
6. The App is successfully deployed on Azure, as shown in the following *Figure 2.15*.

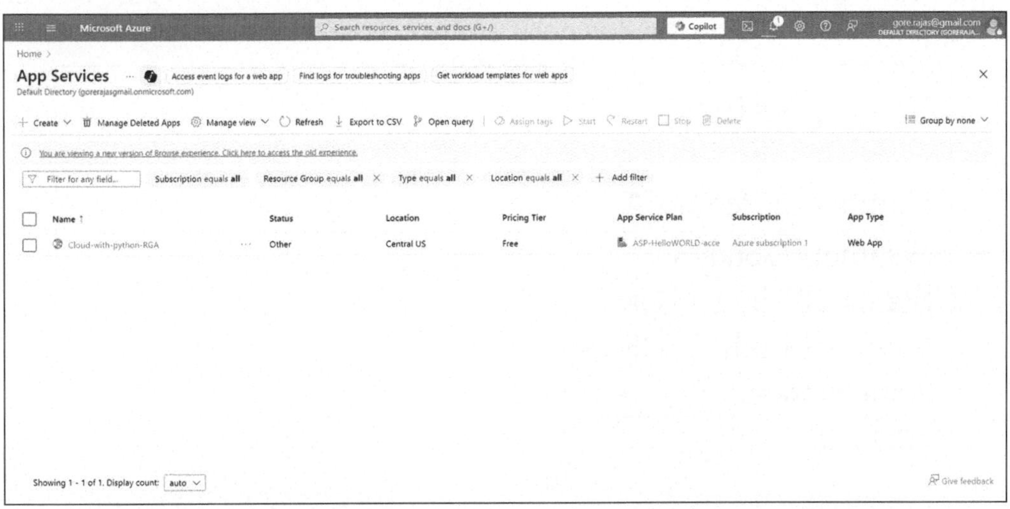

***Figure 2.15**: Successfully Deployed WebApp Named as cloud-with-python-RGA*

7. In the settings of the created app, edit the environment variable as auto-update.

8. Download and install azure cli for localhost (Download for Windows or Unix depending on the machine). Type **az** on the terminal to check, if the installation is successful.

9. Do "**az login**" with the email id of Microsoft account. After login, you have access to the cloud from a local machine.

10. Type "**az resource list**" to see the resource name and service name.

11. Type command "**az webapp deploy -- name <service name> ----resource-group <resource name> --src-path <zip file path>**". *Figure* 2.16 shows successful deployment of flask zip file on the created web app using Azure CLI.

Figure 2.16: *Successful Deployment of Flask zip File Using Web App Deploy Command on Azure CLI*

12. The command runs the file automatically, and deploys the web app onto http://<service-name>.azurewebsites.net/. So, we have successfully implemented our web app, using flask and python on azure cloud.

13. The following *Figure* 2.17 shows a webpage that takes input from users, where the number of people is 2, and the weather is cloudy with both lights on.

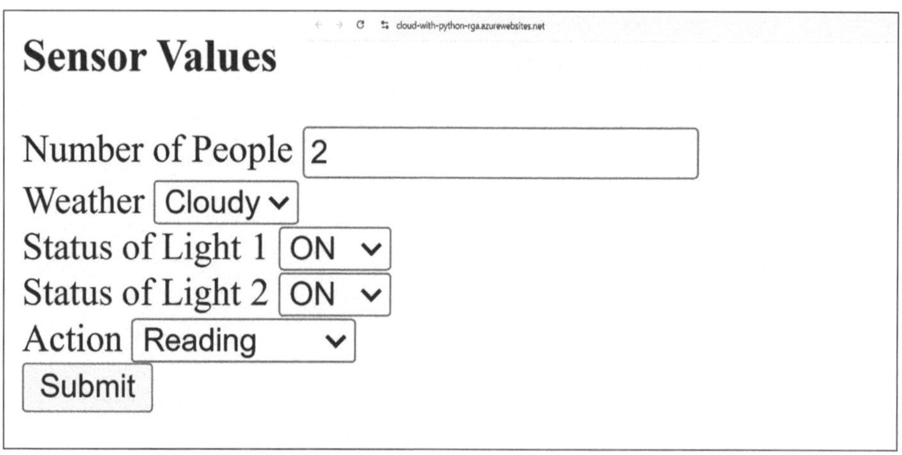

Figure 2.17: *Input Webpage of Flask App Deployed on Cloud IP*

14. The following *Figure* 2.18 shows the prediction of the flask app deployed on Azure Cloud.

***Figure 2.18**: Output Webpage of Flask App Showing Decision*

As we can see, both the clouds have different deployment setups. AWS requires SSH from the localhost, whereas azure has its own command line interface to login and deploy. AWS has more settings compared to azure. However, both have personal information that is stored in the cloud, and are open to hackers. Further, we need to stop the instance in AWS and the app in Azure, when not in use to reduce unnecessary costs. Deployment of even a small web application over a cloud is a lengthy process, but the application can scale to multiple users easily due to a plenty of resources.

Disadvantages with Cloud

Cloud as a concept has been very useful to deploy technologies that are running our worlds today. Social networking sites such as Facebook, OTT platforms like Netflix, e-commerce platforms like Amazon, search engines like Google, and mailing service like Gmail, everything is running smoothly due to cloud computing. Multiple smart applications also require the cloud to operate seamlessly, when accessed by a large population. Cloud has provided infrastructure, platform and software as service, and are available full time with minimal costs. However, all these technologies are exchanging data with clouds over the network. Thus, there is a huge amount of big data over the network. This causes **high network bandwidth consumption** that may lead to downtime, and slower performance of the applications.

The next disadvantage is that once an application is connected with a cloud, it goes into **vendor lock-in**. This means that the application cannot change the cloud service easily with another vendor. Another disadvantage is that building a datacenter for cloud infrastructure consumes lots of machines, and these machines are required to be kept cooled, requiring strong air conditioning. Thus, these cloud data centers consume lots of electricity, and emit lots of heat that is not good for the environment. One more disadvantage is that the data stored at the cloud have **security risks** as multiple applications can access the cloud. It is one of the major issues with the cloud. The recommender systems of some popular websites take our data from the cloud, and recommend similar items, or show similar advertisements to increase their buyers by being more adaptable to customers.

Furthermore, cloud is a **third-party software**. They can increase the cost of their service and users being on cloud lease, have to pay. Further, if for some case the cloud shuts down and goes into repair, all the applications dependent on the cloud have to wait for unknown duration. Therefore, the cloud is a **centralized system** with no backup of its own, even if they are used as backup. They are a point of failure for the whole application, and all the stored data is open for the world to access or hackers to attack even if privacy is set. The last disadvantage of cloud is that with slow internet connection, the application service can get disrupted. Limited network connections impact watching streaming videos, and downloading files over mails. Thus, a **strong and stable internet connection** is mandatory to have cloud benefits.

In fact, today the cloud is an integral part of our lives in the internet world, and with applications having big IoT data, cloud is the solution. But to handle disadvantages of cloud, the application architecture needs to be modified. Thus, came the concept of edge computing to support applications running on the cloud.

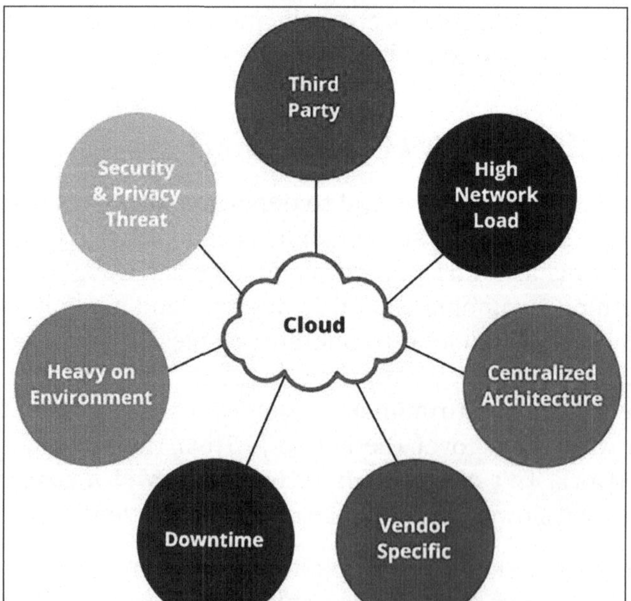

***Figure 2.19**: Disadvantages of the Cloud*

To summarize, the list of disadvantages of cloud as shown in *Figure* 2.19 are as follows:

- High network load
- Vendor lock-in
- Data security and privacy concern
- Third-party software
- Centralized system
- Requires a stable and strong internet connection

Edge with Cloud

IoT applications send the sensed/acquired big data to the cloud for storage and analysis via the Internet. Storage and analysis performed using cloud resources is known as cloud computing. The application developer selects the storage model and analytical model over the cloud according to the application's service. Further, cloud provides scalability and data security as features. To deal with the drawbacks of the cloud, one more layer is added in the IoT applications. The layer lies between sensors/actuators, and the internet connecting to the cloud for data communication. This layer is known as edge layer and storage as well as analysis performed in this layer is known as edge computing.

The data from sensors is communicated to the edge layer, where some of the computations are performed. After the edge layer processes the data, it communicates the data to the cloud for further computations. The communication from sensors to edge devices is within a private network and communication from edge devices to cloud is through a public internet. Therefore, edge computing supports cloud computing in data storage and analysis of an IoT application. Now, we will see what can potentially be edge devices, what computations they can perform and how edge computing is useful. We will consider an IoT application case study that uses edge computing as well as cloud computing. With the case study, it will be easy to understand the benefits of edge computing, and how it resolves drawbacks of the cloud.

Let us assume we are building a smart healthcare IoT application integrated with the cloud. Initial architecture of this application has sensors attached to the patient that communicates data to the gateway, and gateway communicates data to the cloud. The cloud does the storage and analysis of the data, and provides notification. Suppose, the patients that need to be monitored have Parkinson's disease, and the developed application provides early fall detection to the patients remotely. Moreover, it continuously monitors the body movements to detect a disorder as well as contacts hospitals and ambulances in case of emergency. The patient is attached with a wearable device, having sensors that record kinematics.

The data from these sensors have to be stored and analyzed to detect falls and react in an emergency. We select a storage model and an analytical model that takes sensor data as input, and detects falls, or new disorders. We deploy storage and data analysis on a public cloud, and connect the wearable device with the cloud. The data from wearable devices is now communicated to the cloud continuously to autonomously monitor the patient, and react in real-time in an emergency situation.

Assume the application has to monitor 1000 patients living far away from each other. The data from each of the patients is stored and analyzed at the cloud in parallel. There is a huge amount of data over the network and communicated to the cloud at the same time. This can lead to high bandwidth consumption, data loss, noisy data, delay in notifications or delayed detection of emergency conditions. Further, in case of cloud having errors, the developed application cannot afford to have high downtimes. Thus, in such a critical IoT application, completely relying on the cloud can be a disadvantage.

To solve these problems, we will develop our application using both cloud and edge computing. The wearable device is considered an edge device. Edge devices, in general, have very low computational and storage power. Data is then processed at the edge device for fall detection and emergency situations. The data is stored and analyzed in real-time over wearable data. Therefore, data to be communicated to the cloud is reduced. The analysis in real-time cannot be performed continuously at edge devices due to their very limited computational as well as storage power. In most cases, the data is communicated to the cloud for storage and analysis. In case of limited network or downtime of the cloud, the processing is shifted to the edge device for the meantime. You may be thinking that if all the data is still going to the cloud then how the data is reduced over network during good network connectivity?

Solution to this problem is that the edge device pre-processes the data and removes all the outliers as well as filters out data that requires no analysis. For example, if the acquired sensed data is the same for a long time, it is not sent to the cloud for analysis. In simple words, whenever an edge device finds a different reading in the values during continuous acquisition from the sensors, it communicates the data to the cloud for analysis. Through this way, edge devices help in reducing network burden as well as cloud burden. Further, edge devices can be used to contact hospital, relatives and ambulance, in case the application detects a fall.

One more thing to know beforehand is that the edge device cannot run heavy analytical models as they don't have as many resources as the cloud has. Thus, the analytical model running in the cloud may be of greater accuracy but it doesn't matter how much resources it is consuming. The analytical model over edge device needs to be lightweight as well as accurate. Another feature that edge devices can provide is to store sensitive data and not communicate it to the cloud to preserve privacy. For example, the patient's biodata and history record that is very sensitive, can be stored at wearable devices itself to preserve privacy of the patient.

Thus, an IoT application with edge computing has a lot of benefits compared to using only cloud computing. The edge devices are near to sensed location and provide real-time analysis in time-critical situations. Further, it supports cloud computing, reducing data over bandwidth and behaves like cloud during cloud downtime. The drawback of using edge computing is that the number of devices increases at the network edge. Moreover, to scale the computation for multiple persons at the same location, multiple edge devices need to be deployed and configured manually. Apart from these drawbacks, edge computing provides a distributed architecture, avoiding single point of failure, distributing the load, processing in parallel and decreasing the response time during emergency and fall.

Conclusion

In this chapter, we studied cloud components, cloud's layered architecture and type of clouds in detail. Cloud services are discussed and supported with an application use-case example. Next, we got to know world-wide IoT applications such as Vivint, Zoox, Fitbit that utilize cloud for large-scale deployments. Later in the chapter, we have gone through steps to deploy a web application, using flask and python, over amazon AWS and Microsoft azure cloud. Thus, we now have complete knowledge of what cloud is, different types of cloud, its services, its real-world usage, and hands-on deployment of a web app on cloud. At the end of the chapter, disadvantages of cloud are discussed followed by how edge computing is being integrated with cloud to handle the cloud disadvantages in IoT applications.

In the next chapter, we will study about the IoT big data pipeline from data acquisition, pre-processing and analysis.

Points to Remember

- Cloud consists of three main components: Front-end platform, back-end platform, and network.
- Cloud are of three types: Private cloud, public cloud, and hybrid cloud.
- There are three popular cloud services: Software as a Service (SaaS), Platform as a Service (PaaS), and Infrastructure as a Service (IaaS).
- IoT applications like Vivint for home security, Zoox for self-driving cars, and Fitbit for smart healthcare use cloud services.
- Cloud has multiple drawbacks such as downtime, high network load, vendor lock-in, third party software, centralized system, and privacy concerns.
- IoT applications with edge and cloud computing have a lot of benefits such as distributed architecture, privacy, fast computation, and reduced data on the network, compared to using only cloud computing.

Multiple Choice Questions

1. What type of cloud is Amazon AWS?
    a. Private Cloud
    b. Public Cloud
    c. Hybrid Cloud
    d. None of the above
2. If the application is deployed directly on cloud resources, the service is:
    a. Platform as a Service
    b. Software as a Service
    c. Infrastructure as a Service
    d. None of the above
3. If the application is deployed using installed software of the cloud, then the service is:
    a. Platform as a Service
    b. Software as a Service
    c. Infrastructure as a Service
    d. None of the above
4. If the application front-end is deployed on the cloud to access cloud services, the service is:
    a. Platform as a Service
    b. Software as a Service
    c. Infrastructure as a Service
    d. None of the above
5. Which is not a drawback of the cloud?
    a. High network load
    b. Downtime
    c. Single point of failure
    d. Limited resources

Answers

1. b
2. c
3. a
4. b
5. d

Questions

1. How many layers does the cloud have, and what is the functionality of each layer?
2. When to use hybrid cloud for deploying applications?
3. What are the drawbacks of each of the cloud services?
4. How does Zoox operate? What cloud does it run on?
5. How does Fitbit help in smart healthcare solutions?
6. What is the difference between cloud services of Vivint and ADT home security systems?
7. How to create an app service on Microsoft Azure?
8. How does edge computing support the cloud?

Chapter 3
Building IoT Data Pipelines

Introduction

In an IoT application, data from heterogeneous devices is acquired and processed. IoT data has characteristics among 5Vs: volume, velocity, veracity, value and variety. If an IoT data has all 5 Vs combined, it is also known as big data. IoT data needs to be processed either at the cloud or edge device. Processing of IoT data follows a pipeline. The pipeline consists of blocks such as data acquisition, data processing, data analysis, and data visualization. In data processing, the pipeline provides data interoperability, data quality, data storage, and data pre-processing. This chapter discusses each block of the pipeline in detail. Every IoT application will require different tools in the data pipeline depending on the generated IoT data by the application. This chapter will let you understand the IoT application's data, and accordingly model the pipeline.

The chapter mainly focuses on data and techniques used in the pipeline blocks. No one pipeline architecture fits all the IoT applications as data sources are different for each of the applications. Hence, modeling an IoT data pipeline for cloud and edge computing is one of the critical steps during development of an IoT application.

Structure

In this chapter, we will cover the following topics:

- Characteristics of IoT Data
- Data Acquisition
- Data Processing
  - Batch Processing
  - Stream Processing
- Data Storage
  - Relational Database

    - NoSQL Database
    - File System
- Data Pre-processing
    - Data Interoperability
    - Data Quality
- Data Analysis
- Data Visualization

Characteristics of IoT data

Let us start the chapter defining IoT data, and why it is different from normal web data over the network. In an IoT application, data comes from different sources. The main source is sensors attached to different things. The application either uses multiple sensors of different types, or a wireless sensor network of the same sensor, to gather environment data. The only motive to have so many sensors is to have accurate data. For instance, if one sensor fails, the data from other sensors can be used or previously captured data can be used to have data for processing. Data from sensors sometimes is not sufficient to make accurate decisions. In such cases, the sensed data is supported by online data such as weather data, twitter data or a feedback system, to have accurate environment data. The acquired data needs to be very accurate and complete to make trustworthy decisions. A good data will lead to minimum false positives.

However, the data coming from these sources pose different challenges before it can be used for decision making. Getting good IoT data and accurate decisions requires a pipeline. This pipeline combines the data, acquired from different sources, and provides it to an analytical model. Before combining, the data is pre-processed. This data is IoT data that comes from different sources, and is analyzed to have timely and correct service.

IoT data comes from multiple sources, sensors or websites, generating huge amounts of data and hence, voluminous. The data coming from different sources is structured and unstructured and thus, has variety. Further, data from each source is generated at their own rate and thus has high or low velocity. Data from each source may have bias, missing data and inaccuracy as either sensor can be faulty, data can be incorrect or the network is overburdened with data from other applications over limited bandwidth. Thus, IoT data has veracity. Last, each of the IoT data has a value attached. Thus, IoT data requires special processing techniques in the pipeline for accurate, and timely decision-making. Accurate decisions reduce cost, and provide customer satisfaction. Further, changes in data pipeline techniques can improve application performance.

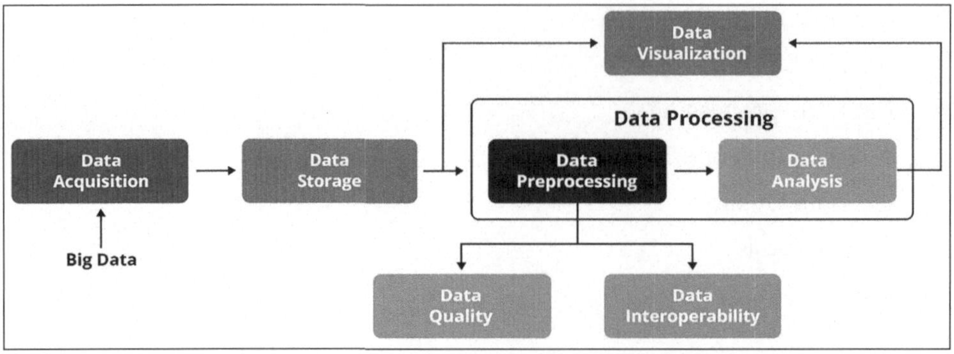

Figure 3.1: *Data Pipeline for Handling IoT Data*

The data pipeline has to be modeled such that the incoming IoT data is handled efficiently to provide accurate decisions. The data pipeline steps are shown in *Figure* 3.1. The first step in the data pipeline is **data acquisition**. This step includes embedded device and network protocols to capture the sensed data. Acquired data needs to be pre-processed for quality improvement, and making it interoperable. **Data pre-processing** includes, removal of noise, imputation of missing data and removing outliers. Two important steps during data pre-processing are providing data quality and data interoperability. Data quality is increased to increase trust in the data. **Data quality** techniques make the data complete, consistent and accurate. Further, data from different sources is heterogeneous and **data interoperability** step resolves heterogeneity to have complete data that can be understood by the application.

Therefore, once the data is pre-processed, quality is checked, data is made interoperable, it is stored. **Data storage** is modeled depending on type of data, either structured or unstructured. From storage, the data is provided to another major pipeline step that is **data processing**. Data processing can be either stream processing or batch processing or both. If data has high velocity and is complete for analysis, it requires stream processing. If data has low velocity and requires previous data to have accurate decision-making, it requires batch processing. There are popular data processing techniques for stream and batch processing. As per the processing choice, the data is analyzed, a decision has to be made. The result from analysis is visualized with the help of charts and graphs in the **data visualization** step. Thus, on the basis of the analysis results and visualization plots, an accurate decision is made by the application.

Data Acquisition

In an IoT application, the sensors are embedded on the things to make them smart. How do things get smart with just a sensor? The data from the sensor is acquired, and then processed for decision-making at the edge device or the cloud. Embedding a sensor over a thing using an embedded device, and then communicating the data from sensor to edge device/cloud are the tasks in the data acquisition block. Steps in the data acquisition block are discussed as follows:

1. **Sensor Data Collection:** Select appropriate sensors and an appropriate embedded device as per the IoT application. These sensors can be analog or digital and convert physical properties to electric signals. These sensors come in raw form with pins. Raw sensors are connected with embedded devices such as Arduino Uno, Raspberry Pi, Jetson, NodeMCU, ESP32 using jumper wires. An embedded device is either a microcontroller or microprocessor and that has capabilities to run software over for a dedicated task. To connect sensors, there are dedicated pins on the embedded devices. These pins are known as GPIO (General Purpose Input/Output).

   The embedded devices do not automatically capture the data. A code has to be written that accesses sensors through specific pins and collects data. In the case of Arduino Uno, the code is written in Arduino App, and then flashed on Arduino Uno. In the case of Raspberry Pi and Jetson, the code is written in python. Arduino Uno has specific pins for analog sensors and digital sensors. In the case of Raspberry Pi or Jetson, an ADC device is required to convert analog signals to digital. Arduino is easy to attach sensors and acquire data with strong capabilities compared to Raspberry Pi/ Jetson Nano. However, Arduino is a microcontroller, it can only be used to acquire data. Raspberry Pi and Jetson are microprocessors that can acquire data as well as process it for decision-making. Further, Arduino Uno does not have wireless communication features. Another device that works similar to Arduino Uno and has wireless capabilities is NodeMCU. A more powerful embedded device is ESP32 that has more computing power compared to Arduino and NodeMCU and has wireless as well as Bluetooth connectivity. Raspberry Pi/Jetson comes with an attached WiFi driver for communication.

2. **Sensor Data Communication:** Once the data is collected from a sensor on the embedded device, it needs to be communicated for processing either at edge or cloud. For data communication, we need to consider the communication range of the embedded device, and accordingly the protocol to be used. Micro-controller devices prefer low communication range due to its processing power, whereas micro-processors have low as well as high communication range. IoT applications have a set of protocols specific for low communication range and high communication range. For low communication range, popular IoT protocols used are Bluetooth, ZigBee, LoRaWAN, and for high range, the popular protocols are CoAP, MQTT and AMQP. If the data needs to be communicated to a nearby edge device, then low range communication protocols are used. However, if the data has to be communicated to a faraway end device or the cloud, high communication range protocol is used. Thus, depending on application architecture, micro-controller/micro-processor is selected as well as communication protocol is selected for data acquisition.

Data from other sources such as social media and mobile vehicles, are acquired via the internet. Mobile vehicles are attached with a camera, microphone, GPS which forms a sensor network within the car. Camera, microphone, and GPS are already embedded devices that do not require coding. The data is directly communicated to nearby edge devices or the cloud.

To get a better understanding, we will go through a use-case. For use-case, we consider data from a PIR motion sensor attached to Arduino Uno. The sensor data captured on Arduino Uno would be communicated to Raspberry Pi, an edge device for the use-case. The hardware required for the use case

First, we need to connect the hardware. For connections, we need to study the pins of Arduino Uno. Arduino Uno consists of 14 digital I/O pins, 6 analog I/O pins and 6 power pins consisting of ground pin, reset pin and two pins of 3v and 5v each. Now, we have to identify if the sensor connected to the Arduino is analog or digital. For this, the sensor manual needs to be studied. PIR motion sensor has 3 pins, ground pin, 5v pin and a digital pin. All three pins of the sensor are connected to respective Arduino pins using female to female jumper wires.

Once the hardware is connected, we need to code the software for Arduino. For that, an Arduino IDE has to be installed on our respective machines. On Arduino IDE, we write code for getting data from sensors and communicating it to the IP address of Raspberry Pi.

In the Arduino IDE, create a new file named "**motion_sensor.ino**". The code for Arduino Uno is called sketch. A sketch has two functions: **setup ()** and **loop ()**. In setup function(), the part of code is written that has to run only once and in loop() function, the part of code is written that has to run continuously. In the new sketch file, before setup and loop function, we need to include required libraries. C++ programming language is used to code in Arduino IDE. Here is a sample sketch to turn on LED when motion is detected else LED is off. It is a default coding language but later we will see deployment of same code using python.

```
int sensor = 3;                // The pin to which the motion sensor
is attached to
int LEDpin = 13;            // The pin to which the LED is attached
to
int state = LOW;               // By default, no motion detected
int val=0;
void setup()
{
  pinMode(sensor, INPUT);     // Initialize sensor as an input
  pinMode(LEDpin, OUTPUT); // Initial LED as output
```

```
  Serial.begin(115200);        // Initialize serial communication
with 115200 bits per second
}

void loop()
{
  val = digitalRead(sensor); // Read sensor value and store in
val variable
  if (val == HIGH) {           // check if the sensor is HIGH
    digitalWrite(LEDpin, HIGH); // LED is ON
    delay(100);                 // delay 100 milliseconds

    if (state == LOW) {
      Serial.write("Motion detected!");
      state = HIGH;       // update variable state to HIGH
    }
  }
  else {
      digitalWrite(LEDpin, LOW); // turn LED OFF
      delay(200);              // delay 200 milliseconds

      if (state == HIGH){
       Serial.write("Motion stopped!");
        state = LOW;       // update variable state to LOW
    }
}
Serial.print(state);
 Serial.print("\n");
}
```

This code is flashed on the Arduino Uno with the help of Arduino IDE by connecting the device to the machine using a USB connector. In the IDE, select the board as Arduino Uno and port as displayed (for example: **com3(Arduino)**), and then click on the top left arrow button for uploading. The above sketch shows how to read sensor data from a digital pin as input and control LED light on a digital pin as output with a single Arduino Uno board.

If there is no Arduino Board to experiment with, there is an Arduino Simulator Wokwi. On it, you can copy paste the above code and design the system setup for simulation using tools. On the page, there is a plus sign to add components to Arduino Uno. We added a motion sensor to the Arduino Uno. To make connections between the Arduino Uno and the motion sensor, we select a pin of the Arduino Uno, for example 3.3 V and connect it to the '+' pin of the motion sensor. Similarly, the GND pin of Arduino Uno is connected to the '-' pin of the motion sensor. The D pin of the motion sensor is connected to digital pin 3 of Arduino Uno. If a connection gets wrongly connected, we can click on the connection and delete it. We can also change the color of the connection. LED is also selected from the drop down menu and added to Arduino

Uno on Pin 13 and GND. The screenshot of the simulator with code and connection is shown in *Figure 3.2*.

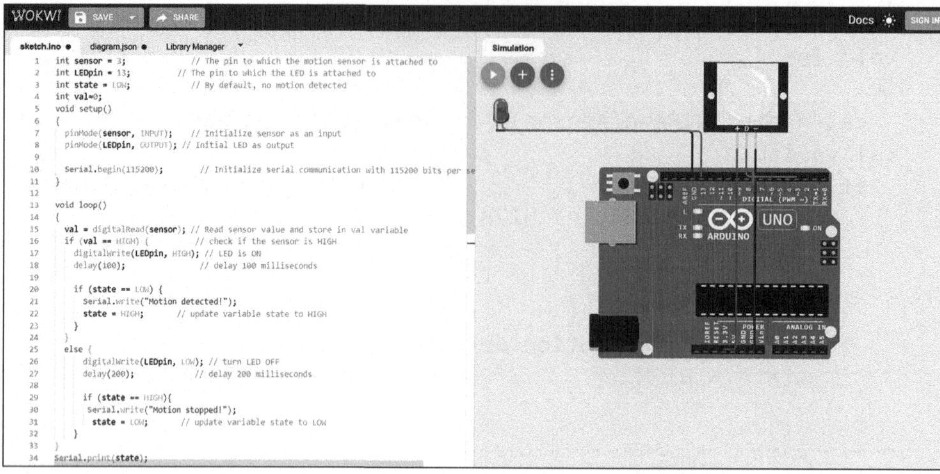

Figure 3.2: *Arduino Attached with Sensors on WokWi Simulator*

Once the connection is made, and code is written on sketch.info, the play button is clicked that starts the simulation. Click on the motion sensor to simulate motion. Click on simulation motion, and you will see the display as 1 and LED blinking. Close the motion simulation to stop the motion, and values get back to 0 with a message that the motion has stopped. Both the simulation results are shown in *Figure 3.3*.

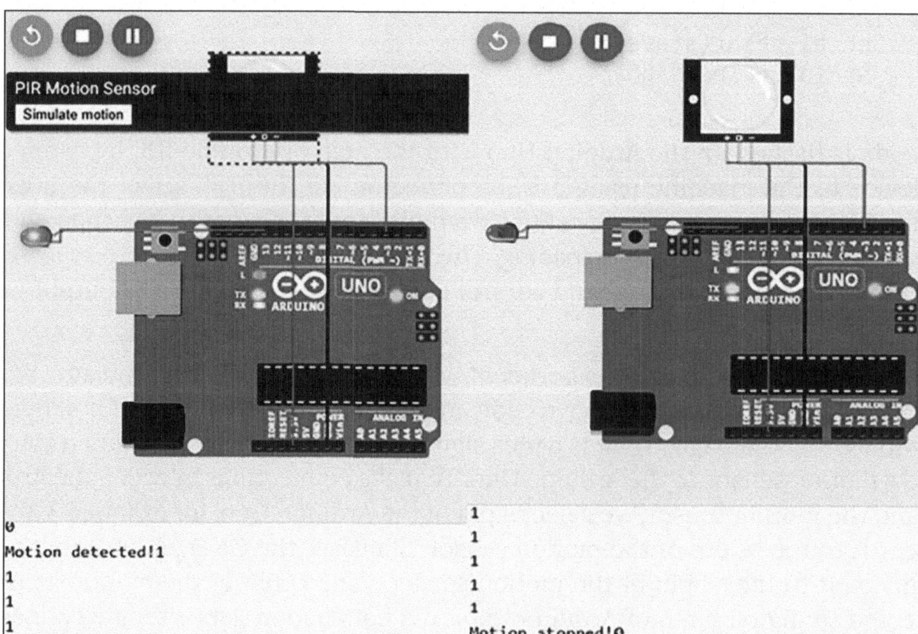

Figure 3.3: *Led is on When Motion is Detected, and LED gets off When Motion Stops*

To code the same in python on Arduino Uno, we need to use micropython. For using micropython, a library named femtoPython Library and femtoPython Board. Micropython is a lightweight version of Python 3, especially designed for embedded devices. Use Micropython on Wokwi - Online ESP32, STM32, Arduino Simulator to code in micropython. We will code the above example on an ESP32 board using micropython language. The interface to code in micropython, and simulate working of ESP32 is shown in *Figure* 3.4.

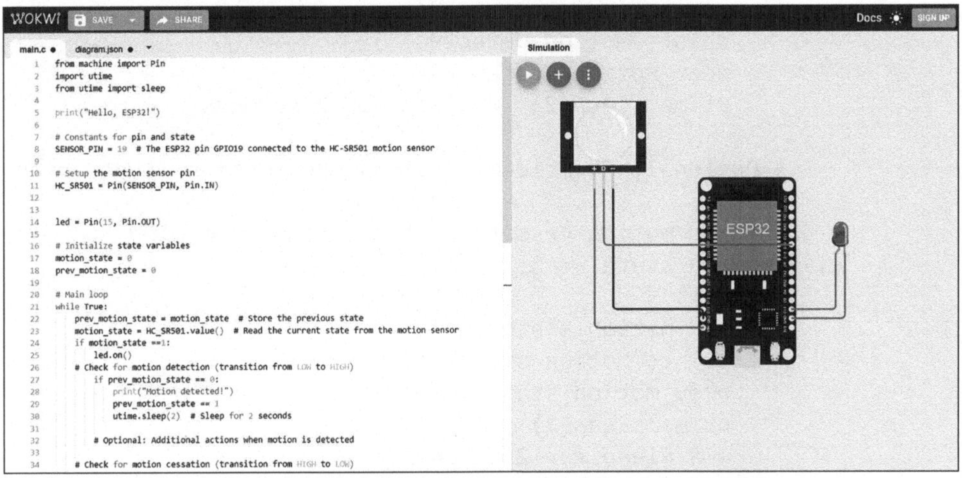

Figure 3.4: *Python Implementation on Simulated ESP32 Device with Attached Motion Sensor and LED Sensor*

```
Micro-python Code of the above code is as follows:
from machine import Pin
import utime
from utime import sleep

print("Hello, ESP32!")

# Constants for pin and state
SENSOR_PIN = 19  # The ESP32 pin GPIO19 connected to the HC-SR501
motion sensor

# Setup the motion sensor pin
HC_SR501 = Pin(SENSOR_PIN, Pin.IN)


led = Pin(15, Pin.OUT)

# Initialize state variables
motion_state = 0
prev_motion_state = 0
```

```
# Main loop
while True:
    prev_motion_state = motion_state  # Store the previous state
    motion_state = HC_SR501.value()  # Read the current state
from the motion sensor
    if motion_state ==1:
        led.on()
    # Check for motion detection (transition from LOW to HIGH)
        if prev_motion_state == 0:
            print("Motion detected!")
            prev_motion_state == 1
            utime.sleep(2)  # Sleep for 2 seconds

        # Optional: Additional actions when motion is detected

    # Check for motion cessation (transition from HIGH to LOW)
    elif motion_state == 0:
        led.off()
        if prev_motion_state == 1:
            print("Motion stopped!")
            prev_motion_state == 0
            utime.sleep(2)
            # # Sleep for 2 seconds
    print(motion_state)
```

The code successfully runs on Wokwi simulator and the LED light of ESP32 blinks on, when the motion is detected. It blinks off, when the motion is stopped. The screenshot is shown in *Figure* 3.5. If the code is successful on a simulator, it is ready to be flashed on the main hardware. Coding on a simulator first guarantees that the code is working and correct. Simulation saves time of re-flashing every time with code errors.

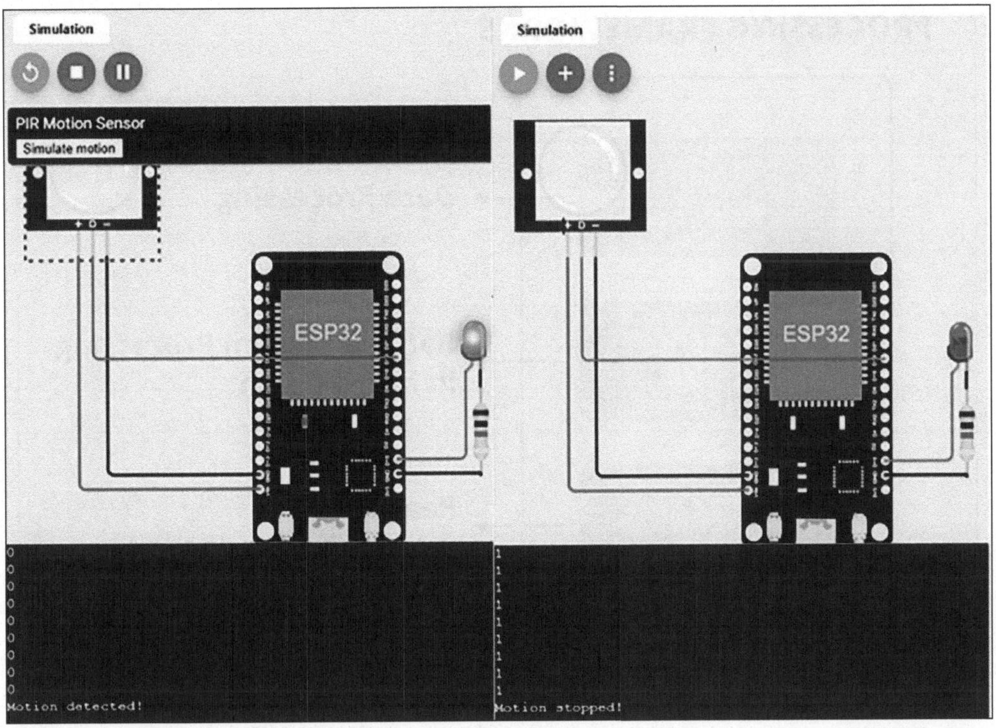

Figure 3.5: *Snapshots of the Simulated ESP32 Device Coded with Micropython*

Data Processing

The data communicated to Raspberry Pi, considered as an edge device, has to be stored and processed. There are mainly two types of processing: Batch processing and Stream processing. In batch processing, a huge amount of stored data is divided into batches, and each batch is processed parallel. Thus, processing is performed after a scheduled interval with a fixed amount of batch size. In stream processing, the data is processed in real-time, near real-time for on-the-fly insights. Most of the IoT applications follow stream processing as they require real-time processing of the environment for suitable instant actions.

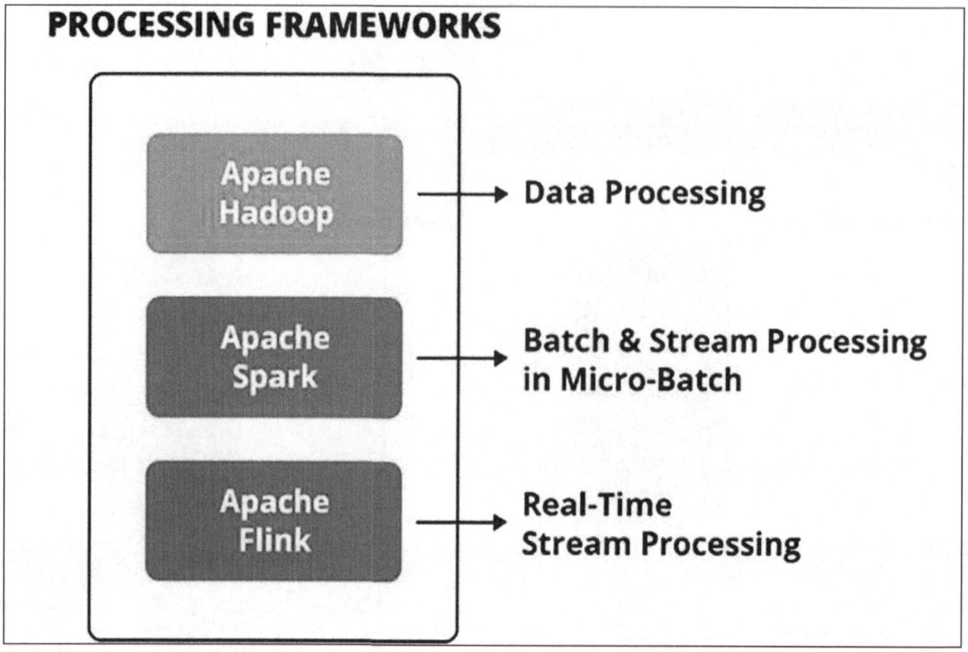

Figure 3.6: *Types of Processing Frameworks for Streaming or Batch IoT Data*

There are three very popular, open-source frameworks for IoT data processing such as: **Apache Hadoop, Apache Spark and Apache Flink** as shown in *Figure 3.6*. These tools work on clusters of computer systems to handle voluminous data, where one machine is a specific master node, and all other machines are slave nodes within the cluster. Apache Hadoop is a software that processes large amounts of data on multiple machines, using map-reduce technique. Apache Hadoop is the first and popular technology for batch processing of IoT data. Apache Hadoop has a fixed processing and storage model. Furthermore, Hadoop processing is only in Java. To overcome limitations of Apache Hadoop, Apache Spark was designed as a processing tool for IoT data. Apache Spark is an engine that provides interfaces and tools for data processing.

Apache Spark supports three programming languages: Scala, Python and R. Apache Hadoop that are popular for batch processing whereas Apache Spark is popular for both batch and stream processing. Apache Spark provides integration with different storage models and platforms to run different machine learning models. Therefore, Apache Spark is considered a better choice than Apache Hadoop. Apache Flink is another processing tool that is popular in IoT applications. It provides real-time processing of streaming data as opposed to Apache Spark that only provides processing of streaming data, considering data as micro-batches. Therefore, latency of real-time response in Apache Flink is very low compared to Apache Spark. Next, we will implement batch processing and stream processing, using PySpark, a python version of Apache Spark, for a better picture on how these two processing types differ.

For installing **PySpark**, we require python, java and Hadoop installed, and after spark download, set environment variables for **`HADOOP_HOME`**, **`SPARK_HOME`**, **`JAVA_HOME`**, **`PYTHON_HOME`** and **`PYSPARK_PYTHON`**. Further add **`SPARK_HOME\bin`** and **`HADOOP_HOME\bin`** to the path. PySpark has tools to run ML algorithms and Graph algorithms.

PySpark works on dataframes, and supports multiple APIs for reading and writing different formats. It has the ability to convert RDD (Resilient distributed datasets) to dataframes. What is RDD? RDD is the basic data structure of Apache Spark. The data is partitioned into multiple slave nodes by driver programs running on the master node, and are represented as RDD. These RDDs are operated in parallel for fast processing of a huge amount of data. RDD has no schema, and is suitable for operations on semi-structured and unstructured data. PySpark dataframe is a high level abstraction of RDDs, and stores data in tabular format with attribute names. Pyspark SQL is used to perform operations on the dataframe. Similar to RDD, dataframes also have transformation operations such as sort, filter, rename, and add. PySpark also has a MLlib library to deploy machine learning algorithms for classification, regression, clustering and much more. Part of the IoT data pipeline from pre-processing to training, and deployment of machine learning models can be implemented on Apache Spark ecosystem via MLlib library.

Batch Processing with PySpark

For batch processing, PySpark follows the map-reduce technique of Hadoop. Pyspark has an advantage over Hadoop as it provides parallel processing, in-memory processing and fault-tolerance. However, batch processing technique of using map-reduce in both as well as other processing frameworks is the same. Thus, we will see the working of map-reduce functions through an example. MapReduce works on Hadoop File System (HDFS). It is a programming model that provides fast processing of voluminous data by computing chunks of data in parallel. The MapReduce technique has two parts: Map and reduce. The client submits a job to map-reduce function. A job consists of a collection of multiple small tasks. Data is provided as input to the map-reduce on which the job has to be performed. In the map-reduce task, the map function divides the data into small chunks and maps it into a <key, value> pair. The key is the id of address, and the value is the actual data. The key-value pairs are re-organized according to the job, and provided to reduce function. The reduce task groups up the key-value pair according to the job, and then provides output. The Master Node runs the job tracker and task tracker to manage the tasks, and the shared data running over clusters of slave nodes. Thus, the Map and Reduce functions are tasks assigned by Job Tracker onto multiple slave nodes, depending on the submitted job. The Task Tracker keeps track of all the tasks mapped onto the slave nodes.

The following example shows how to run batch processing on data using PySpark. The example reads data from csv file, and converts into dataframe with a query. There are two queries. The first query groups the data with respect to Departure station, and prints the average price of each station. The second query groups the data by Arrival destination, and prints the total arrivals. Grouping is a mapping technique and counting, and average computations is a reduced technique.

```
from pyspark.sql import SparkSession
import pandas as pd
# Create SparkSession
spark = SparkSession.builder.appName("BatchProcessing").getOr
Create()
# Read batch data from a file
df = spark.read.csv(r"C:\Users\HP\Downloads\UKTrainRides\railway.
csv", header=True, inferSchema=True)
#Data from https://mavenanalytics.io/data-playground
result = df.groupBy("Departure Station").avg("price")
result.show()
result = df.groupBy("Arrival Destination").count()
result.show()
```

The output is shown in the following *Figure 3.7*. This output shows the framework chose a list of departure stations from the table, and displayed the average price for each. Further, it displayed the number of trains for each arrival destination. The result is observed by Hadoop after batch-processing the whole dataset.

```
+--------------------+------------------+
|   Departure Station|        avg(price)|
+--------------------+------------------+
|Liverpool Lime St...|29.658846744135058|
|              Oxford|19.854166666666668|
|Bristol Temple Meads|             6.125|
|Manchester Piccad...|13.329911504424778|
|  Edinburgh Waverley| 41.03921568627451|
|       London Euston| 22.61707710940654|
|    London St Pancras| 16.18015934207145|
|Birmingham New St...|17.844569288389515|
|             Reading| 17.04882154882155|
|   London Paddington|18.631555555555554|
|                York| 21.08522114347357|
|  London Kings Cross| 47.20974225585245|
+--------------------+------------------+

+--------------------+-----+
| Arrival Destination|count|
+--------------------+-----+
|           Edinburgh|  154|
|Liverpool Lime St...| 5022|
|            Tamworth|  227|
|            Coventry|   65|
|              Oxford|  623|
...
|   London St Pancras|  749|
+--------------------+-----+
only showing top 20 rows
```

Figure 3.7: *Batch Processing Output of Hadoop Framework with Pyspark*

Stream Processing with PySpark

Pyspark processes streaming data using **readStream** and **writeStream** from spark structured streaming tool. Spark structure streaming is an engine for handling streaming data, and is based on Spark SQL engine. It converts the live incoming data into table format incrementally and updates the required results as input data comes in. The table size is unbounded.

Both **readStream** and **writeStream** have common methods of **path()** for fetching file, storage path, format() for having format of the file to be read or file in which data has to be written and option() that takes 'key' and 'value' as parameters. **readStream** has method schema() as schema of the file is highly required in structured streaming, to start reading data as streams from the file. **readStream** cannot detect schema of the file on its own given the file path, it needs to be defined explicitly. **writeStream** has a method called output mode. Three output modes are considered: complete (all rows of the table are written to storage), append (only appended rows are written to storage), update (only extended rows are written to storage). The methods common to both **readStream** and **writeStream** are format(), path() and option('key','value'). Another way streaming data can be captured is via listening to sockets from a specific port. For reading from socket, streaming context is initialized and streaming context has function **socketTextStream** (host, port) for enabling listening to data from socket. From streaming data from socket, create **DStream** (Discretized Stream) and provide processing steps on the **DStream**. These **DStreams** are treated as micro-batches and are processed in real-time. In the following code, the data is provided as input from the json file, and each of the records from the json file is considered as streaming data.

```
import pyspark
from pyspark.sql import SparkSession
import pandas as pd
from pyspark.sql.types import *
from pyspark.sql.functions import *
spark = SparkSession.builder.appName("StreamProcessing").getOr-
Create()
# Read data stream from a socket
jsonSchema = StructType([ StructField("time", TimestampType(),
True), StructField("action", StringType(), True) ])
lines = spark.readStream.option("maxFilesPerTrigger", 1).schema
(jsonSchema)\      .json(r"C:\Users\HP\Downloads\Data")
wordCounts = lines.groupBy("action").count()
query = wordCounts.writeStream.outputMode("complete").format
("console").start()
query.awaitTermination()
```

The following *Figure* 3.8 displays the output after stream processing, using above the code in the Hadoop framework.

```
>>> # Await termination of the streaming query
>>> query.awaitTermination()
24/09/15 08:29:21 WARN ProcfsMetricsGetter: Exception
-------------------------------------------
Batch: 0
-------------------------------------------
+------+-----+
|action|count|
+------+-----+
|  Open|    5|
| Close|    2|
+------+-----+
```

Figure 3.8: *Stream Processing Output of Hadoop Framework with Pyspark*

Data Storage

After the sensor data is acquired, it is stored for processing. The data acquired can be structured or unstructured. Structured data has a specific format and requires specific storage. Unstructured data follows no format, and has to be parsed using metadata. Multiple IoT devices collectively generate huge amounts of either structured data or unstructured data, or both. Analyzing the relationship between these is important to provide smart services. File format, its volume and the relationships with other data, decides the storage system for IoT data. There are three types of storage used in IoT applications: Relational database, NoSQL database and File system. Each of them is discussed in detail below.

Relational Database

Relational database storage is based on a relational model of data, and follows ACID (Atomicity, Consistency, Isolation, Durability) property. The relational model of data is represented as tabular form in rows and columns. Multiple tables are required to completely model an application. A row represents an object.

Columns denote multiple attributes of the object. Relational database is very restrictive in terms of the number of rows, columns and data formats. Any record deleted or inserted in a table impacts the data consistency in multiple tables. Performing joint operation in multiple tables for large-scale data adds on complexity. Due to the above reasons, for large-scale data, managing relational databases in vertical-integrated scalable systems is a challenge. Hence, these databases are suitable for smart city applications whose service is based on historical data evaluation on small-scale data. They are not suitable for large-scale or real-time IoT applications. For example, we have created a table in a MySQL application in the following *Figure* 3.9, entered values in the table as shown in *Figure* 3.10, and then accessed the data through PySpark.

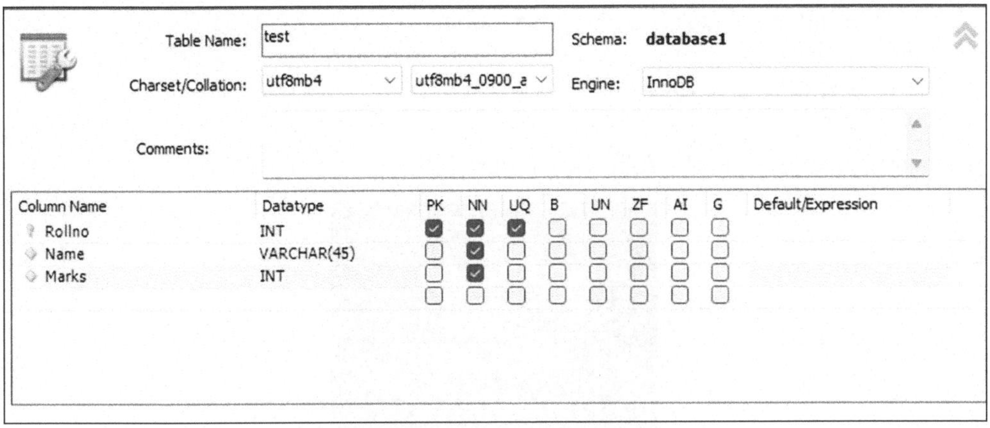

Figure 3.9: *Creation of database1 in MySQL*

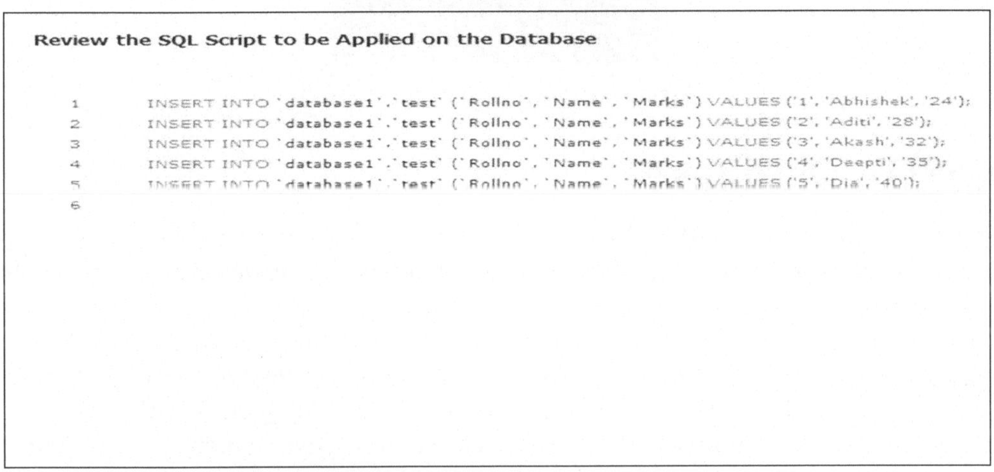

Figure 3.10: *Inserting Values into the Database Using SQL*

The PySpark code is as follows:

```
import mysql.connector
import pandas as pd
pd.DataFrame.iteritems = pd.DataFrame.items
from pyspark.sql import SparkSession
appName = "PySpark MySQL "
master = "local"
spark = SparkSession.builder.master(master).appName(appName).
getOrCreate()
#Establish a connection
conn = mysql.connector.connect(user='root', database='database1',
password='RDBMSMYSQL', host="localhost", port=3306)
```

```
cursor = conn.cursor()
query = "SELECT Name FROM test WHERE (Marks > 30)"
# Create a pandas dataframe
pdf = pd.read_sql(query, con=conn)
conn.close()
df = spark.createDataFrame(pdf)
df.show()
```

The result is displayed in the following *Figure* 3.11.

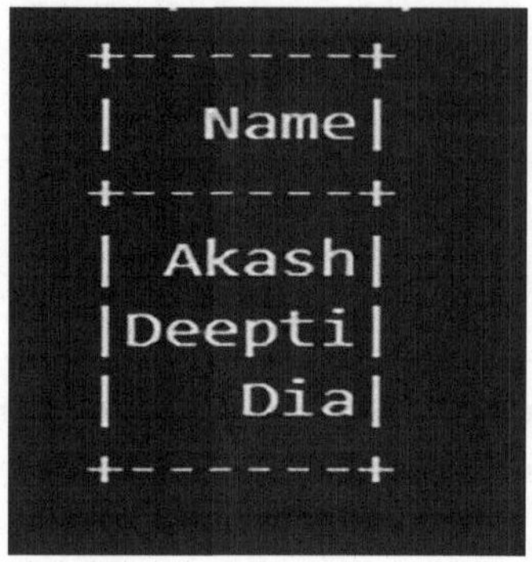

***Figure* 3.11:** SQL *Output on database1*

NoSQL Database

Smart city applications that have to handle voluminous real-time data choose NoSQL databases for storage. This database follows CAP (Consistency, Availability and Partition tolerance) theorem and BASE (Basically Available, Soft State, Eventual consistency) principle. It is developed to resolve consistency and complexity limitations of relational storage. This storage model is flexible because multiple columns and records can be added or removed dynamically. It has the advantage of depicting spatio-temporal relationships between the data which is a drawback in relational databases.

To use a NoSQL database in PySpark, you have to run PySpark on shell followed by -packages that contain a link for the database to be used. The database to be used has to be installed on the device, and the database is accessed through PySpark for processing. An Example is: **`pyspark --packages com.datastax.spark: spark-cassandra-connector-assembly_2.11:2.5.1`** that imports Cassandra spark connector to access Cassandra database. A NoSQL database provides four types of storage models.

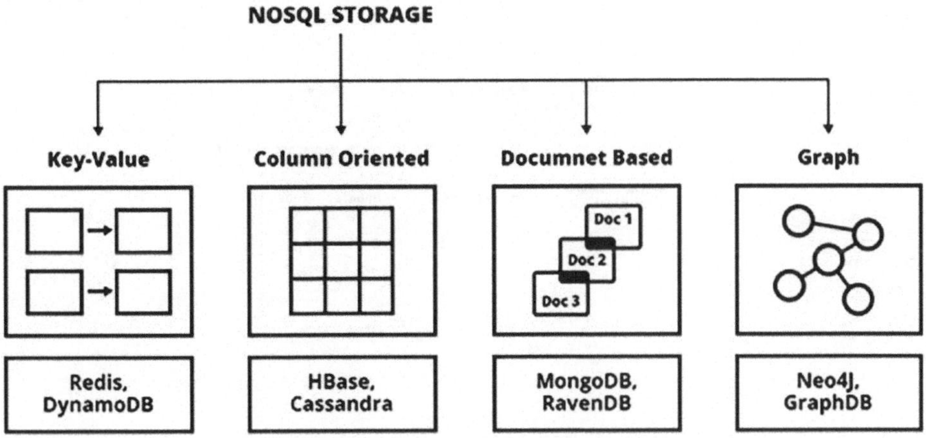

Figure 3.12: *Different Types of NoSQL Database*

These models as shown in *Figure* 3.12 are discussed as follows:

- **Key-value Model**: It is the simplest NoSQL database model. The data is stored in the form of a key-value pair in map data structure. The values are accessed using get, put, and delete operations. It does not provide complex query processing over the data. Examples of key value stores are: Redis, Berkeley DB, and Amazon's DynamoDB.
- **Column-oriented Model**: Data is stored in row-column fashion. In this model, each row has flexible columns. Collection of these columns is defined in a column family. Each column has a key-value pair stored with a timestamp. Some examples of column oriented databases are HBase, BigTable and Cassandra.
- **Document-oriented Model:** Data is stored in the form of documents. These documents are accessed using a key that can be an ID, URL or path. Each document may have different values. Thus, the metadata is stored with the document. Formats in which documents are stored are XML, JSON and BSON. Some databases that are based on this model are CouchBase, MongoDB and Raven. This example shows the use of MongoDB with PySpark to store and retrieve JSON data. The Json data file previously used in stream processing is stored in mongoDB database and the database is made online on localhost as shown in *Figure* 3.13. PySpark access the data from the localhost, and produce results.

Figure 3.13: *Creation of MongoDB Table on Compass*

```
import pyspark
from pyspark import SparkContext, SparkConf
from pyspark.sql import SparkSession, SQLContext, functions as F
from pyspark.sql.functions import *
#pyspark --packages org.mongodb.spark:mongo-spark-connec-
tor_2.12:3.0.2 # spark 3.0
# create a spark session
spark = SparkSession \
.builder \
.master("local") \
.appName("ABC") \
.config("spark.mongodb.read.connection.uri",
"mongodb://localhost:27017/database1") \
.config("spark.mongodb.write.connection.uri",
"mongodb://localhost:27017/database1") \
.getOrCreate()
# read data from mongodb collection "questions" into a dataframe
"df"
df = spark.read \
.format("mongo") \
.option("uri", "mongodb://localhost:27017/database1") \
.option("database", "database1") \
.option("collection", "mongotable") \
.load()
```

```
df.printSchema()
df.filter(df['action'] == 'Open').show()
```

The output of the above-mentioned PySpark code that accesses the MongoDB database is shown in the following *Figure 3.14*.

```
>>> df.printSchema()
root
 |-- _id: struct (nullable = true)
 |    |-- oid: string (nullable = true)
 |-- action: string (nullable = true)
 |-- time: integer (nullable = true)

>>> df.filter(df['action'] == 'Open').show()
+--------------------+------+----------+
|                 _id|action|      time|
+--------------------+------+----------+
|[66e1a83b15a3acf1...|  Open|1469501107|
|[66e1a83b15a3acf1...|  Open|1469501109|
|[66e1a83b15a3acf1...|  Open|1469501110|
|[66e1a83b15a3acf1...|  Open|1469501112|
|[66e1a83b15a3acf1...|  Open|1469501112|
+--------------------+------+----------+
```

Figure 3.14: *Printing the MongoDB Schema through PySpark*

- **Graph-oriented Model:** Databases adhering to this model have graph structure consisting of nodes and edges. Nodes store the data and edges represent relationships between the data. Thus, querying relationships along with the objects is possible in this NoSQL model. This model is useful for storing heavily interconnected data with complex relationships. Neo4J and GraphDB are popular graph model-based NoSQL databases.

These models have different characteristics, and even databases following specific models that differ in their characteristics. To select relevant model for IoT applications, these models are compared over the following parameters:

- **Scalability:** Handling huge amounts of data executing queries fast and storing data on new hardware as per requirement.
- **Real-time Processing:** Real time data is used by the majority of applications. It assists practitioners as well as patients within acceptable time in a critical situation. The application has to deal with temporal data which gets out dated.
- **Availability:** The data can be accessed from storage anytime during read and update operation. The data should be newest and requests should have the same value of data at same time.
- **Reliability:** The storage should be fault tolerant. It should partition the data in various places, such that even if data at one place gets corrupted, data should be available.

- **High Read Throughput:** It denotes a high number of read operations that can be performed per second on heavy load.
- **High Write Throughput:** It denotes a high number of write operations that can be performed per second on heavy load.

The tabular comparison is shown in the following *Figure* 3.15.

Parameter	Redis	Cassandra	MongoDB	Neo4J	DynamoDB	HBase	CouchDB	OrientDB
Data Model	Key value	Column	Document	Graph	Key-Value	Column	Document	Graph
Replication	Master Slave	Master-Master	Master-Slave	Master-Slave	Master-Master	Master-Slave	Master-Master	Master-Master
Scalability	No	Yes	Yes	No	Yes	Yes	No	Yes
Real-Time	Yes	Yes	Yes	Yes	Yes	No	No	No
Reliability	Yes	No	Yes	Yes	Yes	No	Yes	Yes
High Read Thoughput	Yes	No	Yes	Yes	Yes	Yes	Yes	Yes
High Write Thoughput	No	Yes	No	Yes	No	No	No	Yes
Availability	No	Yes	No	Yes	Yes	No	Yes	Yes

Table.2. Comparison between NoSQL Databases

Figure 3.15: *Characteristics of Different NoSQL Databases*

File System

This system is used to store data that has extremely high volume, and of unstructured type that cannot be handled in databases. The file system has no logical model of representation. Data in the file system is stored in a stream of bytes or characters. IoT applications use distributed file systems, maintained over a cluster of computing devices, to handle large-scale data. It stores data and metadata in the files with proper indexing for high data availability. Multiple clients can simultaneously store and retrieve the data or files from a distributed file system server over the network. **Hadoop Distributed File System** is the most popular distributed file systems used in IoT applications.

Data Pre-Processing

Data that is collected from multiple sources cannot be directly used for processing. This is because the data contains lots of errors and noise during data acquisition over the network. Further, all the data that is collected is not required for processing or data has to be derived from the raw data for processing. For example, the data from a motion sensor as 0/1 is raw. IF we calculate people count or access rate from the raw data, the derived information can be used for analysis during data processing.

Pre-processing is the step in the data pipeline that prepares data for analysis. Data pre-processing removes noise, removes erroneous values, handles missing data, detects outliers, removes duplicates, normalizes data if required, and does data integration of data coming from multiple sources (data fusion). Pre-processing has a specific function for each task, and it will be discussed in detail in the next chapter.

There are two types of pre-processing: Offline pre-processing and online pre-processing. In offline processing, the data is collected and stored. The stored data is pre-processed in one go, and is made ready for analysis. In online pre-processing, the collected data is pre-processed on-the-fly, and then stored or provided for analysis. Two important aspects of data pre-processing are data interoperability for seamless fusion of data from multiple sources, and data quality for having quality analysis of the pre-processed data.

Data Interoperability

Connected Things in IoT are heterogeneous. They come in different sizes and power, perform different functions, and speak an endless variety of APIs and physical protocols. Separate applications, and even different Clouds use different data syntax, schemas and formats to describe objects. Interoperability is required to provide the same platform for things to communicate. As the number of devices grows, it will be difficult to handle the heterogeneity, adapting each of them by the IoT. Thus, it is necessary that things and applications share a common data model so that integration and interaction is not an issue. Interoperability has three levels as shown in the following *Figure* 3.16.

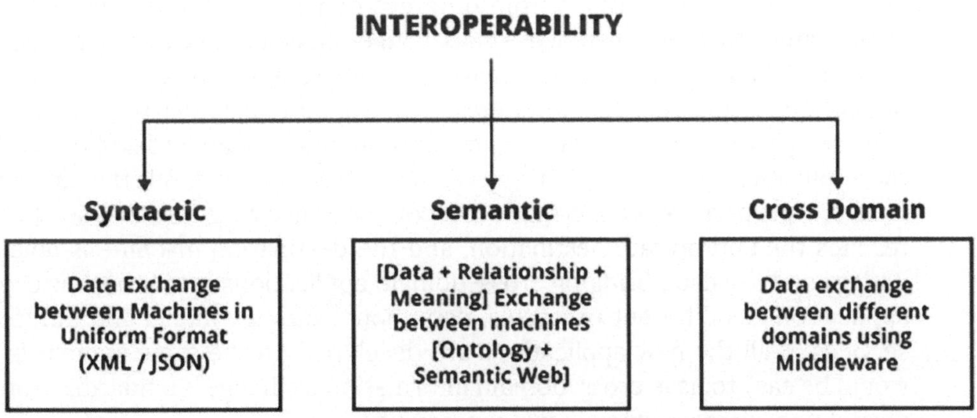

Figure 3.16: *Different Types of Interoperability to be Considered with Heterogeneous IoT Devices*

- **Syntactic Interoperability:** This level of interoperability provides a common data format for increasing compatibility between Things. Common formats to provide syntactic interoperability are JSON and XML. This level of interoperability provides the same language to exchange information. For instance: One machine sends temperature data, and then the format of temperature data should be fixed between two systems (either Celsius or Fahrenheit), for providing syntactic interoperability. Further, the temperature data should be in file format, so that the other machine is able to read.

- **Semantic Interoperability:** This level of interoperability allows two devices to exchange data, and confirms that the meaning of data is perceived similar by both the systems. To provide semantic interoperability, ontologies are used. For example, when one machine sends temperature data, how will the machine know if it is body temperature or room temperature? Body temperature and room temperature are processed differently, and thus, it is very important for machines to know the meaning of data for accurate processing of the exchanged data. In semantic interoperability, the data comes with context. Further, the machine that gets the data understands the data by using universally accepted vocabulary. Semantic graphs are used to store relationships between data and context. RDF is the data format to exchange context enriched data between two machines. There are multiple ontologies for different domains/contexts. The ontology is universally acceptable vocabulary which is fixed by both the machines before data exchange. With semantic interoperability, temperature data would have the context of either room or body, so that the machine receiving the temperature data has an idea of how to process it. Thus, semantic interoperability uses semantic graphs, common ontology and RDF format to provide meaningful communication between machines.
- **Cross-domain Interoperability:** This level of interoperability provides the ability of two different applications from different domains with different services to exchange data. For instance, smart fridge applications can communicate data of picking up items with smart transport applications, depending on prediction of non-availability of items. This will optimize rides to food stores, and save petrol. For this, the data formats should be standardized across all the applications. Further, a gateway is required that understands the data, and routes it properly by converting protocols or converting formats, so that it reaches the appropriate destination, and the destination machine is able to understand the data. Bridging cross-domain applications is toughest as every application has different protocols, data model, storage model and different services. If all the new applications are developed on the same standards, it would be easy to have cross-domain information exchange. Standardization is pivotal to have cross-domain interoperability.

Data Quality

Quality of the data is highly important. Any application with low quality data will impact analysis, decision-making, reducing trust over the application. An example to understand how important it is to have quality data is as follows:

Suppose multiple items from Amazon need to be delivered to a person. The person has selected items, and has added them to the shopping cart as well as paid online. Amazon has the list of paid items, and it estimates the delivery date for each item based on the availability as well distance of item source from the person's address. Each item quantity is provided by the person. If the quality of data is high, then all the items will be delivered on dates predicted, and the person will have full customer satisfaction. In this example, most of the acquired data about items, and address of the delivery are provided by humans as data source. The data from human sources is integrated with item details and item locations. Any discrepancy in data will cause wrong estimation of delivery date, wrong delivery, wrong item dispatched, wrong price paid or wrong quantity delivered. The error in data can be due to human error, machine error or network error. This will reduce customer satisfaction as well as prevent wastage of resources and time. Therefore, data should be entered correctly, accurately, and should have all the information, as well as must be current, and should be the same, wherever it is stored. Then only the data quality will be ensured, ensuring the quality of service.

Thus, the acquired data has quality, if it has the following characteristics:

- **Accuracy:** The data is correct with no errors, and resembles reality.
- **Completeness:** The data has no missing values.
- **Timeliness:** The data is relevant, and up to date.
- **Uniqueness:** The data has no duplicate records.
- **Consistency:** The data is uniform and correct.

Data quality can be ensured during data acquisition as well as in the pre-processing step of the data pipeline. Therefore, the data needs a quality check before it is used.

Data Analysis

Data from multiple sources needs to be "integrated and fused" for analysis to have better insight of the application's environment. Data from individual IoT sources is integrated as a common record in a storage model. This data has to be fused for depicting the complete information of data-driven IoT applications. Data fusion approaches reduce uncertainty in understanding the environment for generating accurate prediction and diagnosis of the environment. It finds correlation between the data, and extracts relevant features in the presence of noisy and faulty data. There exist multiple tools to fuse data for analysis, and predict the state of the environment. The tools are shown in the following *Figure* 3.17, and each tool is discussed in the following subsections.

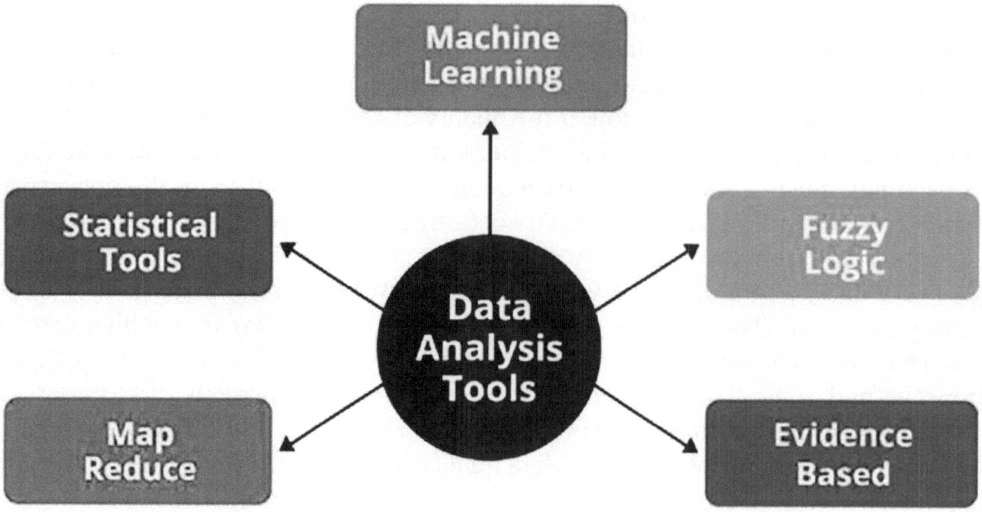

Figure 3.17: *List of Different Tools for Analyzing Data*

Machine Learning

When the application has to learn and predict the current environment state based on the sensed data, the machine is trained for automated and accurate predictions. Training data is collected from multiple sensors and accordingly the services are recognized. Machine training is done by either a supervised, an unsupervised, a reinforcement or a hybrid learning. Supervised learning knows the categories and actions beforehand. The input data is classified based into a category and actions are proposed. In unsupervised learning, the categories are unknown. The application performs data fusion in real-time and forms clusters of similar data. The action on input data is determined by three clusters in which it belongs to. Reinforcement learning decides action in real time and based on the decision, learn with the gain or loss attached with the action. Hybrid model is a mix of supervised, unsupervised or reinforcement learning to pre-train models on some categories, and learn online by dynamically predicting some actions. Neural networks and Deep learning are machine learning methods that learn data with minimum classification error and high accuracy rates. Both of these models require high computational power, but are popularly recommended for applications handling critical IoT data.

Evidence Theory

This technique is used, when a certain situation cannot be decided as true or not true with surety. There is some uncertainty attached with the classification. Evidence theory reduces the uncertainty in data by fusing evidence, and providing a decision closer to what actually happened. It takes into account the unknown states (may be true/ may not be true) with the known states (true/not true), and adds it as a knowledge for evidence. Multiple possibilities based on evidence are considered, and a conclusion is derived. Dampster-Shafer theory is one of the examples of evidence theory that is majorly used in data fusion of IoT data. In this theory, the conclusion is drawn based on the belief of the collected evidence. Conclusion is made by the measure of plausibility. This technique is proven to be efficient for environments having high uncertainty. It requires high computational power, and thus, deploying it on edge devices efficiently is a major challenge.

Fuzzy Logic

IoT applications, where input data is imprecise and fuzzy, use fuzzy logic for fusion. This data does not refer to a particular condition with full confidence. Due to fuzziness, the application is not sure about the exact state of the situation. Dealing with such data is a big issue for applications in predicting and providing services. For instance, an environment temperature cannot be classified only as hot or cold. This is because the degree of hotness varies from person to person, and context to context.

Multiple sets are defined between hot and cold to ease the predictions. Fuzzy logic provides multiple sets to fuse data of an application for predictions that are close to human perception and context. These sets are known as fuzzy sets and the data is classified in one of the fuzzy sets by its degree of membership. Every data will have an associated membership degree in each of the fuzzy sets. Fuzzy rules determine the fuzzy set of the fused data by calculating the membership degree, and combining the degrees of each input data. These rules are in the form of if-then condition, and each rule provides a logical relationship between the data values to determine the corresponding fuzzy set for prediction.

Statistical Tools

Applications that deal with dynamic systems need to estimate the current state based on the previous states. Statistical tools are helpful to model the system mathematically, and predict output, based on input and the prior state. The error in prediction is controlled by a feedback loop that changes system variables. Some of the popular statistical tools are Kalman filter, Bayesian approach, sequential/Monte-Carlo approach. The Kalman filter is a technique used to remove outliers and noise from the data for correct predictions. The Kalman filter is useful for linear systems, but inefficient to predict states for nonlinear systems. Bayesian approach estimates the next state by calculating the posterior probability.

Posterior probability is calculated based on two inputs. First input is the a priori probability of the next state with respect to the current state. The second input is the likelihood of the next state in the probability distribution of all the states. Monte-Carlo approach determines transition probabilities between multiple states a system can have. It is known as a sequential approach because the current state follows a sequence of states to reach the goal state. The Markov model is one of the Monte-Carlo approaches that predicts the next state based on just the previous state and does not consider previous time-series states.

Map-Reduce

Map-reduce technique is one of the most used data fusion techniques to extract summarized knowledge from the data. The map-reduce function comprises a separate ``map" task and ``reduce" task, combined together for data fusion.

The map task filters the relevant data, and the reduce task summarizes the filtered data recursively. In each recursion, the map task splits the dataset followed by summarization by the reduced task. Thus, map-reduce divides the large-scale data into small chunks for distributed processing. It aggregates each chunk for mining complete information. It can also handle streaming data through a method known as micro-benching, but it is not as fast as other techniques for fusing the streaming data.

Data Visualization

This is a very important step of the IoT data pipeline. This step comes either before the pre-processing step, or after the analysis step. In this step, data is represented in image form for better understanding. In other words, it is a visual representation of the data that the human brain can easily study and derive useful insights. This step is very crucial, when the data is big. There are multiple tools and techniques to visualize data, and the techniques are selected with respect to data. There are two types of visualizations: Numerical data visualization and categorical data visualization. Numerical data is the data in continuous or in discrete form. Categorical data is either binary (0/1), or nominal (male/female), or ordinal (range such as low, middle, and high income). Numerical data is represented using bars and graphs, whereas Categorical data is represented using Venn diagrams, and word clouds.

Data visualization provides a way to represent highly complex data or huge amounts of data in a very easy and complete manner. Visualization should be such that the data can be understood easily and no information should get lost. Thus, the impact of visualization depends on the right technique chosen to represent the data. Naturally, our brain visualizes raw data and extract patterns. The visualization step saves time of the developer as well as the customer by conveying information visually so that they don't have to make a picture of numbers in their brains. Further, visualization helps in discovering trends in data, provides multiple perspectives to data and preserves the data context. For example, we have yearly data of population of five countries of the world. When we plot this data with respect to every year, it shows the trend of population in each of the countries. Trend can be either increasing, decreasing or constant. Graphs are mostly used to plot time-series data. Further, if this data is shown as low to high population with percentage, it depicts least populated country and most populated country, showing perspective population-density wise. The other visualization of the same data can be in the context of each country, where for each country, population range is represented. This type of visualization is specific to the context of an individual country. Thus, the same data can be represented in multiple ways, depending on what is required.

To represent data correctly, we should know what tools and techniques are available and how to select the perfect visualization technique based on requirement. Not only technique, but colors, labeling, font are all important to have a good view of the IoT data, conveying exactly the same information and perceived data from visualization is the same for all. Two popular data visualization tools are Tableau and Power BI. These tools convert data to visualizations automatically for better understanding of data as well as for better decision-making. To plot the data by self, python has pandas and matplotlib libraries for creating graphical representations, manually.

Some of the popular visualization techniques are bar charts, line charts, pie charts, scatter plots, histograms, box plots, and heat maps. There are many other techniques that we will not cover here. We will discuss each of the mentioned techniques in detail. For each technique, we will see how each of these are created, using python.

- **Bar Chart:** This chart represents data on X-Y axes, using multiple bars having the same width. The representation can be either with vertical bars, or with horizontal bars. Each bar represents a category and height of the bar is the value in the category. Bar with the lowest height and the highest height means it has minimum value and maximum value, respectively. If the bars are on x-axis and y-axis represents the values and vice-versa. There is also a grouped bar graph, that represents sub-categories within a single category with two different colored bars attached together.

```
import matplotlib.pyplot as plt
import numpy as np
N= 4
r = np.arange(N)
values = [0.4,0.6, 0.7, 1.1]
plt.bar(r, values, color='blue')
plt.xlabel('Years', fontsize = 15)
plt.ylabel('Revenue Growth in IoT devices', fontsize = 15)
plt.xticks(r,['2021','2022','2023','2024'])
plt.title('Bar Chart' , fontsize = 15)
plt.legend()
plt.show()
```

This code creates a bar chart having a blue color. The X values in the bar chart correspond to years, and the Y values in the bar chart correspond to revenue growth. The bar chart is shown in the following *Figure* 3.18.

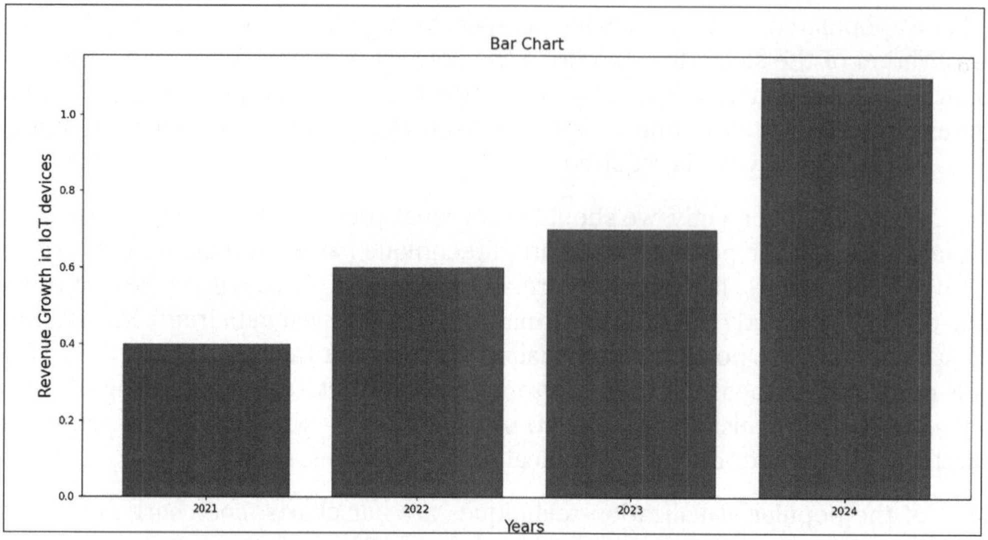

Figure 3.18: *Bar Chart Representation of the Data*

- **Line Chart:** This type of chart is good for plotting continuous data, and is used to depict change in value or trend in data. It only plots data with linear relationships, and consists of points as well as edges connecting the points. It is very crucial to know what is represented by the X-axis and Y axis, and their range of values. Multiple lines can be plotted on the same X-Y axis. Every line has an individual set of (x, y) points. The line is formed, when these points are connected by edges. A single line chart is to depict change for a particular entity, and a multiple lines chart is to show comparison between two entities on the same X-Y axes.

```
import matplotlib.pyplot as plt
import numpy as np
N= 4
r = np.arange(N)
values = [0.4,0.6, 0.7, 1.1]
plt.plot(r, values, color='red')
plt.xlabel('Years', fontsize = 15)
plt.ylabel('Revenue Growth in IoT devices', fontsize = 15)
plt.xticks(r,['2021','2022','2023','2024'])
plt.title('Line Chart' , fontsize = 15)
plt.legend()
plt.show()
```

This code visualizes the data as a line chart. The line color selected is red. X axis shows years, and Y axis shows revenue growth of the IoT devices, every year. The line going upward, every year means that there is an increase in revenue. The line chart is shown in the following *Figure* 3.19.

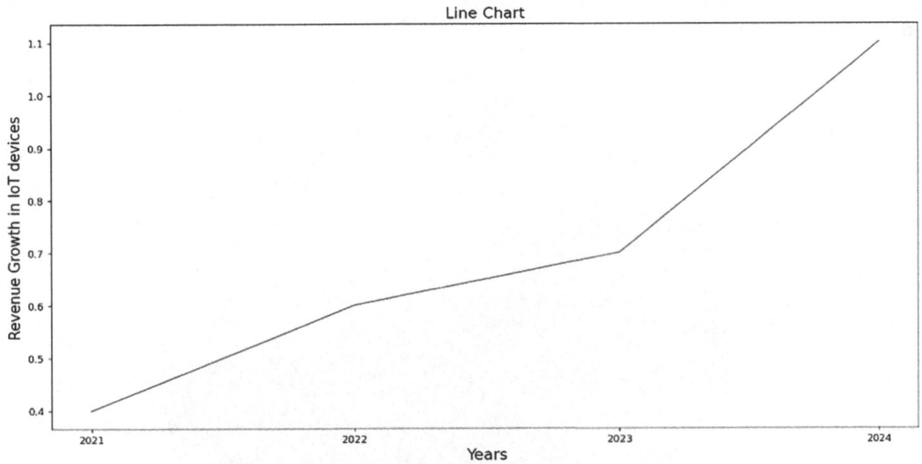

Figure 3.19: *Data Represented in the Form of Line Chart*

- **Pie Chart:** This type of visual representation plots data on a circle. The circle has different pie slices representing a category that data belongs to. Each pie is depicted in a different color. It is best suited to demonstrate the percentage of data in a specific category from total data. Sum of percentages of all the pies of the circle sums up to 100. This type of chart is very popular for depicting percentage distribution amongst different categories.

```
import matplotlib.pyplot as plt
year= [2021,2022,2023,2024]
values = [0.4,0.6, 0.7, 1.1]
fig, ax = plt.subplots()
ax.pie(values, labels=year, colors=['olivedrab', 'rosybrown',
'gray', 'saddlebrown'])
plt.show()
```

This code represents the data of each year in a pie form, and each pie is having a different color. More the value, the pie of that data takes more portion of the circle. The pie chart is shown in the following *Figure* 3.20.

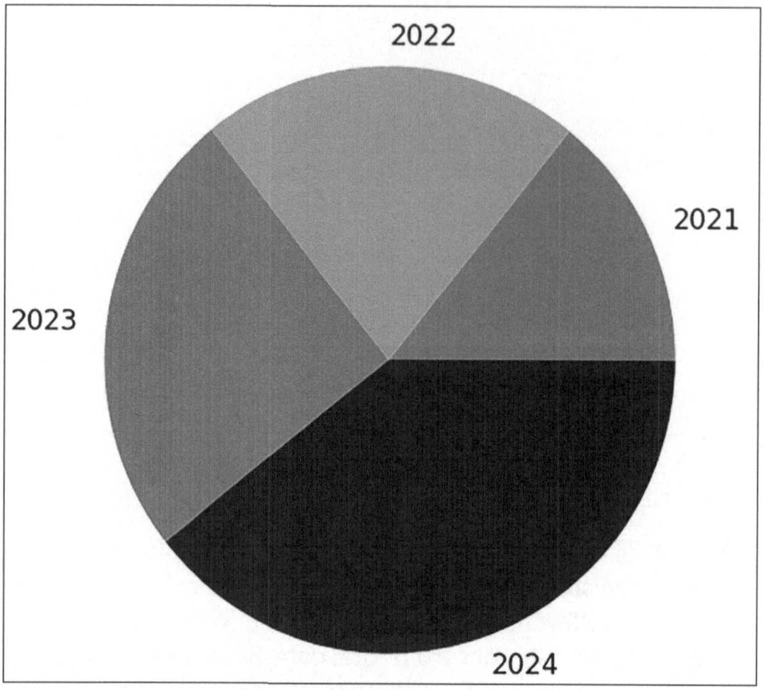

Figure 3.20: *Data Represented in a Pie Chart*

- **Scatter Plot:** This plot is a visualization tool as well as a basic tool to check data quality. It is used to plot bi-variate data. The X axis and Y axis should have the same range. It is used to find outliers in the data quality process. This is popularly used for making clusters of the same type of data. Most important usage of scatter plot is the correlation analysis between the two variables. These two variables have one independent on the X-axis and one is dependent on the Y-axis. As the name says, the points are scattered all over the plot and we try to fit a line through the points, to check correlation between the variables. Some points are left out of the line, then the variables are considered as outliers. Three types of scatter plots are positive correlation (Y variable increasing), negative correlation (Y variable decreasing), and null correlation (no relation between X and Y).

```
import matplotlib.pyplot as plt
import numpy as np
x = np.random.rand(500)
y = np.random.rand(500)
plt.scatter(x, y)
plt.title("Scatter Plot", fontsize = 15)
plt.xlabel("X-axis", fontsize = 15)
plt.ylabel("Y-axis", fontsize = 15)
plt.show()
```

This code plots a scatter plot of values X and Y which shows how much values of X are related to Y. The scatter plot is shown in *Figure 3.21*. If no line passes through the points, it shows that there is no relation between X values and Y values.

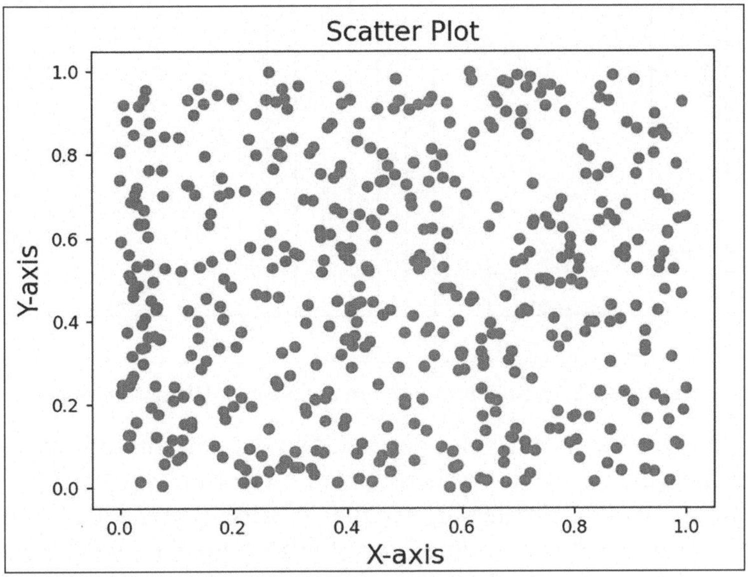

Figure 3.21: *Random X and Y Values Visualized as Scatter Plot*

- **Histogram:** It is a 2-D plot having X axis and Y axis, where Y axis shows distribution/frequency of X axis. They are good to plot data distribution of continuous data such as readings from sensors. Histogram has a set of bins plotted on the X-Y axis. Bins are continuous and overlapping groups, and if a continuous value belongs to a bin, frequency of the respective bin increases. X axis plots a group in continuous data called bin ranges, and Y axis plots frequency by adjusting the height of the bin.

```
import matplotlib.pyplot as plt
import numpy as np
data = np.random.randn(5000)
plt.hist(data, bins=20, color='skyblue', edgecolor='black')
plt.xlabel('Values')
plt.ylabel('Frequency')
plt.title('Histogram')
plt.show()
```

This code represents the random 5000 values in 20 histogram bins. The histogram is shown in the following *Figure 3.22*.

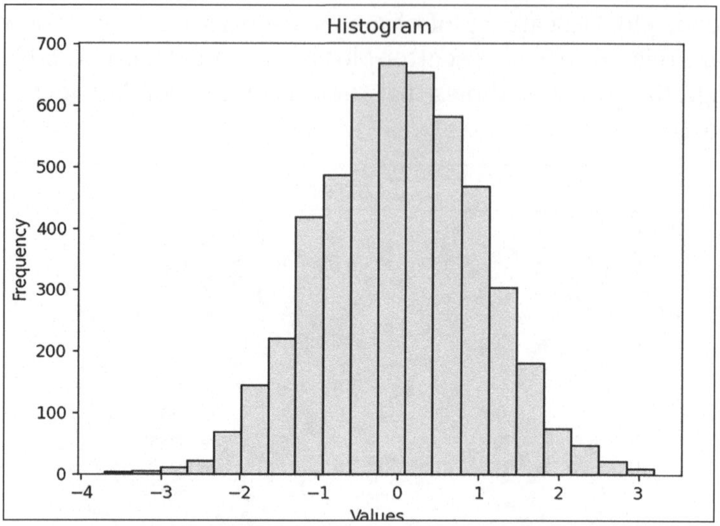

Figure 3.22: *Data Represented in the Form of Histogram Bins*

- **Box Plot:** This is used to plot dataset, and data distribution in a summarized way. The plot has a box with whiskers on both sides. It has 5 parameters: Minimum, First Quartile Q1, Median, Third Quartile Q3, and Maximum. Two whiskers are from minimum value to Q1 value, and from Q3 value to maximum, respectively. The box is represented from Q1 to Q3, having median value dividing the box in two parts. In general, minimum to Q1 represent 25% data, and Q1 to median represents another 25% of data, so, a total of 50 % data. Next, 25% of the data is represented from median to Q3, completing 75% of the data. The remaining 25% is represented from Q3 to maximum. IQR (Inter-Quartile Range) is the difference between values at Q3 and Q1. Outliers are detected from this box plot with the values below (minimum – (1.5*IQR)) ad values above (maximum + (1.5*Q3)). If the median is exactly in the middle, the plot is normally distributed. If the plot has median towards left, and whiskers at left are smaller, then the distribution is right skewed. If the median of the plot is shifted towards the right, and whiskers at right are smaller, then the data is left skewed. This is how box plot helps to identify parameter values, and distribution of the data. Different datasets can be compared using multiple box plots.

```
import matplotlib.pyplot as plt
import numpy as np
# Creating dataset with normal distribution mu=1000, sigma=200,
values=5000
np.random.seed(10)
data = np.random.normal(1000, 200, 5000)
plt.boxplot(data)
plt.show()
```

The code represents data as a box plot, and the output is shown in the following *Figure* 3.23. The box plot shows the maximum value, the minimum value and the median of the data. There are some outliers that are represented in circles, and Q1 and Q3 are quartiles.

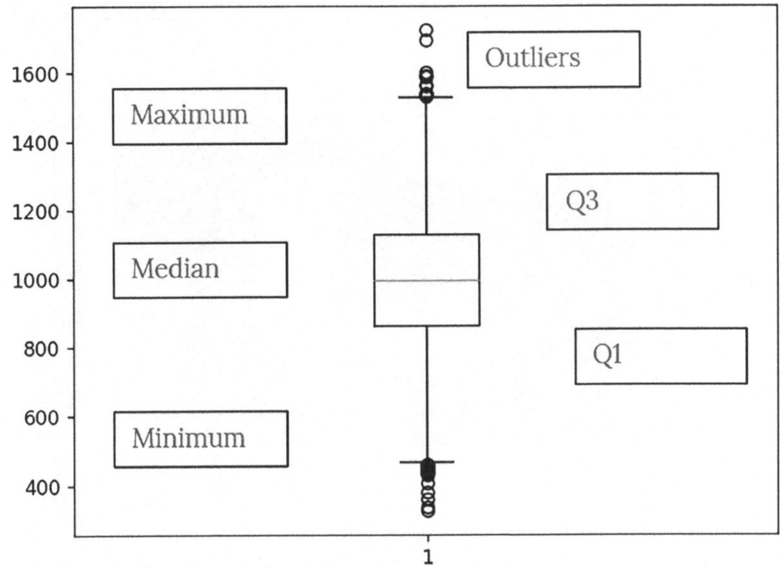

Figure 3.23: *Data Visualized Using Box Plot Showing Minimum, Maximum, and Median Values*

Heat Map: This plot is useful to analyze the highly complex data. The plot has a grid consisting of cells, each cell representing a value. The frequency of values is represented using colors. The cell with lower frequency is represented by cool colors, and the cells with high frequency are represented by warm colors. The heatmap is used to see trends in the data, and the correlation between variables. It is popularly used in website design, market strategies and geographic analysis. The only requirement is to have accurate data to plot heat maps, otherwise heat maps may give erroneous results.

```
import matplotlib.pyplot as plt
import numpy as np
Month= ["January", "February", "March", "April", "May"]
Year = [2015, 2016, 2017, 2018, 2019, 2020, 2021, 2022]
data = np.random.random((5, 8))
plt.imshow(data, cmap='autumn', interpolation='nearest')
plt.colorbar()
plt.title("Heatmap with color bar")
plt.xticks(range(len(Year)), Year, rotation=90)
plt.yticks(range(len(Month)), Month)
plt.show()
```

This code represents data in a heat map in the following *Figure* 3.24. The map color is chosen as autumn. The heat map shows years and months in the X and Y axis respectively. The box that represents the data with dark yellow shows less values, and the light-yellow portions show more values.

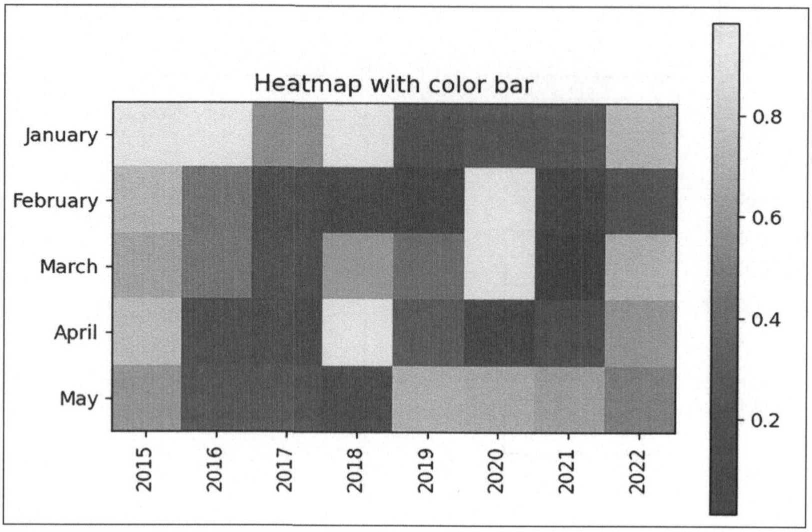

Figure 3.24: *Data Frequency of Each Month in Every Year is Represented Using a Heat Map*

Conclusion

This chapter tells how to process Data in IoT applications, using a data pipeline. Data can be from any source and in any format. They need to be acquired, pre-processed, stored appropriately for analysis. In data acquisition, there are two processes: data collection and data communication. In most of the IoT applications, the sensors are attached to Arduino Uno or Raspberry Pi for data acquisition. After data acquisition, the data is stored. Depending on data type, storage is selected. The different types of storage models are Relational database, NoSQL and File system. For processing the stored data, processing frameworks such as Apache Hadoop, Apache Spark or Apache Flink are used. All the processing operations on stored data are carried out by the processing framework, either in batch or stream. The stored data is then pre-processed to maintain data quality. Further, the data from heterogeneous sources is made interoperable. The data is then provided to analytical tools. Depending on what is expected from the data, the analytical tool is chosen. Data visualization step is a vital step that is used for pre-processing, to check if the data has quality or after analysis, to support decision-making. Using visualizations is very easy to understand the IoT data, and the relationship between data and the analytical results. The data pipeline for IoT data can be easily implemented on edge devices such as Raspberry Pi for stream processing. However, multiple Raspberry Pi supporting clouds are required to process big IoT data for batch processing as this requires huge storage.

In the next chapter, we will go through the *data pre-processing steps* in detail.

Points to Remember

- The pipeline consists of blocks such as data acquisition, data processing, data analysis, and data visualization.
- The data pipeline has to be modeled such that the incoming IoT data is handled efficiently to provide accurate decisions.
- The acquired data needs to be very accurate and complete to make decisions.
- There are mainly two types of processing: Batch processing and Stream processing.
- There are three types of storage used in IoT applications: Relational database, NoSQL database, and File system.
- Data pre-processing removes noise and erroneous values, handles missing data, detects outliers, removes duplicates, normalizes the data, if required, and does data integration of data coming from multiple sources (data fusion).
- There exist multiple techniques to fuse data for analysis, and predict the environment state. The techniques are machine learning, fuzzy logic, evidence theory, statistical tools, and map-reduce.
- To understand data as well as maintain the data quality, or to analyze results, data visualization is an important step in the data pipeline.

Multiple Choice Questions

1. Which of the following is not a part of data pre-processing?
    a. Removing duplicates
    b. Data quality
    c. Data interoperability
    d. Data storage
2. What is the primary language of Apache Hadoop?
    a. Java
    b. Scala
    c. R
    d. C++

3. What is not a characteristic of a NoSQL database?
   a. Flexible schema
   b. Soft consistency
   c. Handles data variety
   d. Follows ACID property
4. Which tool is used to analyze data in batch processing in Hadoop?
   a. Machine Learning
   b. Map-Reduce
   c. Evidence-based
   d. Fuzzy Logic
5. Which analytical tool uses datasets with membership degrees to make predictions?
   a. Evidence-theory
   b. Statistical tools
   c. Fuzzy logic
   d. Machine learning
6. Which data visualization tool plots a grid, and is color-mapped?
   a. Histogram
   b. Scatter Plot
   c. Pie Chart
   d. Heat Map
7. Which visualization tool is used to show data correlation?
   a. Histogram
   b. Bar Chart
   c. Scatter Plot
   d. Box Plot

Answers

1. d
2. a
3. d
4. b
5. c
6. d
7. c

Questions

1. How is data acquired on Arduino Uno?
2. How is the sensed data communicated to edge devices, or the cloud?
3. What are popular processing frameworks?
4. How does stream processing work on PySpark?
5. Why are NoSQL databases popular in IoT applications, and what are its four types?
6. What are different levels of interoperability?
7. How is a machine learning tool different from an evidence-based tool for data analysis?
8. How are box plots used to visualize datasets?

Chapter 4
Integrating Edge with Cloud in IoT Architecture

Introduction

Edge computing with cloud has proved beneficial for IoT applications as well as to the network and the environment. There exists a variety of edge-cloud architectures, and the edge layer modeling depends on the requirements of IoT application. Popular Edge-Cloud architectures are cloudlets, fog computing, mobile edge computing, multi-access edge computing and collaborative edge computing. In this chapter, we will study the origins of edge computing. We will go through each edge cloud architecture, and illustrate it with an IoT application example. Through illustrations, we will get to know which model is suitable for what purpose, and how to build an application over it. Further, for each edge-cloud architecture, we will discuss its characteristics and challenges.

Structure

In this chapter, we will cover the following topics:

- Introduction to Architecture
- Cloudlet
- Fog Computing
- Mobile Edge Computing
- Multi-access Edge Computing
- Collaborative Edge Computing

Introduction to Architecture

The World Wide Web (WWW) was invented by Tim Berners Lee in 1989. When WWW was created, the processing over the devices was transferred to servers. This is when the problem of network congestion was detected. A chance of network breakdown in future was observed, when multiple devices accessed multiple servers located worldwide over the Internet. To stop a complete network breakdown/ Internet shutdown, a group of MIT scientists proposed a solution in 1998. The solution later formed a company named *Akamai*. Akamai is the first concept of Edge-Cloud architecture. At that time, the network was not ready to take a lot of loads like today's network, and the servers had very low computational power compared to a Cloud.

With such servers and a low bandwidth network, the company proposed a content delivery network, where they attached multiple devices between the client and server over the internet for providing content to the client from the network edge. They utilized the concept of caching to serve clients faster without accessing the server all the time. Thus, from handling all the web page requests at the centralized servers, Akamai provided decentralized architecture that provided web content at the network edge. This company is still working on the same concept, and considering big data over the network. Other companies also came up providing solutions on delivering the web content at network edge, and the edge architecture of content delivery network got popular for another decade.

Around the same time, people started accessing the web from mobile devices. Multiple web applications were running on mobile devices. To save battery and resources of the mobile, the idea of pervasive computing came up in 1997. Pervasive devices such as daily appliances were made smart, using embedded devices, and were considered as surrogate servers. In pervasive computing, the tasks from mobile devices were offloaded to nearby surrogate servers, considered as edge devices.

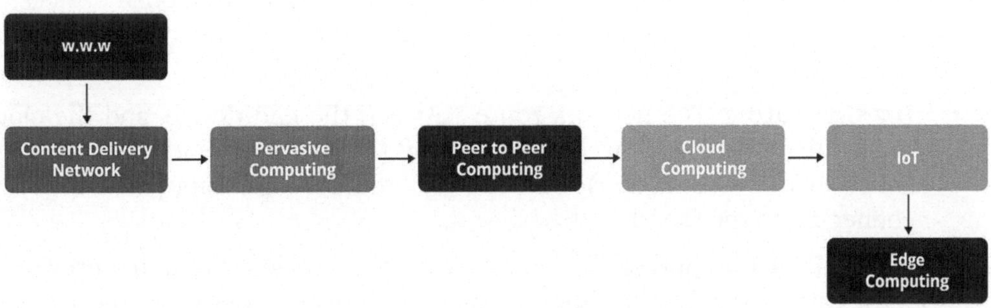

Figure 4.1: *History of Edge-Cloud Architecture*

After the discovery of content delivery network and pervasive computing, a new network model came up to manage the network load that is peer to peer (P2P) network. In a P2P network, the devices are inter-connected, and they have both roles: Client as well as server. The network manages the requests amongst the devices depending on proximity. Napster came as a file sharing system having a P2P network model to share files with the clients over a private network, at the network edge. Multiple peers have the same file after request. If a new peer needs that file, the network will check its global directory and request the nearest peer for the file. Thus, the file reaches the client/peer in minimum hops, and without having a centralized server.

Until 2006, people were using CDN, pervasive computing and P2P to fetch web data faster. However, in 2006, cloud computing became popular with Amazon AWS. Cloud as a server was very much needed as the number of Internet users were increasing, and normal servers were not able to handle all of them. With the cloud, came big challenges on the network that required new edge computing architecture. Further, e-commerce websites like Amazon and Flipkart, and social networking sites such as Facebook and LinkedIn gained popularity worldwide, handling user requests in real-time. In 2009, the Internet of Things (IoT) became popular. IoT was built over a pervasive computing concept connecting pervasive devices together over the Internet, and cloud computing managed the IoT devices and IoT services. In fact, the IoT devices increased the number of devices over the network that surpassed more than the worldwide population. The timeline of edge computing is shown in *Figure 4.1*.

Dealing with such a huge number of IoT applications and big data on the network, the previous technologies (CDN, P2P, pervasive computing, and so on) that provided edge computation were insufficient to reduce network load and service latency. To support new technologies dependent on cloud servers, new edge computing solutions came into the limelight, where some of the processing carried by the cloud is done at edge devices. Some popular edge computing architectures are shown in *Figure 4.2*, and discussed as follows:

- **Cloudlet:** This is a cluster of machines that forms a small data center in a local network to provide Cloud services in nearby proximity to mobile devices. It may or may not be connected to the Cloud, and is maintained independently, or privately.
- **Fog Computing:** The network route between the end device, and the cloud is considered as fog, as well as computing that is carried out on the devices (switch, gateway, or router) in the network route is fog computing. It is always connected to the Cloud.
- **Mobile Edge Computing:** The computations of mobile devices that previously were carried out by the Cloud is taken care of by a device in the route of cellular network (4G or 5G). Thus, there is no need for clouds. The devices in the cellular network behave as clouds at the edge. Devices in cellular network routes via cellular towers are very different from internet network routes.

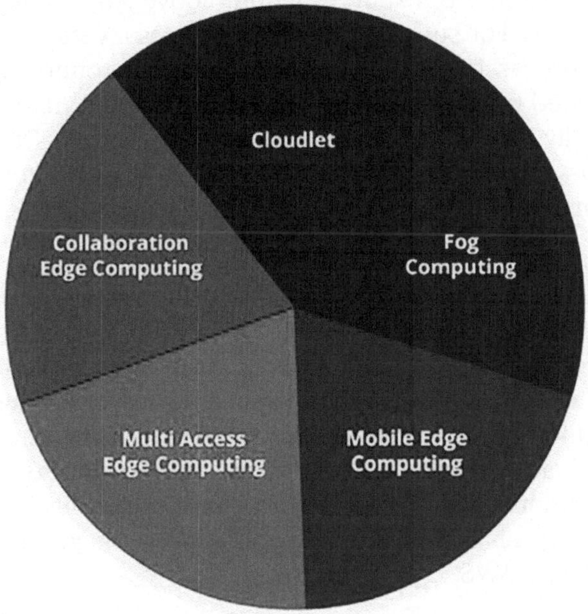

***Figure 4.2:** Different Types of Edge Computing Architecture*

- **Multi-access Edge Computing:** The edge devices collaborate, and form multiple data centers to provide cloud services at the network edge. Distributed cloud architecture over edge devices are used for computation, rather than having a centralized cloud.
- **Collaborative Edge Computing:** Edge devices of specific IoT applications collaborate with each other, and exchange information, resources and services. The exchange is a challenge as each application has its own specifications, and is heterogeneous with each other.

Next, we will discuss more about cloudlets.

Cloudlet

Every smartphone is enabled with a microprocessor, memory chip and a wireless cellular network (3G/4G/5G). In the initial days, the data from mobile devices used to go wirelessly through cellular towers to another mobile device. Nowadays, there is a hybrid model having cellular network and internet for inter-mobile device communication. Further, multiple processes can run on smartphones in parallel.

However, some of the computations are heavy for mobile devices. For example, the speech recognition system of smart phones, such as "*Siri*", is based on Natural Language Processing (NLP). NLP requires powerful computational capability and resources of mobile devices are not enough. Another application on mobile devices that require intensive resources is interactive gaming applications that use Augmented Reality (AR). For such tasks, mobile devices leverage Cloud. The problem of using Cloud for processing is the exchange of huge amounts of real-time data on the bandwidth-limited network. Further, in case of limited network, the timeliness of the data, especially in a real-time application gets affected. Data exchange incurs huge network costs, and if the task processing takes a lot of time, it delays service, decreasing user satisfaction.

Let us think about a situation. We have multiple mobile devices now. Suppose a quarter of these devices are using services of AWS Cloud at the same time. Each of the mobile devices is continuously exchanging information with the cloud and the Cloud is handling processing in parallel. Cloud has high scalability so it can handle a huge number of tasks at a given time instance. However, the network bandwidth is limited. Not all information exchanged between mobile devices and the cloud can fit into the network at once. Some of the data gets lost or gets delayed during the network communication. Further, the network can have serious, long-term shutdown if a huge amount of data is coming at once on the network with more devices having active connections with AWS.

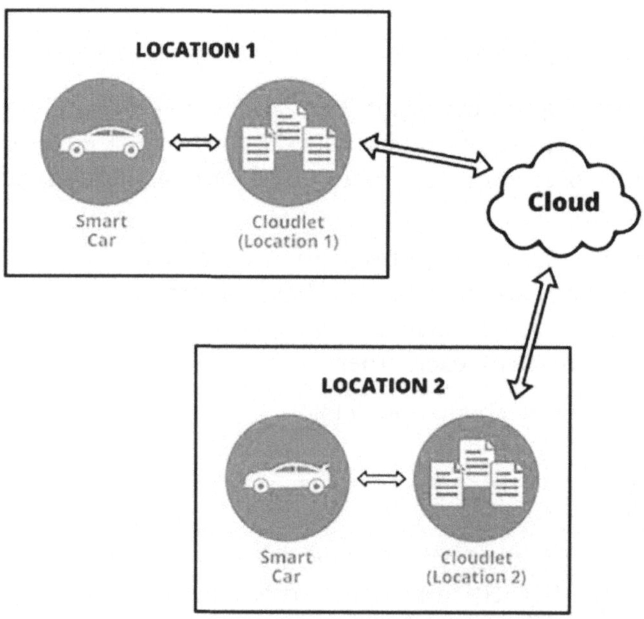

Figure 4.3: *Cars of Different Locations Accessing Location Specific Cloudlets*

Moreover, cellular networks have more latency compared to an Internet connection. Thus, services on mobile devices over cellular networks face more of a latency problem compared to the Internet-based devices. To solve this problem, cloudlets were introduced. Cloudlets are small sized data centers having similar capabilities as a cloud, connected with a fast Internet. The *Figure* 4.3 shows the usage of Cloudlet.

Architecture

It is a **client-server model** that is within proximity. They have no network hops between them. A client is a mobile device, and the server is a cloudlet. The server is managed by a service provider of the Cloud. The services of cloud are migrated to cloudlets, using **virtualization technology**. Cloud services for specific mobile devices are provisioned on the cloudlet. Service provisioning means the services are used in exchange of money. The services are created, launched and deleted on cloudlet, using virtual machines. With the help of virtualization, the services can be migrated to other infrastructures, for example, a base station. The main goal of this architecture is to reduce service latency, and the closest devices/cluster of machines/labs to the mobile device can also serve as a **cloudlet server**.

Applications

- **Shared File Editing:** Suppose, there is a file that is shared by multiple mobile clients over the Internet. The file is stored at the Cloud. If one of the clients edits the file, the updated file is seen by other clients. Thus, the shared file should be consistent among all the clients. The consistency is managed by global consistency management methods. Now, how is the file edited? The steps are as follows:

    1. The client that needs to edit the file, first downloads the file on his local machine from the Cloud.
    2. Once the client edits the file in the local machine, he uploads the new file over the Cloud. The cloud manages upload/download of the files as well as consistency in the file being shared.
    3. If every client continuously uploads/downloads the file from the cloud, it will be a network overburden. The files are then kept in the nearby cloudlets, and chunks of file are downloaded as well as uploaded for editing to reduce download/upload latency.
    4. If a mobile device moves out of the network of the cloudlet, and goes near to another cloudlet that is multi-hop away from the cloudlet, having the file, then the file is either downloaded from the cloudlet, or the cloud to the new closest cloudlet, depending on the round-trip time.
    5. Once the file is edited and uploaded back to the cloudlet, the file is automatically uploaded to all other cloudlets as well as cloud by the consistency management system.

- **Group Chat:** If multiple mobile nodes need to chat, the messages are exchanged via cloud, irrespective of the distance between the two mobile nodes that need to chat. With Cloudlet, the mobile nodes that are within proximity can chat via Cloudlet over a local network, avoiding message exchange through the cloud. The steps are:

1. The cloudlet has a list of all the nearby connected mobile devices. If a mobile device wants to chat with another mobile device, it first checks with the nearby cloudlet.
2. If the cloudlet has the other mobile node in the list, it sends the connection request. Otherwise, it responds as the device is not found. If the device is not found, then the chat request is provided to the Cloud.
3. Cloud knows a list of all cloudlets and mobile devices connected to the cloudlets.
4. If the cloudlet is very close to the cloudlet of the requesting mobile device, the cloudlet forwards the request to the cloudlet in the proximity of the destination mobile device.
5. Thus, the mobile devices communicate over a cloudlet network, if they are in proximity, otherwise they communicate via Cloud. The protocol used by clients to chat over the Cloudlet network is XMPP (Extensible Messaging and Presence Protocol).

- **Streaming Videos:** We have a mobile application on which we can stream videos from the Cloud. The video, while being watched, is cached on the nearby cloudlet. Next time, the video is watched by the mobile device, the video is streamed from the cloudlet and not the Cloud. As opposed to file sharing, the video can be watched, while it is being downloaded. Suppose the mobile device moves towards a new cloudlet that is multi-hop away from the previous cloudlet that has cached the video. The mobile device calculates the round-trip time from the previous cloudlet to the nearest cloudlet, and round-trip time of the cloud to the nearest cloudlet. Depending on the lowest round-trip time, the video is cached on the nearest cloudlet from the previous cloudlet, or the cloud. Thus, there are now two cloudlets that have cached video data, and depending on the current location of the mobile device, the video is streamed either from cloudlet or the Cloud. There is also a case possible, when there is no nearby cloudlet, and then in that case, the video has to be streamed directly from the Cloud.

Challenges

Deploying a cloudlet, and maintaining it is a very challenging task. It is a light version of the cloud. However, it has to be made capable to provide all the cloud services. It is costly to deploy cloudlets in every other location all over the world, where mobile devices can travel.

Fog Computing

Big data is generated by IoT applications, and stored in the Cloud for processing. The device and data explosion due to new IoT applications being deployed over the network on a daily basis, has increased load over network as well as Cloud. Thus, in fog computing, it is not about service latency due to the network. It is about service latency due to huge storage consumption in the Cloud. In fact, Cloud is now very costly and requires intelligent use of storage. Not all data generated by IoT devices need to be communicated and stored in the Cloud. Data can be processed before-hand and only that data is communicated to the Cloud that is relevant and requires high-computational analysis. The processing includes filtering of continuous redundant data, feature extraction and implementing light-weight artificial intelligence on data at the edge. Therefore, most of the processing of the data can be done between the end device and the Cloud. Thus, the concept of fog computing came, that reduces data being communicated to the Cloud in presence of the Big IoT Data over network.

Fog computing is the data computations carried out between cloud and the ground where ground is the network edge. It is a term coined by Cisco. It uses machines that are in the network between end devices and the cloud for computation. Fog computing supports Cloud computing and does not replace it. This means, the fog nodes (machines) do light computations and send only that data to the Cloud which requires huge computation. Fog computing is popular for real-time analytics. It is the most used edge computing architecture for developing Internet of Things applications. Fog computing is a good option for preserving data security and privacy. The computation is done by machines that are more powerful than end devices and less powerful than Cloud. Fog computing enables a decentralized architecture, reduces network bandwidth consumption, and has a fast response time.

Architecture

For deploying fog computing in IoT applications, we follow the most popular OpenFog reference architecture proposed by OpenFog Consortium. The architecture consists of three layers: IoT layer, Fog layer, and Cloud Layer as shown in *Figure* 4.4.

Each layer is discussed as follows:

- **IoT Layer:** This layer comprises sensors and actuators of IoT applications that acquire raw data. The data is then forwarded to the fog layer.
- **Fog Layer:** This layer comprises **N-tiers**. The first tier is near the IoT layer, and Nth tier is near the Cloud layer. The computations are of a higher level with each tier. The cluster of machines in a tier provides more computation and storage power, compared to previous tiers. Thus, the tasks are distributed to each tier accordingly. For example, tier 1 can be filtering the data, tier 2 can

transform the data, and tier 3 can perform real-time analytics on the data, and then the data is communicated to the Cloud for more complex computations or storage. The number of fog tiers depends on the application's requirements. The attributes to determine the number of tiers are work distribution in the tiers, number of sensors, and computation power of the machines being used in each tier, machine availability, and inter-communication latency between tiers and intra-communication latency between machines within the tier. The fog layer consists of fog nodes, where a fog node can be either a gateway, a server or a device. Fog node as a gateway routes data from fog node as a device to the respective fog node as a server. Fog node as a device is used for data storage, and fog node as a server performs data computations. Fog nodes are connected in a network that makes a distributed architecture for data processing. A fog node can either be a physical node (network devices), or a virtual node like virtual machines or cloudlets. It can process or independently as a stand-alone or form a horizontal cluster with other fog nodes for monitoring multiple locations. Functionality of the fog nodes in each tier would be different, and complexity of the functionality would depend on the tier level. Moreover, each fog node is aware of its context and other fog devices in the layer for communication, which makes the fog layer location-aware as well as it provides low latency for real-time analytics. These fog nodes are highly heterogeneous, and are made interoperable to perform tasks.

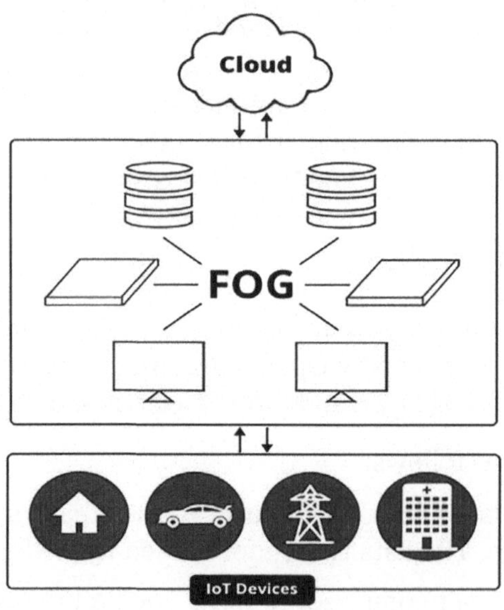

Figure 4.4: *Layers of Fog Computing Architecture*

- **Cloud Layer:** This layer provides storage and computational-intensive services of the Cloud to the reduced and processed data coming from the fog layer.

Applications

- **Video Surveillance:** Suppose, there is a mall having security cameras at each gate, on each level, and inside each shop. These cameras capture video of people for surveillance. These cameras capture video in stream,s and the video streams were traditionally stored at Cloud for processing. With fog computing, these cameras make up the IoT layer and process some of the video stream in-place. Example tasks are noise reduction and filtering video streams. The pre-processed video streams are communicated to the fog layer. Multiple machines can form a fog layer and can be used to store the video streams. One of the fog nodes runs a web server. The web server manages each of the cameras to check if they are working properly or not. The video streams are analyzed in real-time by the fog node and if they find some threat, the video is communicated to the Cloud. If any criminal record matches with the data, the suspect is communicated by web server via web API to user interface.

  Depending on the application, the function of fog nodes is to detect the object or action in real-time and then send the relevant video stream to the cloud for analysis. For example, if theft has to be monitored, the fog node needs to detect theft from the videos using powerful AI tools like deep learning. The fog node has to detect theft in real-time. Suppose if the application needs to check whether everyone has worn a mask or not during the spread of corona, the fog nodes are made capable to detect non-masked objects, filter it and communicate to the cloud for fetching details of that person. If a person is detected without a mask or doing theft, the cloud provides a decision to the fog node and the fog node displays the name of the person with an image on the web server for further actions.

- **Smart Traffic:** The traffic can be monitored according to the current traffic scenario using fog computing. The vehicles are mobile fog nodes that have functions such as navigation, driver assistance, collision avoidance. These vehicles can communicate with each other using cellular network dedicated short range communication protocols. With this Vehicle to Vehicle (V2V) communication, the distance between two vehicles as well as if any vehicle starts malfunctioning, it may directly call assistance or inform another vehicle for calling immediate assistance. V2V communication is also very useful for autonomous driving with collision avoidance. The roads have side cameras to capture the current traffic, and detect road conditions, as well as can directly interact with all the vehicles captured in the video stream to slow down to avoid traffic.

  The road side cameras are the first tier of fog layer. Processed video from each road is communicated to a second tier fog layer that consists of fog nodes monitoring multiple neighborhood locations to which roads are a part. The data from each of the locations is communicated to a third tier fog layer that manages the whole region. With each fog tier, the processing and storage power of fog nodes increases. The data from the regional fog node is shared with the Cloud, and the Cloud captures a global picture of the traffic. The Cloud analyzes the traffic, and creates a plan to avoid congestions. It notifies the fog layer about actions such as managing smart traffic lights, or managing vehicular speed, or changing navigation for particular vehicles with different and efficient routes to their destination. The service of the proposed application is personalized, and only that fog node is informed where there is a detected traffic congestion by the cloud. If a fog node on the roadside sees a traffic congestion, it can also control vehicles and smart traffic lights in real-time, and the data is not communicated further to the upper layers.

Challenges

Although fog computing is close to the device, and the tasks are distributed as well as processed by multiple machines; however, the management of fog nodes is tough and costly. Secondly, fog nodes are heterogeneous systems, and making it interoperable is another challenge. Thirdly, fog nodes increase the number of devices over the local network. Further, the fog does not replace Cloud, that means the fog and cloud needs to be well coordinated and consistent.

Mobile Edge Computing

Mobile phones these days are smart, have huge computational capabilities, and are being used for high-end applications, involving video analytics, speech recognition, augmented reality, virtual reality, gaming etc. The cloud does the back-end processing of all these mobile applications. The devices use cellular networks like 4G/5G to access the Cloud. For better user experience, the edge devices of mobile networks are used to deploy Cloud services. Mobile networks are very different from internet networks. On the Internet, the network devices are switches, routers and gateways. In mobile networks, the devices are base stations and radio network controllers. Mobile network communication for telephone calls follows circuit switching and the Internet follows packet switching. In packet switching, machines exchange information in the form of data packets, where data packets share the same link when multiple machines are communicating at the same time. Advantage of packet switching is shared cost and disadvantage is performance degradation during communication, when the network is flooded with packets. In circuit switching, if a machine starts a communication with another machine, the network between the two machines is reserved until the communication ends. One of the major advantages of circuit switching is guarantee of quality and one of the major disadvantages is the network can be tied up for unknown duration.

Initially, mobile communication followed **circuit switching**, but it now has **packet switching** too. Mobile edge computing is a concept that came up with the 4G/5G network, and it is very essential to know about mobile network advancement from 1G (first generation) to 5G (fifth generation) as well as its components.

- **1G (1980):** It is the analog communication between two mobile devices based on circuit switching technology. These devices were only capable of doing voice communication.
- **2G-GSM (1991):** GSM stands for Global System for Mobile communication. It was also based on circuit switching. The mobile devices, using this technology were now able to digitally communicate with each other, and were able to send SMS with voice communication capability. The GSM infrastructure consists of two systems as shown in *Figure* 4.5: The Base Station Subsystem (BSS) and the Network Switching System (NSS). In the base station subsystem, the mobile stations (MS) have a SIM card for connecting to base transceiver station (BTS), using a radio frequency antenna. These Base Transceiver Stations (BTS) have radio transceivers for handling data coming from Mobile Stations (MS). Multiple BTS are managed by a Base Station Controller (BSC).

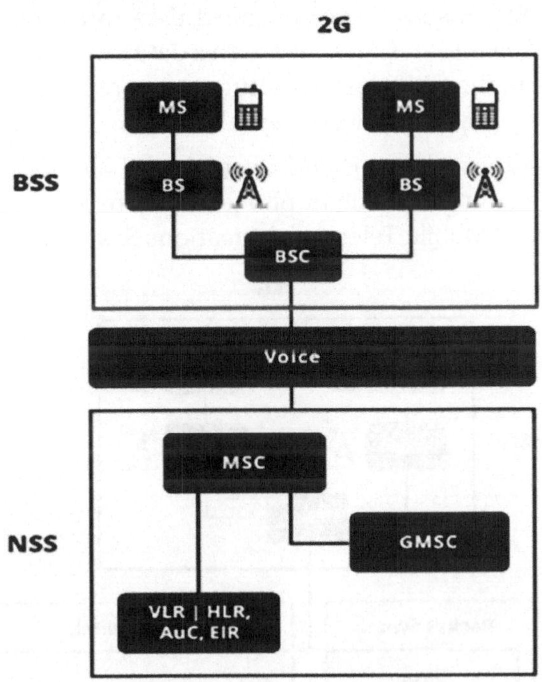

Figure 4.5: *2G Architecture*

BSC communicates the base station subsystem data with a Network Switching System (NSS). NSS has a Mobile Switching Center (MSC), Gateway Mobile Switching Center (GMSC), registers (HLR, VLR, EIR), and an Authentication Center (AUC). MSC does call setup, routing and switching among multiple BSC, and other MSC. GMSC routes call other MSC of another mobile network. They register to store details of mobile devices that are on call. AUC authenticates the mobile devices before placing the calls. This is how a 2G cellular network was first constructed for digital communication, and the devices used are all different from the Internet networks.

- **2.5G-GPRS:** GPRS stands for General Packet Radio System. It is a combination of circuit switching as well as packet switching. It provided internet services, MMS and WAP (connection to wireless router) at a data rate of 56-114 kbps. With GPRS enabled mobile devices, there came a big change in the usage of mobile phones with emails and search engines in-hand, mobile. In the GPRS architecture, two components were added to NSS for accessing internet services via BSC: Serving GPRS support node (SGSN) and gateway GPRS support node (GGSN). SGSN registered the devices, and kept account of charges for use of the internet. GGSN route packet with internal IP to SGSN of other network having external IP address. In this technology, data packets were routed from these two components, and voice communication was carried out through MSC.
- **2.75G-EDGE:** EDGE stands for enhanced data rates for GSM evolution. The edge provided faster internet speed with a data rate of 384 kbps. The protocols were updated in the GPRS infrastructure for increasing the data rate. All other infrastructure components were kept the same.
- **3G (2001):** This network provided a data rate of 3.1 Mbps, allowing video calls and video streaming on mobile phones. This network was standardized as UMTS (Universal Mobile Telecommunications System).

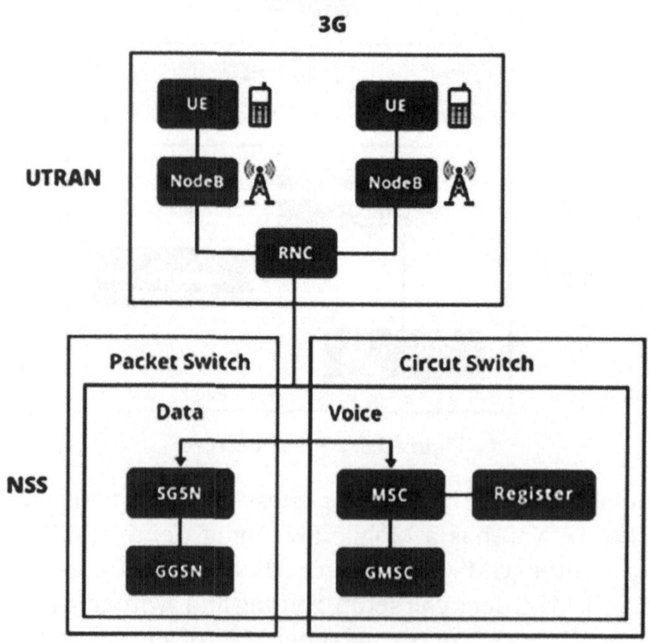

Figure 4.6: *3G Architecture*

The name of BSS as well as names of its components are changed in 3G as shown in *Figure* 4.6. BSS got a new name as UTRAN (UMTS terrestrial radio networks). Mobile stations are termed as user equipment (UE). BST is renamed as NodeB with higher data rates. Finally, BSC is renamed as Radio Network Controller (RNC). 3G mobile phones became popular in every household in a decade globally with video calls, video streaming, SMS, social networking, and many more features.

- **4G (2010):** Circuit switching is completely removed from architecture and the network is based on only packet switching. 4G has LTE support. LTE provides 100 Mbps data rate and 1 Gbps for high and low mobility, respectively. VoLTE or voice over LTE, is a packet switched in 4G which was circuit switched in 2G and 3G. 4G architecture, shown in *Figure* 4.7, is fully based on IP protocol for voice/data communication. There are e-UE and eNodeB in E-UTRAN where everything runs on the internet. The core network is new, named as evolved packet core (EPC) where voice is also communicated over the internet, similar to data, using IP. EPC consists of a database, mobility management, two gateways and rules. The gateways are used to route the voice/data packets to packet data serving nodes (PDSN). PDSN enables sessions between radio networks of mobile phones and the Internet and has similar functionalities as SGSN of 2G/3G architecture. Voice over LTE packets at PDSN are handled by an IP multimedia system.

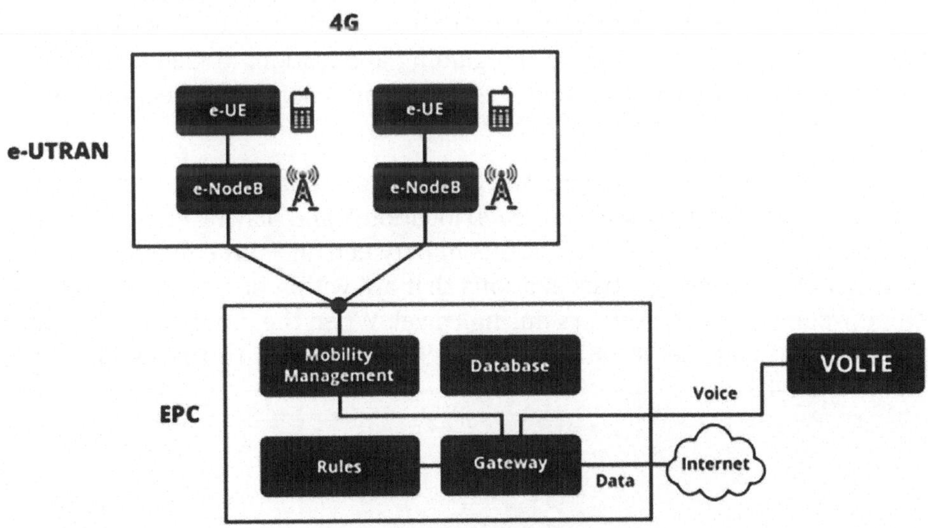

Figure 4.7: *4G Architecture*

- **5G (2019):** These are the latest generation of mobile networks that have high data rates of 20Gbps, and low latency. This network is very useful for IoT, AR/VR, and robotic applications. It has a new generation-RAN replacing e-UTRAN with an increased number of gNodeB, replacing e-nodeB.

For IoT applications, 4G and 5G networks are used for mobile devices, and they are fully internet based mobile networks with packet switching for voice as well as data. Mobile Edge Computing (MEC) is deployed for applications that have mobile phones as edge devices running heavy latency-sensitive applications, using Cloud technology. The mobile edge computing servers are placed near e-nodeB/gNodeB that provide cloud services near the e-UE, before the data is routed to Cloud via the internet. If the data rate is very fast in 4G and 5G networks, then we are using edge computing in mobile networks. The network is fast, however, due to increasing applications over the network, the bandwidth is being shared. This affects the quality of service of the application. That is why the computations are performed within RAN. It is also the best suitable for real-time applications running on mobile devices. Edge devices that can be used to create mobile edge servers having computational resources for implementing cloud services, are mobile phones, base stations, cloudlets, and gateways.

Applications

There are multiple Cloud-based games that can be played on mobile phones. These games require streaming videos with heavy graphics, multiple players, and real-time services. Handling multiple mobile devices running gaming applications by network as well as cloud would be very costly in terms of bandwidth, latency as well as resources. To manage the quality of service of the gaming application, mobile edge computing can be used. Microservice architecture using containerization technology is best suited to deploy cloud services on mobile edge devices.

To illustrate how MEC is deployed, we consider a mobile device, traveling at high speed for an hour from location X to reach location Y and playing cloud games during travel. Suppose, there are 9 base stations in between and three mobile edge servers and each server is covering 3 base stations that are within proximity. Mobile phones switch between three edge servers during travel. When the mobile device is near the edge server, that edge server streams gaming applications to the mobile device as shown in *Figure* 4.8.

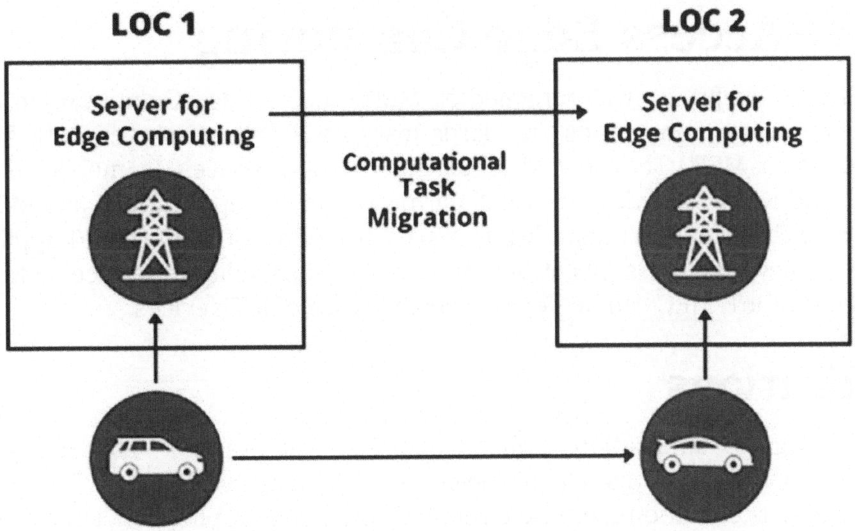

Figure 4.8: *Migration of Tasks in Mobile Devices through Mobile Edge Computing*

The cloud deploys the micro-service of gaming applications on the first edge server. The state of the gaming application has to be preserved, while edge servers change during travel. The edge server detects, when the mobile device is not in its proximity, and migrates the incomplete computation task to the next edge server. The incomplete computation task is migrated, in form micro-service from one edge cloud server to another. If in case, there is no edge server around, the cloud provides the game application services. Thus, the edge servers and the cloud need to communicate continuously, and should be consistent to manage the gaming application in real-time as well as with high quality of service, considering dynamic locations of the phone.

Challenges

The mobile network is highly dynamic with mobile phones changing locations very frequently. A vital task for MEC servers is to handle requests, while managing the mobility. For instance, it is possible that the edge server is processing a request, and the node travels to a base station near another edge server. Mobile networks already have mobility handling capabilities; however, managing mobility between edge servers in parallel to mobility management by mobile network is challenging.

Mobile edge computing was only for cellular phones. Now, Mobile edge computing is known with a new term as "multi-access edge computing". Multi-access edge computing includes all mobile devices such as UAV and vehicles, thus, very useful for IoT applications. The next section will illustrate deployment of multi-access edge computing to current IoT applications.

Multi-Access Edge Computing

Mobile Edge Computing was renamed as Multi-Access Edge Computing in 2017 by European Telecommunications Standards Institute (ETSI). However, both have the same acronym MEC. The new MEC considers edge devices as mobile, Internet-enabled, and wireless devices over cellular networks. IoT applications and MEC have benefited each other with their advantages. With support of MEC, the IoT applications can run latency sensitive applications, and provide the quality of service. In fact, with the support of IoT, MEC can be deployed on all types of IoT devices.

Applications

Smart farming IoT applications utilize Unmanned Autonomous Vehicles (UAVs) like drones to monitor the crops. The drone captures an image of the crop. The crop is 3D modeled, and its condition is checked remotely on mobile application. Drones are very popular for precision farming in smart agriculture applications. UAVs are also used to detect birds and pests that can destroy the crops, and take actions accordingly. Drones are also used in spraying pesticides to increase the agricultural yield.

They are also being utilized to differentiate weeds, and also manage them. Therefore, UAV is nowadays a very popular mobile IoT device that is very beneficial for the IoT applications. Apart from being an IoT device, UAV can be considered as an MEC server in the smart farming application. The UAV is equipped with cloud microservices to process the data on site. Multiple UAVS can form an MEC server if the computational requirements are large. Terrestrial networks are weak in remote areas and are most affected during natural calamities. Such regions are enabled with satellite communication forming a terrestrial-satellite network. If UAV is unable to connect to the cloud via terrestrial network due to some unavoidable situation or requirement of real-time urgent service, then it connects to Cloud via satellite. Moreover, for satellite communication, UAV with more computation power is required compared to UAV used as an IoT device.

Further, regular base stations in terrestrial networks have fixed locations, and cannot be reached during disasters or remote areas. In such cases, these UAVs are being utilized as a base-station, or for relaying data to base-stations, especially for a terrestrial network. UAV-enabled MEC is a popular paradigm, where UAV functions as a flying base station. UAV as a base station provides a reliable network with uplink-downlink communication having very low latency. Once UAV fetches the data, it acts as a base station as well as edge server for the IoT devices. UAV can also relay tasks to MEC servers that are far away but working. Multiple UAVs can collaborate with each other to have powerful computational capabilities for processing tasks as well as have high coverage.

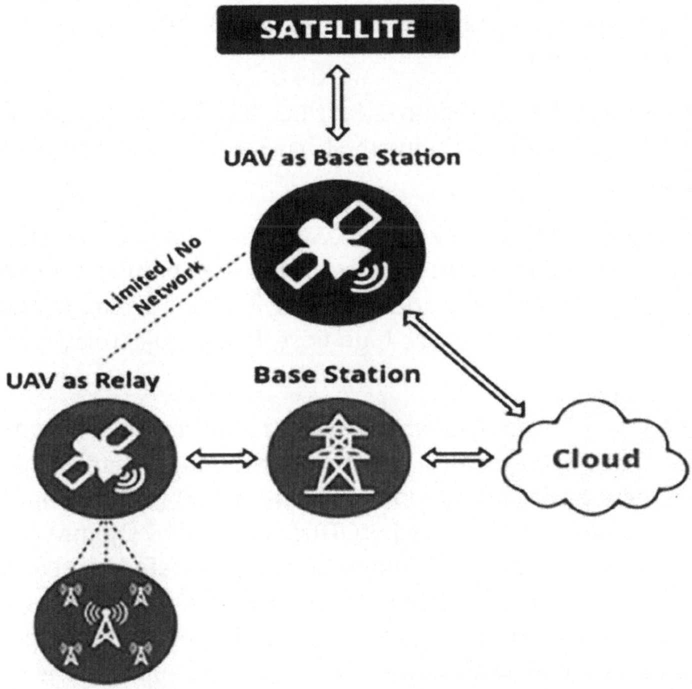

Figure 4.9: UAV *Enabled Multi-Access Edge Computing*

Flying Ad-hoc Network (FANET) is a network for communication between swarms of the UAVS for task offloading. Aerial base stations provide a degree of freedom, improved latency, energy efficiency, and reliable line-of-sight connection between UAVs, and continuous connectivity.

Communication in UAV-enabled MEC architecture for terrestrial-satellite network is shown in *Figure* 4.9, and the steps are described as follows:

1. IoT devices collect data from a location. UAV is also one of the IoT devices.
2. In a good terrestrial network, data from these IoT devices are communicated to the Cloud, using MEC architecture.
3. In a weak terrestrial scenario with no requirement of near real-time service, the UAV can be considered as a MEC server for providing cloud services at the edge as a microservice. Data from IoT devices is uploaded on UAV via base station.
4. In case of real-time service requirements during a weak terrestrial network, the UAV fetches cloud microservices via satellite communication.

5. In case of base station failure of terrestrial network and real-time requirements, the UAV acts as a flying base station for all other IoT devices, and creates a local mobile network.

6. If there are no real-time requirements in a failed terrestrial network, the UAVs may relay the IoT data to the nearest base station that has good connectivity with Cloud.

Thus, with the help of MEC architecture, UAV is now one of the very powerful IoT devices that can be utilized for multi-purpose roles, depending on the situation. UAVS can be utilized in any smart application, even if it is not a part of the application's devices. Challenges to deploy UAV are high cost, flying trajectory, maintenance, and security.

Another application area is the Generative Artificial Intelligence (GenAI), where MEC can be beneficial. GenAI is currently a very popular AI model that learns patterns from training data and generates new random data as per the training in a given context. Github Copilot developed in 2021 and ChatGPT developed by OpenAI company in 2022 are examples of GenAI. GenAI is implemented using transformer-based deep neural networks. There are now a high number of applications that are based on ChatGPT alone. These applications require a huge amount of computational power and thus, are deployed on Cloud. However, requests from all these applications will overburden the network as well as centralized Cloud servers. IoT devices, such as UAVs, smart vehicles, utilize GenAI for autonomous decision making. For applications using GenAI-enabled UAVs and vehicles, MEC is deployed with Cloud to maintain quality of service. GenAI is computationally heavy, so if one edge server is not able to process it, multiple edge servers partition tasks within themselves and collaborate. If edge servers cannot run the model, then Cloud runs the GenAI model.

Thus, MEC is an enhanced edge computing model useful, especially for deploying IoT applications. It has aided in ubiquitous computing with all sorts of IoT devices and edge devices, reducing load on network and Cloud.

Collaborative Edge Computing

In previous edge computing architectures, the tasks from Cloud were offloaded to edge devices or tasks, that is from one edge device were transferred to another edge devices. However, the computation resources were not exchanged or shared. In collaborative edge computing, the edge devices share resources with others, or in other words, make a resource pool. These edge devices that collaborate with each other are from different locations. Suppose, an edge device cannot handle a task that demands heavy computation. It asks for computational resources from edge devices of other nearby locations for completing the task. This concept is very new, and researchers are still working on it.

Applications

For illustration, let us see one example of watching high quality YouTube/Netflix videos from mobile phones. The base stations are considered as MEC edge servers. The video streams from Cloud are cached on the edge server for fast streaming of future requests. However, the edge memory is very low. Therefore, only limited videos are cached. This reduces the hit ratio of caching. The less hit ratio means more downloads from remote Cloud. Video streaming from the cloud increases big data over the network. Thus, accessing Cloud during cache miss is not a good idea. This is where the concept of collaborative edge may help. The edge device asks for the content from the other edge devices, connected on a backhaul network. If content exists, the mobile device will download video streams from the other base station (MEC server), rather than downloading from the Cloud. This will increase the hit ratio, thus reducing latency as well as network bandwidth consumption.

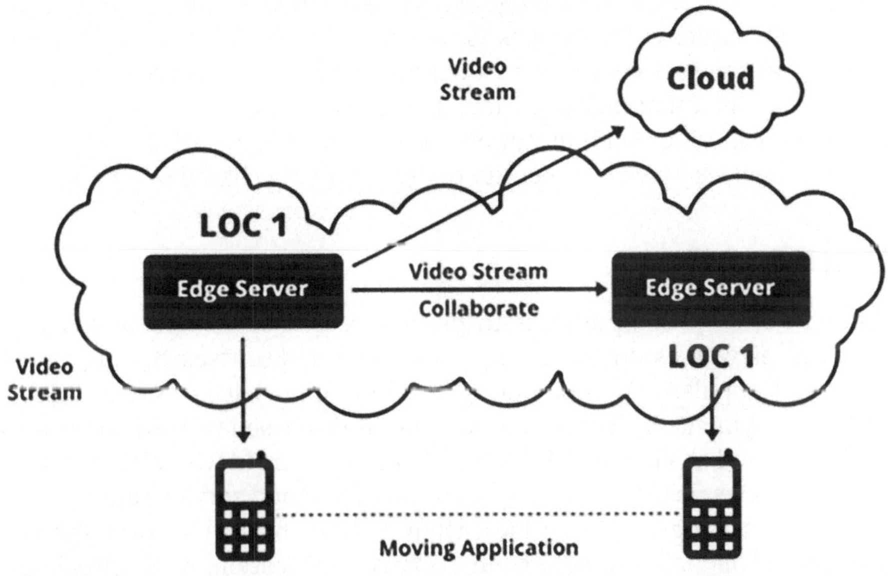

Figure 4.10: *Mobile Applications Performing Collaborative Edge Computing*

Suppose, some devices have low resolution screens. The MEC servers can transcode the data streams to low quality before streaming the data. This will save the network resources. However, it is possible that the cache memory of the edge device is full, and it has no computational resources to transcode. In such a case, the edge device migrates transcoding tasks to another edge device and then the other edge device streams the low resolution version of the video as shown in *Figure 4.10*. For collaboration to be successful, the edge devices need to manage tasks and resources very intelligently. For this, an MEC orchestrator will divide tasks according to the resource power of the edge device, and then combine the result.

Kubernetes is an orchestration technology for managing containerized applications distributed over multiple devices. It is a very popular tool for deployment and management of containerized applications on edge devices. It provides automatic scaling according to the task's computational requirements. Using Kubernetes, edge devices may collaborate and share tasks within themselves in the form of light-weight containers. Thus, collaborative edge devices can provide services as standalone Cloud at the network edge.

Challenges

Collaboration is hard as devices are heterogeneous. The edge devices belong to a heterogeneous network, and their computational power is also heterogeneous. The first and foremost challenge is to provide interoperability. These devices need to have the same platform for communication so that they are fast in collaboration and resource sharing. The second challenge is that collaborative edge computing needs to consider mobility issues of IoT devices as well as mobile edge devices (UAV). A further challenge is that the service (cached video) needs to be discovered automatically as well as with the minimum possible time, so that the time taken using collaborative edge is low, considering communication with Cloud. Lastly, privacy of data shared between edge devices as well as security of devices being shared is very important.

Conclusion

The main aim of edge computing is to provide real-time service, and reduce data over network as well as on the Cloud. This chapter discusses the history of edge computing and popular edge computing architectures that are being used for IoT application deployment. Each of the architecture is discussed with architecture, a use-case application and challenges. The edge computing started with cloudlets that were clusters of machines near the end devices to provide cloud services at the edge using virtualization technology. With an increasing number of devices over the network, cloudlets were challenging to deploy on every other location. After Cloudlets, came the concept of fog computing that provided computing between the end device and the Cloud using internet devices like routers, gateways and switches. For Cloud-based applications running on mobile devices, mobile edge computing was coined. It utilized cellular networks for processing at the edge. Mobile edge computing later renamed as mobile access computing included all kinds of mobile devices/ IoT devices for edge computing. A new architecture is under making known as collaborative edge that aims to share resources to perform heavy tasks.

In the next chapter, we will study different edge platforms and edge devices, and how to deploy IoT applications on edge devices, using edge platforms.

Points to Remember

- Before edge architectures were developed, the Akamai company proposed a Content Delivery Network (CDN). After CDN, came the concept of pervasive computing and P2P computing.
- In pervasive computing, the tasks from mobile devices were offloaded to nearby surrogate servers, considered as edge devices.
- In a P2P network, the devices are interconnected, and they have both the roles of the client as well as the server.
- Cloudlets are the first official edge computing architecture. Cloud services for specific mobile devices are provisioned on cloudlet. The services are created, launched and deleted on cloudlet, using virtual machines.
- In fog computing, the fog nodes (machines) do light computations, and send only that data to the Cloud which requires huge computation.
- Mobile Edge Computing (MEC) is deployed for applications that have mobile phones as edge devices running heavy latency-sensitive applications, using Cloud technology.
- Mobile edge computing is renamed as multi-access edge computing which also includes devices other than mobile network devices in edge architecture.
- In collaborative edge computing, the edge devices share resources with other devices, or in other words, make a **resource pool**.

Multiple Choice Questions

1. In which computing, surrogate servers are used as edge devices?
    a. Cloud
    b. Fog
    c. Pervasive
    d. P2P
2. Akamai Company proposed CDN for:
    a. Processing data near edge device
    b. Caching data at the server
    c. Server handles web requests
    d. Caching web content at the edge

3. What is not a part of fog computing architecture?
    a. Cloud
    b. Base station
    c. IoT device
    d. Fog device
4. Small-scale data center that runs virtual machines to provide Cloud services is called:
    a. Cloudlet
    b. Base station
    c. Surrogate server
    d. Fog node
5. Mobile edge computing is renamed as:
    a. Collaborative edge computing
    b. Ubiquitous computing
    c. P2P computing
    d. Multi-access edge computing
6. In smart farming, UAV cannot do:
    a. Bird watch
    b. Estimate soil temperature
    c. Pesticide spray
    d. Weed detection
7. Which network infrastructure has BSS and NSS?
    a. GPRS
    b. GSM
    c. EDGE
    d. All of the above

Answers

1. c
2. d
3. b
4. a
5. d
6. b
7. d

Questions

1. What is the purpose of CDN, pervasive computing and P2P computing?
2. What are the advantages and disadvantages of Cloudlet?
3. How does fog computing support the Cloud? Describe layers of fog computing.
4. How does UAV help in terrestrial networks with no connectivity?
5. What changed in 4G mobile network compared to 3G network?
6. What is the use of collaborative computing at the network edge? Explain with an example.

CHAPTER 5
Exploring Edge Platforms and Devices

Introduction

With IoT, any object in the world can be made smart with the help of embedded devices. Sensors are attached to the embedded devices to collect the environment data. The data is then stored, and communicated by embedded device to the Cloud. Such smart objects in IoT are labeled as IoT devices/ end devices. These IoT devices can perform edge computing over the embedded device to conserve communication energy, and reduce data over Network. Therefore, IoT devices can also be considered as edge devices.

Other edge devices were listed in *Chapter 4, Integrating Edge with Cloud in IoT Architecture*. These edge devices have very low computational as well as storage power with limited battery life. Further, each edge device has heterogeneous resources and storage. Thus, for performing computation on edge devices, we need to understand how to utilize the limited resources.

For efficient resource utilization, there exists multiple edge platforms that can run on edge devices. This chapter will discuss popular edge platforms for implementation of edge computing architecture in IoT applications. After platforms, we will see characteristics, hardware, and software architecture of edge devices that are being used in deployment of IoT applications.

Further, this chapter will also elaborate on challenges that may be faced during edge computing implementation on different edge devices like smartphones, Raspberry Pi, Jetson and Smartwatch with application use-case.

Structure

In this chapter, we will cover the following topics:

- Edge Platforms
- Edge Devices
- Mobile Edge Devices
- Embedded Edge Devices
- Smart Watch

Edge Platforms

As we have seen in *chapter 4, Integrating Edge and Cloud in IoT Architecture*, cloud has three types of services: Infrastructure, Platform and Software. For edge computing, the clouds have extensions for platform as a service. This means, the cloud providers provide a platform for edge computing. To deploy the platform provided by the Cloud, the edge devices or edge network should be located between end machines and the Cloud. Independent edge platforms are also available that are not connected to the Cloud.

All these existing platforms have a common architecture/stack as Cloud Platforms. Each of these platforms require a specific edge Infrastructure for deployment. Further, the cloud platform needs to monitor, manage and orchestrate distributed edge computing platforms.

Additional functionalities of edge platforms compared to cloud platforms are as follows:

- **Providing Distributed Computing:** The computational tasks need to be efficiently distributed between end machines, edge devices, and the Cloud for maintaining quality of service. Further, the computation is distributed to multiple edge devices, and the computation transactions need to be managed well for proper commits.
- **Managing Traffic between Edge Devices:** The platform optimizes network routes between edge devices and edge-cloud network, with the help of edge gateway and edge cloud connect. The routing considers edge devices for data networking that are available, have plenty of resources, and reduce latency.
- **Orchestrating a High Number of Edge Servers that are Heterogeneous:** The edge devices come in different computation power, storage as well as architectures. Thus, the platform is capable of supporting different types of edge infrastructure. However, not all platforms support all infrastructure. Some platforms require specific infrastructure that needs to be bought, and that is compatible with the platform. For example, the Everyware Software

Framework (ESF) platform requires embedded devices designed by Wire for edge computation, and only uses programming tools called wires for writing codes.

- **Access to IoT Marketplace:** Edge computing is highly utilized in industries to deploy IoT applications. Some of the edge computing platforms also provide specific support to the market of IoT devices and software.
- **Providing Security:** The platforms should have security protocols to keep an eye on incoming data packets. The security is deployed on edge networks to trace data packets between edge devices. Some platforms have no security services of their own, but can be easily integrated with third-party security services.
- **Provisioning of Cloud Services:** Some edge computing platforms are extensions of the existing Cloud computing platforms, and they can be managed through the Cloud portal. Therefore, the Cloud decides the workload distribution to save cost. But some of the platforms are greenfield, and have no connection with Cloud. These platforms should be able to provision Cloud services for consistency in task distribution and orchestration.

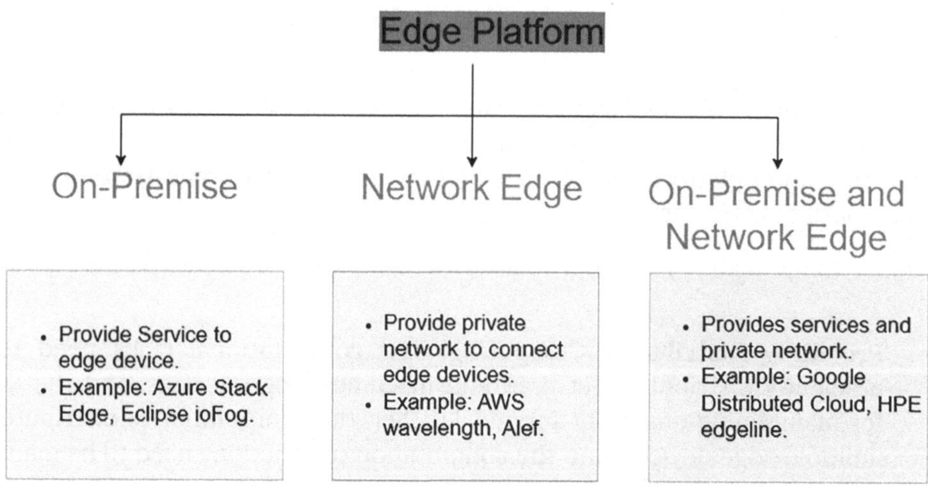

Figure 5.1: *Categories of Edge Platforms*

The edge platforms are divided into three categories as shown in *Figure* 5.1. They are discussed in the next sub-sections.

On-premise Edge

These edge platforms provide services to edge devices. The devices considered can be platform specific, or the platform is open to all kinds of devices. The devices are located near the edge machines, and platforms run independently on them. Examples are: Azure Stack Edge, Eclipse ioFog, and so on.

- **Azure Stack Edge:** Microsoft Azure is a popular Cloud, and it provides an edge computing service namely Azure Stack Edge. The Azure Stack Edge has hardware-as-a-service. The devices need to be bought from the Azure website, and are available in different versions such as mini and pro. The pro devices are with Nvidia GPU and the mini device is specially built for harsh environments.

  The device is then managed by a Cloud server. The device has the capability to cache data locally, and transfer most of the data to the Cloud. The models can be trained on the Cloud, and the trained model is deployed to the device for real-time analysis. The data can be uploaded to the Cloud for re-training of the model. To use it in an IoT application, the azure stack edge is integrated with IoT Hub. The IoT hub is an Azure cloud service that provides connectivity and data communication between devices and the IoT applications. To deploy IoT edge services on the device, The IoT hub migrates the containers to the Azure stack edge device. This platform follows a pay-as-you-go model, and requires specific devices to deploy applications on edge.

- **Eclipse ioFog:** This is a free platform that runs software over edge devices. It behaves as an agent, and provides a platform for running multiple microservices as well as managing them remotely. It also enables communication between two microservices as a broker. We create a network of edge devices near the end machine. Each of these end devices run ioFog agent to communicate with each other, and to perform computations on micro-service architecture. The agent then deploys microservices, using Linux Kernel containers or Dockers. This network of edge devices is called the Edge Compute Network (ECN). Multiple agents are orchestrated by a software called controller. The controller can run on any device that has a static IP address.

- **Greengrass:** It is a software provided by AWS for deploying IoT on edge. It runs Lambda functions and a MQTT broker locally on edge device, and the functions are controlled for updates and debugs by the AWS Cloud remotely. It has automatic device deployment and management feature using AWS IOT console and can be easily integrated with other AWS services. With AWS Greengrass, the IoT application on edge is capable of providing services, even without internet connectivity. It is an open-source software that helps in building, deploying and managing software. It provides local processing, inferences, and tools to accelerate development of the software and secured connection to third party services.

- **Azure IoT Edge:** It is a runtime software that focusses on deploying containerized Linux workloads on edge devices. The containerized workloads aim to bring analytics closer to the sensing for faster insights even in case of no internet connectivity. Any kind of analytics required as per the IoT application's requirement can be fetched from Cloud as a container and deployed on local device with the help of Azure IoT Edge. The business logic is developed at Cloud, packaged as container and then it is easy to reuse on any IoT edge devices. The insights and decision making can then be performed locally, accurately and in offline mode. This reduces bandwidth consumption by avoiding sending of large-scale IoT data. The business logic is deployed on IoT Edge modules that are docker containers, and advanced AI models are easily deployed on the modules. Further, Azure stream analytics and Azure ML can be used to have faster deployment. IoT edge runtime resides on local edge device and connects with cloud for remote management of the operations. It can be deployed on windows machine using Linux virtual machine on top of the Windows OS.

Next, we will discuss the steps to deploy edge computing on Windows OS, using Azure IoT Edge, Azure IoT hub and Azure container registry. First, download visual studio code, an azure cli connected to the azure, and docker desktop.

- Start the docker desktop, and it will run over Windows Subsystem for Linux (WSL), a virtual machine of Linux OS.
- Open visual studio, and add extension of Azure IoT Edge and Azure IoT Hub. After adding extension, create IoT hub from view->command pallet. Follow the instructions and make a with subscription and free tier. I created an IoT hub named **`temp-sense-rj`**, and the screenshot is shown in *Figure* 5.2.

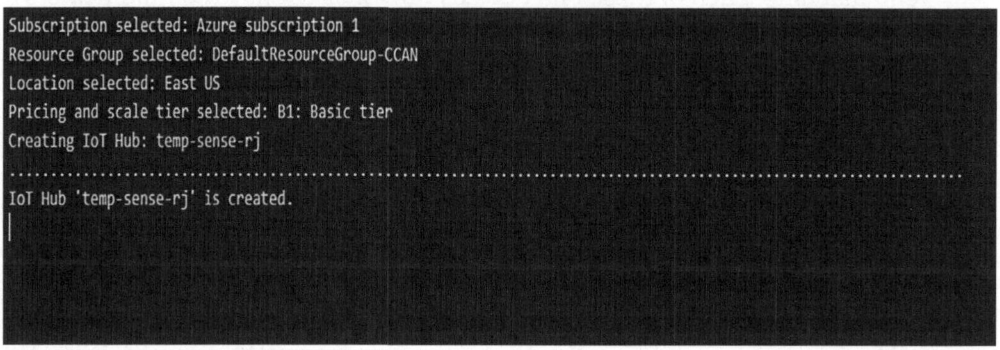

Figure 5.2: *Creation of IoT Hub on Visual Studio Code*

- Create container registry in azure account with the same subscription, and plan as IoT hub. The username and password are shown in access keys under settings, and this is used to login from the edge device, currently our laptop. The following *Figure* 5.3 shows the screenshot of the created container registry.

Figure 5.3: *Container Registry Created on Azure Account*

- After creating an IoT hub and container registry, the next step is to create a new IoT edge solution. During creation, select a folder to store files, and give the azure registry account to connect to the azure container registry. Replace **`localhost:5000/module_name`** with login server **`name/module_name`**.
- Visual studio will automatically open the folder and trust needs to be allowed before making any changes to the files. The folder is shown in the *Figure 5.4*. The folder name is **`Edge Solutiontemp`** and the **`module_name`** is **`TempModule`**.

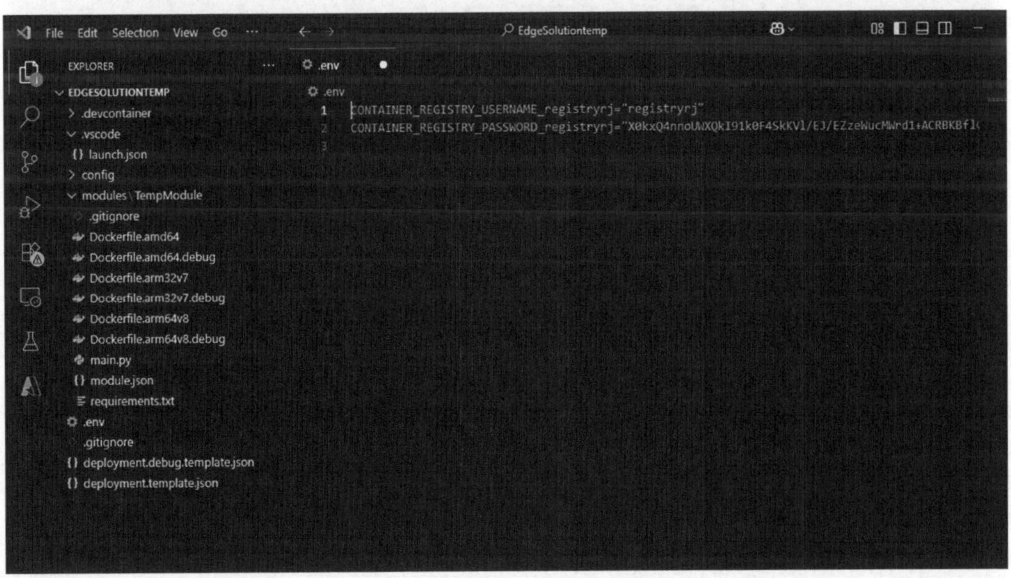

Figure 5.4: *The Folder List on Visual Studio and ".env" File after Creating New Edge Solution*

- Within the folder, there is an .env script file where the username password of registry needs to be stored. The "main.py" file has the python code to be executed and it can be modified.
- We need to containerize this application and send this on azure container registry so that it can be accessed by pull request on any other edge platform.

To connect the device with the azure cloud account and the registry, the following commands need to be executed on the terminal of visual studio.

```
az cloud set -n AzureCloud
az login
az acr login -registryrj
```

- Once the login is successful, the docker needs to be connected to containerize the application, and pushed to azure container registry. The following command connects the docker desktop with azure registry.

```
docker login registryrj.azurecr.io
Username: registryrj
Password:
Login Succeeded
```

- After successful login, right click the "**deployment.template.json**" file, and select "**build and push**". After successful push, the output will look like *Figure 5.5*.

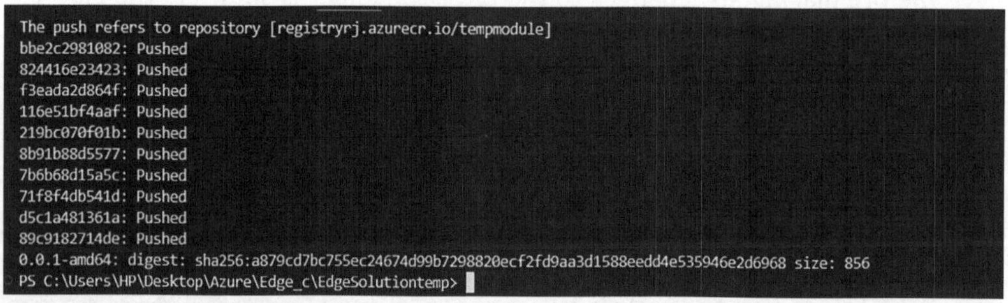

Figure 5.5: *The Folder with the Python File Pushed Successfully to the Azure Container Registry*

Network Edge

In this type, the platform provides a private network that can be used to connect edge devices, and choose IP addresses for each edge device. These platforms are very specific for telecoms. The network of edge devices formed is managed by the platform. Examples are: AWS Wavelength and Alef.

- **AWS Wavelength:** Amazon AWS community has provided an edge computing platform for 5G networks known as AWS wavelength. Their aim is to provide ultra-low latency to mobile devices. For utilizing the platform, the edge devices need to be in the wavelength zone. There are multiple established wavelength zones across the world. To deploy the platform, an Amazon Virtual Private Cloud (VPC) has to be created in a region. The nearest region of AWS cloud is selected for creating the VPC. Within a region, there are three zones: Availability zones (isolated locations), local zones (close to end user) and wavelength zones (5G network edge). The VPC subnets are created in all the three zones. The services are extended from VPC to a subnet of wavelength zones to run ultra-low latency applications. The wavelength zone belongs to a Communications Service Provider (CSP) network. Steps to follow to select the zone are as follows:

1. Firstly, create a VPC in your region, and configure the VPC network with IP address as well as the routing table.
2. Create a subnet in a wavelength zone that is related to the VPC.
3. The subnet in the wavelength zone is accessed by the carrier gateway via the routing table. The routing table is then updated with destination as carrier gateway for VPC devices, within the subnet of the wavelength zone and the subnets.
4. Creation of VPC, subnets, wavelength zones and carrier gateways is managed from the AWS console.
5. The instance in the subnet of the wavelength zone will have a carrier IP address as it is accessed separately through the 5G CSP network.

- **Alef:** This is the first edge computing platform primarily focused on 3G mobile networks, and aims to provide better connectivity between mobile devices. In this platform, the enterprise can create a private mobile network with mobile edge devices, and control the traffic flow between them. The platform offers a collection of Enterprise Mobile Connectivity APIs for creating, configuring and managing the private mobile network. Deploying and maintaining the private edge network is very simple via platform APIs. With the use of APIs, the platform can also be easily integrated with the 5G network for real-time edge computing. Compared to existing mobile network vendors, the deployment and utilization cost of private networks created through the platform is less as well as there is no complex installation. The platform can easily connect to multiple geographically-distributed Radio Access Networks (RANs) over a private mobile network. The network of multiple RANs is managed by the end point of enterprise WAN. The end point is then connected to the Alef Edge Cloud.

On-premise and Network Edge

These platforms provide services that manage edge network as well as connected edge devices. Examples are: Google Distributed Cloud Edge and HPE Edgeline.

- **Google Distributed Cloud Edge:** As all data cannot be processed in the cloud due to data privacy, time-constraints or network issues, Google decided to provide a platform for edge devices leveraging 140+ google edge networks worldwide. The platform can also support other edge networks, edge devices and private data centers. Managing distributed edge centers is done via open-source software called Anthos. Services from the google cloud are extended to these edge devices. It also supports 5G network as well as radio access network. A dedicated edge device known as rack infrastructure has to be bought to deploy distributed edge on 5G network. The rack consists of six servers and switches connecting these servers. These devices are then managed, configured by Anthos. The distributed cloud edge is managed by Anthos running on google Cloud and services are migrated from the Cloud to the dedicated devices created by Google. Another product that Google offers is edge appliance to implement ML models at edge. These devices have Anthons running on bare metal forming a cluster for local management in case of no connection with the Cloud.
- **HPE Edgeline:** This platform is built on a specific edge device that has converged operation technology hardware and software for control/management with IT analytics for autonomous decision-making in presence of limited or no network connectivity. This edge device is HPE Edgeline Converged Edge Systems. The management tool on the provided device helps to manage the other edge devices directly or as a cluster. The management is done through HPE OT link platform. The converged edge systems are created to handle shock, vibrations, dust, extreme temperatures and harsh environment conditions. In this platform, there is no need for data communication to the cloud. The system is independent to do all the operation at the network edge without support of a Cloud. The device price starts from $2500 and there are multiple devices to choose from depending on the edge environment. The data storage is very limited and Cloud is not directly used to store data. Hence, extra storage is required, either to be bought or by connecting a third-party cloud provider with the system for more storage, making it more reliable for analytics at the edge.

Choice of edge platform depends on application specific requirements and costs. Utilizing these edge platforms will help enterprises deal with huge volumes of data communing in high velocity. These platforms will bring a change by reducing data over the network as Clouds won't be able to keep up with the voluminous data.

Edge Devices

A device that is placed on a network edge and has capability to perform computations is called edge device. These edge devices have very low limited computation power and storage compared to the Cloud. They are placed between IoT devices/ end devices and the Internet/Cloud. These edge devices either have their own network connectivity or a network device is attached for supporting data communication. These edge devices can do pre-processing, analysis, and storage of data. Edge devices are popularly used in IoT applications. Depending on different applications, the edge devices are found to be of different types as shown in *Figure* 5.6 and discussed as follows.

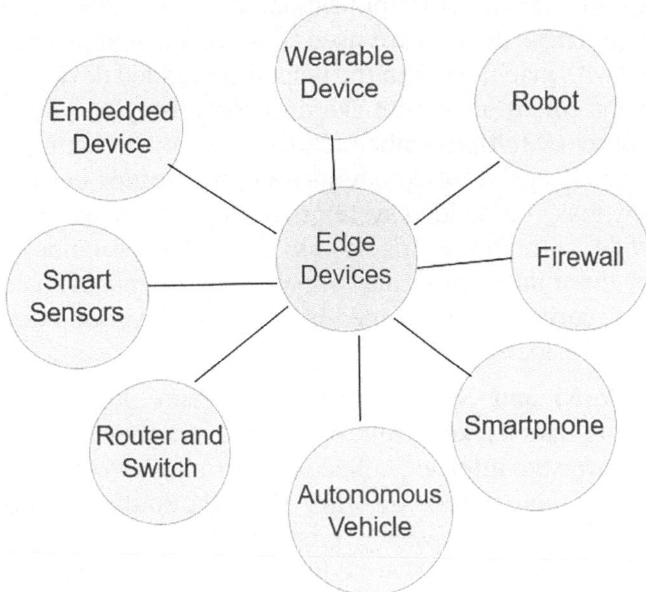

Figure 5.6: *Different Types of Edge Devices in our Surroundings*

- **Smart Sensors** are tiny devices that are used for sensing the environment. Sensors take input in different energy domains and convert it into energy signals suitable for processing. The conversion between energy signals is done by transducers. The input signal is then converted to human readable output. These sensors also have computational capabilities to process the sensed data. These sensors collect data autonomously and accurately and have very low errors. They also communicate data over the internet. A smart temperature sensor can detect overheating of a machine and a smart level sensor detects the oil level of the car and alerts the driver. An example of smart sensor and a popular product of DwyerOmega company is Omega Smart Sensors used in Industrial Internet of Things (IIOT) to monitor temperature, relative humidity, and barometric pressure data. DwyerOmega is a worldwide known company that manufactures edge computing products like sensors, controllers, software and wireless connectors for IIOT.

  IIOT focuses on industries and connects machines via the internet to have an efficient, automated operations pipeline. Smart sensors in IIOT generate machine data to monitor operational processes, making machines smarter.

Benefits of using smart sensors in an IIOT is predictive maintenance and increasing uptime. Smart sensors are plug-n-play sensors that collect environment data in real-time and have automated output with direct connections to alarms and controls even without the internet.

- **Embedded Device and Embedded System:** These devices are small in structure and run a specific application. It has very low computational power and storage. These devices are used to make a machine smarter. Sensors are embedded with machines with the help of embedded devices to detect current environment conditions and make decisions. They can be imagined as very tiny computers. Multiple embedded devices form an embedded system and each device is capable of communicating with other devices. These devices collectively make embedded systems smarter, get in sync by communicating, and provide autonomous decisions. Examples of embedded devices are Raspberry Pi car dashboard touchscreen. An example of an embedded system is a home security system formed by multiple embedded devices like motion sensor, camera, locks.
- **Routers (WAN) and Switch (LAN):** The main purpose of routers is to communicate data packets from one LAN to another LAN. The two LANs are connected over the internet, collectively forming a WAN. The data from WAN can also be communicated to other WAN via Routers. Routers that provide WAN to WAN communication are called core routers and routers enabling communication within WAN are edge routers. To communicate data packets within LAN, a switch is used. In short, a router connects a private network to public internet/internet and switch provides communication within a private network. Apart from data communication, switch and edge routers are used for computations and storage as they reside at the network edge.
- **Firewalls:** It is a software that resides on edge computers to keep an eye on incoming and outgoing packets and also provide security to the device by blocking malwares. It has some predefined set of rules. For example, if a port is not allowed in the firewall, any packet coming from that port number is not allowed to be communicated to the device. The firewall drops the packet. These firewalls are used as a service to provide secured edge computing. A dedicated edge machine serves as a firewall to provide security from multi-access networks.
- **Smartphone:** Mobile phones that have their own mobile OS for deploying a lot of applications, huge memory, embedded systems with multiple sensors, a good connection to the internet is called a smartphone. These devices have all capabilities similar to a normal computer in a compact size. However, to run gaming, social networking, video applications, the computation resources and battery life of smartphones is limited. Smartphones are popular edge computing devices as they do some of the data processing of nearby acquired data. For example, processing of some of the smart home data or health data of

a specific person are carried out on smartphones itself. Smartphones are also considered for providing edge computation to other smartphones. To enable smartphones to be used as edge devices, they are connected to each other forming a mobile cloudlet.

- **Wearable Device:** These devices are built to track and monitor health of the person and these devices are created such that they can be comfortably worn by humans through the day, during all the activities and even while sleeping. They are attached very close to the body and sense vital health conditions like heart rate, speed, distance, calories. Further, they can also be used to monitor the environment around the individual or keep check on the daily actions performed by the person. A wearable device has a microcontroller, sensors, Cloud connectivity and wireless communication capabilities. They have very low computation capabilities, storage capabilities and battery life. Edge computing is very beneficial for wearable devices to avoid long-distance data communication, saving battery life of the wearable devices. Nowadays, wearable devices are also being made capable of performing in-sensor edge computing with the help of OCET arrays. These arrays provide support to run machine learning onto wearable devices. New future in edge computing is AI powered wearable devices that should not compromise with comfort of wearing it all day.
- **Robots:** A robot has a mechanical structure, multiple sensors to detect the surrounding environment and an embedded device that processes sensor data and controls the mechanical movements of the robot accordingly. Thus, embedded devices behave as a small brain connecting sensed data with physical actions. Robots are independent devices; however, these devices are now being integrated with IoT. The new field is the Internet of Robotic Things. Robots sense as well as perform actions in a physical environment. They are provided with AI to solve complex tasks. These tasks are more complex than tasks performed by IoT things. Robots have a good number of computational resources and can run AI at edge, requiring no Cloud to process data. Multiple AI-enabled robots may form collaborative edge computing models over the internet, fusing their collected sensor data, utilize combined intelligence and accordingly take physical actions in real environments like in industrial IoT, smart city.
- **Autonomous Vehicles:** Nowadays, there are self-driving cars that are part of stage 5 autonomous vehicles. Autonomous vehicles mean they do not require much human intervention to operate. They have their own sensing and intelligence capabilities. Stage 0 lists vehicles that have no automation at all. These vehicles are embedded with multiple sensors and machine learning models. They consider data sensed by the vehicle, data collected by other vehicles and road map through satellite, to plan the route in real-time. Further, they have features like reducing speeds, headlights whenever a car comes into

vision, to avoid accidents. These vehicles are capable of performing edge computations. These computations are currently done by Cloud. However, if these cars are considered as edge devices, they can collaborate to provide cloud services to each other via multi-access edge computing models.

Smartphone: A Mobile Edge Device

Smartphone is a mobile edge device that has good computation and storage power with limited battery life. It is equipped with multiple sensors that are helpful to detect environmental conditions. It is one of the most used edge devices in IoT applications as sensing, communication as well as analysis happens in the same place. One of the popular IoT applications is Activity Recognition System. This system aims to detect physical activity in real-time and provide duration for each activity to maintain a healthy lifestyle. For human activity recognition, smartphone sensors are used to capture sensor data and predict activity accordingly.

Linear acceleration and angular velocity data is collected from the accelerometer and gyroscope of the smartphone. To collect the sensor data, the patients' needs to wear the smartphone onto their bodies. There is a popular dataset on Kaggle named as **Human Activity Recognition with Smartphones**. The dataset may be used to deploy the application on a smartphone. The activities recognized in the dataset are walking, walking on stairs, standing and sitting. There exist many other related datasets for use that are collected from smartphone sensors. A supervised classification model or deep learning model is trained on the dataset and the trained model is deployed as a mobile App on the smartphone itself. Another way to sense activities is to place sensors like motion sensors and cameras in the environment, fetch data on the phone, and apply a deep learning model on the phone to detect activities.

To deploy an IoT application on a smartphone, we should know what a smartphone is made of. Smartphones have their own OS, either Android for Samsung, PixelOS or Google Pixel that is the pixel version of android, or iOS for Apple. This device follows ARM architecture and has an application processor unit for running multiple applications. The architecture of smartphone consists of 5 components:

- **Hardware**: Smartphones use System on a Chip (SoC) Architecture that has 3 modules. The first module is an application processor that executes instructions from OS and middleware to run software. The second module is a baseband for radio transmissions of audio and video data. The third module is the interface for peripheral devices.
- **Communication**: The baseband module of SoC architecture provides data communication support and has two main functions, one as transmitter and other as receiver. The baseband module has an OS as well as radio interface. A SIM card is very important during transmission and receiving of data in the form of radio signals. During data transmission, the data to be transmitted is

collected from memory by OS, processed by modern transmission protocols and the transmission is started using a radio interface. During receiving, the incoming data is processed and then the radio OS communicates with peripheral devices, such as speakers for audio and display for video, to provide processed data to the user.

- **Execution of User Application**: The execution of computation-intensive application is done by CPU and graphical intensive application is done by GPU. For the execution of applications, smartphones have a volatile memory and a large non-volatile memory. Linux OS is the base for Android applications.
- **Peripheral Device**: These devices are input/output devices provided to users for communicating with the smartphone. Popular devices are display, touchscreen, camera, keypad, speakers, GPS, Bluetooth, wireless support.
- **Processors**: 8-bit microprocessors are not powerful for running smartphone applications and intel processors used in laptops may drain batteries of smartphones really fast. Therefore, the smartphones are equipped with ARM processors that provide both computational power and also low battery consumption. Current smartphones come with multi-processors cores (2,4,8).

Let us suppose we wish to deploy a deep learning model over smartphones to analyze patient data. Firstly, we will train the deep learning model on a laptop or Cloud, depending on the dataset complexity and volume. There is a specific CNN based deep learning model called **MobileNet** for smartphone deployment. The size of the trained model can be reduced via a technique called quantization. Once the model is trained, it is kept as a back-end. The back-end is deployed using Flask and front-end using JavaScript. The deployment can be done on android as well as Apple phones as shown in *Figure* 5.7. For creating an android app, we need to download Android Studio. The programming language used for Android is Java. To deploy android applications on smartphones, we need to know android architecture for foundation. Install TensorFlow lite library to run trained deep learning model.

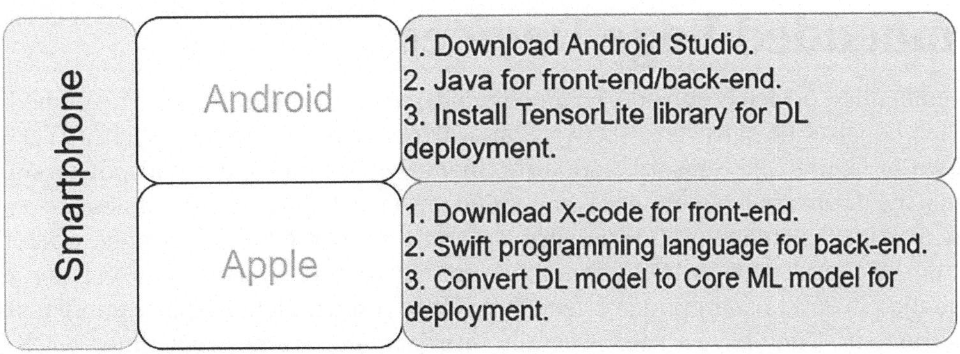

Figure 5.7: *Deployment Steps of Deep Learning Apps on Smartphones*

Android Architecture consists of 5 layers:

- **Applications:** This layer consists of all the pre-installed applications like contacts, messaging and third-party applications like Facebook, twitter, WhatsApp.
- **Application Framework**: This layer provides services to create an application. For each service, there is a class. Services are like notification manager, package manager etc. This layer provides resources as well as manages communication between application and hardware.
- **Android Runtime:** This layer provides an environment to run the application. It consists of a Dalvik Virtual Machine to run multiple instances in parallel. It provides core libraries to develop the application in Java over Linux kernel.
- **Platform Libraries:** These include C++ libraries and Java libraries like SGL for cross- platform communication, SQLite for data storage, SSL for data encryption to provide security to applications, media libraries and web kit.
- **Linux Kernel:** This layer abstracts hardware and provides access to drivers of camera, Bluetooth, audio, display etc. The kernel is responsible for memory management, process management with multi-threading, controlling of devices and security.

If we want to deploy the model on an Apple phone, an iOS application needs to be created that performs data analysis locally using a trained model. To build an iOS app, download Xcode for free and use swift programming language to code for the app. Xcode provides a drop-down menu to create a front-end interface. It has a core ML library to run deep learning models. The deep learning models need to be converted to Core ML format. Swift programming language is used to code back-end service. The app can be tested on an available iOS simulator on Xcode. Once the app is ready, it is submitted to the Apple store for approval. The Xcode can only be used on MAC OS and no other.

Embedded Edge Devices

An embedded device is considered an edge device in IoT applications. The embedded device consists of hardware, software and a real-time operating system (RTOS) as shown in *Figure* 5.8. Sensors, actuators, memory, I/O interfaces and power supply forms the hardware component of embedded devices. RTOS runs, schedules processes and manages memory. RTOS is very different from a general-purpose operating system. General purpose OS cannot communicate with analog waves. Their size, cost and power consumption are very high. They run parallel tasks in a multi-tasking environment. They have a user -friendly interface and are not real-time. RTOS is a dedicated OS programmed to do a specific task. These systems are popular for real-time operations. These systems have less user intervention and have minimal user interface. These systems operate on low power and have low cost in the market. The drawback of these systems is that they are very small and application-specific.

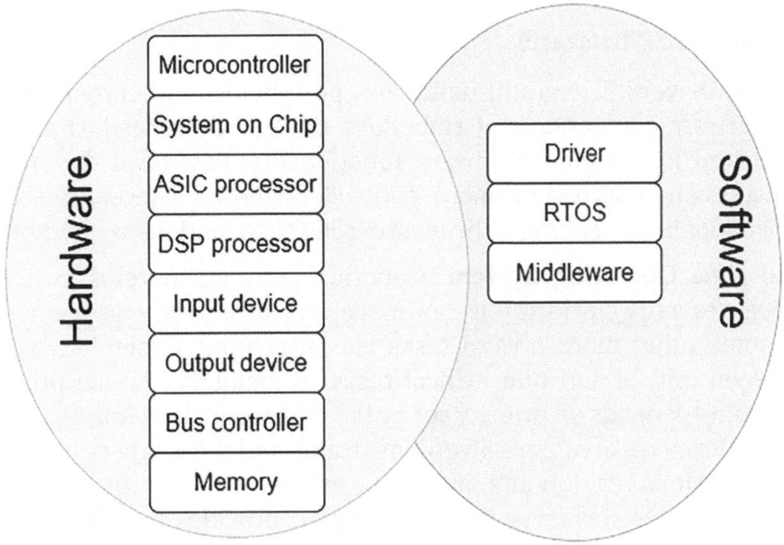

***Figure* 5.8:** *Hardware and Software Components of an Embedded Device*

Embedded Hardware

- **Microcontroller**: A very small computer on a single integrated circuit. It can perform only one task and run only one application. They are especially created for embedded systems and microprocessors are used in general purpose computers. It schedules tasks and allocates memory efficiently.
- **System on Chip**: There is a single IC chip that consists of CPU, peripheral devices, power management circuits and interfaces for communication like universal asynchronous receiver-transmitter (UART) and inter-integrated circuits (I2C).
- **ASIC Processor**: A chip that is dedicated to a specific application.
- **DSP Processor**: This processor is for noise removal from audio and video signals.
- **Input Devices**: These devices sense data from the outside world.
- **Output Devices**: These devices provide output on sensed input. Examples are screen, buzzers, LED, motors etc.
- **Bus Controllers**: These are communication mediums inside the embedded device for data transfer. Examples are SMBus: A system management bus that mainly manages power on/off, USB for data transfer between embedded devices and peripheral devices.

- **Memory**: Embedded devices have non-volatile, volatile and Dynamic RAM to store/retrieve data. Memory devices attached to embedded devices are flash, SD card and EEPROM.

Embedded Software (Firmware)

- **Device Drivers**: Drivers of hardware, peripherals and communication make up software components of embedded devices. Driver is just a code snippet dedicated for specific hardware functionality. Low-level drivers work with registers and controls of micro-controllers and high-level drivers work with applications. The coding of firmware is in C, C++ and micro-python.
- **Real-time Operating System**: General operating systems switch between processes as per priority. It can make a critical task wait for some time to do some other more critical tasks like interrupts. Otherwise, it will switch between critical and non-critical tasks to maintain parallel processing and switching depends on priority set by the developer. Real-time OS ensures that high priority tasks run in a given time frame and there is very less switching or switching for a very low amount of time in between tasks. All other functionality of the RTOS is similar to the OS except it provides real-time response and runs a specific task within a specific time period. This allows running of time-critical applications that require immediate response, such as calling ambulances or police during accidents, or predicting disasters in real-time. The operation of RTOS is sequential, deterministic with no randomness. It also ensures efficient resource allocation and switching is performed on interval quantum. There exists preemptive as well as non-preemptive scheduling of high and low priority applications. However, in RTOS, for releasing resources for a high priority task faster, threads with lower priority are blocked. This principle is priority inheritance. Once the highly critical applications execute its operations, the resources are provided back to the blocked task.
- **Middleware**: It is a piece of software that enables flexible, portable and secure communication of an application with drivers or OS. It also allows multiple applications to communicate with each other through OS or drivers. It is placed on top of the OS or Drivers. The middleware software abstracts the hardware and provides a common medium for communication of application and embedded device hardware and software units. The middleware software provides interoperability between applications and within system components. Examples are: message-oriented middleware (MOM), remote procedure calls (RPCs), database.

We will go through deployment of python code on two embedded devices: Raspberry Pi and Jetson Nano.

Raspberry Pi

Raspberry Pi devices are developed by Raspberry Pi foundation in the United

Kingdom. It is a single board system used for teaching computer science basics in schools. Afterwards, it became popular in making robots, automation purposes and doing projects at home due to its small size as well as low cost as shown in *Figure* 5.9. Raspberry Pi comes in model A, model B, Model B+ with improved arm architecture and cost.

***Figure* 5.9:** *Raspberry Pi used in Schools for Robot Project*

Until now 5 generations of Raspberry Pi came with more improved computational power and improved ARM architecture. Raspberry Pi zero and Raspberry Pi Pico are smallest computers on a single chip priced at $5 and $4 respectively. They have no internet connectivity provided and external devices need to be connected for internet access. Further, memory provided in Raspberry Pi Pico is very low in KBs. Thus, lower the price, lower is the functionality, and more compact is the device. However, each device has its own benefits, and their consideration in the project depends highly on application's requirements.

Next, we will go through installation, sensor connection and deploying of sample python code on Raspberry Pi 4 device.

1. First thing that needs to be done is to install Raspbian OS on Raspberry Pi hardware if the hardware has no pre-installed OS. You require a micro-SD card of minimum 8GB to install the OS.
2. On a microSD card, write the unzipped Raspbian OS using Etcher software.
3. Put the SD card on the Raspberry Pi SD card slot and connect the desktop with Raspberry Pi.

4. Power on the Raspberry Pi and it will automatically boot up the OS. It will ask some configuration questions to set up the OS.
5. Next time you connect the Raspberry Pi device; it will open up on the OS main screen.

Raspbian OS is very similar to Linux.

1. Install python libraries from **sudo apt-get** command on command prompt.
2. Write code on **.py** file and run it on command prompt. The code in the python file takes sensor data input.
3. The sensor data can be pre-processed and analyzed in real-time. Raspberry Pi cannot be used to store much data or run a very heavy trained model for analysis.

The board can be attached to any machine for automation. For example, a robot vehicle having four wheels. It senses the path, and accordingly actuates the motors, which moves the robot accordingly. The python file on Raspberry Pi has the code and the control of code is done remotely from an app known as **RaspController**. This app accesses the Raspberry Pi remotely using SSH and thus, once the OS is installed, there is no need to attach a desktop to it. We can access and run the code on Raspberry Pi from our own laptops. The SSH has to be configured on Raspberry Pi.

Jetson Nano

Jetson Nano is developed by Nvidia to run heavy AI models on embedded devices. It enables deployment of an IoT application on edge device. It can receive data from multiple sensors simultaneously and run tasks in parallel. However, it is a very expensive device. Further, it is not easy to install JetPack, a software development kit created by Nvidia, on the Jetson board.

JetPAck is a bundle of different software. It provides a Linux bootloader, Jetson Linux Kernel and Ubuntu operating system. It also provides libraries for CUDA, GPU, Computer Vision, Deep Learning designed by Nvidia. It also supports DeepStream, Isaac and Riva, which are new software development kits in areas of video analytics, robotics and interactive AI respectively.

For smooth installation, it is recommended to use Linux OS. Steps for installation are:

1. The appropriate JetPack version needs to be downloaded as per device board firmware version, and the downloaded package is written on SD card using Etcher. The SD card is inserted in the board.
2. The device is then connected with the laptop using USB cable and then the device is reset with jumper wires.

3. For flashing, the tool to be used is SDKmanager. The flashing takes a lot of time, can generate multiple errors and even after flashing, it is not necessary that the OS will run.
4. Update firewall settings to allow ssh to the board from laptop to have installation process without error of board disconnections in between.
5. Once JetPack is installed correctly, it is easy to code and run python and other applications on the device.

This embedded device is small in size but has huge computational power because of the GPU. IT can compute faster with parallel processing. An additional storage attachment of 1 TB is provided to the device which makes it suitable for large trained model storage. Nvidia provides CUDA toolkit on Jetson boards to develop, deploy GPU-accelerated applications. The toolkit includes C/C++ compiler, GPU-accelerated libraries, debugging optimization tools. Thus, compared to Raspberry Pi, Jetson is very powerful to deploy heavy edge analytics for applications like augmented reality, gaming and has the same size.

Smart Watch: A Wearable Edge Device

Smartwatch is a wearable device, looks similar to wristwatch and has more functionalities than just telling time. Smartwatch has Bluetooth driver to connect with smartphone. It has a touchscreen and can be used to check messages, calls, listen to music, have a weather report, write emails and much more, without taking out your phone all the time. Smartwatches also have in-built sensors that makes it a very powerful IoT device.

Five main sensors are accelerometer, gyroscope, heart rate monitor, GPS and barometer. The accelerometer determines step count, distance covered and calories burnt. The gyroscope measures angular velocity and helps in step counting and screen rotation. Heart rate monitor calculates heart rate to determine stress level. GPS determines device location from satellites. A barometer is used to measure heights and is very useful during hikes.

In today's era smartwatches are getting powerful with a variety of built-in sensors, strong processing capabilities and wireless protocols. They are the future of edge devices in the Internet of Things. These smartwatches are currently being used for health and fitness monitoring as shown in *Figure* 5.10. They are also being used to make payments. Their processor is now powerful enough to run a deep learning model for edge analytics. In some cases, sensor data from smartwatches is found to be more accurate than sensed data from the smartphone, due to their direct contact with the user's body. Smartwatches have very limited battery life and highly depend on timely battery charging. Due to less battery life, it cannot support heavy sensors like cameras.

Figure 5.10: *Smart Wearable Watches Worn during Workouts to Detect Step Count, Calories Burnt and Distance Travelled*

In early days, smartwatches were an accessory to smartphones, but now they are a standalone device, interfacing with any mobile phone. The smartwatch users are now in millions. Thus, the amount of data these smartwatches generate is big data. Common edge computing architecture that is followed with smartwatches is that smartwatches are considered as IoT devices generating sensor data, smartphones are taken as edge devices to pre-process the data, and the pre-processed data is finally processed at the Cloud. The challenge with such architecture is that the smartphone as edge node is overburdened with other Cloud-driven applications and resources are limited.

Therefore, the idea is to perform preprocessing as well as analysis at the Cloud, saving communication cost of smartphone as well as smartwatch. Reducing communication cost decreases the rate of battery consumption. Another issue is data privacy. The data collected by smartwatches is personal. It has multiple sensors to collect health data of the user to provide personal assistance. To maintain privacy, data should not go into public networks. The analysis is either carried out on a smartphone or smartwatch itself. In the last few years, smartwatches did not have much computational power to perform pre-processing and analysis and data was communicated to smartphones for pre-processing, analysis and decision-making. However, in recent times, the smartwatches are being built with powerful processors and more battery life to support pre-processing as well as analysis of the data at the device itself.

Smartwatch is made of Cortex-A CPU and MALI GPUs and they are of very small sizes to fit into smartwatches. They follow Arm Helium Technology. Helium supports Cortex series and provides a platform for machine learning (ML) and digital signal processing (DSP) on low- powered, small embedded devices. Light-weight deep learning models and ML models are being researched to be deployed on smartwatches for edge analytics. However, analysis on smartwatches is still at infancy stage but has huge future scope with more powerful smartwatches.

Conclusion

Thus, to implement edge computing, we should be aware of existing platforms that support edge computing. This chapter discussed different edge platforms provided by various companies. Edge platforms have similar Cloud functionalities and additional functionalities. The platform is categorized into three types: on-premise, network and platforms that support both. In each of the categories, two edge platform examples are discussed in detail. Except Eclipse ioFog, all have a pay-as-you-go model. Next, the platforms require devices to implement edge computing. These devices do not have similar computational power as cloud; however, they are on the network edge, near to end devices of the application. Edge devices that are popularly used in applications are presented in detail. Later in the chapter, computation deployment on three popular edge devices: smartphone, embedded device and smartwatch are provided. Smartphones have multiple sensors to sense the environment and computation is deployed with mobile apps. An embedded device is a microcontroller, a small-sized computer, having a sensing unit, OS and memory. Embedded devices are only used to run only specific tasks and tasks need to be executed in real-time. Smartwatch is a highly used wearable device for monitoring physical activity of users. These devices sense the data and do some edge computation on the device. Therefore, this chapter is all about how to implement edge computing using platforms and edge devices in IoT applications.

The next chapter discusses popular networking protocols and technologies for edge computing.

Points to Remember

- For edge computing, the clouds have extensions for platform as a service.
- Microsoft Azure is a popular Cloud and it provides edge computing service names as Azure Stack Edge. Azure stack edge is an on-premise platform.
- Amazon AWS community has provided an edge computing platform for 5G networks known as AWS wavelength. AWS wavelength is a network edge platform.

- Google decided to provide Google distributed Cloud edge platform for edge devices leveraging 140+ google edge networks worldwide. The platform can also support other edge networks, edge devices and private data centers.
- Choice of edge platform depends on application specific requirements and costs.
- The new field is the Internet of Robotic Things. Robots sense as well as perform actions in a physical environment. They are provided with AI to solve complex tasks.
- The embedded system consists of hardware, software and a real-time operating system (RTOS).
- Apart from data communication, switch and edge routers are used for some computations and storage as they reside at the network edge.
- Compared to Raspberry Pi, Jetson is very powerful to deploy heavy edge analytics for applications like augmented reality, gaming and has the same size.
- RTOS is a dedicated OS programmed to do a specific task. These systems are popular for real-time operations. These systems have less user intervention and have minimal user interface.
- Low powered smartwatches follow Arm Helium Technology to support Cortex series and provide a platform for machine learning (ML) and digital signal processing (DSP).

Multiple Choice Questions

1. Which edge platform provides both device and network edge computations?
    a. Eclipse ioFog
    b. Azure stack edge
    c. HPE Edgeline
    d. AWS wavelength
2. Which is the first edge platform?
    a. HPE Edgeline
    b. Alef
    c. Google Distributed Cloud Edge
    d. AWS Wavelength

3. What edge platform does not do?
   a. Orchestrating heterogeneous edge server
   b. Traffic between edge devices
   c. Centralized computing
   d. Security
4. Robot is a popular IoT edge device because of
   a. Sensing
   b. AI-enabled
   c. Mechanical structure for action
   d. All of the above
5. Which is not an edge device?
   a. Robot
   b. Autonomous vehicle
   c. Sensor
   d. Routers
6. Which deep learning model is used on smartphones?
   a. CNN
   b. Mobile Net
   c. RNN
   d. Transformer
7. Why wearable devices cannot support cameras?
   a. Low battery
   b. Low memory
   c. Low computational power
   d. Mobility

Answers

1. c
2. b
3. c
4. d
5. c
6. b
7. a

Questions

1. What are the additional functionalities of the edge platform?
2. What Azure stack edge and AWS wavelength provide as edge platforms?
3. How autonomous vehicles can be deployed as edge devices?
4. What are the five components of a smartphone?
5. How to deploy a robot application on Raspberry Pi?
6. What are the hardware components of embedded devices?
7. Who developed Jetson Nano, and for what purpose?
8. How are wearable devices enabled to deploy lightweight ML models?

CHAPTER 6
IoT Data Networking at Edge

Introduction

The data is captured by sensors, and processed on edge devices as well as Cloud in a general IoT application. The data captured is an IoT data and some IoT data has characteristics of big data. Communicating IoT data over the network is a challenge as it consumes a lot of network bandwidth. Thus, the communication of data between sensors, devices and the Cloud need to have less network cost. HTTP is a default application layer protocol used for communicating web data between clients and servers. However, the HTTP protocol generates a high overhead on IoT devices that have low computational power. Further, edge devices should utilize such protocols for data communication that are lightweight so that they can utilize most of their resources in processing. There exist multiple communication protocols as well as application protocols that are dedicated to lightweight communication, and are very useful for IoT applications as well as big data communication.

This chapter studies multiple communication protocols and application protocols. Further, the chapter studies and demonstrates working with three popular application protocols: Constrained Application Protocol (CoAP), Message Queuing Telemetry Transport (MQTT) and Advanced Message Queuing Protocol (AMQP). Later, the chapter also discusses network technologies, Software Defined Network (SDN), Information Centric Networking (ICN) and Content Delivery Network (CDN) that are used to provide efficient data networking with big data in IoT applications.

Structure

In this chapter, we will cover the following topics:

- Communication Protocols
- Application Protocols
- CoAP Protocol

- MQTT Protocol
- AMQP Protocol
- Software Defined Networking
- Information Centric Networking
- Content Delivery Network

Communication Protocols

ICT (Information and Communication Technology) is an infrastructure that provides communication technologies for device to device, device to things, and things to things communication. ICT has already provided multiple protocols, software and hardware for Cloud, edge devices and things. IoT applications demand more from ICT compared to an application that is based on traditional hardware, software and protocol used by earlier IT applications. This is because IoT connects all objects (IoT things) that exist around, and thus produce big data. Data communication within things, and things to devices require lightweight communication protocols. Communication protocol helps data exchange within a short range and within a network. Since these things have very low power, we should avoid use of application protocols for communication. Application protocols are protocols designed for long communications across networks. Communication protocols are for specific devices used for communication between two machines.

Generally, two communication devices are used in any machine-to-machine communication: Ethernet and Wi-Fi. The communication can be done via MAC address without connecting to the Internet. Both have different communication protocols. Ethernet requires a cable for communication and Ethernet ports on both the machines. Cable length depends on how far the machines are placed. Though Ethernet provides high speed and reliable data communication, it is hard to set up the cables when multiple things are communicating that are located anywhere. Further, Ethernet restricts mobility, and mobile IoT devices cannot utilize Ethernet communication protocol.

Wi-Fi provides wireless connectivity between devices using radio waves. Wi-Fi adapters are very popular in every household. The device creates a wireless hotspot and multiple devices can connect to the adapter to communicate with each other as well as to communicate data onto the internet. Since it is a very commonly used communication protocol and is suitable for mobile devices too, it is one of the most used communication protocols in IoT devices. However, Wi-Fi communication requires a lot of power and is not suitable for some of the IoT devices. For such devices, the communication protocols used are Bluetooth, Bluetooth Low Energy, RFID. Another limitation of Wi-Fi is limited connectivity range and limited connections. To overcome this limitation, IoT devices have the option to choose from other communication protocols like Z-Wave, LoraWAN, WiMax, 6lowPAN, Cellular and ZigBee.

- **Bluetooth:** It supports wireless communication over short distances and it connects with a maximum seven nearby devices. It enables simplex communication with only one device at a time. It communicates data on a short wavelength and on a very high frequency radio channel. For enabling Bluetooth communication in resource-constrained IoT devices, Bluetooth 4.0 device is developed. It consumes less time and less power compared to Bluetooth devices attached to machines and smartphones. It communicates using master -slave architecture and uses two frames for communication: advertising and data. Slave sends the advertising frame to master, master accepts and sends the data frame. It is highly suitable for creating a personal area network between IoT devices. It has capability to send data even in noisy environments. HC-05 module is used to connect to embedded devices to enable Bluetooth communication.
- **Bluetooth Low Energy (BLE):** This is a variation of traditional Bluetooth specifically designed to operate under low energy consumption. These devices are suitable for battery-operated IoT devices.
- **RFID** is a radio frequency identification device that uses electromagnetic fields to transfer data and are used for tracking, monitoring, contact less payment, and automated toll collection. RFID has three components: tag, antenna and a reader. Reader emits radio waves via antenna and tags reflect the waves. There are two types of RFID, Active and Passive. Active RFID comes with a battery and they communicate their identity to other readers directly. They continuously broadcast their information and can communicate data over a long range. They are most popularly used in applications that require real-time location monitoring. Battery life of an active RFID reader is 3-4 years. Passive RFID works on the reader's battery power. They provide information only when they get in contact with the reader. Passive RFIDs tags are very cheap and are very popular in supply chain management.

  It can be as ultrathin as possible and can be easily attached to anything big or small. One question that comes to mind is whether RFID tags are similar to QR code. The answer is no. The tag has a chip and the chip has an inventory number. The data is communicated from tag to reader via antenna. QR codes do not use radio waves for communication, they are based on barcode technology. These codes can be read horizontally or vertically. It is a data encoding scheme and these days' smartphones have QR code scanners. However, RFID readers are costly.

  Active RFID tags are used in IoT applications as things. They are connected with sensors and are used to communicate sensor data through radio waves. There are three kinds of active RFIDs: Beaconing RFID that sends encrypted data after a specific time interval, transcoding RFID is a hybrid version of passive as well as active RFID that responds when the reader requests the data, and intelligent RFID where one RFID tag senses data from multiple beaconing tags, calculates location of data from beacon tag and send location, information to the reader. Intelligent RFID replaces the scenario of having multiple readers for each beaconing RFID at every location.

- **Zigbee**: ZigBee is a protocol suite that covers network, transport, and application layers. ZigBee can connect 65,536 devices to a network. In order to connect ZigBee devices to the Internet, an application-level gateway is required. It communicates data on the frequency 2.4 GHz. It is a good choice for time-critical applications. It is one of the most popular, low-cost, low-throughput, and low-power wireless mesh networking standards. To create a mesh network of low powered devices, it is the most used protocol for smart home applications. It does not have a centralized point. The devices either communicate directly at line of sight or some of the devices that are in between serve as repeaters. Huge number of products have Connectivity Standards Alliance (CSA) that support ZigBee communication. A project named "CHIP (Connected Home over IP" has an alliance with ZigBee protocol. In this project, the smart devices would have a logo and name of "MATTER" to know that they are compatible with each other. These devices then connect and communicate with each other using ZigBee protocol. This project has made smart home applications popular and has increased the usage of ZigBee protocol.
- **Z-Wave**: This is a reliable, low-latency wireless communication protocol designed to facilitate machine to machine communication and can connect 232 nodes in a Z-Wave network. It provides interoperability between the devices. It provides communication on 908.42 MHz and thus, is slow data transfer compared to ZigBee devices.
- **6lowPAN (IPv6 over Low Power Wireless Personal Area Networks)**: This protocol aims at enabling IP based communication for small low powered devices with limited processing capabilities. It is based on IPv6 protocol and encapsulates the communicated data onto smaller data frames. These small frames consume less power while being transmitted and received by the resource-constraint IoT devices. It connects the devices to the internet as well as to the Cloud. It has good scalability and is compatible with Bluetooth, Wi-Fi and ZigBee enabled devices. It is a very lightweight IP protocol and is the future of IoT-Internet-Cloud connectivity.
- **WiMax (Worldwide Interoperability of Microwave Access)**: WiMax can be considered as a standardized wireless version of Ethernet. It focuses on enabling broadband access to users. This provides a higher data rate and higher number of connections compared to Wi-Fi and thus, is also called "Wi-Fi on steroids". It is suitable for Metropolitan Area Network (MAN) and connectivity range is 50 Kms. However, WiMAX signals cannot easily penetrate

walls and they cannot provide connectivity to mobile devices. This protocol is highly suitable for rural and remote locations to provide coverage as well as connectivity with the internet.

- **Cellular**: The mobile network that we use to communicate with our mobile phones is a cellular network. We discussed it in the previous chapter where we studied all generations. The data is communicated over the existing cellular networks. A land area is divided into cells and each cell is controlled by a base station. A cell has multiple frequency channels and a base station of respective frequency. Cellular can communicate over 35 km using GSM and 200 km over HSPA. Radio waves are used for communication and this protocol is very good for mobile devices. However, cellular communications costs in terms of both money and power and are not usually preferred for resource-constrained devices.
- **LoraWAN**: This protocol allows battery-operated sensors to communicate over long distances. It is a highly low-powered device which stays for 10 years on battery. Very suitable for long range communication of small data such as data from sensors. LoraWAN gateways deployed in a building or tower can connect to sensors more than miles away. The LoraWAN protocol works on Lora hardware. Lora is a modulation technique that encodes radio waves into chirp pulses. Chirp signals are signals used by bats and dogs to communicate with each other.

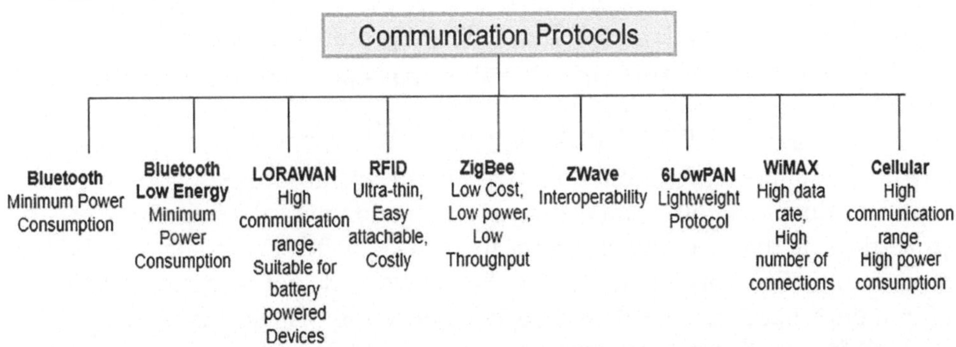

Figure 6.1: *Different Communication Protocols in IoT and Their Characteristics*

Each protocol has its own special characteristics as shown in *Figure* 6.1. For selecting particular communication protocol for IoT application, parameters are listed as follows:

- High communication range is Cellular, WiMax, and Lora WAN.
- Best bandwidth is WiMax.
- High power consumption is Cellular.
- ZIGBEE has low cost, low power, and low throughput.

- WiMax (IEEE 802.16) has higher speed over great distances as compared to Wi-Fi and provides microwave access.
- LoraWAN is best for battery powered sensor communication over long distance.
- Minimum energy consumption is provided by low-power Wi-Fi, IEEE 802.15.4, and Bluetooth Low-Energy.

Application Protocol

HTTP protocol is a popular application protocol that is used to access web servers and communicate webpages. It follows a client-server architecture. However, HTTP is not sufficient in an IoT application as IoT has more requirements than a normal network. An IoT application in general consists of three layers, IoT layer having low-powered devices or things, fog layer and a Cloud layer. HTTP protocol is very heavy for a low-powered device to communicate data to the Fog and Cloud layer. Thus, multiple application protocols have been developed depending on the requirement of the layer that needs to communicate data.

To make it easy for developers to select a protocol, communication in an IoT application is categorized into three types: D2D (device to device), D2S (device to server) and S2S (server to server). D2D is within things, D2S is from edge to fog or fog to cloud or edge to cloud, S2S is within cloud or within fog.

- For D2D, IoTivity, HyperCAT and AllJoyn protocols are used.
- For D2S, HTTP, XMPP, MQTT, DDS, AMQP and CoAP protocols are used.
- For S2S, HTTP and AMQP are the only protocols.

There is no common agreement on the reference architecture or adopted standards of application protocols. Thus, one of the fundamental challenges for system engineers is to choose the appropriate protocol for their specific IoT system requirements. For this challenge to be addressed, some general architecture requirements need to be taken into consideration. These include: Devices that can range from resource constrained devices to high performance cloud systems, data generated to be processed between the cloud and the fog layer, the types of wireless connectivity that can be used, or security and privacy solutions, just to name a few. The candidate application protocols differ in their interaction models. Two popular interaction models are request-reply and publish-subscribe as shown in *Figure 6.2*.

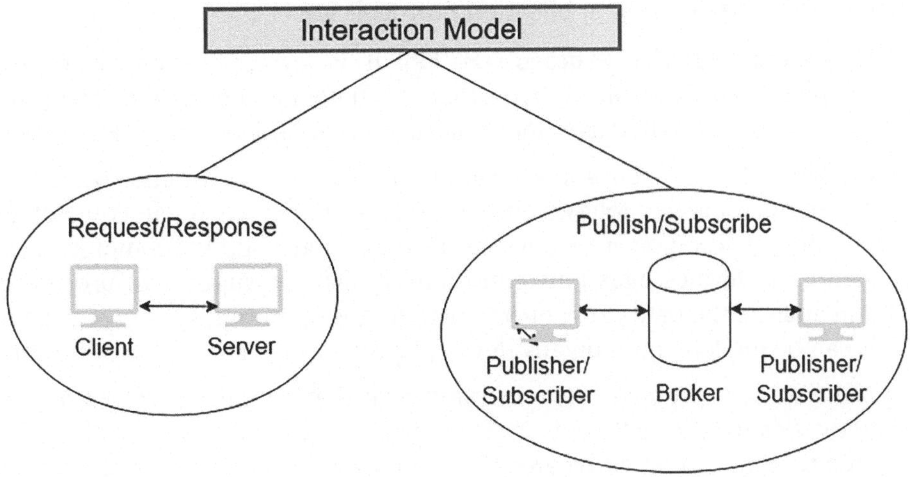

Figure 6.2: *Two Types of Interaction Model are Request/Response and Publish/Subscribe*

- **Request-Reply:** The request-reply communication model is one of the most basic communication paradigms. It represents a message exchange pattern especially common in client-server architectures. It allows a client to request information from a server that receives the request message, processes it and returns a response message. Information for the client-server style is usually managed and exchanged centrally. The two protocols based on the request/reply model known the most are REST HTTP and CoAP.
- **Publish-Subscribe:** The publish-subscribe model emerged out of the need to provide a distributed, asynchronous, loosely coupled communication between data generators and destinations. Components of the publish/subscribe model are: publisher, subscriber and a broker. The publisher publishes data with a topic. The subscriber listens to the topic and when data arrives over the topic, it captures the data. The publisher and subscriber are connected to the broker. The broker has a buffer that stores and routes data as per topic-based subscription. The publisher and subscriber need not to be online at the same time for communication. Publish/Subscribe architecture also ensures quality of service. The broker stores the message until the subscriber acknowledges if it has received or not. There are many standardized messaging protocols currently implementing a publish/subscribe interaction model, most known are MQTT, AMQP and DDS.

Finally, some protocols support both request-reply and publish-subscribe interaction models. This includes XMPP protocol.

The specifications of different application protocols are:

- **Hypertext Transfer Protocol (HTTP):** It is an application layer protocol designed for distributed hypertext documents and media. Hypertext is structured text. HTTP uses more battery, is less reliable, and a lot slower.
- **IoTivity:** It is an open-source framework and acts as a middleware for D2D communication and follows client-server architecture. It can connect a large number of low-powered devices securely and support communication of standardized messages between them. It also has support to process, store and analyze the data exchanged. Further, it is operating system (OS) agnostic. It can be implemented on any device, laptop or cellular, having different OS.
- **AllJoyn:** It is an open-source framework that connects devices in the P2P network and follows Remote Method Invocation (RMI) with publish/subscribe architecture. It communicates data in binary format. It has been integrated with IoTivity making IoTivity a leader in D2D communication protocol.
- **HyperCAT:** It is an open standard for IoT developed by 40 UK-based companies. It is an interoperability layer between smart devices that are from different IoT applications. The aim of this protocol is to make interactions and services exchanges possible between devices having heterogeneous specifications. It can browse data among devices that is required by any device in the network. Thus, it allows sharing of information across heterogeneous smart devices.
- **Extensible Messaging and Presence Protocol (XMPP):** It is a message-oriented protocol designed for (near) real-time communication. It uses XML to format and model its data.
- **Message Queue Telemetry Transport (MQTT):** IT is a lightweight protocol with header size 2 bytes. It is not designed to be fast or real time. MQTT is a binary protocol that performs asynchronous communication.
- **Constrained Application Protocol (CoAP):** It is an open standard application-level protocol specifically designed to enable communication between resource constrained devices. CoAP integrates with XML, JSON, CBOR, or any data format.
- **Advanced Message Queuing Protocol (AMQP):** AMQP is a secure and reliable protocol that supports queuing and routing. AMQP is mostly used in business messaging where it was initially being developed to support banking applications.
- **Data Distribution Service (DDS):** This protocol aims to enable scalable, real-time, dependable, high-performance and interoperable data exchanges using a publish/subscribe pattern.

CoAP Protocol

CoAP or constrained application protocol is a popular IoT application layer protocol. It is a suitable protocol for low-powered, resource constrained IoT devices. This protocol is mainly designed for constrained environments in 2014 by IETF (Internet Engineering Task Force). It is a lightweight version of HTTP protocol and has similar client-server architecture with REST (Representational State Transfer). In REST, the protocol performs CRUD operations on the resources and resources are considered as objects having a unique identifier. The identifier is URI (Unique Resource Identifier). The CoAP client requests for a resource with a URI and the CoAP server responds with the resource.

Differences between CoAP and HTTP are:

1. CoAP uses UDP as transport layer protocol whereas HTTP uses TCP.
2. CoAP has a lightweight payload compared to HTTP.
3. CoAP request/response is energy efficient as well as fast compared to HTTP request/response.
4. CoAP supports multicast communication whereas HTTP does not.
5. CoAP does not require synchronous communication like HTTP.
6. CoAP is suitable for harsh environments unlike HTTP.

Message Format

CoAP protocol consists of two layers: messages and request/response. The messages layer interfaces with UDP protocol and provide asynchronous communication between client and server. The request/response layer communicates data between client and server using a method and a response code. There are four methods and four response codes. Methods are GET, PUT, POST, DELETE similar to HTTP. Response codes are 0 for confirmable, 1 for non-confirmable, 2 for acknowledgement and 3 for reset. More specifications of CoAP protocol are provided in RFC 7252. An important fact about CoAP is that the message is encoded in binary (0/1) format. Message has a header and a payload as shown in *Figure* 6.3. The header is 4 bytes long and includes version, type, option, code and message ID. Version tells the CoAP version. Type tells the response codes. Option tells the size of optional data in the message. Code tells whether it is an empty message or a request/response message. Last, the message ID is the unique ID for a message to detect duplicate messages.

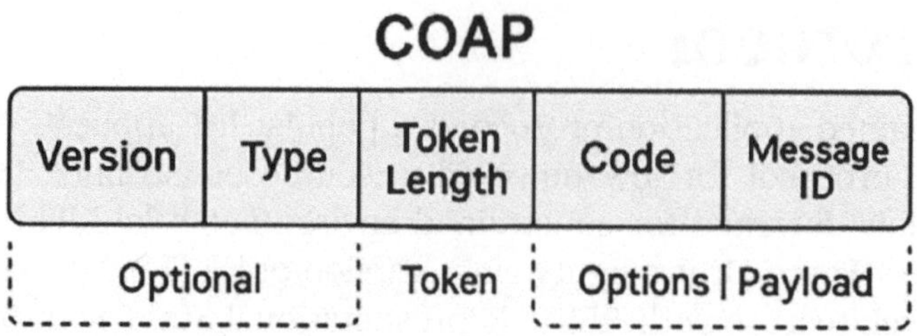

***Figure 6.3.a**: Header of CoAP Protocol*

Byte	Bits	Field	Description
0	2	Version	Always 01 for CoAP version 1
	2	Type	Confirmable, Non-confirmable, etc.
	4	Token Length	Length of token (0–8 bytes)
1	8	Code	Request or response code (e.g. GET=1)
2-3	16	Message ID	For message deduplication
4+	var	Token	Optional token for matching responses

***Figure 6.3.b**: Header of CoAP Protocol and Description of Each Field*

Confirmable and Non-Confirmable Messages

Confirmable message is a type of message that has critical information and is reliable. This kind of message is definitely communicated from client to server. This message is sent continuously to the server until the server responds with the acknowledgment message. The message ID of confirmable message and acknowledgment message is the same. If the server is not able to get the message, it sends a reset message rather than an acknowledgment message. Non-confirmable messages are not at all critical, they don't have any important information and are not prioritized. The client does not get acknowledged by the server about the receiving of the message. However, these messages also have unique IDs. Sensor readings are examples of non-confirmable messages.

Message Communication

CoAP client and server communicate in request/response. If the client sends a confirmable message that has reliable information, then the server sends an acknowledgment message. If the acknowledgment is not received by the client, it again resends the confirmable message.

If the server cannot handle the request, it sends a reset message. If a client sends a message that is not critical, the client communicates data as non-confirmable messages. Server accepts the data and does not acknowledge the client. In case of limited network connectivity or an unreliable environment, COAP makes sure that the data reaches the server using confirmable messages. Further, it saves bandwidth by not acknowledging non-critical packets when sent as a non-confirmable message.

Further, data that is critical is stored at IoT devices until it is acknowledged. However, all other data that will not cause any issues if got lost or missing are not stored after it is communicated to the server as no-confirmable message. Previous communication is when a client sends data to a server with a POST method. However, if the client requests data from the server, it sends a request using the GET, PUT method. If the server is not able to respond with the data, it sends an empty message to the client with the same message ID of request. Once the server gets the data, it sends the data as a response to the client.

Implementation

To implement CoAP protocol on IoT devices like Arduino Uno, there are multiple libraries that are developed. One of the libraries that is popular is **`coap_client.h`** when Arduino Uno is connected to NodeMCU to communicate data over Wi-Fi. Link to the file and implementation is https://github.com/IoT-CoAP/CoAP-using-NodeMCU/blob/master/coap_client.

One implementation example is:

```
#include <ESP8266WiFi.h>
#include <ArduinoJson.h>
#include "coap_client.h"

//instance for coapclient
coapClient coap;

//WiFi connection info
const char* ssid = "your-wifi-ssid";
const char* password = "your-wifi-password";
String DEVICE_SECRET_KEY  = "your-device_secret_key";

//ip address and default port of coap server in which your
interested in
IPAddress ip(52, 17, 209, 228);
int port = 5683;
char* path = "events";

StaticJsonBuffer<200> jsonBuffer;
JsonObject& root = jsonBuffer.createObject();
```

```
// coap client response callback
void callback_response(coapPacket &packet, IPAddress ip, int
port) {
  char p[packet.payloadlen + 1];
  memcpy(p, packet.payload, packet.payloadlen);
  p[packet.payloadlen] = NULL;

  //response from coap server
  if (packet.type == 3 && packet.code == 0) {
    Serial.println("ping ok");
  }

  Serial.println(p);
}

void setup() {
  Serial.begin(115200);

  WiFi.begin(ssid, password);
  Serial.println(" ");
  // Connection info to WiFi network
  Serial.println();
  Serial.println();
  Serial.print("Connecting to ");
  Serial.println(ssid);
  WiFi.begin(ssid, password);
  while (WiFi.status() != WL_CONNECTED) {
    yield();
    Serial.print(".");
  }
  Serial.println("");
  Serial.println("WiFi connected");
  // Print the IP address of client
  Serial.println(WiFi.localIP());

  // client response callback.
   coap.response(callback_response);

  // start coap client
  coap.start();
}

void loop() {
  root["name"] = "temperature";
  root["data"] =  21.5;
  root["accessToken"] =  DEVICE_SECRET_KEY;
```

```
  String data;
  root.printTo(data);
  char dataChar[data.length() + 1];
  data.toCharArray(dataChar, data.length() + 1);
  bool state;


  //post request
  //arguments server ip address,default port,resource name,
payload,payload length
  int msgid = coap.post(ip, port, path, dataChar, data.length());

  state = coap.loop();

  delay(5000);
}
```

To implement CoAP protocol over Raspberry Pi, Jetson Nano or any system, **aiocoap** library written in python 3 needs to be downloaded. The library can be cloned from GitHub link: https://github.com/chrysn/aiocoap.

CoAP Server: This is the python code for CoAP server that needs to be executed first in a separate terminal. This code lets the CoAP server bind to default port 5683. The code defines a class BlockResource that fetches content from the file and prints it to the output file having path and file name. In the main function the resource is added referring to the class and a URI is provided "other/block". This URI is used by the CoAP client to send the file.

```
import datetime
import logging
import asyncio
import aiocoap.resource as resource
import aiocoap

class BlockResource(resource.Resource):

    def __init__(self):
        super().__init__()
        self.set_content(b"This is the resource's default
content. It is padded "\
                b"with numbers to be large enough to trigger
blockwise "\
                b"transfer.\n")

    def set_content(self, content):
        self.content = content
        while len(self.content) <= 1024:
```

```
            self.content = self.content + b"0123456789\n"

    async def render_get(self, request):
        return aiocoap.Message(payload=self.content)

    async def render_put(self, request):
        print('PUT payload: %s' % request.payload)
        self.set_content(request.payload)
        c=0
        filee="";
        pay=str(request.payload,'utf-8')
        for line in pay.splitlines():
            if(c==0):
                fname=line
                c=c+1
            else:
                filee=filee+line+"\n"
        print(filee)
        path="/usr/local/spark/" + fname
        with open(path , 'w+') as f:
           print('file opened')
           f.write(filee)
           print('written to file')
           f.close()
        return aiocoap.Message(code=aiocoap.CHANGED,
payload=self.content)


# logging setup

logging.basicConfig(level=logging.INFO)
logging.getLogger("coap-server").setLevel(logging.DEBUG)

def main():
    # Resource tree creation
    root = resource.Site()

    root.add_resource(('.well-known', 'core'),
    resource.WKCResource(root.get_resources_as_linkheader))
    root.add_resource(('other', 'block'), BlockResource())
    asyncio.Task(aiocoap.Context.create_server_context(root))

    asyncio.get_event_loop().run_forever()

if __name__ =
```

CoAP Client: This python code implements CoAP client. The method code is selected as "PUT" and the URI starts with the protocol name CoAP, followed by the server's IP address and the URI "other/block". The port need not be instantiated as it knows the default port. The file is read and converted to byte format to be stored as payload. Payload with data in byte format is then sent to the server as requested. The client waits for the response and prints the response code once it gets the acknowledgement from the server.

```
import logging
import asyncio

from aiocoap import *

logging.basicConfig(level=logging.INFO)

async def main():
    filename='sensor_data.csv'
    protocol = await Context.create_client_context()
    payload = bytes(filename, 'utf-8')+ bytes("\n", 'utf-8') +
open(filename, "rb").read()
    request = Message(code=PUT, payload=payload, uri="-
coap://172.31.135.30/other/block")

    try:
        response = await protocol.request(request).response
    except Exception as e:
        print('Failed to fetch resource:')
        print(e)
    else:
        print('Result: %s\n%r'%(response.code, response.payload))

if __name__ == "__main__":
    asyncio.get_event_loop().run_until_complete(main())
```

MQTT Protocol

MQTT (Message Queue Telemetry Transport) is an application layer protocol that is designed for M2M communication that suffers with a low bandwidth, high latency network. It is a very lightweight protocol suitable for IoT devices. It is a TCP-based protocol and follows a publish-subscribe architecture. It is the most popular IoT protocol. Due to the underlying TCP protocol, it provides reliable communication in a harsh environment. The communication between clients is taken care of by a third party called as MQTT broker. The broker is connected to multiple MQTT publishers and subscribers called as clients. There is no server in the publish/subscribe communication paradigm. In case of packet loss, or packet coming out of sequence,

MQTT makes sure it is received correctly by the server. The MQTT broker retains the message until the acknowledgment is not received by the subscriber. The subscriber gets the message from the broker whenever it is online. The publisher does not need to wait for subscribers to send a message. The message goes to the respective subscriber with topic-based routing.

QOS level of MQTT is a measure of guarantee of messages that are communicated from publisher to subscriber via broker using MQTT protocol and is applied in two parts. The first part guarantees published messages are received by the broker and second part guarantees subscribed messages are received by the subscriber. Thus, both publisher and subscriber have its QOS level with respect to the broker. MQTT protocol supports three types of QOS level: 0, 1 and 2 in which the default QOS level is 0.

- **QOS 0:** In this level, a message is sent by sender (publisher or broker) with no guarantee of receiving by respective receivers (broker or subscriber). Messages may get lost during disconnection and the sender is unaware. Thus, it is suitable for applications that will face no disconnections or any lost message will make no difference.
- **QOS 1:** In this level, message is buffered at sender side (publisher or broker) until it is received by respective receiving end. If a message is lost during disconnection, message is resent until its acknowledgement is received. The receiver (broker or subscriber) may get more than one duplicate of the lost message. Thus, this QOS level is suitable for applications that require guaranteed delivery and can handle duplicate messages.
- **QOS 2:** This level is similar to QOS 1 but there is no problem of duplicate messages. Exactly one message is received by the receiver (broker or subscriber) after a message is lost during disconnection. Sender and receiver performs four-way handshake to guarantee message delivery and thus this level is slowest of all. It is suitable for applications that need guaranteed delivery, is not time critical and cannot handle duplicate messages.

MQTT Broker

MQTT broker plays a vital role in establishing communication and exchange information between MQTT publishers and subscribers. First, it routes the data to appropriate subscribers. Next, it provides scalability and handles large connections at once, with a large number of publishers publishing the data and subscribers listening to the data. Third, it provides data security and uses encryption and authentication like username and password before communicating the data. Fourth, it can be easily integrated with communication protocols, IoT platforms and Cloud platforms. The ease of integration makes MQTT very useful in IoT application deployment. Fifth, it checks upon subscribers continuously to see if they are online or not and ensures the messages reach the subscriber in case of frequent disconnections. For managing disconnections, MQTT provides persistent sessions where if we set persistent sessions before communication, the broker will retain important messages. This session also lets subscribers be connected even with disconnections and the subscriber does not need to reconnect again and again whenever the network is available. There is also a clean session flag available. If the clean session flag is 1, the publisher/subscriber gets disconnected immediately if the connection is lost and its state is also removed from the broker. If the clean session is set to 0, the connection persists even if there are disconnections.

MQTT Routing

The routing technique followed by MQTT is Topic-based routing. Every data published by the publisher is attached with a topic. Every subscriber connected to MQTT broker listens to a topic. This topic lets the broker decide which message from the publisher is to be communicated to which subscriber. When one broker is connected to multiple publishers as well as subscribers, the topic differentiates them into different M2M communication channels. A topic is a text to label a message. For example, if a publisher publishes temperature data on topic "temperature" then only the subscribers who are subscribed to topic "temperature" will receive the temperature data. Topic can also be a sequence of words with "/" as a separator forming a hierarchy just like a file directory. For example, "**home/temperature**", "**body/temperature**" will differentiate temperature data for body and home and will provide it to respective subscribers subscribed to either of these topics.

The topic used for subscribing can contain wildcards. Wildcard enables a subscriber to fetch data from multiple publishers with the use of generic topics. There are two types of wildcards: + and #. + is for ignoring one level of hierarchy. For example, "**+/temperature**" will capture data from publishers with any word in place of + followed by /temperature. + cannot be used in multiple levels however, # ignores the rest of the levels and can be used only once in the topic. For example, if there are topic "**room/motion**" and "**room/temperature**" and subscriber is subscribed to "**room/#**", then the subscriber will get data from the temperature sensor as well as a motion sensor placed in the room.

MQTT Payload

MQTT has a fixed header of size 2 Bytes as shown in Figure 6.4. The first byte is the control field that tells the type of message published in 4 bits and the control flag in next 4 bits. The second byte tells the length of payload and variable header combined. MQTT has 15 kinds of control packets that are **CONNECT**, **CONNACK**, **PINGREQ**, **PINGRESP**, AND **DISCONNECT** for **connection/disconnection**, **PUBLISH**, **PUBACK**, **PUBREC**, **PUBREL**,

PUBCOMP, for publishing data and **SUBSCRIBE**, **SUBACK**, **UNSUBSCRIBE**, **UNSUBACK** for subscription.

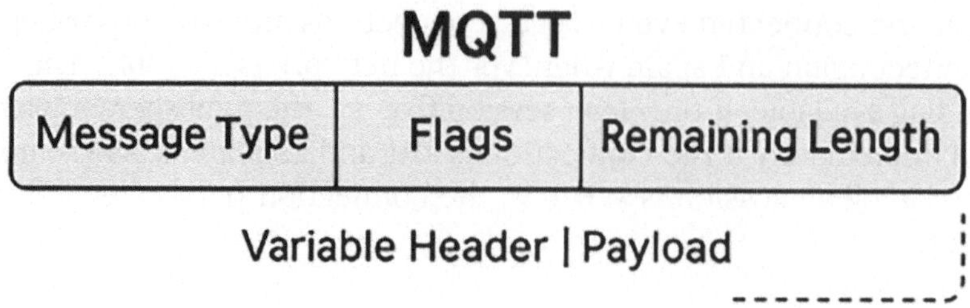

***Figure 6.4.a**: Header of MQTT Protocol*

Byte	Bits	Field	Description
0	4	Message Type	CONNECT, PUBLISH, SUBSCRIBE, etc.
	4	Flags	QoS level, DUP, RETAIN
1+	var	Remaining Length	Length of next part of message

***Figure 6.4.b:** Header of MQTT Protocol and Description of Each Field*

PINGREQ message is from MQTT client to MQTT broker asking for availability and **PINGRESP** is message that broker replies with to the client. The **DISCONNECT** message informs the broker that the client is disconnecting and will not anymore publish or subscribe. A **CONNECT** message is sent by the client to connect with the broker.

There are seven flags: **DUP**, **QoS**, **RETAIN**, **Clean session**, **Will**, **Username** and **Password**.

- **DUP** is set to one 1 by publisher when a duplicate message is being published after no acknowledgment is received.
- QoS can be either 0, 1, 2 and is set by the publisher.
- **RETAIN** if set to 1 by publisher means the message has to be stored otherwise it may be dropped if not received by the subscriber.
- Clean flag is set to 1 for persistent sessions and is used with **CONNECT**.
- Will is set to 1 that means a will message has to be saved on the server.
- Username and password flags with **CONNECT** packet if set to 1 tells that the connection is secured with a username and a password.

A Will message is generated by a client that has a message consisting of notification if the client itself goes offline. The will message has the same specifications as a normal message and it is the last message by the client. This message lets all the subscribers know that the publisher is no longer active. The broker stores the will message and publishes only when connectivity to the publisher is lost. To include a will message during CONNECT, the Will flag needs to be set to 1. The purpose is to let subscribers know that publisher-topic is not active and they can go for alternate actions/topics.

MQTT Implementation

There are many software tools to implement the MQTT protocol. Mosquitto MQTT is the most popular among them. To install mosquito on Unix platform of edge devices like Raspberry Pi, Jetson Nano or any personal computers oh home or office, we need to run following two commands on the terminal:

```
sudo apt-get install mosquito

sudo apt-get install mosquitto-clients
```

The first command is for installing MQTT broker on the system and the second command is to make a device MQTT publisher or subscriber. Once the installation of the broker is successful, it starts running automatically on port 1883. Once the mosquito client is installed, the device can behave as a publisher or as a subscriber and connect to a broker. The connect message from publisher is as follows:

```
mosquttio_pub -t "MQTT_learn" -m "Hello python coders! Welcome to
IoT world"
```

where,

- t tells the topic on which the message is published on broker
- m tells the message to be sent to broker
- u is the username of publisher choice
- p is password of publisher choice

The subscriber device needs to run the following command to have data from the topic.

```
mosquitto_sub -t "MQTT_learn"
```

The subscriber listens to the topic and since the publisher published one message, it is printed on the subscriber's terminal. To publish another message on the same topic, the publisher needs to run a new command every time. This can also be automated using shell scripting.

To have a secure MQTT connection, we can save username and password. With this facility, the data from the publisher is protected and can only be accessed by subscribers that know the username and password. Mosquitto comes with the **mosquito_passwd** command to set username and password. The following command creates a file **/etc/mosquitto/passwd** and saves a username and password.

```
sudo mosquitto_passwd -c /etc/mosquitto/ user-pass Rajasi
Password: python
```

I have chosen my username as Rajasi and password as python. You can multiple user and password sets with the following command.

```
sudo mosquitto_passwd -b /etc/mosquitto/ user-pass IoT network
```

where, IoT is the username and network is the password. To delete username IoT and password, run the following command.

```
mosquitto_passwd -D /etc/mosquitto/user-pass IoT
```

This file needs to be added to the conf file of **mosquitto**. To do this the steps are as follows:

1. Open **default.conf** file: **sudo nano /etc/mosquitto/conf.d/default.conf**
2. Paste two lines in the file.

   allow_anonymous false

   password_file /etc/mosquitto/ user-pass
3. Save the file
4. Restart mosquito: **sudo systemctl restart mosquito**

The publisher now publishes data on username and password otherwise it is not authorized to communicate with the broker. The updated commands to publish data is:

```
mosquttio_pub -t "MQTT_learn" -m "Hello python coders! Welcome to
IoT world" -u Rajasi -p python
```

Also, the subscriber needs to update their command.

```
mosquttio_sub -t "MQTT_learn" -u Rajasi -p python
```

By using mosquitto, we can have multiple publishers, subscribers connected to the MQTT broker and communicate data using the publish/subscribe paradigm.

Following code implements MQTT on Arduino Uno with NodeMCU, as mosquito is not compatible with Arduino.

```
#include <PubSubClient.h>
#include <ESP8266WiFi.h>

boolean connectWifi();
boolean wifiConnected = false;
const char* ssid     = "iPhone"; //enter your ssid/ wi-fi(case
sensitive) router name - 2.4 Ghz only
const char* password = "wifirjg123";   // enter ssid password
(case sensitive)
const char* mqtt_server="172.20.10.11";
WiFiClient espClient;
PubSubClient Client(espClient);
```

```
String con=" ";
const char* mssg;
void setup() {
  // Open serial communications and wait for port to open:
  Serial.begin(115200);
  while (!Serial) {
    ; // wait for serial port to connect. Needed for native USB
port only}
  }
    wifiConnected = connectWifi();

  if(wifiConnected){
    Serial.println(«success»);}
    Client.setServer(mqtt_server,1883);

}

void loop() { // run over and over

    if(wifiConnected){
  Serial.println("success");}
   if (Serial.available()) {
    mssg=»hello»;
    con.concat(mssg);

   }
    if(!Client.connected())
    {
      reconnect();
    }
  Client.loop();
  Client.publish(«topic»,»hello world»);
}
void reconnect() {
  // Loop until we›re reconnected
  while (!Client.connected()) {
    Serial.print(«Attempting MQTT connection...»);
    // Create a random client ID
    String clientId = «ESP8266Client-»;
    clientId += String(random(0xffff), HEX);
    // Attempt to connect
    if (Client.connect(clientId.c_str())) {
      Serial.println(«connected»);
      // Once connected, publish an announcement...
      Client.publish(«topic», «hello world»);

    } else {
```

```
            Serial.print(«failed, rc=»);
            Serial.print(Client.state());
            Serial.println(« try again in 5 seconds»);
            // Wait 5 seconds before retrying
            delay(5000);
         }
      }
   }
```

AMQP Protocol

AMQP (Advanced message queuing protocol) follows publish/subscribe as well as client-server paradigm. It also broadcasts. The protocol uses RabbitMQ broker for managing connections as well as data exchanges. It follows rules that are known as bindings. Moreover, it is a programmable protocol where clients declare queues, exchanges, binding and is not controlled by the broker. The broker follows what the client expects from it. AMQP has extra components with publisher, consumer and a broker. The publisher is connected to exchange. The exchange is connected to the queues. The consumer is connected to specific queues. Exchange, Queue are part of RabbitMQ broker.

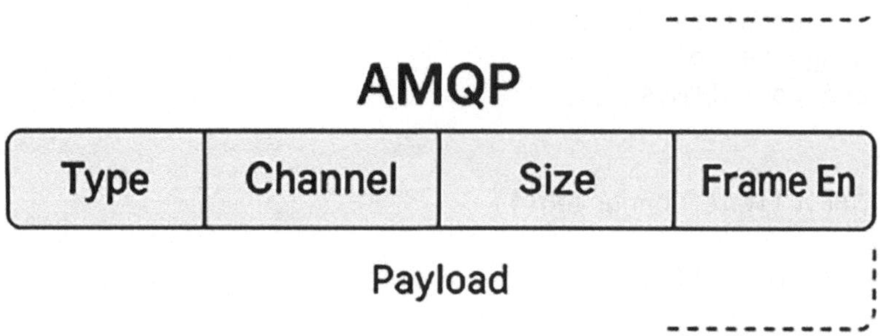

Figure 6.5.a: *Header of AMQP Protocol and Description of Each Field*

Bytes	Field	Description
0	Type	Frame type (method, header, body)
1-2	Channel	Virtual channel number
3-6	Size	Frame payload size
7	Frame End	Always `0xCE`

Figure 6.5.b: *Header of AMQP Protocol and Description of Each Field*

The header of RabbitMQ is shown in *Figure* 6.5. All components of RabbitMQ are explained as follows:

- **Exchange:** This component fetches data and places them in the appropriate queue. It has four types: Fanout, Topic, Direct, Header and Default.
  - Fanout exchange places the message to all the queues that are bound to the message.
  - Topic exchange has a message routing key with published data and the key is matched to a wildcard pattern that is bound to the queue and accordingly placed into the queue.
  - Direct exchange routes the message having a message routing key to the queues bound to the same routing key.
  - Header exchange routes the message as per header values and not routing key and the queue that receives the message has the same header values.
  - Default exchange is a direct exchange where the name is empty.
- **Channel:** A virtual connection between peers that follows multiplex communication.
- **Message Queue:** Data structure that stores messages and also has some additional properties. It has a unique name, Queue name that starts with "**`amq`**" is reserved. The queues can be made durable to save messages in disc so that the message is not lost until the recipient successfully receives the message. There can be an exclusive queue for a specific connection. When the connection is closed, the exclusive queue is deleted. The queue also has the property of auto-delete that is deleted automatically when the last subscriber unsubscribes.
- **Binding:** It is predefined rules for delivery of messages from exchange to appropriate queue.
- **Virtual Hosts:** The broker can have multiple isolated environments in the form of virtual systems known as virtual hosts, that have all the components of a broker, to manage message exchanges in parallel.

AMQP Communication

The publisher publishes the message to exchange. Queues bind to exchange using a binding key. Exchange performs routing depending on exchange type. The steps to create connections are as follows:

1. The publisher/consumer client communicates with RabbitMQ using the "**`exchange.declare`**" method to declare an exchange having a name, type and other attributes.

2. The broker responds with "**exchange.declare-ok**" once the exchange is declared.
3. The publisher/consumer client then declares a queue in the broker with the "**queue.declare**" method having a name.
4. The broker responds to the publisher client with "**queue.declare-ok**" once the queue is created.
5. The publisher/consumer client then creates channel binding between queue and exchange with a binding key.
6. Once everything is declared by the client, the broker communicates the data as per exchange type to the respective subscriber.

The publisher connects to the virtual host of RabbitMQ to create an exchange, queue and binding. The virtual host has a name and is secured with username and password. To create a virtual host in RabbitMQ, we need to follow the steps below.

1. Login to RabbitMQ and then on RabbitMQ portal, go to **Admin** > **Virtual Hosts**.
2. Add a new virtual host.
3. Add a new user with username and password within the new virtual host.
4. Connect to the newly created virtual host.

With virtual hosts, multiple applications can utilize a single RabbitMQ broker. This makes the AMQP protocol platform-agnostic as it can connect any application for message exchange. It exchanges messages in different data formats too.

AMQP Implementation

Install Erlang and RabbitMQ on Unix OS with the following commands:

```
sudo apt-get install -y erlang-base \
                        erlang-asn1 erlang-crypto erlang-eldap
erlang-ftp erlang-inets \
                        erlang-mnesia erlang-os-mon erlang-
parsetools erlang-public-key \
                        erlang-runtime-tools erlang-snmp
erlang-ssl \
                        erlang-syntax-tools erlang-tftp
erlang-tools erlang-xmerl
sudo apt-get install rabbitmq-server -y --fix-missing

To run the RabbitMQ broker, type following command on terminal:
service rabbitmq-server start

Create two files: publisher.py and consumer.py.
```

publisher.py

```
import pika
connection = pika.BlockingConnection(pika.ConnectionParameters
(host='localhost'))
channel = connection.channel()
channel.queue_declare(queue='python')
channel.basic_publish(exchange=' ', routing_key='python',
body='Hello from IoT world!')
print("[x] Sent ''Hello from IoT world '")
connection.close()
```

consumer.py

```
import pika
connection = pika.BlockingConnection(pika.ConnectionParameters
(host='localhost'))
channel = connection.channel()
def callback(ch, method, properties, body):
    print("[x] Received %r" % body)
channel.basic_consume(queue='hello', on_message_callback
=callback,auto_ack=True)
print('[*] Waiting for messages. To exit press CTRL+C')
channel.start_consuming()
```

For windows, Erlang has to be downloaded first separately and then RabbitMQ is installed using GUI interface. RabbitMQ server is installed from official website. Complete installation and from terminal, move to rabbitmq sbin directory. Enablc plugins using command "rabbitmq-plugins enable rabbitmq_management". Restart RabbitMQ service and open localhost:15672/ on the browser with username and password as guest. For macOS, the command is "brew install rabbitmq" and the command installs Erlang as well as RabbitMQ scripts.

Differences between MQTT and AMQP

AMQP is a more complex protocol compared to MQTT. It provides publish-subscribe as well as point to point communication whereas MQTT provides only publish-subscribe communication. AMQP prioritizes messages and no message is lost during communication whereas MQTT has three qualities of service and de\interes on what QoS level is chosen, it acts accordingly. Next, It is easy to set up an MQTT connection whereas in AMQP the client needs to set up everything with the broker before communication. Thus, AMQP has more message exchanges during connection phase compared to MQTT. This property of AMQP is not suitable for resource-constrained devices and limited networks. AMQP has better functionalities compared to MQTT overall but MQTT is suitable for IoT network and devices and AMQP between fog-cloud and cloud.

Software Defined Networking

Software Defined Networking (SDN) was proposed in 2008 to replace manual configuration of routers and switches. It provides a virtual layer over physical network resources. It virtualizes all the network resources and utilizes them to meet the application requirements accordingly. It is most used in the Cloud so that the workload can be distributed as per network resource availability. SDN is important because it has the ability to control large distributed networks in a centralized manner. Without SDN, routers have a routing table and according to it, the router forwards the packet from source to destination.

They have no intelligence to adjust the routing table dynamically and select destinations where resources are available. SDN provides control over the routing of packets using software.

SDN	Overlay Network	NFV
• Controls routing of network packets. • Implemented on Switched and Routers.	• Logical network over physical network. • Its of three types: Structured, Unstructured and Hierarchical.	• Creates virtual machine. • Runs above hypervisor and physical resources.

Figure 6.6: *Differences between Software Defined Network (SDN), Overlay Network and Network Function Virtualization (NFV)*

SDN is often confused with overlay network and network function virtualization (NFV), although they are different as shown in Figure 6.6 and they may execute together to provide better network management. We should know each of them so that we get clear picture of what SDN actually is. Overlay network is a logical communication network that abstracts the complexity of underlying physical network. These are built using software to encapsulate packets with extra header for communication and provide redundancy, fault tolerance as well as virtualization. Due to virtualization, two nodes from different network can also communicate easily.

There are three types of overlays: structured, unstructured and hierarchical. Structured overlays connect nodes in a topology and each node has equal distribution of resources. Mapping of data to a specific node is done via distributed hash tables. In unstructured overlays, nodes have random connections with other and use flooding, gossiping technique to get the data. They can easily adapt to dynamic network changes. Third is hierarchical overlay that has cluster of nodes where each cluster has a super node. This makes searching of node very efficient.

Routing in overlay is selecting of most efficient path considering overlay as well as underlying network. Network function virtualization creates virtual machines that run software to accomplish network functions over physical network. It provides load balancing, routing of packets as well as firewall security. NFV runs above a hypervisor and defines software for doing the tasks, however, it utilizes underlying physical network resources. SDN controls the routing of the packet by implementing software directly on network resources like switch and routers.

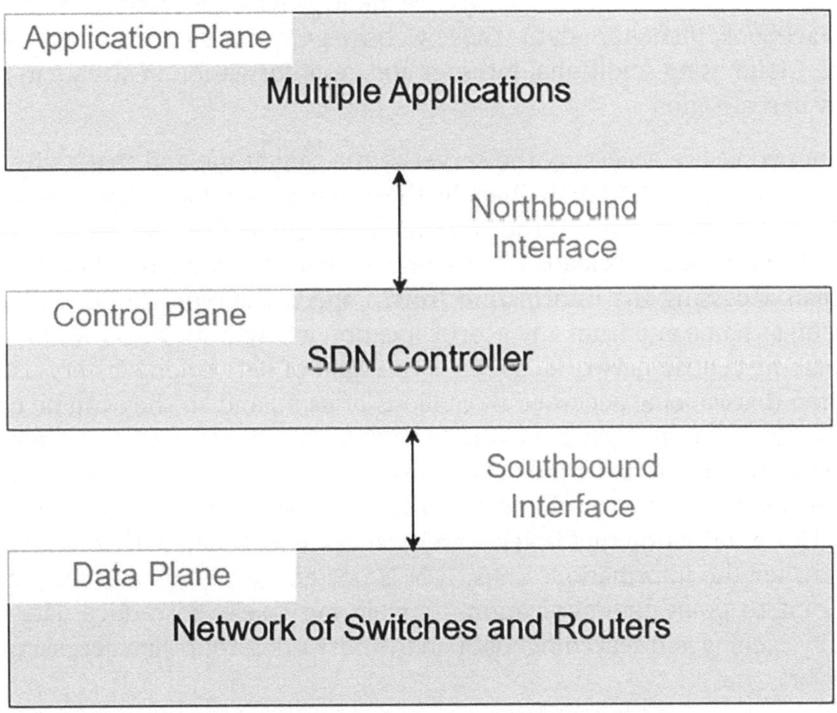

Figure 6.7: *Layered Architecture of SDN*

SDN has three layers as shown in *Figure* 6.7: Application layers, control layer and infrastructure layer. Application layer runs applications that tell network requirements to the control layer. Control layer manages the network of the infrastructure layer. Infrastructure layer consists of all network devices like switches and routers. The control layer has two APIs: Northbound and Southbound. Northbound to communicate with the application layer and southbound is to communicate with the infrastructure layer. Thus, SDN 's main purpose is to divide the network into data planes and control planes. The data plane can be controlled by a control plane and dynamically routes packets from switches/routers as per the requirements of multiple applications from the application layer. OpenFlow protocol is the protocol used by SDN to administer data traffic through routers and switches through the control plane. OpenFlow has a controller, flow table, and network devices like OpenFlow Switches.

Thus, SDN can be integrated with IoT applications to manage the network for improved performance.

Information-Centric Networking

Today, a lot of people are using Netflix and Amazon Prime to watch movies. Already YouTube is being used worldwide even for little children. Further, not only audio/ video data, there are other data that are frequently being accessed by multiple users such as Facebook, Instagram data. These websites request data from respective host servers in Cloud using traditional Internet and get information in stream in response to display in real-time.

Millions of people are accessing the server at the same time and that's why all these popular websites have Cloud to handle the request simultaneously. However, the information is all over the internet continuously going from server to millions of clients and vice-versa. This leads to network bottlenecks as the bandwidth is limited. Rather than accessing the information from a specific server, the idea is to access information as name and from any nearby location where it may be available. This led to information-centric networking (ICN). This kind of networking is very useful with information that is being accessed by millions of users and so they can be cached to save server time as well as save network bandwidth. If a user requests for information, the ICN searches and fetches the information from the nearest server by the unique name provided to the information rather than requesting the main host server. It is not useful for information that is very rarely accessed and then in that case the server is accessed for the information. Thus, ICN is not here to eliminate internet client-server, point-to-point communication. Its main purpose is to reduce data over the network by caching and searching "data" in the network rather than accessing a single point server.

Salient Features

- Data is split into small chunks called named data objects.
- Each of the Named Data Object (NDO) is named uniquely.
- Routers in ICN forward packets similar to traditional networks and also store named data objects in their limited memory.

- Caching is a service that is open for all network devices and independent of the application.

Naming Scheme

To search for the information in the network, it requires a name. For example, if we want to get recent news about Narendra Modi, the ICN will search for this information and find the closest cache server.

The cache server has stored the information about Narendra Modi with a unique name like "news modi" and ICN is aware of the name. The naming is very important so that exactly the same information is provided to the user that he made a request for. The name is used to search for the information rather than a location of the server. There are four types of naming techniques:

- **Flat:** A single name provided to the information.
- **Attribute-based:** An attribute of the information is selected as a name.
- **Hierarchical:** Name in tree-like structure similar to file path.
- **Hybrid:** Combining flat and hierarchical naming to provide name to the information.

Caching and Replacement

ICN cache named data objects (NDO) so that the access is faster and the data need not be requested to the same target location every time, saving time and network cost.

Default caching policy is Leave Copy Everywhere (LCE) in which the object that is requested will leave its copy on the way to the receiver. Disadvantage is that too many copies of the same object are created, eating up limited space unnecessarily. Another Caching policy is Leave Copy Down (LCD) in which the copy is cached only in direct downstream nodes. The third strategy is Move Copy Down in which the object is copied on a direct downstream node and deleted from the previous target node after it is moved.

Fourth scheme is Copy with Probability (Prob) where each node in the path has a probability assigned and accordingly the object is cached. The fifth scheme is Randomly Copy One where the object is cached at a random node. Sixth scheme is Probabilistic Cache where each node is assigned with an increasing probability while going downstream. With this scheme, the object is easily cached at the network edge, faster than other schemes. Replacement of a cached data is also important to optimize the use of limited memory. Random Replacement, Least Recently Used, Least Frequently Used, and Max Diversity Most Recent. Max Diversity Most Recently stores each object with its producer name and replaces the object from the same producer.

Routing Scheme

Routing in ICN is in two parts: Routing of NDO requests and routing of NDO response. There are two approaches in routing. In the first approach, the request is routed to Name Resolution Service (NRS) node where name is converted into a source address. The NRS node stores the named object and its source address. Once the source address is known, the request is routed to that address. Data as response is then routed from source to the requester. For this approach, name-resolution routing might be followed during routing to the NRS node and once the IP address is known then topology-based routing might be a good choice. In the second approach the request message is directly routed to source and the source responds back to the requester. The routing is heavily dependent on the namespace. Name-based routing is suitable for the second approach.

Content Delivery Network

As we read in *Chapter 4, Integrating Edge with Cloud in IoT Architecture*, Content Delivery Network (CDN) gave rise to the idea of edge computing in an IoT application. In this network, the frequently fetched web contents are cached at a nearby server so that whenever the same content is requested later, the content is fetched from the local server machine. This network reduces the request/response latency and the main server is free to handle requests from other clients. It is a cluster of systems that are distributed at the network edge that work together for fast webpage loading. CDN delivers static contents like images, documents, pages, scripts, etc. The CDN is being widely used in popular websites like Netflix, Amazon, Facebook, etc and has proved to be very effective when handling millions of user requests at once. There are dedicated CDN edge servers created and deployed all around the world for use by any web developer.

Working Steps:

Step 1: A user/client requests a server for web contents such as HTML pages, CSS, images, JavaScript files to load a webpage onto his device.

Step 2: Closest CDN server is assigned to the request.

Step 3: The CDN server responds with the cached content.

Step 4: If all the requested content is not available with the selected, remaining files are requested from another CDN server.

Step 5: If the requested content is not available on any of the CDN servers or the content is stale, the contents are requested from the original web hosting server.

Step 6: The response from the original web host server is cached on the previously requested CDN server for future reference.

Architecture:

Thus, a CDN network consists of a client, DNS server, CDN servers, Load Balancing, and a main server as shown in Figure 6.8. Client requests for the content. The request is first routed to a DNS server. The DNS server is enabled with CDN and Load Balancing in a CDN network. The CDN's DNS has a lookup table with IP address of CDN edge servers and it selects the edge server on the basis of distance from the client's location, load on the main server and network conditions. Load Balancing in CDN ensures that all the edge servers are equally utilized and hikes in data traffic is handled efficiently. If we are hosting a webpage on the main server, we need to sign up for CDN services and provide the URL of the content to be distributed. The CDN then copies the content to all the edge servers or provides the copy when requested by the edge server. The edge server caches the contents. The CDN also updates the cached data on edge servers automatically whenever the main server web content is updated. This ensures the content provided by CDN is always fresh.

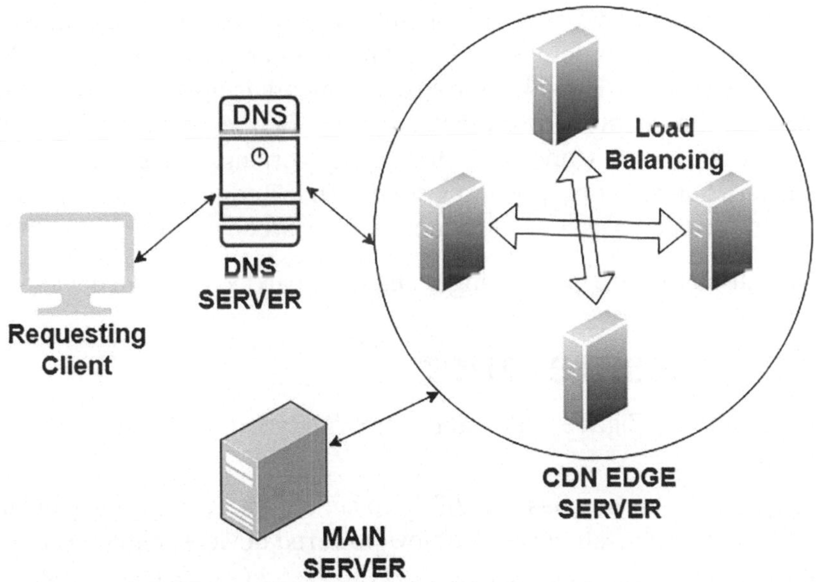

Figure 6.8: *Architecture of Content Delivery Network (CDN)*

Caching

- **Push Caching:** The main server pushes the content to CDN edge servers so that the content is available whenever requested.
- **Pull Caching:** Whenever a CDN server is requested for a web content and the content is not available, it requests the content from the main server.

Benefits

- The web content loads very **fast** on the client's machine when requested from anywhere around the world.
- Multiple people can access the website at the same time without **overloading the main server**.
- Load and download **latency** of web contents is reduced.
- It increases **scalability** of the main server by distributing the handling of requests from a large number of users to CDN edge servers.
- Network **bandwidth** consumption is reduced.

Conclusion

In this chapter, we studied different communication protocols and application protocols that are popularly used in IoT applications. These protocols are designed for low-powered resource constrained IoT devices. Two architectures that are used in IoT communication: request/response and publish/subscribe are also presented. Further, CoAP protocol, MQTT protocol and AMQP protocol are discussed in detail. Moreover, implementation details of these protocols are also provided. When to use which protocols as per IoT application's requirements is also studied in the chapter. After protocols, the chapter introduces Software Defined Networking, Information Centric Networking and Content Delivery Networking. These are very popular networking paradigms that may be integrated with IoT edge applications to efficiently utilize network resources as well as reduce service latency of the application.

Next chapter discusses pre-processing techniques carried on edge devices.

Points to Remember

- Bluetooth 4.0, ZigBee, RFID and LoraWAN are popular IoT communication protocols.
- Bluetooth 4.0 device has capability to send data even in noisy environments and to create a mesh network of low powered devices, ZigBee is popular.
- RFID uses electromagnetic fields to transfer and LoraWAN is suitable for long range communication of small data.
- Communication in an IoT application is categorized into three types: D2D (device to device), D2S (device to server) and S2S (server to server).
- Two popular interaction models are request-reply (CoAP) and publish-subscribe (MQTT, AMQP).
- CoAP is a lightweight version of HTTP protocol and has similar client-server architecture with REST (Representational State Transfer).

- MQTT is a very lightweight, TCP-based protocol where the MQTT broker retains the message until the acknowledgment is not received by the subscriber.
- AMQP protocol is platform-agnostic as it can connect any application for message exchange using a virtual host.
- SDN controls the routing of the packet by implementing software directly on network resources like switches and routers.
- ICN reduces data over the network by caching and searching "data" in the network rather than accessing a single point server.
- CDN is a cluster of systems that are distributed at the network edge that work together for fast webpage loading. CDN delivers static contents like images, documents, pages, scripts, etc.

Multiple Choice Questions

1. Which protocol is called as "WiFi-on-steroids"?
   a. 6lowPAN
   b. LoraWAN
   c. WiMax
   d. RFID
2. Which communication protocol is based on IPv6?
   a. LoraWAN
   b. ZigBee
   c. Cellular
   d. 6lowPAN
3. Which protocol is used for D2D communication, and is OS agnostic?
   a. MQTT
   b. IoTivity
   c. CoAP
   d. Alljoyn
4. The CoAP packet that has critical information:
   a. Non-confirmable
   b. Confirmable

   c. Reset
   d. Acknowledgement
5. Which MQTT does not have the following characteristics?
   a. Publish/Subscribe
   b. Persistent connection
   c. Topic-based Routing
   d. CRUD method
6. In AMQP, if a message is routed as per the header value, it is:
   a. Header Exchange
   b. Topic Exchange
   c. Direct Exchange
   d. Fanout Exchange
7. Which paradigm creates clusters of Virtual Machines (VMs) over a physical network?
   a. SDN
   b. ICN
   c. NFV
   d. Overlay

Answers

1. c
2. d
3. b
4. b
5. d
6. a
7. c

Questions

1. How is ZigBee and RFID used as a communication protocol in an IoT application?
2. Explain publish-subscribe model, and how is it different from request-reply?
3. Why is HTTP application layer protocol inefficient for an IoT application?
4. Explain the message format of CoAP protocol.
5. How does MQTT route the message from publisher to subscriber?
6. What are the components of RabbitMQ broker?
7. Discuss the layered architecture of SDN.
8. How is data cached in ICN?
9. List the benefits of CDN.

CHAPTER 7
Pre-Processing Data on Edge Devices

Introduction

The IoT big data is collected from multiple IoT devices, and various other sources such as social platforms, web applications, media, location, and so on. The collected data from each source is raw, consisting of erroneous, missing data and outliers. Further, the data from individual sources are insufficient to provide complete information alone. This data is made informative, when it is fused with data from other sources. Data preprocessing is a crucial step to increase the data quality for accurate decision-making, and perform data fusion. Data quality is maintained, when data accuracy and completeness is given priority, while fusing data from heterogeneous sources. With Fog-Cloud IoT architecture, the data processing step is carried out in a distributed manner, with data pre-processing step implemented on the network edge near to the source, and data analysis step implemented at the cloud. Data pre-processing is a light-weight process, and can be easily deployed on edge devices having limited computational power.

Data pre-processing includes cleaning of data by filtering, smoothing and outlier detection, imputing missing data and fusing data from heterogeneous sources to generate relevant information. We will study pre-processing of the batch as well as streaming Big Data. The pre-processed data is then communicated to Cloud for the data analysis step. This chapter discusses different data pre-processing methods, and provides details on techniques used in each of the methods.

Structure

In this chapter, we will cover the following topics:

- Data Cleaning
- Missing Data Imputation

- Heterogeneous Data Fusion
- Python Implementation

Data Cleaning

Cleaning is a very important step during data pre-processing. It is absolutely necessary to capture the correct and complete data for increasing trust in decision-making. Cleaning includes filtering data to reduce size, removing errors, and detecting outliers in the data. For cleaning, we should choose the appropriate strategy to have reliable data analysis. Cleaning process enhances the data quality which directly impacts trustworthiness of the decisions made by the analytical model. The cleaned data is the soul of accurate functionality of any IoT application, and thus, it is very crucial to know how to clean the captured data. Hence, for cleaning the data, first, we will detect the outliers. Next, we will remove error/noise from the data by a smoothing process. At the end, we will filter the data to remove duplicates and redundant values.

Outlier Detection

Outlier is a data point that is an anomaly in the acquired data due to measurement errors, variations or unusual events. To understand the outlier better, let us assume, we have a daily transaction data of a credit card to analyze. Every day, for a year, there are minimum zero transactions or maximum three transactions. However, one day, the collected data shows a total of 11 transactions a day, which is not usual. This data, showing a high peak in the transactions, is considered as an outlier, and is specially handled to confirm a fraudulent transaction due to stolen card. Another example is of an application that detects heart attacks in real-time. If there is a sudden spike or dip in heart rate, this data is considered as an outlier, indicating signs of an attack. Thus, before analyzing the data, if the outlier is detected, the situations of emergency can be handled immediately.

Outliers are of five different types. These are as follows:

- **Univariate:** The outlier is in a specific feature only.
- **Multi-variate:** The outlier is explicitly determined by combining multiple features.
- **Global:** The outlier differs from other data points by a huge margin.
- **Contextual:** The outlier belongs to a specific context.
- **Collective:** Collection of multiple data points forming an outlier, and each of the data points within the collection may or may not be an outlier.

Outlier is an unusual pattern, and needs to be detected before performing analysis. These data are handled separately, or if undetected can lead to miscalculations of mean, and variance of the data. Miscalculations will lead to misleading decisions from the analytical model. Detecting and handling outliers first, before analyzing the data improves accuracy, quality of data and performance of the application.

Techniques that are popularly used to detect outliers are:

- **Standard Deviation:** This parameter measures the spread of the data points in a normal distribution. Outliers are points that are at end points of the spread. Points that are located further than three times the standard deviation can be considered as outliers. The spread is positive at the right side of the mean, and negative at the left side of the mean.
  Given a dataset, calculate the mean (μ) and the standard deviation (σ). Next, calculate if any result is greater than +/- (3* σ).
- **Boxplot:** This is a visualization tool that shows five values: Minimum, maximum, medium, first quartile and third quartile. Whiskers join the minimum with the first quartile, and the maximum with the third quartile. Calculate the difference between 1.5 times the interquartile range, and minimum value as O1. Calculate the sum between 1.5 times the interquartile range and the maximum value as O2. Data points that are less than O1, and greater than O2. The value 1.5 is considered is heuristic, and not a strict number. IT is because at value 1, the relevant data points are considered outliers, and at value 2 the outliers are considered the relevant data points. Hence, to preserve range sensitivity, the value 1.5 is considered. This range is only for Gaussian distribution. For an exponential distribution, the number "1.5" changes as per the data.
- **Z-Score:** Different data features have different ranges. For example, values in Age feature and weight feature differ in range. Even within weight features, the range of values in pounds and kilometers are different. It is difficult to estimate how far the value is from the mean by just looking at the value. Z-score is a numerical method that calculates how far is the data point from the mean. Process of transforming each of the data values to its respective z-score is called standardization. Z-score is calculated as the difference between data point and the mean, and the resultant is divided by the standard deviation. Data point having a z-score greater than 3 is considered an outlier and is very far away from the mean of the actual range.
- **Clustering:** This method divides data points in multiple subsets. Each subset is a cluster of data points having similar properties. There are four clustering approaches: Partition methods, Hierarchical methods, Density-based methods, Grid-based methods. In partition-based methods (K-mean) creates mutually exclusive clusters each having a defined center. The Hierarchical Method divides the data points into different hierarchical levels as tree-structure, based on distance, density and continuity. There are two types of Hierarchical Clustering: Agglomerative and Divisive.

Density-based clusters, for example, DBSCAN, create clusters for data having arbitrary shapes that have a density threshold, and the cluster grows with data points until it reaches the threshold. Parameters that define these clusters are eps (distance between two points within cluster is less than or equal to eps) and MinPts (number of points within the eps radius). Grid-based method clusters the data points in grid cells. Due to grid structure, processing is very fast. Data point that does not belong to any cluster is an outlier. If the data point is outside of the closest cluster, then it is an outlier. Further, if the data point is part of a small cluster, then all the data points in that cluster are outliers.

- **Isolation Forest:** This is a popular method that finds outliers in less time. The outliers are isolated from the data through recursive binary partitioning in a tree-structure. There are three concepts: Isolation, partitioning and anomaly score. In isolation, the uniqueness of each of the data points is identified. In partitioning, the data points are split by random feature selection. Anomaly score tells the number of splits for each data point to be isolated from the data. Higher anomaly score means the data point requires fewer splits to be isolated. There is a threshold score over which the data points are classified as anomalies. This method efficiently detects an abnormal pattern in the data, and is computationally very inexpensive.

Detecting outliers is a challenging task. The choice of threshold value that separates the outlier data point from other data points is very difficult. Detecting whether the outlier is an unusual pattern in data, or just a noise due to measurement error is a big problem. Outlier that is a noise results in false analysis of the situation. For instance, if the transaction details 11 is an error due to human error, the fraud detected by the system is not actually a fraud. This results in reduced performance of the system.

The outlier detection is also helpful in finding unauthorized access to sensitive data, network attack, a mechanical failure of an equipment, disease outbreak.

Data Smoothing

The errors in data need to be eliminated, and the process to eliminate them is smoothing. Errors in data can be generated due to multiple factors.

The error generation can be due to human error in data entry, measurement error of the sensor (faulty sensor), network transmission noise, or malicious attack. The errors can be random or systematic. The outliers can also be an error, and hence, requires elimination as it arrives. Data with error is a noisy data, and needs to be treated to avoid incorrect analysis.

Some of the popular data smoothing methods are:

- **Exponential:** There are three types of smoothing processing depending on the time-series data. These are:

- **Simple Exponential:** This method removes noise from time-series data that has no seasonality or trend. A single parameter is used known as smoothing factor α with value between 0 to 1. This parameter tells how much the impact of past observations should be minimized. Smaller value of smoothing factor means a higher weightage to the past observation. As the observation gets far away from the data point, its weight diminishes exponentially.

  The formula used for smoothing is $O_t=\alpha E_t+(1-\alpha)\ O_{t-1}$

  where O_t and O_{t-1} are smoothened values of data points of current timestamp t, and previous timestamp t-1, respectively. E_t is the noisy data point of current timestamp t that is smoothened to $O_{t,}$ using the formula.

- **Holt's Trend:** This method smoothens the time-series data with trend, but no seasonality. Two parameters are required to smooth the data: alpha (α) and beta (β). Beta implies the effect of the changing trend, and decays as the observation gets far from past observatio by ns.

- **Holt-Winters:** This method considers three parameters to smooth time-series data. The first two parameters are alpha and beta having the same functionality as previous two exponential methods. The third parameter is gamma that controls the effect of seasonality on the time-series data smoothing. This method is the most popular and very precise, yet very complicated, and requires large data.

* **Moving Average:** This technique is very common to remove data noise, and is quite simple. A new time series data is created having an average of the past observations. There is a window width that specifies how many previous observations are considered to calculate the average value for the current observation. The window moves over current observation, and calculates the average of the current observation, using the total number of recent previous observations specified as window width.
* **Random Walk:** This technique generates data randomly, and is independent of previous observations. The data generated is based on probability, and can approximate actual data. The current observation can be smoothened by the synthetic data produced by random walk.
* **Exponential Moving Average:** This method is a kind of moving average technique that also provides weight to the previous observations. The number of previous observations considered is calculated from the window width. Simple moving average applies the same weight to all the observations in that window; however, this method assigns different weights to each of the observations in the window. The smoothing constant K assigns weights to the

observation, and is calculated as 2 divided by (window width + 1). The formula to calculate exponential moving average (EMA) is

$EMA(O_t)=(K*O_t) + (1-K) *EMA(O_{t-1})$ where O_t is the current observation and O_{t-1} is the previous observation.

- **Binning:** The data is divided into multiple bins, and each bin is treated for noise separately. To create bins, the data needs to be sorted first. Bins are either created by equal frequency distribution that means each bin is of the same size. Another method to have a total number of bins is to divide the range of the total data with a constant number. The bin numbers or bin frequency is adjusted to have more smooth data. The values within a bin are smoothened either by mean or boundary.

  For example, suppose a bin has value 2,3,7,8,10. Bin mean smoothing replaces all the values in the bin with their mean. After mean smoothening, the bin is 6,6,6,6,6. Bin boundary smoothing calculates the minimum and maximum value of the bin, and assigns each of the bin elements, either the minimum value or the maximum value, whichever is the closest from the observation. After bin boundary smoothing, the bin values are 2,2,10,10,10.

- **Kernel Smoothing:** This is a non-parametric technique that use probability density function for smoothing the data. A kernel function is placed over each of the data point to smooth it. The kernel function is a non-negative and symmetric probability distribution like Gaussian, Epanechnikov, or uniform. The data is smoothened depending on its distance from all the observations covered in the by the function spread. The smoothing highly depends on the choice of the function applied over each observation. Selection of kernel function bandwidth is very critical as small bandwidth can cause overfitting, and large bandwidth may over smooth the data removing valid features.

Data smoothing helps in identifying trend and seasonality in the data by eliminating noise. These algorithms are successful in removing most of the noise from the data. They also help in determining a certain data pattern, and the data that do not follow the pattern are considered as **noise**. However, in this process, relevant information can also get lost, including meaningful outliers.

Data Filtering

This pre-processing reduces the data size by removing data that is irrelevant for analysis. The removal is based on a certain criterion. If a data point satisfies the criteria, it is kept otherwise deleted. Data filtering increases the information relevancy, and enhances data accuracy. Further, the reduced data saves computational resources as well as time of processing, and provides faster decision-making.

The different types of Data filtering are:

- **Basic Filtering:** Basic techniques consist of range filter and set membership filter. Range filter specifies the required data range. The data points outside the data range are automatically filtered. In set membership, the filter selects the data points that are members of specific set, for example, season, gender, country, and so on.
- **Filtering by Criteria:** The data is filtered using multiple criterions. For instance, age greater than 30, and pay greater than 50000 rupees. The filtering results into smaller data that are above 30, and have income more than 50000 rupees.
- **Filtering by Time Range:** Data within a specific time period can be selected to analyze the trend. The obtained data is good to analyze the data within a certain time period. This filter is popular during stock analysis.
- **Text Filtering:** Keywords and pattern matching are used to filter the data. This filter is popular on social websites. Filtering by keyword finds the most suitable post out of huge twitter data, and with pattern matching the posts with hashtags (#) are filtered out.
- **Numeric Filtering:** This filter is used to set the threshold value for numerical data, and the operation is defined based on whether the values that need to be filtered should be greater than threshold, or less than threshold. For example, to filter patients having high blood pressure, the filter is applied as values that are greater than 90/140.
- **Custom Filtering:** Filters can also be designed and customized depending on specific application requirements from the given dataset. These filters are more complex, and need to be carefully designed to get the accurate data.

To do data filtering, the objectives should be very clear. Three questions that need to be addressed are:

- What are the specific insights we are looking for?
- How to know the relevancy of data?
- How is the filtered data useful?

The filtering process differs for data of different data types. Further, filtering may affect the other related data values in a multi-column dataset. Relationships in data that provide useful information need to be preserved. Multiple filters can also be applied, when the data to be captured is complex. Validate the data after every filtering, and keep the back-up of the original data, until correct filtering technique is not identified.

Missing Data Imputation

There is no guarantee that the data would be acquired. Some data goes missing due to the following reasons:

- Errors by humans during data entry.
- Malfunctions of IoT device/sensors/ network.
- When there is no response in user survey, feedbacks.
- When critical data gets missed during sensing/collecting of information.
- Unreliable low-cost sensors.

Records with missing data can be deleted, however, it may cause loss of relevant information. There are two deletion methods that are popular: List-wise deletion and pairwise deletion. In list-wise deletion, the records with any one column missing are completely deleted. In pairwise deletion, records with one or two missing values are preserved, and only available values in that record are considered for analysis. Pairwise deletion reduces the number of deletions and information loss compared to list-wise deletion. The deletion process may lead to inaccurate or biased analysis and decision-making. A better way is to impute the missing data with a predicted value to have accurate analysis.

Strategy other than imputation, and deletion is to implement multiple sensors/ IoT devices in the same area to have back-up for missing data. These backup sensors/ devices in the area are geographically co-located, and have spatial and temporal correlation. The first step in imputation of missing data using correlation is to find a proximate sensor with the help of geographic coordinates of the missing data. The next step is to find the correlated data from these proximate sensors, and impute the value. Imputing is the process of assigning a related, approximate value to the missing data for generating unbiased information. This strategy works well with a wireless sensor network that implements multiple sensors of the same specification to monitor an area, for example, sensor network over a forest to detect a fire beforehand. However, increasing the number of devices over the network is not a good idea, when there is a requirement of one sensor per application.

When there is no backup sensor, there are statistical and machine learning techniques to impute the missing data.

Classification of the Missing Data

For accurate technique selection, we first need to understand the missing data frequency, and the cause. For ease in identifying the best suited technique, the missing data is classified into three types:

- **Missing Completely At Random (MCAR):** This is a type of missing data that is completely unrelated to observed and unobserved data of its own field/attribute/column, and other fields in the dataset. The missing trait is random, and the recovery of the data is not at all possible. Missing data in this type is extremely rare. This may be caused by data not captured at the first place due to battery die out, or due to humans that are unable to fill out surveys due to time or network constraints.

- **Missing At Random (MAR):** This type of missing data occurs, when the data is not being provided due to some personal reasons. For example, wrong placement of the sensor leads to missing data or humans that did not attend the concert, or did not provide a musical concert survey. Missing data in this type is related to the observed data, and can be predicted from past observations from one's own field or other fields. However, these data are independent of the unobserved data. For instance, if humans not entering survey information are found to be of the same gender or the same age (an observed data), then such type of missing trait is known as MAR. With known observed data, it helps to have unbiased analysis with the missing data.
- **Missing Not At Random (MNAR):** When the humans interested in music also do not fill the form intentionally, then the missing data generated from such humans is considered in this type. It is related to the unobserved data, and not the observed data. There is no reason why the source denied providing the information and thus, it is non-random, intentionally generated missing data. The data that is missing is very important for unbiased analyses, and needs to be fetched/imputed/re-surveyed to have a complete set of data.

Missing Data Pattern

Data that needs to be analyzed is generally multivariate, and these variables are inter-related. Missing data can affect the complete information of an individual record as well as the whole dataset. Missing data have different patterns, and according to which techniques are applied. These patterns are classified as:

- **Univariate:** When data is missing in a single field/column/attribute.
- **Multivariate:** When data is missing in multiple fields/columns/attributes in a single record.
- **Monotone:** When data is missing for subsequent time periods for a particular field due to discontinuity.
- **Non-monotone:** When data is missing in intermittent fashion for subsequent time periods for a particular field.

Large and Small Missing Data Gaps

Missing data can be missing for a short or long time period, and it affects imputation of a time-series data where each observation is inter-dependent. Missing data with gaps has limited past observations to predict the future data, and mostly, future observations are predicted on imputed past observations. Large gaps of the missing data have more effects on imputation accuracy compared to small gaps.

Imputation Techniques

Imputation is a method to predict the missing values, and the prediction is based on previous and current non-missing observations. There are various techniques for imputation, and this depends on the data to be imputed on what technique is best suitable.

- **Simple Imputation:** The missing column value is imputed with the mean, median or mode of the whole column, it belongs to. It is very simple, but performs poorly in case of big data or data of high dimensions.
- **Regression:** The column variable with missing value is selected as a dependent variable. The related variables to the dependent variable are considered as independent variables. The available values from dependent and independent variables are fitted onto a regression model. The model can then be chosen as linear or logistic, depending on the data. The missing value is predicted from the regression plot.
- **Hot-Deck:** The missing value is imputed from hot observations (observations that has been recently processed). A common method following the hot deck technique is the "Last Observation Carried Forward" (LOCF) that imputes the missing value/s of the column with previous value/s. This technique increased the bias in data, and affected decision-making negatively.
- **Cold Deck:** In this method, the values are replaced by studying the values of similar objects in datasets collected previously. Other similar datasets are considered as doors to impute the missing values in the current dataset.
- **Expectation-Maximization:** It is an optimization technique that imputes the missing value or values by following three salient steps: Impute, estimate and iterate. The iteration process further includes two steps: Expectation and maximization. The expectation estimates a value for the missing data, and maximization estimates probability of the whole data with replacement of the missing values. The technique converges, when the probability of whole data in maximization steps is approximately close to the maximum likelihood of the entire data.
- **Multiple Imputation by Chained Equation (MICE):** This technique is also iterative with pre-defined 'k' iterations. For every iteration, for columns with a missing value, a regression plot is created separately, using other two related columns. The other two columns are made complete by imputing missing values with an approximate value. The missing value is then predicted from the regression plot. Similarly, missing values in the other two columns are

imputed. The new imputed missing values are then provided as new data for the next iterations. This creates a chain between each iteration. Finally, after kth iteration, the imputed values are the final values for the missing data.

- **Miss Forest:** Random Forest is trained to predict the missing value. The model is trained by a complete dataset with missing values replaced by mean, median or mode. Through predictions from trained Random Forest, impute original missing values, and replace previously imputed values. New dataset is used to train the Random Forest model again, and new predictions are used for imputation of the missing values. This iterates until convergence, or a maximum number of iterations.
- **K-Nearest Neighbor:** This method imputes the missing values of a column by using values from the same column. The imputation is independent from values of other columns. Krow values are selected that are near to the missing row value in the column. The mean of these K row values is calculated and used for imputing the missing value. Repeat this process for each row in the column, and then proceed with the next column of the missing values.
- **ARIMA:** ARIMA model is a statistical model that integrates auto-regression with the moving average, and is applied on time-series data with trend or pattern and non-seasonality. It forecasts the data in time-series based on lags in past observations and forecast errors. The ARIMA model has three parameters: p, d and q. To make the time-series data stationary, differencing is performed in the ARIMA model with the parameter d. Value of d determines the number of differencing to be performed to make the time-series stationary. Auto-Regression (AR(p)) model forecasts depending on lags of the previous observations and p is defined as order of lags to predict the missing data. Moving Average (MA(q)) model forecasts based on past forecast errors and q is defined as order of lagged forecast errors. ARIMA is used for missing data imputation by taking into account all the past observations before the missing value in that specific column.

Heterogeneous Data Fusion

In an IoT application, data from multiple platforms/sources are gathered to provide intelligent service. Different datasets add more information, context to the situation/ environment to be analyzed. For example, in a smart farming application, data comes from soil sensors, images collected from drones, weather sensors, and so on. Final fused data is called IoT data that has to be analyzed and proper fusion of these datasets increases the quality of the data, provides complete and accurate information, as well as provides unbiased analysis. However, fusing datasets from different sources is a very complex task. This is because the datasets are heterogeneous in nature as well as dimensionality. Furthermore, merging of the datasets needs to preserve the information, relationship within datasets, and relationship between the datasets.

The data fusion techniques are classified based on five different domains:

- Data Source Configuration
- Level of Abstraction
- Input/ Output
- Classification by JDL

Data Source Configuration

An IoT source can either be implemented as a support to other sources, or as a backup during failure, or for generating new information. As per the source's relationship with other sources, the fusion method is classified into three types.

- **Complementary:** In this fusion, the sources acquire information from the same environment on different points of view to provide the complete information.
- **Redundant/Competitive:** In this fusion, the sources acquire data from the same environment just to increase confidence, and the fused data is used during failures as a fault-tolerance.
- **Cooperative:** In this fusion type, the two sources provide different information, and their combination generates a new complex information.

Level of Abstraction

The fusion process is categorized into three levels, and how the data is processed for analysis from raw sensor data to feature extractions from the sensor data, ultimately analyzing the features for decision.

- **Low-level fusion:** Multiple sensor data that measure the same environment attribute is combined at this level to have more accurate information about the attribute.
- **Medium-level fusion:** In this level, the features are extracted from the raw sensor data, and a feature vector is created for analysis.
- **High-level fusion:** The feature vector is provided as input to the analytical model, and a decision is generated in this level.

Input/ Output

This classification is proposed by Dasarathy, and provides a fusion type based on what input is provided, and what output is expected. The input/output is based on the level of abstraction classification.

- **Data in-data out:** This type of fusion is implemented on raw data, and is either in the form of signal or image processing. Resulting data is updated, corrected, and transformed to enhanced raw data.
- **Data in-feature out:** This fusion type is used for extracting relevant features/ characteristics from the raw data.

- **Feature in- feature out:** The features extracted are combined in this fusion type to form new features or refine features to have complete information.
- **Feature in-decision out:** Decisions are made by analyzing the input feature set in this fusion type.
- **Decision in-decision out:** This type of fusion combines multiple decisions or refine decisions or make new decisions from decisions as input.

JDL Classification

This is a popular model that has conceptualized the fusion process, and its origin is from the military domain.

- **Level 0, source preprocessing:** In this level, raw sensor data is processed on pixel level, signal level. This level filters out irrelevant data and produces important information for analysis.
- **Level 1, object refinement:** The data from previous level is fused for refined object definition and the fusion is performed via correlation, clustering, association, spatio-temporal alignment, and combining extracted features.
- **Level 2, situation assessment:** The fused data with important features about the object from level 1 is analyzed in this level for studying the current conditions to identify situations. At this level, analytical models are applied for inference.
- **Level 3, impact assessment:** From the identified situations, the impact is evaluated in this level. Impact includes future risks and vulnerabilities. This level evaluates the impact and makes a logical decision.
- **Level 4, process refinement:** As per the solution in previous level, the whole process from level 0 to 3 is refined to minimize the impact of the situation as well as managing resources and sensors efficiently.

For fusion, techniques used are categorized into three types:

- Probabilistic methods like Bayesian network
- Artificial Intelligence (AI), including neural network, reinforcement learning, and fuzzy logic
- Evidence-based theory

Python Implementation

In this section, we will see how to implement pre-processing steps, using python libraries. To implement python in your system, you can either use command prompt, or visual studio code, or Jupyter Notebook. Once the code is running in your system, you can deploy it in any system with .py file extension. There are three parts in common for each step. First part is importing the appropriate library. Second part is importing or generating data, and the third part is passing the data to the function. The function either detects outliers, or detects noise or filters the data or handles missing values. Data fusion from scratch is implemented in the next chapter, where we will study the analysis of the data.

The code implementations for each step are as follows. For data cleaning, dataset on flight schedule (Link: https://maven- datasets.s3.amazonaws.com/Airline+Flight+Delays/Airlines+Airports+Cancellation+Codes+%26+Flights.zip) is considered. The dataset is shortened to the first 100 records only for ease of understanding. For missing data imputation, the dataset is generated using the panda's library. We will start the code with importing the library, and defining a data frame.

```
import pandas as pd
import numpy as np
import matplotlib.pyplot as plt
df = pd.read_csv('flights.csv')
print(df.head())
```

The following *Figure* 7.1 shows the first five rows of the imported csv dataset as output of **`df.head()`** command.

```
   YEAR  MONTH  DAY  DAY_OF_WEEK AIRLINE  FLIGHT_NUMBER TAIL_NUMBER  \
0  2015      1    1            4      AS             98      N407AS
1  2015      1    1            4      AA           2336      N3KUAA
2  2015      1    1            4      US            840      N171US
3  2015      1    1            4      AA            258      N3HYAA
4  2015      1    1            4      AS            135      N527AS

  ORIGIN_AIRPORT DESTINATION_AIRPORT  SCHEDULED_DEPARTURE  ...  ARRIVAL_TIME  \
0            ANC                 SEA                    5  ...         408.0
1            LAX                 PBI                   10  ...         741.0
2            SFO                 CLT                   20  ...         811.0
3            LAX                 MIA                   20  ...         756.0
4            SEA                 ANC                   25  ...         259.0

   ARRIVAL_DELAY  DIVERTED  CANCELLED  CANCELLATION_REASON  AIR_SYSTEM_DELAY  \
0          -22.0         0          0                  NaN               NaN
1           -9.0         0          0                  NaN               NaN
2            5.0         0          0                  NaN               NaN
3           -9.0         0          0                  NaN               NaN
4          -21.0         0          0                  NaN               NaN
```

Figure 7.1: *Five Rows of the Dataset "flights.cv" on which Examples are Implemented*

Outlier Detection

1. **BoxPlot**

   a. To detect an outlier:

```
import seaborn as sns
df = pd.read_csv('flights.csv')
sns.boxplot(df['ARRIVAL_DELAY'])
```

The following *Figure* 7.2 shows a boxplot of **`ARRIVAL_DELAY`** column in the dataset depicting outliers.

<Axes: ylabel='ARRIVAL_DELAY'>

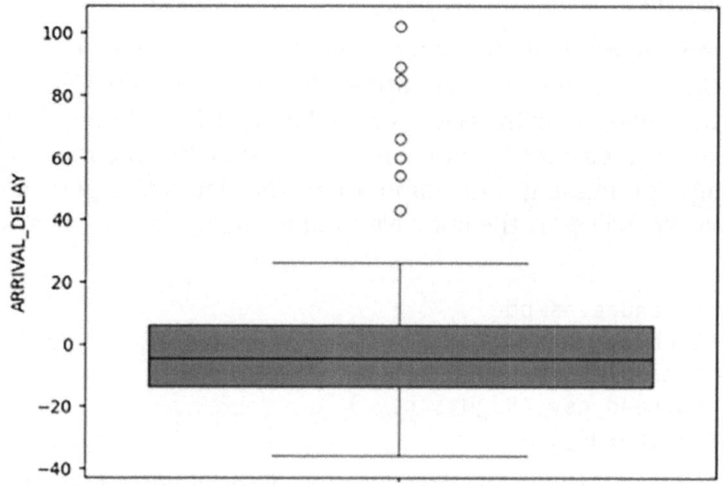

Figure 7.2: *Boxplot to Detect Outliers*

b. **To remove an outlier:**

```
outlier_indices = np.where(df['ARRIVAL_DELAY'] > 40.0)
no_outliers_df = df.drop(outlier_indices[0])
sns.boxplot(no_outliers_df['ARRIVAL_TIME'])
```

The following *Figure* 7.3 shows a boxplot of **`ARRIVAL_TIMe`** column in the dataset with outliers (>40) detected, as well as removed.

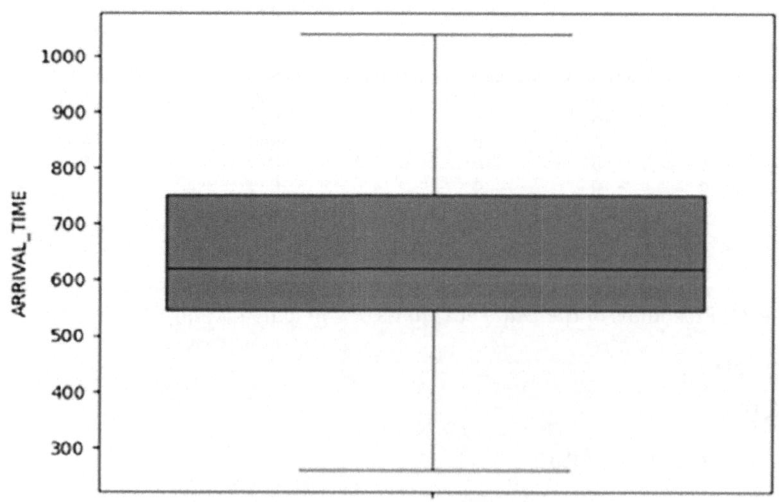

Figure 7.3: *Boxplot with Removed Outliers*

2. **Clustering**

 a. **To detect an outlier**

```
fig, ax = plt.subplots(figsize=(6, 4))
ax.scatter(df['ARRIVAL_TIME'],df['DESTINATION_AIRPORT'])
ax.set_xlabel('(Time)')
ax.set_ylabel('(Airport)')
plt.show()
```

The following *Figure* 7.4 shows a scatterplot of **DESTINATION_AIRPORT** with respect to **ARRIVAL_TIME** in the dataset, depicting outliers.

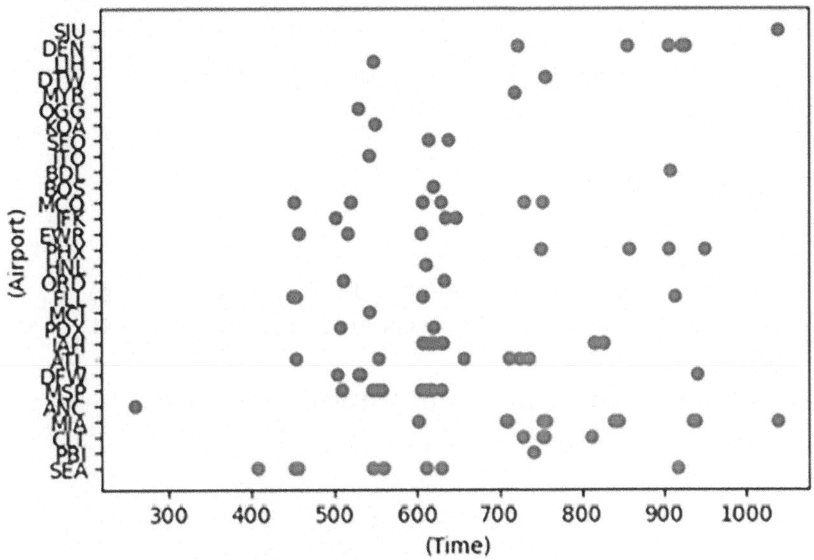

Figure 7.4: *Scatterplot for Detecting Outliers*

 b. **To remove an outlier**

```
outlier_indices = np.where(df['ARRIVAL_TIME'] > 925.0)
no_outliers_df = df.drop(outlier_indices[0])
fig, ax = plt.subplots(figsize=(6, 4))
ax.scatter(no_outliers_df['ARRIVAL_TIME'],no_outliers_df
['DESTINATION_AIRPORT'])
ax.set_xlabel('(TIME)')
ax.set_ylabel('(AIRPORT)')
plt.show()
```

The following *Figure* 7.5 shows a Scatterplot of **DESTINATION_AIRPORT** with respect to the **ARRIVAL_TIME** with outliers (>925) detected, as well as removed.

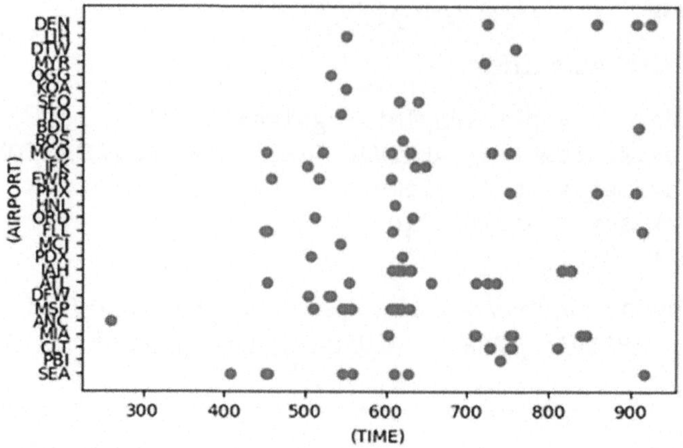

***Figure* 7.5:** *Scatterplot with Removed Outliers*

3. **Z-Score**

   a. **Detect Outliers**

```
import scipy.stats
df = pd.read_csv('flights.csv')
df.dropna(subset=['ARRIVAL_TIME'], inplace=True)
z_scores = scipy.stats.zscore(np.abs(df['ARRIVAL_TIME']))
print(z_scores)
```

The following *Figure* 7.6 shows Z score of **ARRIVAL_TIME** column values to detect the outliers.

```
0     -1.659154
1      0.459598
2      0.904981
3      0.555037
4     -2.607185
         ...
94     0.936794
95    -0.132126
96    -0.214840
97     2.355658
98    -0.342092
Name: ARRIVAL_TIME, Length: 94, dtype: float64
```

***Figure* 7.6:** *Z_score of* ARRIVAL_TIME *Column*

   b. **Remove Outliers**

```
threshold_z = 2.0
outlier_indices = np.where(z_scores > threshold_z)
no_outliers = df.drop(outlier_indices[0])
print("Original DataFrame Shape:", df.shape)
print("DataFrame Shape after Removing Outliers:", no_outliers.
shape)
```

The following *Figure* 7.7 shows the removal of outliers using Z score.

```
Original DataFrame Shape: (94, 31)
DataFrame Shape after Removing Outliers: (92, 31)
```

Figure 7.7: *Datashape before and after Outlier Removal Using Z_score*

Smoothing

1. **Moving Average**

```
df['moving_average'] = df['ARRIVAL_DELAY'].rolling
(window=3).mean()
print( df['ARRIVAL_DELAY'].tail())
print(df['moving_average'] .tail())
plt.plot(df['ARRIVAL_DELAY'], label='Original Data')
plt.plot(df['moving_average'], label='Moving Average Smoothing')
plt.legend()
plt.show()
```

The following *Figure* 7.8 depicts sharp edges in the original data as blue line, and how it is smoothened, using moving average as shown in orange line.

```
94    14.0
95   -15.0
96   -25.0
97    19.0
98   -21.0
Name: ARRIVAL_DELAY, dtype: float64
94    14.333333
95     0.666667
96    -8.666667
97    -7.000000
98    -9.000000
Name: moving_average, dtype: float64
```

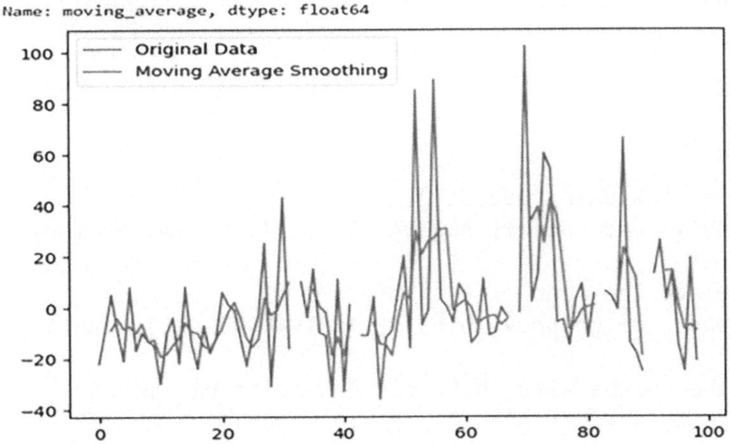

Figure 7.8: *Line Plot of* ARRIVAL_DELAY *and* ARRIVAL_DELAY *after smoothening using Moving Average*

2. **Simple Exponential**

```
from statsmodels.tsa.api import SimpleExpSmoothing
model =SimpleExpSmoothing(df['SCHEDULED_DEPARTURE']).fit
(smoothing_level=0.2)
smoothed_data = model.fittedvalues
plt.plot(df['SCHEDULED_DEPARTURE'], label='Original Data')
plt.plot(smoothed_data, label='Simple Exponential Smoothing')
plt.legend()
plt.show()
```

The following *Figure* 7.9 depicts sharp edges in the original data as blue line, and how it is smoothened, using simple exponential shown in orange line.

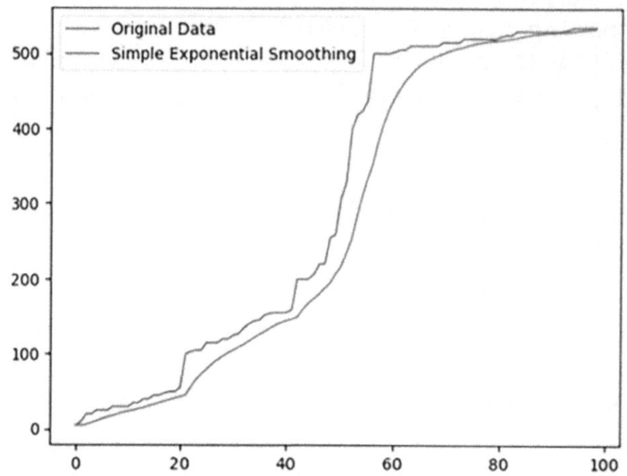

Figure 7.9: *Line Plot of the* SCHEDULED_DEPARTURE *original and* SCEDULE_DEPARTURE *after Simple Exponential Smoothening*

3. **Binning**

```
num_bins = 5

# Create bins using pd.cut()
df['bins'] = pd.cut(df['ARRIVAL_DELAY'], bins=num_bins)

# Calculate the mean of each bin
bin_means = df.groupby('bins')['ARRIVAL_DELAY'].mean()

# Replace values with their corresponding bin means
df['BINNING'] = df['bins'].map(bin_means)

plt.plot(df['ARRIVAL_DELAY'], label='Original Data')
plt.plot(df['BINNING'], label='Smoothing with Binning')
plt.legend()
```

```
plt.show()
df = df.drop('bins', axis=1)
df = df.drop('moving_average', axis=1)
df = df.drop('smoothed_values', axis=1)
df = df.drop('BINNING', axis=1)
```

The following *Figure* 7.10 depicts sharp edges in the original data as blue line, and binning has tried to smoothen it, but some are increased. With change in the number of bins, it can be smoothened further.

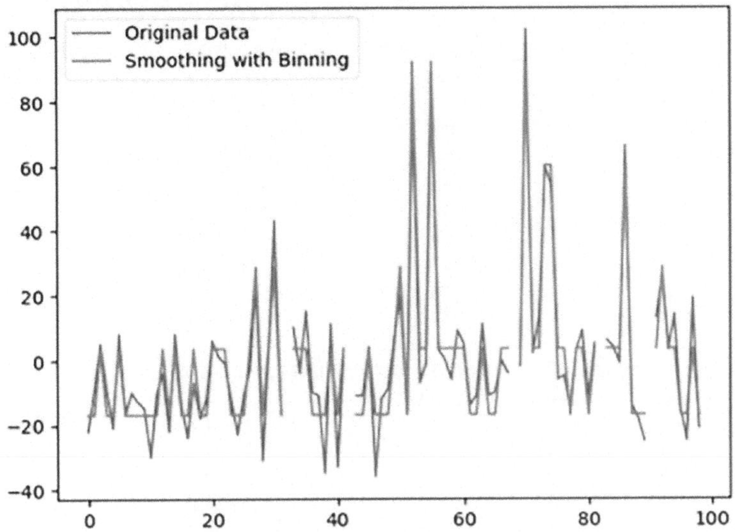

Figure 7.10: *Line Plot of* ARRIVAL_DELAY *and* ARRIVAL_DELAY *after Smoothening Using Binning Technique*

Filtering

```
filtered_df = df[df['FLIGHT_NUMBER'] > 100]
filtered_df = df.query('ARRIVAL_DELAY < 40')
filtered_df = df[(df['ARRIVAL_TIME'] > 500) & (df['DESTINATION_
AIRPORT'] == 'MIA')]
names = ['ANC', 'SFO']
filtered_df = df[df['ORIGIN_AIRPORT'].isin(names)]
filtered_df = df[df['AIRLINE'].str.startswith('A')]
print(filtered_df.head(10))
print(df.shape)
print(filtered_df.shape)
```

The following *Figure* 7.11 shows the filtered data in the dataset after applying filter to **FLIGHT_NUMBER**, having greater than 100, **ARRIVAL_DELAY** and less than 40, **ARRIVAL_TIME** is greater than 500, **DESTINATION_AIRPORT** as Mia and **ORIGIN_AIRPORT** not from '**ANC**', '**SFO**'.

	YEAR	MONTH	DAY	DAY_OF_WEEK	AIRLINE	FLIGHT_NUMBER	TAIL_NUMBER	\
0	2015	1	1	4	AS	98	N407AS	
1	2015	1	1	4	AA	2336	N3KUAA	
3	2015	1	1	4	AA	258	N3HYAA	
4	2015	1	1	4	AS	135	N527AS	
8	2015	1	1	4	AA	1112	N3LAAA	
11	2015	1	1	4	AA	1674	N853AA	
15	2015	1	1	4	AS	108	N309AS	
18	2015	1	1	4	AS	122	N413AS	
21	2015	1	1	4	AA	371	N3GXAA	
23	2015	1	1	4	AA	115	N3CTAA	

	ORIGIN_AIRPORT	DESTINATION_AIRPORT	SCHEDULED_DEPARTURE	...	ARRIVAL_TIME	\
0	ANC	SEA	5	...	408.0	
1	LAX	PBI	10	...	741.0	
3	LAX	MIA	20	...	756.0	
4	SEA	ANC	25	...	259.0	
8	SFO	DFW	30	...	532.0	
11	LAS	MIA	35	...	753.0	
15	ANC	SEA	45	...	455.0	
18	ANC	PDX	50	...	507.0	
21	SEA	MIA	100	...	939.0	
23	LAX	MIA	105	...	839.0	

	ARRIVAL_DELAY	DIVERTED	CANCELLED	CANCELLATION_REASON	AIR_SYSTEM_DELAY	\
0	-22.0	0	0	NaN	NaN	
1	-9.0	0	0	NaN	NaN	
3	-9.0	0	0	NaN	NaN	
4	-21.0	0	0	NaN	NaN	
8	-13.0	0	0	NaN	NaN	
11	-10.0	0	0	NaN	NaN	
15	-14.0	0	0	NaN	NaN	
18	-18.0	0	0	NaN	NaN	
21	1.0	0	0	NaN	NaN	
23	-12.0	0	0	NaN	NaN	

Figure 7.11: *New Dataset after Filtering*

Data Imputation

```
missing_df = pd.DataFrame({'A':[1, np.nan,24], 'B':[np.nan,
12,14], 'C': [5, np.nan,15], 'D':[8, 10, np.nan]})
print(missing_df)
```

The following *Figure* 7.12 displays the dataset considered for performing imputation techniques to handle the NaN values.

	A	B	C	D
0	1.0	NaN	5.0	8.0
1	NaN	12.0	NaN	10.0
2	24.0	14.0	15.0	NaN

Figure 7.12: *DataFrame with the Missing Data*

1. **Simple Imputation**

   a. **Mean**

```
from sklearn.impute import SimpleImputer
imputed_df = SimpleImputer(strategy="mean")
print(imputed_df.fit_transform(missing_df))
```

The following *Figure* 7.13 displays the dataset after using mean for data imputation.

```
[[ 1.   13.    5.    8. ]
 [12.5 12.   10.   10. ]
 [24.   14.   15.    9. ]]
```

Figure 7.13: *DataFrame after Mean Imputation*

   b. **Median**

```
imputed_df = SimpleImputer(strategy="median")
print(imputed_df.fit_transform(missing_df))
```

Figure 7.14 displays the dataset after using median for data imputation.

```
[[ 1.   13.    5.    8. ]
 [12.5 12.   10.   10. ]
 [24.   14.   15.    9. ]]
```

Figure 7.14: *DataFrame after Median Imputation*

2. **Hot Deck**

```
def hot_deck_imputation(df, column):
    df_copy = df.copy()
    for i, value in df_copy[column].items():
        if pd.isnull(value):
            impute = df_copy[column].dropna().sample(1).values[0]
            df_copy.at[i, column] = impute
    return df_copy

imputed_df_1=hot_deck_imputation(missing_df,'C')
imputed_df_2=hot_deck_imputation(imputed_df_1,'D')
print(imputed_df_2)
```

The following *Figure* 7.15 displays the dataset after using the hot deck technique for data imputation.

	A	B	C	D
0	1.0	NaN	5.0	8.0
1	NaN	12.0	5.0	10.0
2	24.0	14.0	15.0	10.0

Figure 7.15: *DataFrame after Hot Deck Imputation*

3. **Cold Deck**

```
cold_deck = pd.DataFrame({'A': [11, 15,13],'B':[8, 12, 24],'C':
[1, 8 ,15],
                    ‹D':[7, 10, 13]})
def cold_deck_imputation(df, column, cold_deck):
    df_copy = df.copy()
    for i, value in df_copy[column].items():
        if pd.isnull(value):
            impute = cold_deck[column].dropna().sample(1).
values[0]
            df_copy.at[i, column] = impute
    return df_copy
imputed_df_1=cold_deck_imputation(missing_df,'B',cold_deck)
imputed_df_2=cold_deck_imputation(imputed_df_1,'C',cold_deck)
print(imputed_df_2)
```

The following *Figure* 7.16 displays the dataset after using cold deck technique for data imputation.

```
      A     B     C     D
0   1.0   8.0   5.0   8.0
1   NaN  12.0   1.0  10.0
2  24.0  14.0  15.0   NaN
```

***Figure* 7.16:** *DataFrame after Cold Deck Imputation*

4. **K-Nearest Neighbor**

```
from sklearn.impute import KNNImputer
imputer = KNNImputer(n_neighbors=2, weights="uniform")
imputer.fit_transform(missing_df)
```

The following *Figure* 7.17 displays the dataset after using KNN for data imputation.

```
array([[ 1. , 13. ,  5. ,  8. ],
       [12.5, 12. , 10. , 10. ],
       [24. , 14. , 15. ,  9. ]])
```

***Figure* 7.17:** *DataFrame after KNN Imputation*

5. **MICE**

```
from sklearn.experimental import enable_iterative_imputer
from sklearn.impute import IterativeImputer
imputer = IterativeImputer()
imputed_df = imputer.fit_transform(missing_df)
print(imputed_df)
```

The following *Figure* 7.18 displays the dataset after using the MICE technique.

```
[[ 1.          9.98844347  5.          8.        ]
 [12.53322645 12.         10.01444592 10.        ]
 [24.         14.         15.         11.98847416]]
```

Figure 7.18: *DataFrame after MICE Imputation*

Conclusion

This chapter introduces data pre-processing steps, and discusses techniques in each step. Edge computing is popular for data pre-processing because pre-processing is faster on edge devices compared to the Cloud due to low data volume as well as close proximity. Data pre-processing transforms the data so as to have complete, accurate information for better analysis. This is carried on the edge of the network to reduce load on the network as well as the Cloud.

The major three steps discussed in this chapter are **data cleaning, data imputation and data fusion**. Data cleaning removes outliers, noise and captures only the relevant data from large datasets. This increases data quality and prediction accuracy of an IoT application. Data imputation replaces the missing values with an approximate value derived from past observations and related fields. Deleting records having missing data is not considered as a good option as it can create bias in the dataset, affecting the decision-making. The cleaned imputed raw sensor data is then considered for heterogeneous data fusion, to be fused with values from other sensors and other datasets.

At the end of the chapter, pre-processing steps are implemented, using python libraries to showcase how the data is cleaned, imputed and fused. The implementation has computationally low requirements, and can run on resource-constraint edge devices with ease. In the next chapter, we will see how to analyze, or in other words, perform high-level data fusion in an IoT application.

Points to Remember

- Data preprocessing is a crucial step to increase the data quality for accurate decision-making, and perform data fusion.
- Data pre-processing includes cleaning of data by filtering, smoothing and outlier detection, imputing the missing data, and fusing data from heterogeneous sources to generate relevant information.

- Outlier is a data point that is an anomaly in the acquired data due to measurement errors, variation or unusual events.
- Techniques to detect outliers are Standard Deviation, Boxplot, Clustering, and Z-Score.
- The errors in data need to be eliminated, and the process to eliminate them is smoothing. Popular smoothing techniques are Exponential, Moving Average, and Binning.
- Data filtering increases the information relevancy, and enhances data accuracy by removing the data that is irrelevant.
- Missing data is classified into three types: Missing completely at random, missing at random and missing not at random.
- Imputation is a method to predict the missing values, and the prediction is based on previous and current non-missing observations.
- Fusing datasets from different sources is a very complex task because of the dataset heterogeneity and dimensionality.
- The data fusion techniques are classified based on five different domains: Data Source Configuration, Level of Abstraction, Input/ Output and Classification by JDL.

Multiple Choice Questions

1. Data Cleaning comprises:
    a. Outlier detection
    b. Smoothing
    c. Filtering
    d. All of the Above
2. Outlier detection is done for:
    a. Error removal
    b. Finding unauthorized access
    c. Filtering
    d. Fusion

3. Noisy data is a:
    a. Heterogeneous data
    b. Missing data
    c. Erroneous data
    d. None of the Above
4. Data filtering reduces:
    a. Size
    b. Accuracy
    c. Quality
    d. Error
5. Missing at random occurs when a:
    a. Person of a specific category do not fill the survey
    b. Person do not fill the survey due to network error
    c. Person intentionally do not fill the survey
    d. None of the above
6. Technique with 'k' iterations that creates regression plot to impute the missing value:
    a. KNN
    b. MICE
    c. Miss Forest
    d. Expectation Maximization
7. Which fusion process is provided by Dasarathy?
    a. Low-level Fusion
    b. Complementary Fusion
    c. Data in-Feature out
    d. Object Refinement

Answers

1. d
2. b
3. c
4. a
5. a
6. b
7. c

Questions

1. Explain data preprocessing requirements, and briefly discuss the steps.
2. What is data cleaning, and why is it critical?
3. How Boxplot detects outliers?
4. How does Exponential Smoothing remove noise, and it works on what type of data?
5. What are different filtering methods?
6. Why is missing data imputation important?
7. How does ARIMA impute the missing data?
8. Classify the missing data techniques into univariate and multivariate.
9. What are the similarities and differences in KNN based imputation and Miss Forest?
10. Discuss fusion classification by JDL.
11. What are fusion abstraction levels?

CHAPTER 8
Leveraging Edge Intelligence

Introduction

An IoT application consists of multiple real-world things such as cars and buildings as data sources, and it is very challenging to fuse, analyze and predict future insights. To analyze heterogeneous data from different IoT devices, there are multiple information fusion models. The fusion model is selected depending on the type and complexity of the IoT data. Most IoT applications either collect the unstructured data such as images and texts, or collect different environmental conditions that have no direct relationships. Such applications require an artificial intelligence model for fusion and analysis. **Machine learning** and **deep learning** models are the most popular information fusion models that are based on artificial intelligence. Rather than deploying these AI models on the Cloud, the current IoT applications deploy them on edge devices. Intelligence provided by machine learning and deep learning models running over edge devices is known as edge intelligence, and it improves latency, provides data security and preserves privacy of the user. However, these AI models, especially deep learning models, are very heavy to be deployed on edge devices. In this chapter, we will study different information fusion models, and optimization of deep learning models for deployment on edge devices. Further, we will discuss different types of analysis requirements of the IoT application, and how they are handled at the edge device.

Structure

In this chapter, we will cover the following topics:

- Information Fusion Models
- Deep Learning and Tensor-Lite
- Real-Time Analysis

- Event-Driven Analysis
- Context-Aware Analysis
- Collaborative Analysis

Information Fusion Models

IoT applications utilize information from different sources, and fuse it to derive a more accurate and reliable interpretation of information. The process of fusion of information from multiple sources is carried out by information fusion models. It is applied in the data analysis of IoT data; however, it is different from an analytical model. An analytical model runs through data from a single source and applies classification, regression, and statistical tools, to predict the future. Information fusion models consider data from different sources, and different modalities and fuse it to predict the future. Both have predictions in common but the data in analytical models is fairly simple compared to data in information fusion models. As IoT applications acquire data from multiple sources, analysis of IoT data is performed by an information fusion model. Information fusion models and analytical models can be the same but their approach is different. For example, if a random forest is used to predict traffic congestion from multiple sources of information, then the random forest is an information fusion model. If a random forest is used to predict whether an employee will take leave from the company, based on his previous records, then the random forest applied here is an analytical model. Thus, the information fusion model is applied when the prediction is complex and requires the study of information from multiple individual sources. IoT applications apply information fusion models for data analysis to predict the future. Common information fusion models are the Bayesian network, Kalman filter, Fuzzy logic, Evidence theory and ML/DL. We have already discussed these tools theoretically in Chapter 3. Here, we will see the implementation of the fusion models on IoT data.

Bayesian Network

These are information fusion models that are based on probability, and represent data graphically as directed acyclic graphs. Multiple attributes in a data are represented as nodes, and the relationship between them is represented as edge. The relationship between attributes/nodes is probabilistic.

These networks can accurately fuse and analyze data in the presence of uncertainty and noise. Suppose we have data from three sensors. To model a Bayesian Network, we first need to define a structure that means relationship. Next, we need to determine Conditional Probability Distribution (CPD) for each of the relationships. These probabilities represent the dependency of one sensor value with another. With the created model, we directly make inferences.

Bayesian Network has been widely used for risk assessment, anomaly detection, and sensor malfunction in IoT as well as the smart home is the most popular IoT application that utilizes the Bayesian network as an information fusion model. Following is the code structure of the Bayesian network implemented in Python, using the library pgmpy. In this code, there are two sensor nodes, rain and humidity. This network predicts humidity probability in the presence of rains P(humidity|rain).

```
from pgmpy.models import BayesianNetwork
from pgmpy.factors.discrete import TabularCPD
model = BayesianNetwork()
model.add_node("Rain")
model.add_node("Humidity")
cpd_rain=TabularCPD(variable="Rain", variable_card=2,
values=[[0.4],[0.6]])
cpd_humidity=TabularCPD(variable=''Humidity", variable_
card=3,values=[[0.8],[0.2]],evidence=["Rain"],evidence_card=[2])
model.add_cpds(cpd_rain,cpd_humidity)
from pgmpy.inference import VariableElimination
inference = VariableElimination(model)
print(inference.query(variables=["Humidity"], evidence={"Rain":
1}))
```

In this code, we have a function **`TabularCPD`** that calculates the conditional probability of each node. The **`TabularCPD`** has five parameters: **`variable`**, **`variable_card`**, **`values`**, **`evidence`**, and **`evidence_card`**. The variable card tells the states of the sensor. Values is a 2D array of elements forming a table. Evidence is a node on which the probabilities are calculated and an evidence card is the number of states of the evidence node. **`Variable_card`** of Rain is 2 as it has two states that are 'Yes' or 'No'. **`Variable_card`** of humidity is also 2 as it has two states 'High' and 'Low'.

This example is for two sensors; however, it can be expanded to multiple sensors. CPD values have to be calculated manually to create the model. Further, defining the structure and CPDs for multiple sensors will increase the complexity of the network. Further, the prediction is highly subjective, and the values should be calculated efficiently to represent dependency. Calculation of CPD is also dependent on an expert and thus, the inference can be biased.

Kalman Filter

This is also a probability-based information fusion model. It assumes data in normal distribution, and the probability calculation is based on the Bayes Theorem. It is a suitable fusion model for sensor data that is noisy.

It is lightweight as it represents the sensor data in the form of a system model, and the system model is updated as per the new values. Updating a system model means updating the mean and variance of the data distribution. The most critical step is to create a system model of the Kalman filter. The system model is a mathematical representation of the data. This information fusion model is mostly applied in IoT applications that monitor trajectory or navigate either vehicles, robots or planes. The updates in the system model to have better predictions happen in real-time. For implementing Kalman filters in Python, the filterpy library is available.

```
import numpy as np
from filterpy.kalman import KalmanFilter

# Create a Kalman filter object
kf = KalmanFilter(dim_x=2, dim_z=1)

# Add the state transition matrix
kf.F = np.array([[1, 1], [0, 1]])

# Add the measurement matrix
kf.H = np.array([[1, 0]])

# Add the control transition matrix
Kf.B= np.array([[0.5], [1]])

# Add the process noise covariance matrix
kf.Q = np.array([[1, 0], [0, 1]])

# Add the measurement noise covariance matrix
kf.R = np.array([[1]])

# Initialize the state
kf.x = np.array([[0], [0]])
# Initialize the covariance
kf.P = np.array([[1, 0], [0, 1]])

# Simulate measurements and run the Kalman filter
measurements = [1, 2, 3, 4, 5]
for z in measurements:
#Predict Current system state based on previous state
   predicted_state= kf.predict()
#Update the predicted system state based on current measurement
    updated_state=kf.update(z)
```

The dimensions of the state model are passed on when initializing the Kalman filter. **dim_x** are a number of state variables, for example, (position and velocity). To represent 2 state variables, a 2D matrix is created. **dim_z** depicts the number of measurements at the current time t. A measurement means raw sensor data, for example, current position value derived from a GPS. For fusing data from multiple sensors, the **dim_z** value will increase accordingly. The state model denoted as F is represented as a state transition matrix of X and Y coordinates, and it describes the rate of change of state over linear time t. The current values of X and Y coordinates are calculated, provided by multiple sensors. A noise covariance matrix Q is designed to show covariance between X and Y in 2D form for the process which is the system state model. Measurement matrix H has the value of current measurements of X and Y, derived from the sensor data. A measurement noise covariance matrix is calculated with a constant current measurement value, and is denoted as R.

The Kalman Filter follows two steps: predict and update. In prediction, the current state is multiplied by matrix F to predict the state transition matrix at the next time step. Similarly, the covariance matrix is also predicted. The current state covariance matrix is multiplied by matrix F and F transpose and then Q is added to the output of the product to predict the covariance matrix of the next timestep. These predictions do not consider current measurement data for predicting the state of the system at time step t. With new matrix values, the Kalman Filter updates the system model. In an update, the filter calculates gain and noise, using matrix H and R that has current measurements of timestep t, and derives a new state matrix F and noise covariance matrix Q.

The limitation of the Kalman filter is that it assumes a linear system, and works on data with a Gaussian distribution. Thus, it cannot be applied to more complex real-world problems where the system state cannot be mathematically derived.

Fuzzy Logic

This information fusion model has human-like reasoning. It is part of Artificial Intelligence, and it enables thinking as a human. However, it requires expert knowledge to be designed appropriately. This fusion model is also a part of soft computing that uses approximation to solve a problem that are impossible to solve by existing tools. Soft computing is utilized for non-linear and complex real-world problems. Fuzzy logic is mostly applied to a recommender system that takes input from humans in real-time and produces expert-like decisions.

To design a fuzzy-logic-based information fusion model, popularly known as the Fuzzy Inference System, we need to know the steps to follow. The first step is to take input as antecedent and define output as consequent. The next step is to define membership functions and fuzzy sets for input and output variables. The third step is to design rules that map input to output. The rules have an if part and then part that maps input to output. The if part is known as Antecedent and then part is known as Consequent. The fourth step is to add rules to the Fuzzy Inference System and build it. The fifth step is to predict output with new inputs on the built fuzzy inference system.

We will go through the steps using a Python code sample. The **Skfuzzy** library is used to implement fuzzy logic and to import this library we need to install the scikit-fuzzy library in Python.

```
Import numpy as np
Import skfuzzy as skf
from skfuzzy import control as ctrl

# 1. Fuzzification
Temperature_sensor = ctrl.Antecedent(np.arange(15, 41, 1),
'temperature')
Light_sensor = ctrl.Antecedent(np.arange(0, 801, 1), 'light')
recommendation = ctrl.Consequent(np.arange(0, 101, 1),
'recommendation')


# Membership Functions
Temperature_sensor ['low'] = skf.trimf(Temperature_sensor.
universe, [15, 15, 25])
Temperature_sensor ['medium'] = skf.trimf(Temperature_sensor.
universe, [20, 27, 30])
Temperature_sensor ['high'] = skf.trimf(Temperature_sensor.
universe, [25, 40, 40])

Light_sensor['low'] = skf.trimf(Light_sensor.universe,
[0, 0, 450])
Light_sensor['high'] = skf.trimf(Light_sensor.universe,
[300, 800, 800])

recommendation['low'] = skf.trimf(recommendation.universe,
[0, 0, 50])
recommendation['medium'] = skf.trimf(recommendation.universe,
[20, 50, 80])
recommendation['high'] = skf.trimf(recommendation.universe,
[50, 100, 100])

# 3. Fuzzy Rules
rule1 = ctrl.Rule(Temperature_sensor ['low'] & Light_sensor
['low'], recommendation['low'])
rule2 = ctrl.Rule(Temperature_sensor ['medium'] | Light_sensor
['medium'], recommendation['medium'])
Rule3 = ctrl.Rule(Temperature_sensor ['high'] & Light_sensor
['high'], recommendation['high'])

# 4. Fuzzy Inference System
recommendation_ctrl = ctrl.ControlSystem([rule1, rule2, rule3])
recommendation_sim = ctrl.ControlSystemSimulation(recommendation_
```

```
ctrl)

#5. Output

recommendation_sim.input['Temperature_sensor'] = 25
recommendation_sim.input[' Light_sensor '] = 700

# Compute output
recommendation_sim.compute()

# Print the recommendation score
print(recommendation_sim.output['recommendation'])
```

In the preceding code, the data from the temperature sensor and light sensor is acquired as Antecedents and their fuzzy sets are created. The fuzzy set of temperature sensor data has three values: low, medium and high. The fuzzy set of light sensors has two values: low and high. A recommendation variable to recommend fan speed is considered as output (consequent). A triangular membership function is considered to map input values to fuzzy sets. Each fuzzy set has a range of membership functions. Next, three rules are created with antecedent and consequent. Finally, the fuzzy inference system mode is designed by adding the rules and simulation.

Fuzzy logic requires a good number of resources for computation and storage for large-scale IoT applications with a high number of sensors, each having a large number of fuzzy sets and rules. Thus, this fusion model may not be feasible for edge devices. Further, the if-then rules are highly subjective to experts, and thus, can cause bias in predictions.

Evidence Theory

The Dempster-Shafer's Theory which is based on evidence theory is used as a tool to fuse IoT sensor data. The Dempster-Shafer Theory is a mathematical expression that collects information from different sources as evidence, combines them with belief and takes a judgement. It is like a detective brain that is joining cases to solve a situation. It is a useful tool when there is uncertain information or conflicting evidence.

When different sensors or other data sources provide an environmental state, and when we are confused about which source to believe the most, Dempster-Shafer comes to the rescue. It comes up with the most accurate environment state combining all environment states predicted by different IoT sensors. There are four terms that need to be known before implementation. These are:

- **Frame of Discernment:** A collection of hypotheses that are possible. For example, the weather can be sunny, cloudy, rainy, snowy or windy, or whether performance can be excellent, good, average, or poor.

- **Focal Set:** The set of hypotheses is the assigned mass and the new set is called focal set. The sum of assigned masses is 1 but these hypotheses can overlap each other. Mass is not similar to probability. The mass denotes evidence or degree of belief. It shows the weightage of each hypothesis.
- **Dempster-Shafer combination rule:** It combines the masses from different evidences and the combination is known as joint mass. This rule calculates the degree of overlap. For example, to find joint mass for hypothesis A and masses provided by evidence 1 and evidence 2 is m1 and m2, respectively, then according to the rule, the formula is (m1 ⊕ m2) (A).
- **Belief:** It is a quantity that tells total support for a hypothesis and is represented in (0,1) where 0 is no support and 1 is very certain about the hypothesis.
- **Plausibility:** It is a quantity that shows a lack of support for a hypothesis and is represented in (0,1). The equation is Plausibility (Hypothesis A) = 1 – Belief (Negation of Hypothesis A).

Following is the code for detecting, whether there was an intrusion in the house with respect to motion sensor data attached to the door, and data from the vibration sensor attached to the gate.

```
import dempster_shafer as ds
fod = ds.FrameOfDiscernment(['In', 'Out'])
# Sensor 1
motion_sensor_data = ds.FocalSet(fod,{"Out": 0.6, "In": 0.2,
"Out,In": 0.2})

# Sensor 2
vibration_sensor_data = ds.FocalSet(fod,{"Out": 0.5, "In": 0.4,
"Out,In": 0.1})

# Combine evidence using the dampster-shafer rule in user-defined
function dempster_Shafer_combine

combined_data = Dempster_Shafer_combine(motion_sensor_data,
vibration_sensor_data)

lattice = ds.Lattice(fod, combined_data)
belief = lattice.bel()
plausibility = lattice.pl()

print("Belief:", belief)
print("Plausibility:", plausibility)
```

Dempster-Shafer theory is computationally expensive, and is dependent on masses assigned which is subjective, and can cause bias in results. Further, if the data from multiple sensors is highly overlapping, then the results can be counter-intuitive, which means, it would not be as expected.

Machine Learning and Deep Learning

Machine learning is a tool that utilizes intelligence to fuse data from multiple IoT sensors. Machine learning techniques are classification, clustering, and regression. With learning algorithms, the data is provided and it somehow learns the pattern of the data and then accurately predicts the future insights. The best of this tool is that it can model large-scale data and a high number of sensors with ease. Libraries that provide machine learning in Python are TensorFlow, Keras, Torch and Scikit-learn.

The machine learning models need to be trained on the huge data. Then the trained machine learning model is tested on some unknown data. If the model accuracy is good during testing, then the model is implemented in real-time applications. The biggest advantage of using Python is that the code can be converted to automation scripts that can run independently on the cloud or edge.

Some ML models that are being popularly used as information fusion models are:

- Random Forest
- K-Nearest Neighbor
- Neural Network
- Support Vector Machine
- Deep Neural Network

We will see each of these ML models performing information fusion on IoT sensor data. We will consider the dataset "Heart Failure Clinical Records" (Link: https://archive.ics.uci.edu/dataset/519/heart+failure+clinical+records) which is available in the UCI repository in CSV format. The libraries that are common in all algorithms are:

```
import pandas as pd
import numpy as np
import seaborn as sns
import matplotlib.pyplot as plt
df = pd.read_csv("heart_failure_clinical_records_dataset.csv")
X = df.iloc[:,:-1].values
y = df.iloc[:,-1].values
from sklearn.model_selection import train_test_split
X_train, X_test, y_train, y_test = train_test_split(X, y, test_
size=0.2, random_state=42)
```

To train the machine learning models, the dataset is imported, and a train-test split is performed on it. Train-test split means the dataset is randomly divided into training dataset and test dataset. The value of test data is 0.2 in the above code, which means 20% of the randomly selected dataset is test data and the remaining 80% is for training.

Random Forest

Random forest is an ensemble-based method that combines the results of multiple decision trees running in parallel. Decision-tree splits data based on a decision and each node has one decision to make. The final decision is at the leaf nodes. The leaf node that the data reaches in a decision tree. This is the final decision for that data. The trees created in random forest are uncorrelated and thus every data will not reach the same leaf node in each of the decision trees. This way, a random forest makes a better decision compared to a decision tree alone. This model is best suitable for both classification and regression models and performs supervised learning. In the code, **n_estimators** is the number of decision trees and **random_state 0** means generating different results after every execution.

```
# import Random Forest classifier
from sklearn.ensemble import RandomForestClassifier
# instantiate the classifier
rfc = RandomForestClassifier(n_estimators=100, random_state=0)
# fit the model
rfc.fit(X_train, y_train)
print(rfc.predict(X_test))
```

K-Nearest Neighbor

It is a classification machine learning algorithm that finds the nearest neighbor of the data for classification. The value of k is selected that denotes the number of neighbors. The parameter is n_neighbors which has a value of K. It is a distance-based classification and groups the data points that are neighbors. It can follow the Manhattan distance, hamming distance, minkowski distance and Euclidean distance and the default is minkowski. The distance can be provided as a parameter metric in the classifier.

```
# import KNNclassifier
from sklearn.neighbors import KNeighborsClassifier
# Instantiate the classifier
knn = KNeighborsClassifier(n_neighbors=7)
# fit the model
knn.fit(X_train, y_train)
print(knn.predict(X_test))
```

Multi-Layer Perceptron

These machine learning models are efficient in modelling non-linear, complex data relationships. It is a neural network having an input layer, hidden layer and output layer. The input layer has nodes equal to the number of features. The hidden layer is hyperparameters. The output layer is the prediction. If it is a binary classification, the output layer has one node. One node of the output layer can also produce continuous results in a regression. The parameters in the classifier are hidden layer dimensions, maximum iterations to train the ML model and random_state similar to a random forest.

```
# import MLP
from sklearn.neural_network import MLPClassifier
# Instantiate the classifier
mlp = MLPClassifier(hidden_layer_sizes=(64, 32), max_iter=1000,
random_state=42)
# fit the model
mlp.fit(X_train, y_train)
print(mlp.predict(X_test))
```

Support Vector Machine

This machine learning model is good for regression as well as classification, but more accurate in classification problems. It finds a hyperplane that clearly separates the classes. If the data points are not easily classifiable, SVM implements a technique called kernel that maps the data points to high dimensional space, and the data becomes separable there. Support vectors are data points that lie closest to the hyperplane and thus these points help decision-making. There are three parameters passed into the classifier, C as the regularization parameter, kernel type tells SVM kernel such as linear, polynomial, sigmoid, or radial basis function (rbf, also known as Gaussian) and default is rbf. Scale is the kernel coefficient of rbf.

```
# import SVM
from sklearn.svm import SVC
# Instantiate the classifier
svm = SVC(kernel="rbf", gamma=0.5, C=1.0)
# fit the model
svm.fit(X_train, y_train)
print(svm.predict(X_test))
```

Deep Neural Network

Once the preceding machine learning models are trained with huge amounts of data, they can be saved using Python's Pickel library. The pre-trained model is low in size and can be easily implemented on edge devices providing real-time predictions.

However, a deep neural network is trained on more complex data and thus, has a high number of hidden layers. Popular deep neural network models are Convolutional Neural Networks, Recurrent Neural Networks, Long-Short Term Memory Neural Networks, Gated Recurrent Units and Encoders-Decoders.

- **Convolution Neural Network (CNN):** These networks are used for computer vision-related tasks. They are good at representing images in a 3D model, extracting features and classifying the data. For example, it can train from known cat and dog images to predict an unknown image has either cat or dog accurately.
- **Recurrent Neural Network (RNN):** CNN has no memory but RNNs are popular as they have a memory that considers prior information too to predict future information from the current. It preserves the context of the input data with a hidden state.
- **Long-Short Term Memory (LSTM):** It is a type of RNN and it has a cell in the hidden layers. Each cell has three gates: input gate, output gate and forget gate. These gates control the flow of information, and important repetitive words are preserved for a really long time and unused words are dropped after looking into long-term data.
- **Gated Recurrent Units (GRUs):** This model works similarly to LSTM but the difference is it has only two gates in the cell, a reset gate and an update gate. Since the architecture is simple, it is more computationally efficient.
- **Encoder-Decoder:** This type of ML model is used for sequence-to-sequence tasks where input and output are sequences. It is popularly used for language translations carried out by a machine. Encoding comprehends the input sequence and decoder outputs a sequence, depending upon understanding. Encoder-decoder maps complex relationships between sequences by understanding the context.

The architecture of pre-trained deep neural network models is large, and is not feasible to run on edge devices. To utilize deep learning on edge devices, python came up with a tensor-lite library that optimizes the size of pre-trained models for edge implementation.

To perform an infusion fusion model in deep learning with the input of different modes, the architecture is different. For example, self-driving cars require video+ LiDAR data. For each input mode, a deep learning model is created. The results from each of the DL models are then fused for predictions. The model's fusion happens in the encoding phase. Once a single output is captured, it is decoded. A popular information fusion model in deep learning is image captioning (image + text), and it requires deep study for implementation.

Model	Strengths	Limitations	Suitable For
Bayesian Network	Works with uncertainty	Manual Cumulative Probability Distributions	Smart Homes, Risk Assessment
Kalman Filter	Lightweight, real-time	Linear-only, assumes Gaussian	Navigation, Robotics
Fuzzy Logic	Human-like reasoning	Subjective, Resource heavy	Recommendation systems
Evidence Theory	Deals with conflicting information	Biased, computationally heavy	Intrusion detection, Belief models
ML/DL Models	High accuracy, Scalable	Requiring large data, training time	Complex IoT applications, Real-time edge computing

Table 8.1: *Comparison of Different Information Fusion Models*

Challenges in machine learning and deep learning as information fusion models are that they require huge amounts of data to train, the training requires a lot of time for good accuracy and hyper-parameter tuning is extensive as it needs to be most optimal. However, once trained, they are easy to deploy on a real-time application at edge devices with the help of optimization techniques. *Table* 8.1 compares the information fusion models as per strengths, weakness and suitability. In the next section, we will study the optimization techniques with an application example.

Deep Learning and TensorFlow-Lite

It is challenging to implement a deep learning model on edge devices as these models are very huge in size and require high computational power. On the other hand, edge devices have very limited computation power as well as battery life, to run a DL model autonomously. To efficiently utilize edge devices for implementing deep learning models, the models are optimized during training or after training. Two popular optimization techniques are model pruning and quantization. These techniques are provided by TensorFlow as well as PyTorch with libraries such as TensorFlow lite and PyTorch mobile respectively.

- **Model Pruning:** In this type of optimization, the neural connections that have insignificant weights are removed. This way the size of the model is reduced, and it becomes faster to load and process on edge devices. Pruning can be done before or after training.
- **Quantization:** It is an optimization technique that converts float datatype weights into integers, or 16-bit float numbers. This way the weights stored in the memory consume less space, optimizing the memory utilization of the model.

IoT applications that deploy deep learning on edge using optimization techniques are wearable health monitoring devices, real-time object tracking, augmented reality and smart homes. To showcase optimization, we will implement a convolution neural network, using the TensorFlow library, and then optimize it using tensor-lite. With optimization, a tinyML model is created that can be deployed on edge devices with ease.

Steps to optimize the deep learning model before deployment on edge devices are:

1. **Import Libraries:**

```
import tensorflow as tf
import pandas as pd
import numpy as np
from tensorflow import keras
from keras.datasets import mnist
import matplotlib.pyplot as plt
from tensorflow.keras.models import Sequential
from tensorflow.keras.layers import Dense, Flatten, Conv2D,
MaxPooling2D, Dropout
```

2. **Load and Pre-Process MNIST Data:**

```
(x_train, y_train), (x_test, y_test) = mnist.load_data()
print(type(x_train))
x_train = (x_train/ 255) - 0.5
x_test = (x_test/ 255) - 0.5
x_train=np.expand_dims(x_train, axis=3)
x_test=np.expand_dims(x_test,axis=3)
print(x_train.shape) # (60000, 28, 28,1)
print(x_test.shape) # (10000,28,28,1)
print(y_test.shape)  #(10000,)
```

3. **Create a Convolution Neural Network**

```
CNN=Sequential()
CNN.add(MaxPooling2D(pool_size=2))
CNN.add(Flatten())
CNN.add(Dropout(0.5))
CNN.add(Dense(120,activation='relu'))
CNN.add(Dense(10,activation='softmax'))
CNN.compile(optimizer='adam',loss='crossentropy',
metrics=['accuracy'])
from tensorflow.keras.utils import to_categorical
CNN.fit(x_train,to_categorical(y_train),epochs=50)
predictions = CNN.predict(x_test)
```

Model training for 50 epochs with increasing accuracy and decreasing loss is shown in *Figure* 8.1. We can see from figure that epoch 42 and epoch 50 have overall the same values of accuracy and loss, and thus, training can be reduced to 42 epochs to save training time.

```
1875/1875 ━━━━━━━━━━━━━━━━━━━━ 22s 12ms/step - accuracy: 0.9924 - loss: 0.0242
Epoch 42/50
1875/1875 ━━━━━━━━━━━━━━━━━━━━ 21s 11ms/step - accuracy: 0.9923 - loss: 0.0233
Epoch 43/50
1875/1875 ━━━━━━━━━━━━━━━━━━━━ 21s 11ms/step - accuracy: 0.9919 - loss: 0.0249
Epoch 44/50
1875/1875 ━━━━━━━━━━━━━━━━━━━━ 21s 11ms/step - accuracy: 0.9917 - loss: 0.0242
Epoch 45/50
1875/1875 ━━━━━━━━━━━━━━━━━━━━ 21s 11ms/step - accuracy: 0.9923 - loss: 0.0226
Epoch 46/50
1875/1875 ━━━━━━━━━━━━━━━━━━━━ 21s 11ms/step - accuracy: 0.9917 - loss: 0.0238
Epoch 47/50
1875/1875 ━━━━━━━━━━━━━━━━━━━━ 21s 11ms/step - accuracy: 0.9920 - loss: 0.0233
Epoch 48/50
1875/1875 ━━━━━━━━━━━━━━━━━━━━ 21s 11ms/step - accuracy: 0.9922 - loss: 0.0223
Epoch 49/50
1875/1875 ━━━━━━━━━━━━━━━━━━━━ 21s 11ms/step - accuracy: 0.9925 - loss: 0.0227
Epoch 50/50
1875/1875 ━━━━━━━━━━━━━━━━━━━━ 21s 11ms/step - accuracy: 0.9921 - loss: 0.0223
<keras.src.callbacks.history.History at 0x192ce3a8920>
```

Figure 8.1: *Screenshot of Model Training from 42 to 50 epochs*

4. **Check Results**

```
from sklearn.metrics import confusion_matrix
cm = confusion_matrix(y_test, predicted_labels)
plt.imshow(cm, interpolation="nearest", cmap=plt.cm.Blues)
plt.colorbar()
plt.xlabel("Predicted class")
plt.ylabel("Actual class")
plt.show()
```

The following *Figure* 8.2 shows the confusion matrix between actual value and predicted value, and the diagonal is marked with blue, confirming that the predicted value is close to actual.

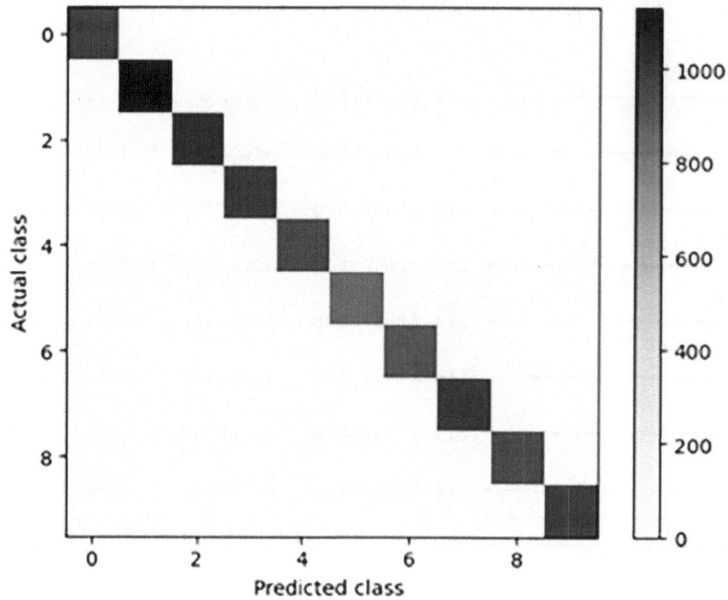

Figure 8.2: *Confusion Matrix of Actual and Predicted Values*

5. **Check the size of the model, and save the model as '.keras' for optimization**

```
CNN.summary()
CNN.save('CNN_edge.keras')
keras_model=tf.keras.models.load_model('CNN_edge.keras')
```

The following *Figure* 8.3 summarizes every layer of the model, describing its shape and total parameters. Further, it shows the total size of the trained model which is 1.87 MB. It also shows parameters that can be optimized.

Model: "sequential_3"

Layer (type)	Output Shape	Param #
conv2d_3 (Conv2D)	(None, 26, 26, 8)	80
max_pooling2d_2 (MaxPooling2D)	(None, 13, 13, 8)	0
flatten_2 (Flatten)	(None, 1352)	0
dropout_1 (Dropout)	(None, 1352)	0
dense_4 (Dense)	(None, 120)	162,360
dense_5 (Dense)	(None, 10)	1,210

Total params: 490,952 (1.87 MB)
Trainable params: 163,650 (639.26 KB)
Non-trainable params: 0 (0.00 B)
Optimizer params: 327,302 (1.25 MB)

Figure 8.3: *Summary of the Trained Model*

6. **Optimization with Pruning**

```
import tensorflow_model_optimization as tfmot
prune_low_magnitude = tfmot.sparsity.keras.prune_low_magnitude
CNN_pruning = prune_low_magnitude(CNN_original)
CNN_pruning.compile(optimizer='adam',
              loss=keras.losses.SparseCategoricalCrossentropy
(from_logits=True),
              metrics=[‹accuracy›])
CNN_pruning.summary()
```

The following *Figure* 8.4 shows a summary of the trained model after pruning. After pruning, parameters in each of the layers are reduced, reducing the overall size of the model to 1.25 MB.

```
Model: "sequential_1"
_________________________________________________________________
 Layer (type)                Output Shape              Param #
=================================================================
 prune_low_magnitude_conv2d  (None, 26, 26, 8)         154
  (PruneLowMagnitude)

 prune_low_magnitude_max_po  (None, 13, 13, 8)         1
 oling2d (PruneLowMagnitude
 )

 prune_low_magnitude_flatte  (None, 1352)              1
 n (PruneLowMagnitude)

 prune_low_magnitude_dropou  (None, 1352)              1
 t (PruneLowMagnitude)

 prune_low_magnitude_dense   (None, 120)               324602
 (PruneLowMagnitude)

 prune_low_magnitude_dense_  (None, 10)                2412
 1 (PruneLowMagnitude)

=================================================================
Total params: 327171 (1.25 MB)
Trainable params: 163650 (639.26 KB)
Non-trainable params: 163521 (638.78 KB)
```

Figure 8.4: *Summary of the Pruned Model after Training*

7. **Optimization with Dynamic Quantization**

```
converter = tf.lite.TFLiteConverter.from_keras_model(keras_model)
converter.optimizations = [tf.lite.Optimize.DEFAULT]
tflite_quant_model = converter.convert()
#Save the model in a .tffile
open("tflite_quant_model.tflite", "wb").write(tflite_quant_model)

#Reduced size of TFlite file
import os
# Get file size in bytes for a given model
```

```
file_size_bytes=os.stat('tflite_quant_model.tflite').st_size
file_size_mb = file_size_bytes / (1024 * 1024)
file_size_mb=round(file_size_mb, 2)
print(str(file_size_mb) + " " + "MB")
```

The following *Figure* 8.5 displays the size of the trained model after dynamic quantization, and the size of quantized trained model is 0.16 MB.

```
Saved artifact at '/tmp/tmpdsozjp4u'. The following endpoints are available:

* Endpoint 'serve'
  args_0 (POSITIONAL_ONLY): TensorSpec(shape=(None, 28, 28, 1), dtype=tf.float32, name='input_layer')
Output Type:
  TensorSpec(shape=(None, 10), dtype=tf.float32, name=None)
Captures:
  139486516663824: TensorSpec(shape=(), dtype=tf.resource, name=None)
  139486516664400: TensorSpec(shape=(), dtype=tf.resource, name=None)
  139486516663248: TensorSpec(shape=(), dtype=tf.resource, name=None)
  139486516665552: TensorSpec(shape=(), dtype=tf.resource, name=None)
  139486516665744: TensorSpec(shape=(), dtype=tf.resource, name=None)
  139486516664208: TensorSpec(shape=(), dtype=tf.resource, name=None)
0.16 MB
```

Figure 8.5: *Output Screenshot Showing the Size of Model after Dynamic Quantization*

8. **Optimization with 16-bit Float Quantization**

```
converter = tf.lite.TFLiteConverter.from_keras_model(keras_model)
converter.optimizations = [tf.lite.Optimize.DEFAULT]
converter.target_spec.supported_types = [tf.float16]
# Converting the model.
tflite_fp16_model = converter.convert()

# Saving the model.
with open('fp_16_model.tflite', 'wb') as f:
  f.write(tflite_fp16_model)
#Reduced size of TFlite file
import os
# Get file size in bytes for a given model
file_size_bytes=os.stat('tflite_quant_model.tflite').st_size
file_size_mb = file_size_bytes / (1024 * 1024)
file_size_mb=round(file_size_mb, 2)
print(str(file_size_mb) + " " + "MB")
```

The following *Figure* 8.6 shows that the output size of the trained model has decreased to 0.16 MB after performing 16-bit quantization.

```
Saved artifact at '/tmp/tmp0sml02mz'. The following endpoints are available:

* Endpoint 'serve'
  args_0 (POSITIONAL_ONLY): TensorSpec(shape=(None, 28, 28, 1), dtype=tf.float32, name='input_layer')
Output Type:
  TensorSpec(shape=(None, 10), dtype=tf.float32, name=None)
Captures:
  139486516663824: TensorSpec(shape=(), dtype=tf.resource, name=None)
  139486516664400: TensorSpec(shape=(), dtype=tf.resource, name=None)
  139486516663248: TensorSpec(shape=(), dtype=tf.resource, name=None)
  139486516665552: TensorSpec(shape=(), dtype=tf.resource, name=None)
  139486516665744: TensorSpec(shape=(), dtype=tf.resource, name=None)
  139486516664208: TensorSpec(shape=(), dtype=tf.resource, name=None)
0.16 MB
```

Figure 8.6: *Output Screenshot Showing the Size of Model after 16-bit Quantization*

Clearly, the optimization technique has decreased the size of the model, and the optimized size fits in the limited memory of edge devices. As is seen in the model summary in step 5, the original CNN size is 1.85 MB. After pruning in Step 6, the size of the model is reduced to 1.25 MB. In steps 7 and 8, Quantization has reduced the size of the model to 0.16 MB.

Advantages of Edge Deployment:

- Data Privacy
- Real-Time Service
- Personalized
- User experience increased
- Neural networks, once trained, are transferable solutions to any device
- Independent of Limited Network
- Cloud cost reduced
- Offline service
- Low battery power consumption

Disadvantages of Edge Deployment with Optimization:

- The reduction of computational complexity of a model can negatively affect accuracy.
- Hardware incompatibility for low-bit quantization.

Real-Time Analysis

Real-time analysis is a very crucial and in-demand analysis type. Some of the IoT applications such as a heart attack detector, or car accident detector, require timeliness in response. These are time-critical applications that require real-time analysis and highly accurate decisions. An ordering meal app or a flight booking application requires real-time service as it can lead to delays in bookings, leading to inconvenience to the user. The main two steps in real-time analytics are quick data ingestion and quick analysis and reporting of decisions. Real-time data is known as streaming data and to store the data for analysis from a huge number of sensors, there exists real-time databases.

It is expected that real-time analysis provides insights in the blink of an eye even when streaming data is too large. Streaming platforms, real-time databases and analytics framework as shown in *Figure* 8.7. A real-time analytical framework empowers the user to query information in real-time and visualize data in motion. The data for analysis is a time-series data where the timestamp of the data is the most important factor and next is accurate service. Real-time machine learning provides insights instantly and is suitable for dynamic environments. The ML model for real-time learns as well as adapts as the new data comes in. Some applications for real-time ML are fraud detection, smart grid management, route optimization during travel in a vehicle, surveillance through video, and so on.

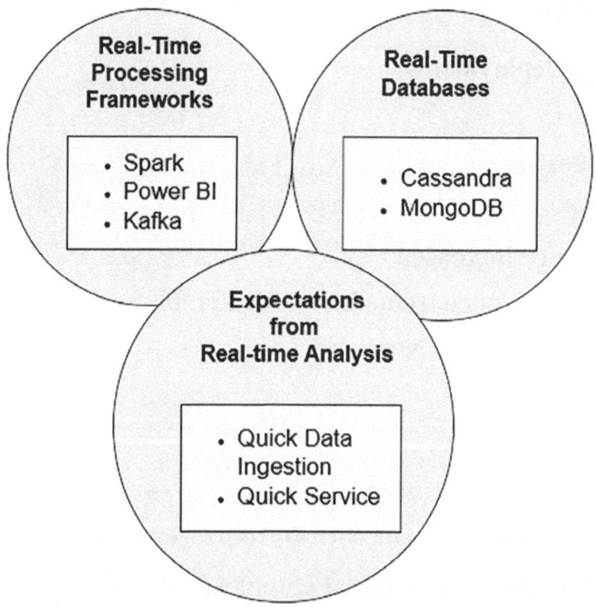

Figure 8.7: *Components of Real-time Analysis*

The steps to model real-time ML is to train the model with the collected dataset, and then test it. If the test accuracy is good, then the pre-trained model is deployed for analyzing the online data. If the model is not performing well in real-time, it is again re-trained, re-tested and re-deployed. The continuous train, test and deploy process gets easier with the help of containerization technology. Thus, real-time analysis on complex real-time large-scale data is usually done by pre-trained, optimized machine learning and deep learning models at the edge device to deliver faster service.

Real-time databases are part of Online Analytical Processing (OLAP) databases that provide fast, complex, and parallel queries on large-scale data. The data in real-time analytics gets stale in seconds, the expected delay in service is in milliseconds, and is collected from 1 million users at a given instance. Popular real-time tools are Power BI (a visualization tool), Kafka and Spark (Streaming platforms), Cassandra and MongoDB (Real-Time Database). We will study streaming platforms for real-time analysis in the next chapter.

Real-time analytics is now growing and serving applications in the area of AR/VR, self-driving cars, UAVs, and healthcare, and is very crucial as well as beneficial these days as well as in the near future.

Event-Driven Analysis

This is a new type of analysis that has provided a major breakthrough in IoT applications. Rather than studying continuous sensor data and extracting patterns, events are captured and acted upon in real-time. What exactly is an event? Well, to explain it nicely, we will take an example of an IoT application that predicts, prevents, or tackles forest fires in real-time. To predict and prevent forest fires, we need continuous sensor data that detects fire. But if there is already a fire, then it is considered an event. The event-based sensor data is analyzed to call fire stations in real-time, telling them the fire location and the number of resources with respect to its spread. Other events that can be captured by this application are smokers and campfires through cameras, calling forest officials in real-time to prevent the fire, and also alerting the people in the forest with an alarm system.

We can see how event-driven analysis has opened a lot of capabilities and possibilities in an IoT application. Thus, events can be a user response on a website with clicks, a disaster, a critical health-related problem, activities of an old person, suspicion, fraud, video surveillance, motion detection, maintenance issues or failure. Event-based analysis is similar to real-time analysis, and the only difference is streaming events, and not the streaming data. There are some hardware and network-based events that are considered to do optimized resource utilization and computational offloading on edge devices. Event-driven analysis has improved services, user experiences, accuracy in real-time decision-making, and trust in applications.

Complex Event Processing (CEP) is popular in IoT to deal with event-driven analysis on streaming events. The events may or may not be stored for analysis. This processing involves capturing multiple events and analyzing the "Cause and effect" relationship between them in real-time. The analysis is based on mapping the events over a pattern, and determining action in real-time. Complex event processing can be implemented on Spark, Flink, Hadoop and other streaming data platforms. Complex event processing is different from stream processing in the way data is collected and analyzed. In stream processing, the data of an individual event is collected, processed and analyzed.

However, in event-driven analysis with CEP streams of multiple events are captured at the same time, analyzed and mapped to a pattern to exactly understand the current situation. The current situation is considered a complex event that cannot be directly sensed, and requires a fusion of multiple events.

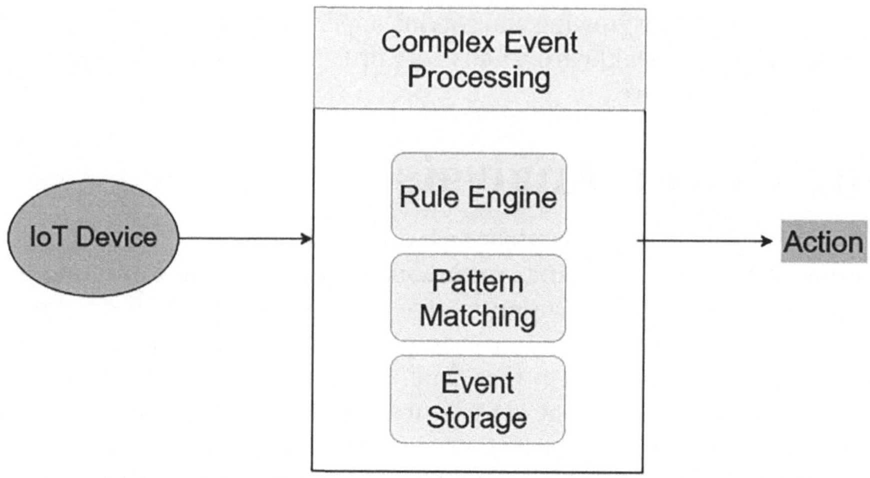

Figure 8.8: *Architecture of Complex Event Processing* (CEP)

Three functions are required to build a CEP: Event Patterns, Event Abstraction and Event-driven Architecture. The architecture is shown in *Figure* 8.8. The event patterns, that are to be matched with generated complex events, are predefined and stored in the rule engine. The events are combined to get a complex event with the higher-level abstraction of events that made it up. To provide real-time analysis of streaming event inputs performing complex event processing, an event-driven architecture is mandatory. The publish/subscribe model is a popular event-driven architecture that most IoT applications utilize to implement event-driven analysis.

Designing event patterns is the toughest part of designing an event-driven analysis. Another challenge is event correlation to find a complex event. Deploying CEP takes a lot of time in learning the concept, query language, and pattern designing. Further, it requires a huge number of resources to acquire and process large numbers of events, and may cause delayed responses.

CEP can be implemented on a stand-alone edge device if the number of events is low, event correlation is not very complex and event patterns are less. If a full-fledged CEP needs to run on edge, the edge devices need to be collaborated to deploy CEP. There exists CEP-based event-driven analysis on mobile devices that perform real-time event analysis on edge. The IoT applications with mobile device-based event-driven analysis activity monitoring systems, smart home and recommendation systems. Sensor data from a mobile device is leveraged to capture events and provided to the CEP engine that is specifically designed for mobile devices. Define event patterns and event-triggered actions that need to be manually coded in the CEP engine. Deploying CEP on edge devices needs consideration of battery consumption and network connectivity issues.

Context-Aware Analysis

Context means the surroundings. This book is in the context of IoT applications. The chapters in this book are dependent on, and related to the context. Similarly, every environment has a context. The sensor senses an entity's activities but the activities are highly influenced by the context in the current environment. Let us take a general example to understand the context. Suppose an IoT application autonomously controls the lighting of the home. Just sensing if the environment is dark or lit will not provide efficient light control. However, it will consider other contexts, such as if there is a person in the room, or time of the day or the weather outside, mood of the person, then how many lights need to be turned on in the given room can also be managed. Another example is a self-driving car that depending on the current context, drives autonomously and efficiently. The context around a vehicle is traffic, weather, road type, country rules, current speed limits, and so on.

Basically, the context adds meaning to collected data. This meaningful data then provides more accurate information about the current state. Some of the existing context-aware applications are automatic screen brightness adjustment, Google Map directions update in real-time and recommendations on streaming platforms based on view history where a person's history is the context. Even in the healthcare sector, the context may be able to decode the illness and provide accurate medications. Even a general physician asks all the context of the patient such as food, activities, sitting time, how many family members, and sleeping time, before prescribing medicines.

Context collection in IoT is done via specific sensors separately. For example, a camera sensor, GPS and other web sources that tell current weather or social network data help in providing the context of the system, entity, or user. Once the contextual data is collected, it is analyzed using machine learning techniques and accordingly, the IoT application adapts the context and provides relevant service.

The advantage of context-aware analysis in IoT applications is that it personalizes the application, providing user satisfaction and as well as provides efficient service. When an edge device acquires data with context, analyses it and adapts in real-time, the computing is known as context-aware edge computing. Smartphones and wearable devices are popular context-aware edge devices.

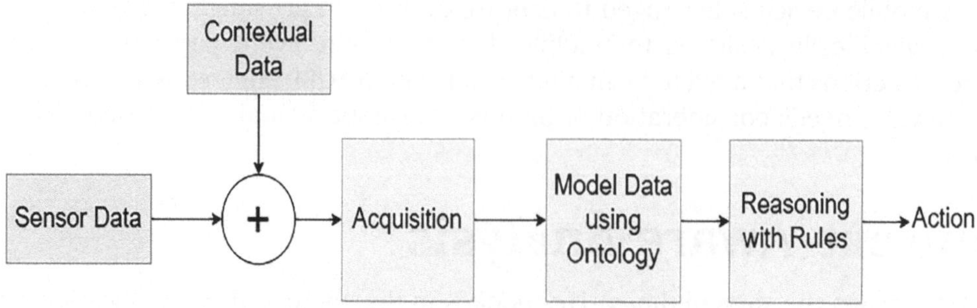

Figure 8.9: *Steps of Context-aware Analysis*

The steps for context-aware analysis as shown in *Figure* 8.9 are as follows:

1. **Context Acquisition:** Contextual data from sensors are collected and pre-processed in this step.
2. **Context Modelling:** A structured representation of context is modelled using ontology and semantics. The modelling includes developing algorithms that efficiently combine the contextual data from multiple sensors, and define relationships between the context. This step builds a bigger picture of the environment or entity context.
3. **Context Reasoning:** Train machine learning models with rules to infer high-level information from the context data. This high-level information helps in adapting to the current environment in real-time, and provides accurate decision-making.

The reasoning engine helps in building a context-aware system. This engine is intelligent, and mimics the human brain with the help of rules and logic to make contextual and adaptive decisions. A reasoning engine has three main components: A knowledge base to structure the raw context, an engine and a user interface. Reasoning are of four types: Rule-based, probabilistic, semantic, and hybrid. Rule-based reasoning has a predefined set of rules on which intelligent decisions are made. Probabilistic reasoning utilizes statistical models to infer. Semantic reasoning utilizes ontologies, and knowledge graphs to deduce context for inferences.

A popular reasoning engine in IoT applications is Complex Event Processing (CEP). It analyses the streaming data to detect context with the help of rule-based reasoning.

Collaborative Analysis

The analysis that is distributed to multiple devices, and carried out in collaboration is known as collaborative analysis. This is a popular analysis in edge computing as individual edge devices have limited capabilities to analyze IoT data alone. This analysis is specific to IoT applications where data is very large-scale, streaming and requires real-time results. Collaborative learning is also known as team-based learning, peer-based learning, and cooperative learning.

An IoT application that can benefit from collaborative analysis at the edge is a traffic light management system. The traffic lights may have an attached Raspberry Pi that detects current traffic through a camera, and then performs collaborative analysis on overall traffic. Inferring from analysis, they adjust the time of individual traffic lights where traffic is higher to reduce road traffic, and mitigate blockages.

Communication between edge devices performing collaborative analysis follows the following steps:

1. Each device performs analysis locally and produces a summary.
2. The analysis summary from the edge device is communicated to all other edge devices in the network.

Federated Learning

Federated Learning is a part of the collaborative analysis. It is a distributed approach to train machine learning models. This learning aims to keep the data private by training models at the network edge, and not at a global, centralized server such as Cloud. Therefore, the main aim of federated learning is to work with the sensitive data, and provide privacy as well as security.

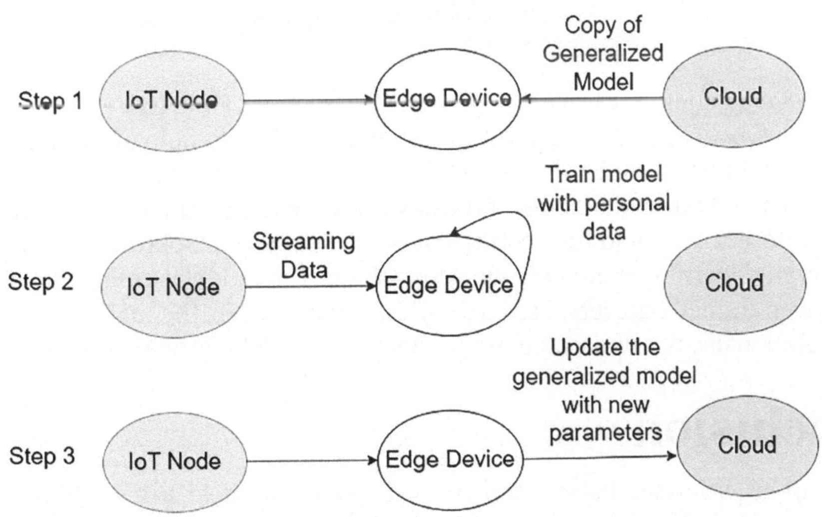

Figure 8.10: *Centralized Federated Learning of ML Model by Edge Devices*

The machine learning model architecture is created at a global server that is generic. A copy of this model is then shared with the edge devices. These edge devices then train the model with the local data they acquire. With time, the models on each of the edge devices get personalized, and provide a better user experience.

The next step is that the trained models are shared with the global server, and through secure aggregations from different inputs, the model at the global server is updated with new parameters. This model is then shared with edge devices to be trained on local data in the next cycle. In every cycle, we get an optimized model at the global server, and then on the edge devices. As we can see, the training does not happen on a global server, but a global server manages federated learning, and is not replaced.

This type of federated learning with a global server managing the model training is known as Centralized Federated Learning as shown in *Figure* 8.10. A centralized approach may face a bottleneck, and thus, for such situations, there is a decentralized federated learning. In decentralized learning, edge devices update their models with parameters shared from connected edge devices. The efficiency of the model is fully dependent on the network topology all devices are connected in. Another type of federated learning is HeteroFL which assumes edge devices to be heterogeneous as in an IoT application.

A real-life federated learning application is Siri on the Apple iPhone. Each of the Apple phones has Siri that trains its model based on its user and provides a personalized experience. The data of the user is kept private over the smartphone. Apple periodically collects trained models to update the global model and sends the updated model back to each of the Apple phones. This global model makes Siri better as an assistant with experiences from all around the world.

To implement federated learning, python has a TensorFlow federated library which is developed by Google. A usual ML training model has to upload the dataset, split it into train and test, compile the model with a train dataset, and evaluate it with a test dataset. In a federated ML model, if the edge devices are 10, the training dataset is split into 10 different sets, and the testing dataset is unaltered. Splitting of data simulated the federated learning model on a local machine. The model is trained locally on each of the given trained datasets. For each of the edge devices, the main model is updated iteratively. Finally, the updated main model is evaluated on the test data.

Conclusion

This chapter discusses information fusion models used in IoT applications to fuse and analyze data from multiple sources. From probability-based fusion to AI-based fusion, different IoT applications utilize the models based on their requirements. Deep learning models are heavy to be implemented on edge devices, however, they are the most used model in recent IoT applications, involving smartphones and wearable devices. We studied optimization techniques using tensorflow-lite to reduce the size of the model: Quantization and pruning. Next, we studied four different analytical models that an IoT application selects, depending on the type of service.

Real-time analysis stores and analyzes streaming data in the blink of an eye and is used in time-critical applications. Event-driven analysis is a real-time analysis of streaming events using complex event processing (CEP). The events are fused to get a complex event that describes the current environment state and is matched with predefined patterns for decision-making. The context-based analysis is for personalized IoT applications that adapt to context in real-time. CEP is used for context analysis with contexts considered as events. CEP extracts context from multiple sources and models it using semantics for reasoning. The fourth type of analysis is collaborative analysis where multiple edge devices collaborate to train machine learning models locally and then transfer the learning to optimize learning models at the global level. One type of collaborative learning is federated learning which is currently popular in edge computing. The next chapter discusses streaming data frameworks for data analysis and visualization.

Points to Remember

- The process of fusion of information from multiple sources is carried out by information fusion models.
- Bayesian networks are based on probability, and represent data graphically as directed acyclic graphs.
- Kalman Filter assumes data in normal distribution, and the probability calculation is based on Bayes theorem. The limitation of the Kalman filter is that it assumes a linear system.
- Fuzzy logic is mostly applied to a recommender system that takes input from humans in real-time, and produces expert-like decisions.
- Dempster-Shafer theory is a mathematical expression that collects information from different sources as evidence, combines them with belief, and takes a judgement.
- Machine learning techniques are classification, clustering, and regression. With learning algorithms, the data is provided, and it somehow learns the pattern of the data. Then it accurately predicts the future insights.
- To efficiently utilize edge devices for implementing deep learning models, the models are optimized during training, or after training using model pruning and quantization.
- A real-time analytical framework empowers the user to query information in real-time, and visualize data in motion.

- Complex Event Processing (CEP) is popular in IoT to deal with event-driven analysis on streaming events.
- The advantage of context-aware analysis in IoT applications is that it personalizes the application, providing user satisfaction and efficient service.
- Federated learning, a part of collaborative learning, aims to keep data private by training models at the network edge, and not at a global and centralized server such as Cloud.

Multiple Choice Questions

1. The probability-based model follows two steps: predict and update:
    a. Bayesian Network
    b. Fuzzy Logic
    c. Evidence theory
    d. Kalman Filter
2. Which fusion model calculates belief and plausibility?
    a. Bayesian Network
    b. Fuzzy Logic
    c. Evidence theory
    d. Kalman Filter
3. Ensemble-based machine learning with multiple decision trees is called:
    a. Random Forest
    b. K-nearest neighbor
    c. Multi-layer perceptron
    d. Support vector machine
4. A technique called kernel that maps the data points to high dimensional space:
    a. Random forest
    b. K-nearest neighbor
    c. Multi-layer perceptron
    d. Support vector machine

5. Deep learning method for sequence-to-sequence task:
    a. Encoder-Decoder
    b. Recurrent Neural Network
    c. Convolution Neural Network
    d. Gated recurrent units
6. Optimization technique that removes insignificant weights:
    a. Quantization 16 bit
    b. Dynamic Quantization
    c. Pruning
    d. None of the above
7. Complex event processing is used in:
    a. Real-time analysis
    b. Event-driven analysis
    c. Collaborative analysis
    d. All of the above
8. Apple Siri works on what type of analysis?
    a. Real-time analysis
    b. Event-driven analysis
    c. Collaborative analysis
    d. None of the above

Answers

1. d
2. c
3. a
4. d
5. a
6. c
7. b
8. c

Questions

1. Explain the working of the Kalman Filter.
2. What are the steps of fuzzy logic?
3. Discuss terms used in evidence theory.
4. What is the difference between RNN, LSTM and GRU?
5. What are the advantages and drawbacks of optimization of deep learning?
6. How does CEP work, and explain its three functions.
7. Discuss the steps of context-aware analysis, and its benefits.
8. Explain how Apple Siri does federated learning.

CHAPTER 9
Streaming Data Processing

Introduction

Nowadays, fitness and health status can be tracked on wearable devices and mobile phones. These are edge devices that handle the streaming data in real-time to predict heart rate, calories burnt, number of steps, and so on. The analysis on these edge devices is very lightweight. However, there are some predictions that require heavy analysis of data streams from multiple sources. Examples of IoT applications that work on streaming data are live traffic updates, supply chain tracking, and real-time monitoring of industrial equipment in real-time. In this chapter, we will study how to model such applications with streaming data, and what is the processing framework for multi-source data streams. Further, we will see the usage of popular processing frameworks in IoT applications, and how to choose between them. We will also study use cases of IoT applications on each of the frameworks, and how to choose among them, depending on the IoT service requirements.

Structure

In this chapter, we will cover the following topics:

- Data Stream Processing Framework
- Layered Architecture
- Apache Spark
- Apache Flink
- Apache Kafka
- Esper

Data Stream Processing Framework

Before we discuss the processing frameworks, we should know what streaming data is, and why it is challenging to handle it in IoT applications. IoT applications have multiple sources such as sensors or social media, audio inputs in natural language or cameras capturing video continuously. Most of the data input in an IoT application is streaming data, and it has to be analysed in real-time to provide autonomous and efficient service. The data can be of size a few bits to megabytes. The sources continuously emit data, and every data it communicates is relevant.

The streaming data is required for deep analysis such as sentiment analysis from Twitter data or product feedback via a number of clicks, reviews and purchases updated in real-time.

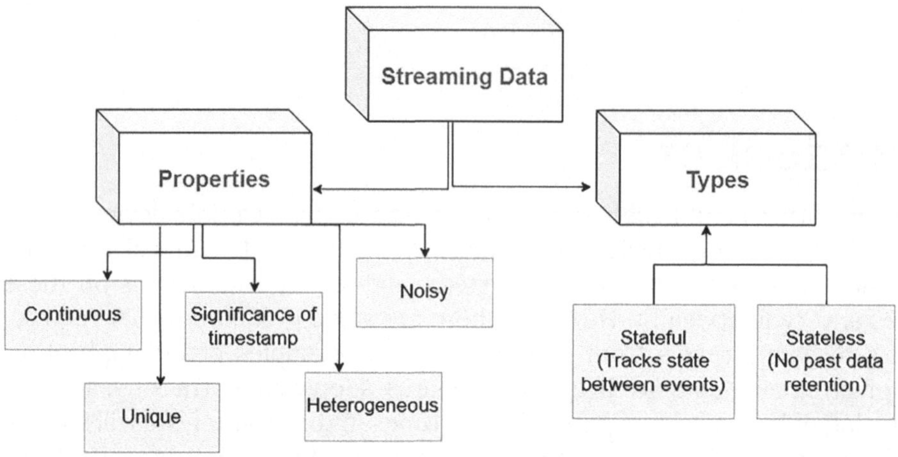

Figure 9.1: *Characteristics of Streaming Data and Types of Stream Processing*

Characteristics of streaming data as shown in *Figure 9.1* are:

- **Continuous:** The source generates data until the device runs, and has no start or end points as well as no breaks. If there is a break, it means there is a failure of the network or device.
- **Unique:** Once the data is available, it has to be processed in real-time, and has no retransmissions, so it is a huge problem, if not processed. Any data in the stream if lost can cause loss of important information, and is uniquely identified from other data.
- **Heterogeneous:** Data streams can be in multiple formats and data types. These need to be stored and handled in real-time to fetch as well as analyse data of specific data types and specific file formats.
- **Noisy/Erroneous:** Due to network or sensor failures, there can be missing data in streams. With continuous data, it is challenging to impute data, and validate it.
- **Significance of Timestamp:** Streaming data is fresh, if it is handled in time, otherwise it gets stale, and loses its significance for real-time service and decision-making.

The success of an IoT application is highly dependent on data, and how it is processed. As streaming data is mostly acquired in an IoT application, they need to be processed efficiently. Traditional data processing frameworks process data in batches. They acquire data from multiple sources, form a storage model and then analyse. In streaming data, the storage model on the voluminous data has to be updated in real-time, validating data and handling data velocity in parallel. We can say from the concepts that streaming data in an IoT application is Big Data.

Streaming data processing frameworks are a new technology that handles streaming data. The framework needs to be available all the time, should provide results in real-time, must be able to scale, and has to be fault tolerant.

We studied the properties of streaming data, and what is required by a processing framework that handles streams. Now, we will see what stream processing is all about. It is a data management technique that processes data streams, and processing includes filtering, validating, transforming, and analysing in real-time. The processed stream is then passed on to the application, storage or another stream processing pipeline.

The benefits of the stream processing framework are:

- It is used for developing applications that are adaptive and responsive in real-time.
- It benefits businesses by improving decisions with real-time analytics.
- It provides decisions faster and more accurately by analysing data streams from multiple sources.
- It improves user experience by providing real-time service.
- It captures the current context, and provides personalized decisions.

There are two types of stream processing as shown in *Figure* 9.1:

- **Stateless Stream Processing:** In this type of processing, the data or event is considered individual. This processing type does not require history or past events to analyse data. The information from the data is sufficient for analysis and decision-making. Thus, it is called stateless because there is no requirement to track the states of the system with data or events.
- **Stateful Stream Processing:** It is a very complex type of processing where the state between events has to be tracked. It requires complex tools such as widowing, joining streams with keys, and tracking continuously. It is important in scenarios where the output or decision is based on accumulated knowledge from all past observations and current observations. This processing requires a scalable framework with good memory, and needs to perform a lot of computations.

Next, we will study two use cases of stream processing in an IoT application, and how it benefits the user.

A popular IoT application is the Smart Monitoring of Industrial Machines. The machines are attached with sensors on embedded systems. The operational status is detected by sensors that capture vibration, pressure, power consumption, and temperature. This data is continuously captured by sensors, and communicated as well as processed using a stream processing framework to predict machine health in real-time.

Real-time monitoring is very important for industrial machines as it can prevent major problems by detecting issues as early as possible, and communicating them in time. This will provide maintenance to industrial equipment in time and on proper problems. So, as a result, the industry keeps running successfully, and the quality of the product is important, saving costs. Another popular IoT application that processes the streaming data is traffic data monitoring. The vehicle is attached with a sensor that provides real-time streaming information about the car's speed, fuel level, path from source to destination, GPS position of the vehicle, and so on. Other information is collected from cameras on traffic lights to detect traffic in real-time. Further, it also collects information from weather stations to know the current climatic conditions, or to be relevant to other weather advisories. Depending on the vehicle's information, traffic information, and weather information, the vehicle's path is updated in real-time, and the updates are communicated to the user. The application also highlights traffic congestion, and alerts about accidents around.

There are various other IoT applications that are successfully using streaming data processing frameworks, and the demand for processing frameworks in the concept of smart city is very high. That is why it is necessary as well as an interesting topic, if we need to develop an efficient real-time IoT application that analyses the streaming data, and provides smart solutions. Stream processing frameworks are set to grow in future with GenAI, serverless computing and edge intelligence.

Architecture of Stream Processing

Data is increasing day by day and traditional systems of processing are not able to cope up with the voluminous data streams. Data streaming platforms continuously ingest data, and process and empower businesses with useful insights. Processing of data streams is done in six steps. These steps are as follows:

1. **Data Production:** Multiple sources generate data in streams and the sources may be cameras, microphones, sensors, the web, or social media. The data may be in different file formats (JSON, CSV), data types (integer, string), and coming from different application layer protocols such as HTPP or MQTT.

2. **Data Ingestion:** The produced data from the previous step is stored in a message broker. Streaming platforms and technologies consume data from

brokers to handle the velocity, veracity and volume of data. Here, the data can be validated and cleaned.

3. **Data Processing:** The ingested data, that is cleaned and validated, is processed in the next step. Processing involves filtering, transformation, and data enrichment while in motion. After this step, the data is ready to be analysed. This processing can be integrated with the ingestion platform or paired with another processing tool for better-processed data, ready to be analysed.
4. **Streaming Data Analytics:** In this step, the scientists analyse and interpret the data using Python Notebook and Power BI to visualize streaming data. The scientists utilize technologies to do predictive, descriptive analysis. The analysis generates reports and produces real-time alerts.
5. **Data Reporting:** The analysed data is converted into a report summarizing key metrics and trends. The report formats can be documents, emails, or dashboards.
6. **Data Visualization and Decision-making:** Visualization is a tool that displays data in a lucid manner so that leaders and business people can understand. The tools used are graphs, maps and charts. Decision-makers can think of optimizing processes and improving products and user experience in a timely manner.

All stream processing frameworks follow these steps. Thus, to process data, every stream processing architecture has the following five main components.

- **Stream Processing Engine:** This is the heart and soul component of stream processing. It performs various operations on streaming data such as filtering, aggregation, enrichment, transformations, and analysis in real-time. It can be integrated with CEP (Esper) to find anomalies and patterns in streaming data. Popular engines are Apache Kafka, Apache Spark and Apache Flink. Appropriate engine is selected based on properties of IoT data, processing complexity, scalability and reliability, is easily integrated with other components and is compatible with formats and connections of other tools.
- **Message Broker:** This component stores data as a buffer from data sources. The data of the broker is consumed by the stream processing engine. This is the place where data from different formats is converted to a standard message format (JSON or AVRO). Brokers can scale, have fault tolerance, and do load balancing and partitioning. The tools are Apache Kafka and Amazon Kinesis Streams.
- **Data Storage:** This component stores structured and unstructured data, either in raw form, or in processed form. Since streaming data has a huge volume and variety, cloud storage is used to store the data. The storage is

known as an operational data lake. The tools to store the streaming data are Amazon S3, HDFS, and Cassandra.

- **Data Ingestion Tools:** Acquire data from multiple sources, resolve its heterogeneity and forward it to storage models. These tools ingest structured, and unstructured data in real-time. They also validate the data quality for further processing. Some popular ingestion tools are Apache Flume and Amazon Kinesis Firehose.
- **Data Visualization and Reporting Tools:** These are tools that provide ways to explore the processed data streams to analyse and visualize them. These tools provide real-time insights and they plot maps and graphs on streaming data. Popular tools that are integrated with streaming frameworks are Grafana, Kibana, Tableau and Power BI.

There are two popular architectures that data streaming processing follows. These are: Lambda architecture and Kappa architecture.

Lambda Architecture (Data at Rest)

This architecture performs batch processing and stream processing together to handle large amounts of data. It has three layers: a batch layer, a speed layer, and a data serving layer. In the batch layer, the architecture follows two steps. The first step is to manage the master data to preserve historical data and keep track of status. The master data is immutable and read-only. In the next step, it stores the batches as precomputed views for faster reuse. The data serving layer acquires the batch view from the batch layer periodically and these views are indexed for querying purposes. The indexing is done in batches and while one batch is being indexed, the next is kept in a queue. Since the batch layer has higher latency, the speed layer reduces this latency and keeps the processing balanced for real-time analysis. The speed layer performs faster indexing of the batches and makes it query-ready. Once the batch views are indexed and pre-computed, the data is deleted. Query is submitted to both the data serving layer and speed layer, and the results are merged before being provided to the user. Query processing is very fast with batch views and pre-computed data, making it a good architecture for processing data streams.

Kappa Architecture (Data in Motion)

This architecture has only a stream layer, and no batch layer such as Lambda Architecture. Key components of this architecture are Data sources, a stream processing engine that performs processing tasks such as filtering, transformations, enrichment, data storage such as NoSQL database for historical data and event replays, a serving layer that provides dashboards to perform real-time analytics on data, and the last component is re-processing/replay mechanism. The replay mechanism is the new concept provided by this architecture. This mechanism is implemented to eliminate the need to have a separate batch processing system. In this mechanism, the data is ingested, processed and stored in a database for analysis. This data can be replayed for batch processing to keep event logs. These logs can help fix bugs in the processing and improve algorithms. Thus, this architecture considers incoming data streams as events and handles all data in real-time.

In the recent times of technological advancements, Kappa Architecture is replacing the Lambda Architecture. Companies such as Disney, Twitter and Uber are benefiting from kappa architecture and have got good results without Lambda Architecture. The reason is that the big data volume has increased a lot, and balancing data velocity as well as having real-time analysis is getting challenging. Further, Lambda Architecture has to maintain two distributed systems, keep the systems coordinated for data quality, and has added complexity. However, Kappa Architecture is easy to implement. It has high data loss chances, and has limited tools compared to Lambda Architecture. Although it seems Kappa Architecture is better than Lambda, and is currently popular as shown in *Figure* 9.2, it really depends on the application, you are implementing that will determine what architecture to choose for stream processing.

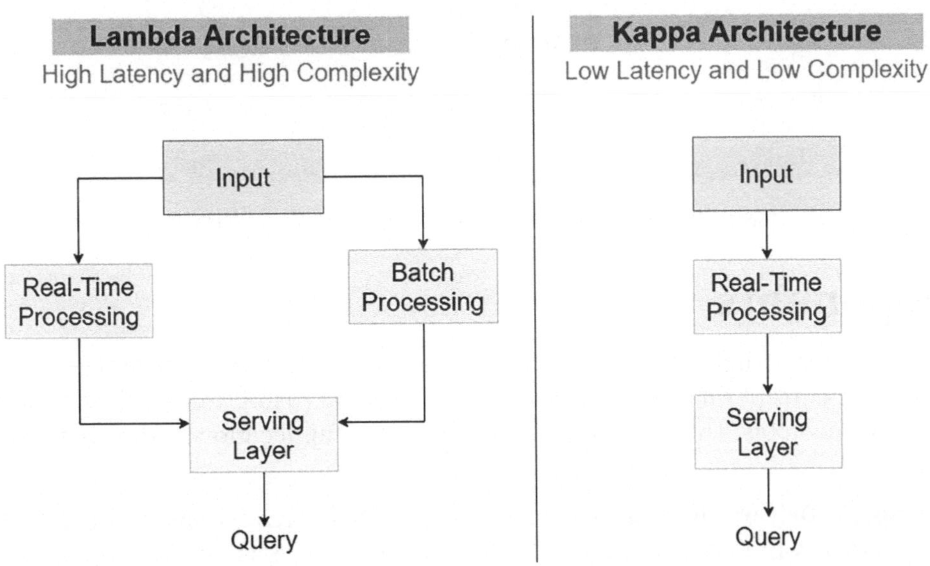

Figure 9.2: *Differences between Lambda Architecture and Kappa Architecture*

Apache Spark

Apache Spark is a batch/stream processing framework that follows master/slave architecture. It is a very popular framework used by thousands of companies, including 80% of the Fortune 500, and has over 2,000 contributors to the open-source project from industry and academia. Batch and Stream processing, using Pyspark is already discussed in *Chapter 3: Building IoT Big Data Pipelines*, which has a brief description of how Spark works, and implementations for both batch and stream processing, discussing commands and libraries. In this section, we will see more about Apache Spark, mainly its components, and two use-case applications that can be built on Spark, following simple steps.

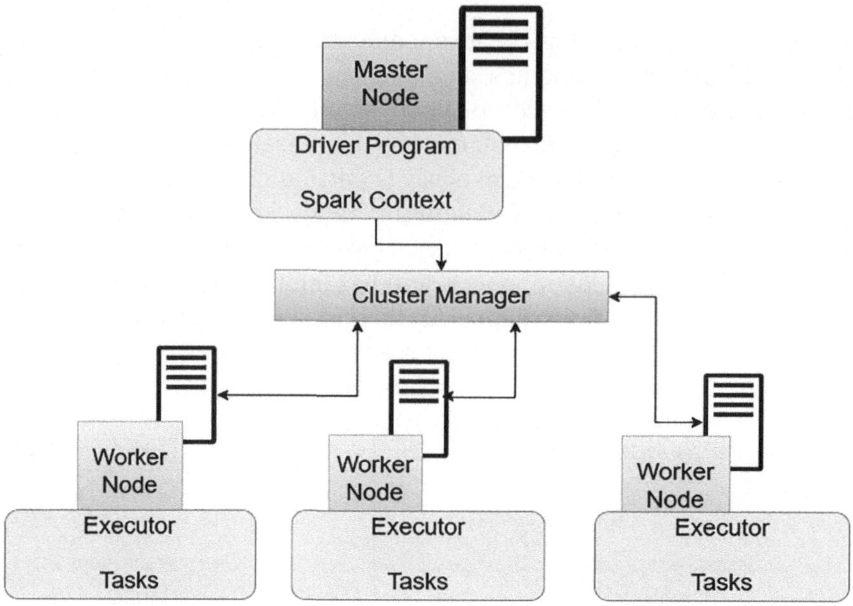

Figure 9.3: *Architecture of Spark Processing Framework*

Components

Spark processes a high number of datasets, and it is the foremost active Apache project of the current time. It is open-source, and can be customized by the developer by creating new tools. The main components of a spark application as shown in *Figure* 9.3 are:

- **Spark Driver:** It runs the main function that creates spark context, and connects the context to the cluster manager. This is where the execution starts, and the code is implemented.
- **Spark Executor:** They are launched on worker nodes that execute tasks of the applications. These coordinate with the driver and cluster manager. The tasks are executed parallel, and the data to be used while execution is stored in immediate memory or cache.
- **Cluster Manager:** They manage the resources of the cluster by assigning resources as per the task requirements of the worker node.

- **Spark Context:** It is initiated by Driver where RDDs and variables are created, and only one context is active as well as running at a time. It can also access the services of Spark, and perform jobs.
- **SQL Context:** The context that allows the creation of Schema RDD and running relational queries.
- **Streaming Context:** The context is created for working with streaming data, and the creation of Dstreams from various input sources.
- **Spark Session:** This is the entry point to access SQL Context, Streaming Context and Spark Context. It allows programming with spark libraries, and creating datasets as well as data frames. There can be multiple spark sessions running at once.

The components of the Spark application are very important before developing Spark because it follows a hierarchy like Spark driver, then Spark Context, and then Spark Session or SQL session.

Use-Case Applications

Monitoring of Traffic Using IoT and Spark

IoT applications on traffic data monitoring will have three main modules: IoT Data Producer, IoT Data Processing and IoT Data Dashboard. We assume that the IoT Data is produced in Json format and is being produced from connected vehicles. The vehicle data that is produced is vehicle ID, vehicle Type, Route ID, timestep, fuel and current position in terms of latitude and longitude. For understanding, assume that there are three routes only. The vehicle type may be a "truck", "car", or "bus". Thus, the steps to design an IoT data processing module in the IoT application are:

1. To store vehicle data, create a Cassandra table having columns from vehicle data attributes. Multiple tables can be created using different attributes of vehicle data. Further, each of the tables needs to be created based on an objective to be calculated.
2. In our application of traffic monitoring, two tables need to be created. The first table calculates the total number of vehicles of one type on a particular route at the current time instance. The table is named "total_traffic" and consists of attributes such as current timestamp, vehicle ID, vehicle type and total count. The second table is about a point of interest, named "poi", and is created having columns as vehicle ID, vehicle type, distance and timestamp. The tables will be filled with data via Spark. Objectives can be increased and with them, the number of tables can be increased.
3. During the ingestion of IoT data from the producer, Spark deserializes the string in JSON format into the Object IoTdata.

4. On an IoTdata object, map transformation is applied to get Dstreams of the IoTdata object.
5. The Dstream of the object is then converted to a key, value pair where the key is vehicle ID, and the value is the remaining attribute value in the IoTdata DStream.
6. The first objective is to calculate the total number of vehicles. For this objective, we need to keep track of past Dstreams. Spark's stateful operation is utilized to keep track of all the unique IDs previously processed.
7. Spark stored the state in RDD format on multiple machines of Spark Cluster.
8. Once the data is paired and state preserved, a transformation operation is applied to the data that calculates the total number of vehicles for different types in each route. A new pair is created with the key as an aggregate key having route ID and vehicle type together, and the value will be the total number of vehicles.
9. The data is then sent to the Cassandra database of "**`total_traffic`**", we created in step 1 using the **`saveToCassandra()`** method.
10. The next objective is to calculate the point of interest, which means the number of vehicles that are in a specific range from the point of interest.
11. A point of interest object named **`poiData`** is defined with a latitude and longitude value and acceptable radius.
12. To calculate the distance of the car from the point of interest, we will use the vehicle's latitude and longitude data on "**Haversine Formula**".
13. Another pair of Dstream is created having key as route ID, vehicle type and value as distance from poi.
14. The values are passed to Cassandra table "poi" using the **`saveToCassandra()`** method.

    The processed data for each of the objectives are in the tables, appended in real-time as the data is ingested. The table values, which are continuously being updated, can be used to plot and update graphs in real-time on dashboards to have more advanced analysis.

    The Cassandra data is then directly passed on to the third module of the application, the IoT data dashboard. IoT data dashboard shows the table as a graphical representation such as a bar chart or pie chart to easily visualize patterns in the data. The charts on the dashboards are updated periodically as new streams produced from the first module "IoT data producer" are processed by the second module "IoT Data Processing" of the application.

Predictive Maintenance of Industrial Machines

The machines in the industry have sensors on embedded devices that produce IoT data. The sensor data may include temperature, vibration, sound, and pressure and each data is uniquely identified by the machine's ID. The objective is to predict the future health of the machine so that the machine can be repaired beforehand with scheduled maintenance. This will not let the machine fail completely, giving the machine more life to run. The steps are as follows:

1. Collect the data in any centralized NoSQL database or HDFS.
2. Clean the data in the table, using Spark.
3. Summarize the upcoming data. Update the mean and standard deviation of a normal distribution with the streaming data for anomaly detection.
4. If data values are known that caused failures in the data, label the incoming data accordingly.
5. Choose an ML model from the MLlib library that can predict a machine's health, based on the labelled data. It should be able to classify a machine as healthy or unhealthy.
6. Train and test the model to have the best accuracy.
7. Use the trained model on real-time streaming data from the machine to predict the health of the machine on the fly.
8. Based on the model's decision, the alerts can be sent to workers and maintenance departments automatically.

Both the use-case applications had different techniques of using Spark, and the technique is based on the objective of IoT applications. The common objective of both applications was to process streaming data in real-time and analyse objectives. The first technique used in-memory transformations to predict objective values. The second application used the ML model from the MLlib library, trained it and then used the model to predict the health of machines. This ensures that Apache Spark streaming can be utilized in a variety of IoT applications. The only problem is that the streaming data is considered a micro-batch. Spark processes data in micro-batches, which may introduce minor latency compared to true event-by-event systems like Flink. For that, Apache Flink is a popular framework, discussed in the next section.

Apache Flink

It is a distributed stream processing framework that provides stateful processing of unbounded and bounded datasets. It follows the Kappa Architecture. Streaming data is considered as an unbounded dataset and batch data is considered as a bounded dataset. Stream processing has low latency and processing is done on data as it is ingested. It performs computation in-memory, has high availability, removes a single point of failure and scales horizontally, by adding multiple servers in the architecture. It provides a unified programming interface for batch as well as stream processing. The two streams it handles are discussed as follows:

- **Bounded Stream**: Bounded data, such as tables, are finite and have start and stop. The algorithm processing the bounded data will stop at a finite time and provide a result. Complete data can be ingested before performing computations. Ordering is not necessary as they are sorted.
- **Unbounded Stream**: Data that has started but has no end. It is generated by the source continuously and indefinitely. The processing algorithm to process this stream never stops, and needs to run for an infinite time. The data must be continuously processed, and results should be provided in real-time. The ordering of events is very important for ingestion and analysis to reason for the results captured.

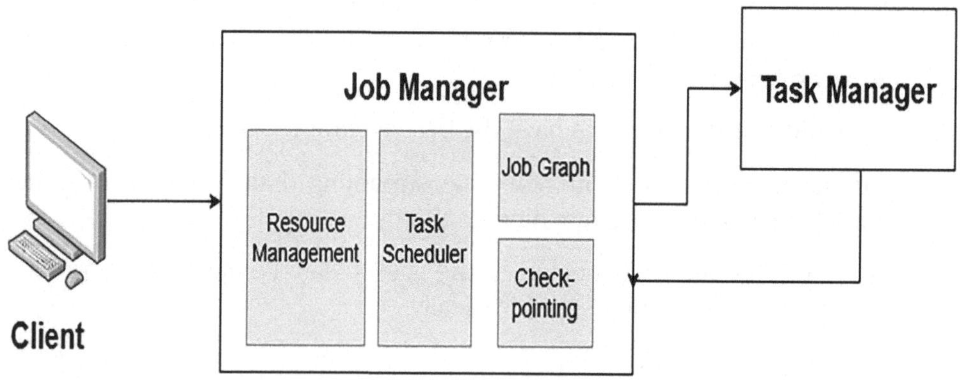

Figure 9.4: *Architecture of Apache Flink*

Components

Flink is a high-throughput low-latency stream processing framework. This is possible due to the following components that process data in collaboration, providing efficiency as well as scalability. The architecture is shown in *Figure* 9.4, and is discussed as follows:

- **Datastream API/Batch API:** Datastream API is provided for stream processing and Batch API is provided for batch processing. These APIs allow developers to process data in a high-level manner.
- **JobManager:** It is a software component that coordinates the execution of Flink jobs by dealing with job submission and task scheduling.

- **TaskManager:** It handles the execution of tasks within a Flink job. It executes tasks in parallel on multiple machines by creating parallel instances of the same task.
- **JobGraph:** It provides a graphical representation of the flow of data within the Flink process. The representation is in the form of a directed acyclic graph (DAG) where nodes are tasks and edges are dependencies between tasks.
- **Task:** Smallest unit in a Flink job that has operations such as map and reduce.
- **CheckPointing:** To ensure fault tolerance, this software saves snapshots of the job's current state. This makes the system fault-tolerant. It also ensures "exactly once processing semantics". This semantics means that the data is processed one time only, no duplicate processing occurs, and no data is missed even if the system suffers failures.
- **State:** It is a representation of the current Flink state during processing, saved in the form of key-value or user-defined data structure.
- **DataStream and DataSet:** DataStream represents unbounded data, whereas Dataset represents the bounded data.
- **Windowing:** This is a tool to aggregate data for analysis in a specified time interval. The window can be fixed, sliding or time-bounded.
- **Source and Sink:** Source is the input to Flink, and Sink is the output. Flink supports multiple sources, and sinks for integration with the help of connectors.
- **Apache Gelly:** It is a graph-processing library, incorporated by Flink, to process graph-based data.
- **Table API/ SQL API:** To provide results to a real-time query, the event data is stored in a relational database, and this API allows to declare tables, save data in it, and query it using SQL. The queries can run batch as well as stream inputs, and results will be fetched from the relational table.
- **Connector Libraries:** Flink has a variety of connector APIs to connect and integrate with different data sources, and sinks such as Apache Kafka, and Apache Hadoop for data communication.
- **Library Ecosystem:** Flink has multiple libraries that provide more functionalities to data processing, and it is increasing. FlinkML library provides ML tools and FLinkCEP provides complex event processing.

Apache Flink has excellent performance while processing both bounded as well as unbounded streams. It takes data from the source, ingest it as a job, partition it into tasks and distributes the tasks to run on multiple machines. The tasks are computations such as transformation, filtering, map, reduce.

The transformed data is stored in a relational database and then queried for results using SQL. The output is provided to the sink. Two features of Flink are, first, it saves the state of the process to provide fault-tolerance and second, it shows the flow of data in the process using graphical representation.

Benefits

- **Scalability:** It is scalable due to distributed architecture having multiple data centres working together in a cluster. Processing is parallelized by partitioning the task into multiple machines and managing their execution in real-time.
- **In-memory Performance:** The data is partitioned into multiple machines, and thus when a task runs on a particular machine, it fetches data from its local data which is in-memory.
- **Exactly One-state Consistency:** Flink stores the current state of the process and it ensures that the process runs exactly once even in the presence of failures.
- **Wide Range of Connectors:** Flink has connector APIs for popular streaming engines, data storage, search engines and file systems. Some popular sources and sinks are Kafka, Amazon Kinesis Data Streams, RabbitMQ, DynamoDB, HBase, Apache Pulsar, ElasticSearch, and so on.
- **Multiple Levels of Abstractions:** There are four levels of abstractions and we will go from low to high. The lowest is the ProcessFunction API which provides fine-tuning of processes and states with event handling. The next level is DataStream API provides enrichment, windowing and mapping of data streams. Next is Table API creates tables by using SQL API to perform operations on tables. The highest level of abstraction is StreamSQL which is used to do complex queries on tables having events. For querying, the table values, the data ingestion into the table and the state preservations, event handling, and how the process is working are all hidden.
- **Support for Multiple Programming Languages:** The computations can be coded in Java, Kotlin, Scala and Python and the query uses streamSQL for complex query in streaming data or unbounded data.

Apache Kafka

It is a popular tool developed by LinkedIn in 2011 for their own use. This tool is a high throughput message broker that stores messages/events as well as efficiently communicates them from sender to receiver. When LinkedIn was successful, they open-sourced it, and later donated it to Apache Software Foundation. Currently, Kafka is the most used streaming platform that has big Fortune 500 companies as customers such as Netflix, AirBnB, and Microsoft. It is capable of ingesting and processing trillions of events per day, and has no scaling issue with huge volumes of data. The software has three capabilities:

- It provides a messaging broker, and enables publishers and subscribers to communicate as well as receive events.
- It stores events in a time-series manner, and provides durability as well as fault tolerance.
- It provides real-time processing of the events.

Kafka has four popular APIs to make developers capable of leveraging the software's capabilities.

- **Producer API:** This API allows a producer to publish a stream of events. The publisher needs to decide a Kafka topic under which the events will be stored and the events can be recognized by the subscribers through this topic. Once the record of the event is published to the Kafka broker, it cannot be altered or deleted. Kafka broker keeps it for two days or until memory space is free. The time to keep the record can be pre-configured during the instantiation of the Kafka broker.
- **Consumer API:** This API enables consumers or subscribers to subscribe to multiple topics. It also enables subscribers to ingest and process the records within the topic before consuming. The ingestion and processing can be both real-time or batch as per the requirement of the subscriber.
- **Streams API:** This API adds complex processing capabilities and is bounded by Producer API and Consumer API. It enables applications to fetch, process in real-time and again publish on the same topic. With only producer API and consumer API, the application provides simple stream processing. However, this API combined with the preceding two APIs enables the development of complex event stream applications.
- **Connector API:** This API allows developers to connect with producers and consumers and automate the integration of multiple event sources into the Kafka cluster. A Kafka cluster is a distributed architecture spanning multiple data centres and servers to store incoming events within a topic.

Kafka is mostly used for log aggregation, stream processing, commit logs and clickstream tracking. To get how Kafka works, we will go through its architecture.

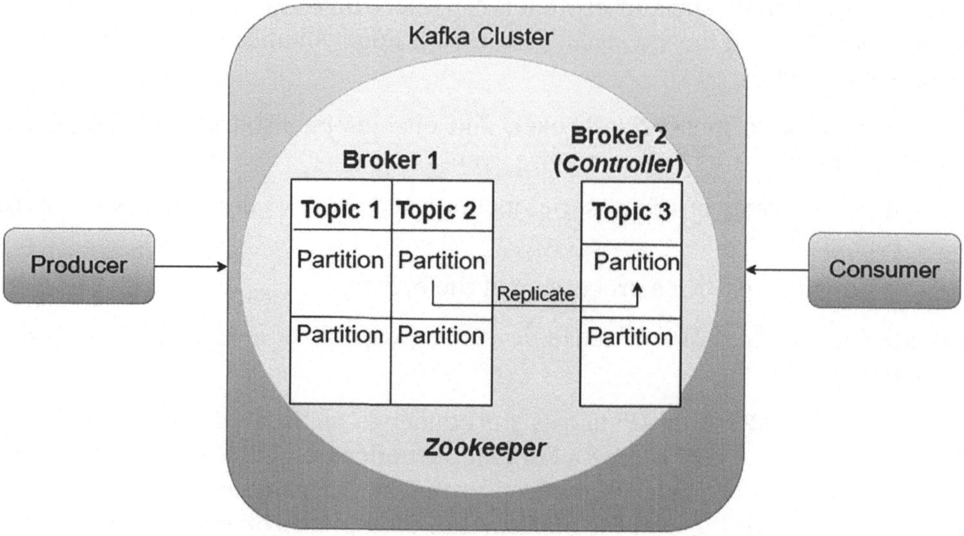

Figure 9.5: *Apache Kafka*

Event-Driven Architecture

Apache Kafka stores events provided by producers as messages with a topic name as shown in *Figure* 9.5. These messages are consumed by the subscribers, and the subscriber listens to specific topics to consume the events. Therefore, Kafka is also known as the pub/sub model. An event has a key, value and a timestamp. The message/ event is stored on the Kafka cluster of multiple data centres and the cluster spreads the data evenly among the distributed systems. Thus, the Kafka cluster can scale without any problem of increasing the volume of streaming data. Next, we will discuss the components of the Kafka Architecture in detail.

- **Broker:** It represents a Kafka server. It receives events as messages from the producers and the messages are consumed by the subscribers. The messages from the producers are stored on a disk with an offset, a unique identifier. Offset is incremented with new incoming messages to preserve the temporal characteristics of the event. Every partition has unique offsets. Offset is also important for recovery after failure, thus making the server fault-tolerant. As per the partition request from the subscriber, the broker provides the message.
- **Controller:** A cluster of Kafka brokers shares information with each other. One of the brokers in the cluster is the controller. The controller manages partitions and replicas of each broker. The controller broker has administrative tasks of registrations, re-assignments of replicas/partitions, creating/ deleting topics, and handling failures. It also periodically checks the health of

brokers in the cluster. Every broker in the cluster is a controller, but only one broker is a controller at a given point in time.

The controller starts up automatically with the start of the broker. It writes system problems in controller logs which is different from a server log.

- **Partitions:** It is a popular fundamental element in a distributed system. The topic on which the producer sends messages is divided into multiple partitions. Partition is a log file that stores the messages in an append-only method.

  Thus, records being stored under a topic are actually divided and stored in partitions in the Kafka cluster. The partitions are distributed within the cluster which provides parallelism and improves scalability. With multiple partitions in multiple brokers, it can send events under topic, to multiple subscribers at a time-instance. This is a huge advantage of Kafka for the real-time processing of streaming data. The replicas of the partitions are created and they are distributed within the cluster. The replicas provide fault tolerance. If any broker fails, the data can be fetched from another broker. Thus, every broker keeps a copy of the "state" of other brokers in the cluster. Kafka also makes sure that the subscriber consumes data within a topic in the same order in which it was published by the producer.

- **Topics:** It is a name that categorizes events. Storing events with a common topic name is similar to storing files in a specific folder or generating a log. Topics are provided by developers. They are partitioned into a Kafka cluster. The event of a topic is appended to the topic log file. Topics can be accessed by multiple producers and consumers, which means they can write data on the same topic and consume data from the same topic. Multiple producers and consumers are handled due to the partitioning of topics in the Kafka cluster providing parallel input/output on the same topic.
- **Zookeeper:** It stores the metadata of the brokers and coordinates the operations within the Kafka cluster. It keeps track of brokers, topics, and partitions within clusters. It eases communication between brokers. Zookeeper elects a broker as a controller from the cluster. If the elected controller fails, it selects a new controller immediately. It is very useful software as it keeps track of where the data is, which broker has the data, and assigns a leader to a topic and its partitions for smooth management and efficient communication with subscribers. It makes sure that the data expected by the subscriber is exactly communicated by the broker.

In upcoming versions of Kafka, zookeeper is set to be removed because it makes the Kafka cluster a centralized point of failure. Zookeeper is so important that if it fails, the Kafka cluster will not be able to operate at all and provide functionalities it is good at.

- **Queues:** Events published on Kafka broker are stored in a queue data structure following first in first out operation. This way, it preserves the order of events while consumed by the subscribers. The queue size is considered unlimited due to the cluster of brokers and thus, deletion of events due to memory shortage is not common in Kafka.

- **Schema Registry:** It is a registry that routes message schema to the relevant topic log. Schema registry has message schema saved for every topic. The schema of the incoming message is checked with the stored schema of the topic before it is added. A schema ID is generated for the schema. The schema's namespace is provided by the producer with the record/event. Then the reader in schema deserializes the data with respect to schema and produces a schema ID. The publisher communicates with the schema registry to fetch ID. Next records published by the producer contain the schema ID and not the namespace every time. When a subscriber requests, the schema registry sends data serialized with schema ID, to the subscriber. This way, the registry does not store every incoming message with its schema in the topic log, saving a lot of memory.

Drawbacks of Kafka: It has very limited querying capabilities due to relational databases. The data is never deleted automatically in log-based storage, which leads to events that are not useful at all taking up space. Further, the message size it can handle is a maximum of 1MB, which can limit the applications that have streams of large-sized events. Performance degrades as Kafka splits the large messages into multiple messages to fit in. Kafka do scale horizontally well and it has good storage however, due to limited query capabilities and message size, the scaling is limited. Scaling can be achieved by adding more brokers or utilizing external database.

Esper

It is a Java platform that is developed by EsperTech. It provides Complex Event Processing (CEP) and Event Stream Processing (ESP). It has tools and frameworks that support event-based applications. The framework has three editions, and each edition provides different dimensionality to the application. The editions are:

- **Esper Engine:** Here the main application code is developed that has processing logic. The application code uses algorithms of CEP and EEP combined. It is an open-source software with GPLv2 license.
- **Esper Enterprise Edition (Esper EE):** It packages the codes, integrates, and deploys the application.
- **Esper High Availability (Esper HA):** It provides security, fault tolerance, high availability, and persistence to the processing logic.

We will go through each of the components one by one.

Esper Engine

It is the edition where the processing logic is implemented. The implementation can be carried out in Java or .Net. Java which is mostly used as a language for engines as it can be easily integrated with other editions. The engine is a JAR that has its own Java AP and XML configuration file.

Thus, the Esper engine runs along with logic, GUI, and other frameworks inside a Java application. How does Esper process complex event streams? It follows simple steps:

1. Event is considered as a Plain Java Object (POJO), and stream is considered as a pipe of events where events belong to a class.
2. With streams, the events are fed into the engine. An output of one event is chained with the input of another event inside the Engine, allowing statement composition.
3. Statement composition is the collection of continuous queries, registered with the engine, to continuously monitor streams.
4. The language used to write statements(queries) is EPL which has very similar functions as SQL such as aggregation, projection, selection, joins (named as correlation in EPL), and named windows (similar to SQL views). To consider the temporal characteristics of the stream, EPL provides sliding windows and pattern-matching tools.
5. The statements are triggered by incoming events, evaluated on them and the matched event is forwarded to another statement in case of chaining or to an associated event listener.
6. If stream data has to be correlated with historical data or has to be enriched with lookups stored in relational databases, SQL query is joined with the stream.

Thus, the main job of the Esper engine is to match events with respect to patterns, and remove complex events. It simplifies complex events by storing the history of events triggered at every stage so that theoutput events are fine-tuned. It provides high-volume event correlation within the event stream. It is able to accept data from multiple sources, and has a very high throughput with 10000 -200000 events per second. It provides adapters to connect databases. It is written in Java, and thus easily integrated with other Java applications.

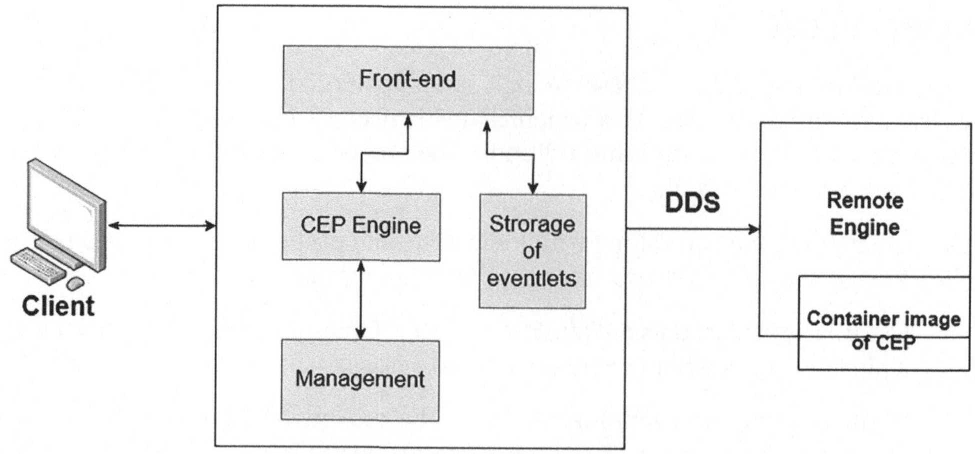

Figure 9.6: *Esper HQ Architecture*

Esper EE

Esper EE provides a collection of plugins. The most widely used plugin is Esper HQ.

Esper HQ

It is an application providing complex event processing, and its architecture is shown in *Figure* 9.6. that has 4 components: Runtime container, management console, basic IDE and frontend to the local CEP engine. Runtime container deploys a CEP application as a container on a different host OS without hassle.

The container image consists of a CEP application packaged as WAR archives. Management console manages hosts on remote servers. Basic IDE for creating statements and eventlets. For eventlets creation, the application has a wizard. Front-end allows users to manage the local CEP. Management includes writing/updating statements and variables, providing query as well as seeing results.

To create statements, Esper HQ provides a comprehensive EPL designer, and eases the task of writing complex EPL codes. Eventlets are time-driven and event-driven continuous displays that are subscribed to events produced by the engine, and with changes in events, the display changes accordingly. It is easy to integrate historical data into eventlets. It is easily launched on the dashboard with the help of a URL.

Other plugins are:

- **Esper IO:** It is a collection of adapters to import data from multiple sources. It supports well-known protocols and file formats. More specific sources that are not available directly can be built up by custom connectors built on top of SDK.

- **Esper JDBC:** It converts Esper statements from a Java application to JDBC calls for easy integration with reporting tools.
- **Esper JMX:** It is a set of industry-defined APIs and standards in Java that enables runtime management of ESP from external tools, exposing the Engine for remote access. In remote access, JMX provides full control to the remote user on ports, security, connectors and managed objects of the engine.
- **Esper DDS:** It is a plugin to host an EPS engine on a remote server.

EsperHA

This plugin provides persistence to event data. The plugin stores the internal state of the CEP engine after a scheduled interval as checkpoints. Each statement is stored one by one, with annotations and XML configurations. In case of engine failure, the statements are already backed up. Once the system runs again, the backed-up CEP engine state is loaded automatically. The state loaded will be until the previous checkpoint hence there may be some data loss during recovery.

Persistence is a serialization overhead and impacts performance. The four persistence profiles to choose from are:

- **Transient:** It has no persistence and it is a default profile. This means, it does not backup any data and hence cannot recover the engine after failure.
- **Durable:** This profile automatically restarts backed-up statements after the system starts running. There is no need to register and bind the statements to the engine.
- **Resilient:** This profile stores everything, from statements to the state of the engine.
- **Overflow:** When memory is low, this profile can free up space by flushing stored events for storing new ones.

Esper HQ provides data recovery and also tools to switch between the current engine and the backed-up engine. Other features such as load balancing, global persistence and message passing, are done from outside the engine and for that management facility of Esper EE edition can be used.

Drawbacks of Esper: The interface is not user-friendly. It has no backtesting or enhanced simulation features. It is not designed for storing static data. The use of relational databases slows down the engine. The engine cannot scale dynamically. The scale is set up during implementation.

Table 9.1 summarizes the characteristics of each framework.

Framework	Strength	Weakness	Ideal for
Spark	Scalable, MLLib integration	Micro-batching, not strict real-time	Data heavy applications
Flink	True real-time, stateful, CEP	Complexity, resource-heavy	Stateful, low latency applications
Kafka	Scalable, pub-sub, fault tolerant	Limited analytics	Log ingestion, ETL pipeline
Esper	Strong CEP, low latency	Hard to scale, limited UI	Complex pattern recognition

Table 9.1: *Comparison between Processing Frameworks*

Conclusion

This chapter discussed about streaming data, and its relevance in the Internet of Things (IoT) applications. Traditional systems are only capable of batch processing, and thus, for processing streaming data, data stream processing frameworks are created. These frameworks handle streaming big data in real-time. In IoT applications, the properties of streaming data are discussed. Further, we learned stateful and stateless stream processing. We studied Lambda and Kappa architectures used for processing data streams.

Popular frameworks such as Apache Spark, Apache Flink, Apache Kafka and Esper are discussed in separate sections. We went through pseudocode steps to create a Spark application for streaming IoT data from vehicles and machines. Further, we explored bounded and unbounded datasets, components of Flink Architecture and its benefits. Later in the chapter, we studied the role of Kafka as a message broker and Esper as a CEP engine with their drawbacks.

The next chapter discusses how containerization technology is used to deploy applications on the edge device for providing edge computing on IoT data in batch/stream.

Points to Remember

- Most of the data input in an IoT application is streaming data, and it has to be analysed in real-time to provide autonomous and efficient service.
- In streaming data, the storage model on the voluminous data has to be updated in real-time, validating data and handling data velocity in parallel.
- Data processing frameworks are used for developing applications that are adaptive and responsive in real-time.
- The stream processing frameworks capture the current context, and provide personalized service.

- Processing of data streams is done in six steps: Data production, Data ingestion, Data processing, Streaming data analytics, Data reporting and Data visualization.
- Apache Spark is open-source, processes a high number of datasets, used by multiple IoT applications, and it is the foremost active Apache project of the current time.
- Lambda architecture performs batch processing and stream processing together to handle large amounts of data. It has three layers: a batch layer, a speed layer, and a data serving layer.
- Kappa architecture has only a stream layer, and no batch layer such as Lambda architecture. Key components of this architecture are data sources, stream processing, data storage, serving layer, and reprocessing/replay mechanism.
- Apache Flink is a distributed stream processing framework that provides stateful processing of unbounded and bounded datasets.
- Apache Flink has excellent performance while processing both bounded as well as unbounded streams.
- Apache Kafka is a high throughput message broker that stores messages/ events as well as efficiently communicates them from sender to receiver.
- The message size Kafka can handle is a maximum of 1MB, which can limit the applications that have streams of large-sized events.
- Esper simplifies complex events by storing the history of events triggered at every stage so that output events are fine-tuned. It provides high-volume event correlation within the event stream.

Multiple Choice Questions

1. What are the tools for stateful stream processing?
   a. Windowing
   b. Ingestion
   c. Validation
   d. Job execution
2. Which is not a characteristic of streaming data?
   a. Heterogeneous
   b. Noisy
   c. Significant even after hours
   d. Continuous

3. What are the steps in data processing?
    a. Filtering
    b. Enrichment
    c. Both of the above
    d. None of the above
4. A popular message broker in stream processing is
    a. Spark
    b. Flink
    c. Cassandra
    d. Kafka
5. What is the architecture for data at rest?
    a. Kappa Architecture
    b. Lambda Architecture
    c. Flink Architecture
    d. None of the above
6. Which component of Apache Spark launched on worker nodes for task execution?
    a. Cluster Manager
    b. Spark Executor
    c. Spark Driver
    d. None of the above
7. What does the JobGraph component do in Apache Flink?
    a. Represent the flow of data graphically
    b. Visualize results graphically
    c. Ingest graph-based data
    d. None of the above

8. What is the drawback of Kafka?
    a. Scalability
    b. High-latency
    c. Low throughput
    d. Poor storage management

Answers

1. a
2. c
3. c
4. d
5. b
6. b
7. a
8. d

Questions

1. Explain the components of a stream processing framework.
2. What is the difference between Lambda Architecture and Kappa Architecture?
3. What are the steps to implement traffic monitoring with the objective of total traffic count on Apache Spark?
4. How does Apache Flink process data streams?
5. What are the benefits of Apache Flink?
6. What are the different APIs used in Kafka?
7. What is the role of Zookeeper and Schema Registry in Kafka?
8. What are the steps followed by the Esper Engine?
9. What are the four persistence profiles in EsperHA?

Chapter 10
Containerization Technology for Edge Intelligence

Introduction

IoT applications have multiple sensing enabled things providing data, and the data is pre-processed at the edge as well as analyzed at the cloud. To increase scalability of the cloud with good quality of service, virtualization techniques came up. Virtualization supports multiple OS independently on a single machine with the deployment of Virtual Machines (VMs). In some cases, where edge intelligence has to be scaled, virtualization cannot be used as edge devices are resource-constraint, deployment of virtual machines is complex, and managing them is challenging. To scale edge intelligence, a pool of edge devices is considered.

To provide further scaling at the network edge to handle multiple IoT applications simultaneously, containerization techniques gained popularity. Containerization is a part of virtualization technique where the environment of the edge intelligence and the analytical model is packed in a container, and the container can run on any edge device. In this chapter, we will go through virtualization, containerization, tools in containerization and edge device orchestration with running containers.

Structure

In this chapter, we will cover the following topics:

- Containerization vs Virtualization
- Containerized Edge Intelligence
- Docker
- Kubernetes Orchestration

- Container Scheduling
- Container Auto-scaling

Containerization vs Virtualization

We will go through an example to understand what virtualization is capable of. After the example, we will study more about virtualization technology. Suppose, we have deployed an edge intelligence in our machine, and assume our machine has Ubuntu 18.04 OS. Assume edge intelligence model is convolution neural network deploying on python and it takes input from 1GB dataset having labelled images. Now, we face an error while running the edge intelligence model and we need help from our project partner who is good at it. The project partner is travelling, and has a laptop with only Windows. The partner needs to install OS, dataset, python libraries, and then he runs the code. This will take a lot of time, and when the partner is travelling, error resolution will take more time. What is the solution then?

The solution is virtualization. But how to go about it? We will install a software known as virtual box, and it is a very popular virtualization software. We will ask our project partner to download VirtualBox. We will make a replica of our OS with a dataset, software, libraries, and edge intelligence model. The replica is saved as an .iso image file. The file is then communicated to the partner via cloud app. The partner downloads the iso file and runs it on a virtual box on its windows machine. Now, the partner has everything on his machine with Ubuntu OS as a virtual machine running on Windows OS. The Ubuntu OS virtual machine has the same environment setup. When the partner runs the code in the virtual machine, he gets the same error instantly. The partner resolves the error, creates a new ISO file with corrected code from the virtual machine and sends it to us through Cloud. This type of virtualization is application virtualization.

The first advantage is that a lot of time is saved. The second advantage is that only hardware and a virtual box are needed to run any virtual machine, and work on the same project in parallel. Now, we know how virtualization is advantageous. The cloud has multiple virtual machines, and client applications can select virtual machines with respective OS as well as set its environment to deploy applications.

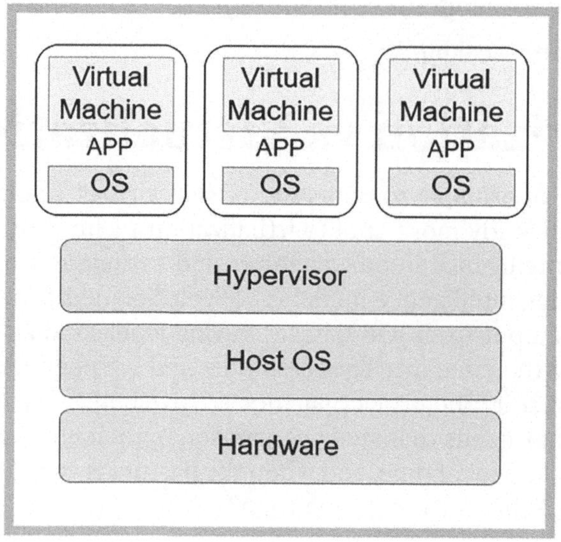

Figure 10.1: *Architecture of Virtualization Technology*

Virtualization, as seen by example, runs multiple OS on a single host machine, and these OS independently are known as Virtual Machines (VMs). These virtual machines share hardware capabilities of the host machine such as storage, memory and processor. The operating system of the machine that runs multiple VMs is known as Host OS. Virtualization allows the user to partition the host machine into multiple machines, each running different applications on different environments. The architecture of virtualization technology as shown in *Figure 10.1*.

Virtualization runs multiple machines on the host OS with the help of a software known as hypervisor. Hypervisors allocate resources to VMs, and it keeps each machine isolated. It allows multiple machines to run simultaneously on the same hardware resources. Thus, it is a very important part of application virtualization. There are two types of hypervisors. Hypervisors of type 1 directly control hardware resources on bare metal, and they do not need a host OS. Hypervisors of type 2 are installed on host OS, and they manage hardware resources through OS. VirtualBox installed on both the machines in the example is a type 2 hypervisor.

We studied Cloud Architecture using virtualization technology in *Chapter 2, Conventional Cloud vs Edge*. Further, we studied Virtualization technology used to deploy cloudlets on network edge in *Chapter 4, Integrating Edge with Cloud in IoT Architecture*. Thus, Virtualization is very popular in the Internet of Things and edge computing domain. However, these days, the edge devices are very small with very limited hardware resources. To have more resources and scalability, multiple edge devices are connected as a cluster for edge computing.

Two popular virtualization technologies in IoT with edge devices are embedded virtualization and network virtualization. Embedded virtualization runs multiple VMS on IoT device. Network virtualization techniques are SDN and NFV, we studied in *Chapter 6, IoT Data Networking at Edge*. Containerization is a type of virtualization technology that is popular on edge devices. This technique runs multiple applications packaged as a container on the host operating system. The resources of the host OS are virtualized and shared within containers. The architecture is shown in *Figure 10.2*.

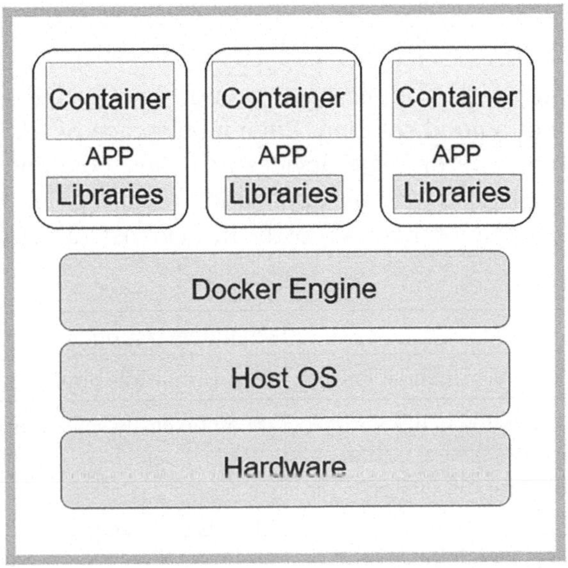

Figure 10.2: *Architecture of Containerization Technology*

Thus, virtualization is good for applications that have independent components, whereas containerization is best suited for homogeneous applications. With these advantages over virtualization, containerization is nowadays very popular in IoT and edge computing having resource-constraint edge devices.

Containerized Edge Intelligence

We know that containerization has major benefits in IoT edge computing, but how it is utilized in an IoT application is a very important concept to know. In *Chapter 8, Leveraging Edge Intelligence*, we learnt about different analytical models that can be deployed on edge devices like Raspberry Pi and Jetson Nano. The deployed edge intelligence is a pre-trained model that is trained and tested at Cloud or normal PC. Deployment of pre-trained models on edge devices is done via containerization.

Next, we will see another situation. In *Chapter 8*, we also studied federated learning, in which the model is trained at edge in a distributed model, and shared to the cloud for developing a global model. Collaborative model training without sharing sensitive data in federated learning is done through containerization technology. The edge intelligence model deployed on edge which is either pre-trained, or is part of federated learning is known as containerized edge intelligence. The containerized edge intelligence provides real-time analysis.

Why edge intelligence has to be on a container when it can be directly implemented on the host OS of an edge device? Containers provide portability, process isolation and management of microservices of the application. If the application can be divided into multiple independent services, each termed as micro-service, containerization is very beneficial.

On the other hand, if the application cannot be divided into microservices, containerization is not a good solution. Edge intelligence of IoT can be deployed in a microservice architecture on edge devices and thus, containerization technology is very useful. IF there is a very simple application requiring only one edge device for computation, containerization may be costly. In that case direct deployment is more suitable.

	Virtualization	Containerization
1.	It runs multiple OS on the host OS.	It runs multiple applications on Host OS.
2.	It can scale up and down, but with each up-scale, there is new virtual machine overload on the host OS.	It can be easily scaled up and down.
3.	It provides isolation to every machine running, which means the applications are more secure.	It runs isolated processes on the same OS, and thus, they are less secure.
4.	It runs on host OS and portability may be an issue.	Containers are compatible with host OS hardware and thus, they are a more optimal solution for heterogeneous edge devices.
5.	Image file of a virtual machine is very large as it includes its own OS.	Image file is lightweight and suitable for embedded devices.
6.	The virtual machine needs to have a hypervisor of type 1 or type 2 to manage hardware resources.	The software to run containers is docker engine which is very lightweight compared to hypervisor.
8.	It supports multiple applications running on the same machine in parallel.	It supports running multiple instances of the same application as microservices on the same machine.

Table 10.1: *Comparison between Virtualization and Containerization*

The benefits of containerized edge intelligence are as follows:

- Containers are a package of application and supporting environment as well as dependencies, and it can be easily deployed on any edge device with similar architecture and OS. This is how it provides portability. Packaging is similar to virtual machines, except it does not package the OS.

- The containers are easy to be deployed on Cloud or other edge devices providing light-weight transfer and consistent deployment. This is beneficial when intelligence is deployed on Cloud or Edge, depending on the service requirement.
- Containers can be easily created, started, stopped, scaled and managed over a cluster of edge devices.
- There is never a dependency conflict with the host OS as the container already has its own host OS with dependencies. This makes the container independent of the host OS.
- If one container fails, the other containers are not affected.
- If a container fails, it can be recovered through its image file. The image file is updated from the running container.
- If there is a large-scale IoT application, the intelligence model can be updated to Cloud, and migrated to geographically distributed edge devices by containerizing it. This provides real-time intelligence model updates on edge devices.

Containerization edge intelligence keeps the edge intelligence consistent across edge devices. There are multiple IoT applications that deploy containerized edge intelligence. To deploy containers on edge, docker and Kubernetes are popular tools. Docker creates images and deploys containers. Kubernetes is an orchestration tool that manages containers across clusters of edge devices.

To illustrate the use-case of containerized edge intelligence, we will see a smart home application based on federated learning. To check if lights are on, if the door is open, if there is smoke, the data from the door, smoke detector and lights need not go to the cloud for analysis. They can be analyzed as different microservices each running in a separate container at the network edge. The microservices running edge intelligence is updated and then the updated model container is migrated to Cloud for global update. The data does not move directly to the Cloud, preserving smart home privacy. Migration is very easy, managing these microservices on the network edge is very easy with the help of containers.

Docker is a building block of images and running containers and Kubernetes is a container orchestration tool. Both are very important technologies to build a containerized edge intelligence application. Next two sections will focus on Docker and Kubernetes to deploy containerized edge intelligence.

Docker

It is a platform to build images and run containers and deploy the running containers on the host machine. It is the most used containerization tool worldwide. It has a docker image repository known as Docker Hub which keeps docker image files that have built software. These files can be taken from the hub and used on any host machine, to directly use the software. Some popular docker image files are python, node, mongo, tensorflow, nginx, and ubuntu. From examples, it is clear that docker images can have an OS, a database, an application. These images are considered as base images when we build our application on it. Once our application is complete, we can create the application's image and save it on the docker hub for future use. Multiple hosts can work on the same base image simultaneously and commit it on the local host. The base images on docker hub cannot be altered. We can keep copies of images on localhost to develop applications in offline mode.

To fetch images from the docker hub onto a local machine is **PULL** operation, and to store the newly created image running application at docker hub is done via **PUSH** operation. To Pull or Push images between the local host and docker hub, docker needs to be installed on the local machine.

Installation Steps on Ubuntu OS distribution:

1. **`sudo apt-get install docker-ce docker-ce-cli containerd.io docker-buildx-plugin docker-compose-plugin`**
2. **`sudo docker run hello-world`**

Step 2 will ensure successful docker installation if it shows the hello world message by pulling the hello-world image from installed docker files, and running it as a container. To utilize Docker on Windows, we need to install Docker Desktop.

Docker follows a client-server architecture. Some popular tools of docker are:

- **Docker Host**: Physical or virtual machine that runs docker and has docker-engine compatible OS.
- **Docker Engine**: It is a client/server software consisting of a docker daemon, docker API, and a command line interface to interact with daemon via API.
- **Docker Daemon**: It is a server that is responsible for creation and management of docker images.
- **Docker Client**: It provides a CLI to access Docker API for interacting with daemon with the help of UNIX sockets or network interface.
- **Docker Objects**: It is a docker component that packages applications for distribution. The package consists of images, containers, volumes, environment, plug-in, network.

- **Docker Image**: It consists of executable source code with libraries, dependencies and environment variables. It has layers where previous layers define the previous versions of the application. These versions provide roll back features.
- **Docker Containers**: When an image runs on the Host OS, it is a container. It is a live component, and users can communicate with it. From a single docker image, multiple containers can be created as instances. This helps in making applications scalable.
- **Docker Build**: It is a command that provides tools to create a docker image.
- **Dockerfile**: It is a file having CLI instructions to create docker images. These instructions are handled by docker engine. The list of commands in Dockerfile for creating images are standardized. This file, when executed, automates creation of image, and running a container of it.
- **Docker Hub**: It is a public repository, a cloud storage for docker images. The image can be shared with anyone with public access over the hub. Anyone can create versions of the image if it is publicly available.
- **Docker Compose**: It is a tool of docker that defines multiple containers of the application, and runs multi-container applications with ease. The definition of each container consists of image name, network, environment, dependencies, and so on. The container definitions that collectively run for an application are saved in a YAML configuration file.

Micro-Service Architecture

Docker supports a micro-service architecture. This architecture is different from monolithic architecture and service-oriented architecture. To explain these architectures in terms of real-life examples, we will see operations in our house. If a person does chores of the house like cooking, laundry, vacuum cleaning, dish cleaning every day, it is a monolithic architecture where the person is the single code that is running and doing chores sequentially. If the person hires a maid for a day to do all the chores, and pays the maid for all the chores, it is a service-oriented architecture. Here the maid needs to schedule all the tasks in a day, and provide the work as a service to the house owner.

Another service can be pest control or gardener; a person can take to keep his house nice. These services are independent and together they do the work for the person. However, service from the maid, gardener is huge and has multiple microservices like watering plants, sowing seeds for gardener and laundry, cooking for maid. In microservice architecture, the micro-services like cooking, vacuum cleaning, grass cutting are made independent of each other. Automated micro-services will do work for the person such as washing machines, dishwashers, and cleaning robots, are all micro-services, and together they keep the house clean. Now, we will study each architecture from a technical point of view.

A monolithic architecture has all applications in a single code. This architecture helps in application development as well as deployment with tight integration and easy management of the whole application within one code. All the components of the application in monolithic architecture work on shared memory and store their data in a centralized, common database. The components of the application are specified as layers in the code, which makes code structure modular. Drawback of monolithic architecture is that it is not easy to scale or adapt to changing needs due to tightly coupled components of the application. When a monolithic code runs, it takes more time to be deployed and if the code fails, the whole application fails. Further, monolithic architecture utilizes more resources of the system where code runs.

In contrast to monolithic architecture, service-oriented architecture combines different services from the internet and creates an application. There is a service provider and a service consumer and they agree to use service based on SLA. The application is a collection of loosely coupled services.

According to service requests from the consumer, the provider will aggregate information from other services or create a workflow of services. Services can be re-used by any application and they do not need to know how the services are being coded. Thus, service-oriented architecture is platform dependent, and these services are available to anyone on request. These services can belong to different business domains, different applications and are accessed through the internet. Drawbacks of service-oriented architecture are high investment on services, service interoperability as they are from heterogeneous providers and their management in a workflow pipeline, when delay in one service can delay in other services.

Microservice architecture is very similar to SOA and it divides the application into fully independent services. The services in SOA are business processes handling high-level logistics. However, in microservice architecture, the services focus on specific tasks and are of very small code size. Thus, the services in which an application is divided in microservice architecture is known as a *microservice*. These services are light-weight and easily scalable. Drawback is communication between services adds complexity and every service has its own data storage and managing multiple storage is tough. Go and read the example provided at the start of this section once again and now we will understand it more clearly.

Micro-services are bundled as a docker image and stored on docker hub. The application that requires the micro-service, pulls the image from the hub and runs it as a docker container. Multiple microservice-based containers running together form a micro-service architecture of the application.

Docker Swarm

To manage containers in the docker environment running on multiple devices, docker swarm is a container orchestrator tool. It is a pool of devices called nodes that consists of a manager node and multiple worker nodes. A running container is called a task. A service defines how to run a container. For communication, docker swarm creates an overlay network. It has two planes: Control Plane and Data Plane. Control plane manages sets of the swarm of nodes, schedules tasks, performs scaling, updates the services whenever required and provides an API to users for interactions. Data plane run containers and tell the status of the running containers to the manager node.

Docker swarm is installed with docker installation. To initialize swarm, the command is:

"**sudo docker swarm init – advertise-addr <IP>**" where <IP> is the IP address of the manager node.

Implementation

Now let us see how to implement an edge intelligence model on a single Raspberry Pi device using Docker. Steps to follow are:

1. Install Docker on Raspbian OS using **`apt-get`** command on terminal.
2. Since Raspberry Pi has an arm architecture, pull python base image for arm architecture.

   Command: `sudo docker pull armhf/python: latest`
3. We can view the downloaded image on the localhost machine; we can even give a new name to the docker image using docker tag command.

   Command: `sudo docker images`
4. Once the image is downloaded, run the image as a container and once the container is running, a terminal on the base image opens with installed python3.

   Command: `sudo docker run -it armhf/python:2.7 /bin/bash`
5. We can even check the status of the running containers through another terminal.

   Command: `sudo docker ps`
6. Within the container, on the terminal of base image, install all python libraries to deploy edge intelligence.

Command:

```
sudo su
apt-get update
apt-get python-numpy
apt-get python pandas
apt-get python-sklearn
apt-get python matplotlib
apt-get network
```

7. Check the folder where the python is installed in the base image.

   Command: `which python`

8. To check where the python library is installed in the base image.

   Command: `dkpg -L numpy`

9. Create a python file importing the libraries and deploying an edge intelligence model. A sample code is listed here that classifies data as per labels using random forest. On Raspberry Pi, we are not training the edge intelligence model. We are preparing the model to be deployed for real-time analysis using a pre-trained model. **`X_val`** is the sensor value on which prediction is made in real-time and **`y_pred`** is the prediction value.

   Python Code:

```
import numpy as np
import matplotlib.pyplot as plt
import pandas as pd
import pickle


filename = 'finalized_model_rasp.sav'
loaded_model = pickle.load(open(filename, 'rb'))

# Predicting the Test set results
y_predv = loaded_model.predict(X_val)
# Predicting the Test set results
y_pred = classifier.predict(X_test)
print(y_pred)
```

10. When the edge intelligence written in python files using a pre-trained model runs successfully on docker, the docker container state needs to be saved to have a new image having edge intelligence with pre-trained model and related libraries. Container-id can be found in Step 5. **`raspberrypi_Code`** is the new name of the base image. More commits to the new image, more layers will be added.

    Command: `sudo docker commit "container-id" raspberrypi_Code`

11. Create a docker hub account with username and password and save the newly created image file. Upload the newly created docker image to the created account by login into docker hub through the local host.

    Command:

    ```
    sudo docker login -u <username>
    sudo docker push raspberrypi_Code
    ```

12. This docker image can be pulled by any other Raspberry Pi device, and or Jetson Nano device for direct deployment on real-time data. Run once, save it as an image, and utilize it multiple times. That is Docker for us.

Kubernetes Orchestration

It is developed by Google to manage thousands of containers running on clusters of large numbers of nodes. Google made it an open-source platform in 2014, and Microsoft, Red Hat as well as IBM are all utilizing Kubernetes for managing containers.

Characteristics

- It deploys containers on nodes, and keeps them in the state they are supposed to bc.
- The container can be used as service over the Internet with a specific IP address.
- If any container needs more resources, it can have storage from a local machine or from Cloud.
- It provides load balancing by distributing workloads over clusters of nodes efficiently. Distribution can be based on CPU or other metric specific.
- It provides auto-scaling where the containers are upscaled or downscaled dynamically, depending on incoming load and scaling of service spreads on to multiple nodes.
- It provides high availability as well as it recovers by itself. It can start a container automatically when it fails to prevent downtime of the application.
- It provides a feature of rollouts. Rollout means the process of adding newer updates to the pods and old ones are removed.
- It provides a feature of roll back, through which pods can go to the previous version if rollout doesn't work.
- It manages stateful applications, and to save states, it provides persistent storage.

Architecture

Kubernetes is a cluster of nodes, and nodes are either physical machines or virtual machines as shown in *Figure 10.3*. Each node consists of pods. Pods are a group of containers that share resources, and are connected to a common network.

Therefore, cluster, node and pods together form a worker node, and ensure a successful Kubernetes deployment, managed by a control plane. But there are more Kubernetes components that are required for deployment of pods, creation of nodes and managing a cluster. Kubernetes components are divided into two parts: Components belonging to the control pane, and components that manage nodes.

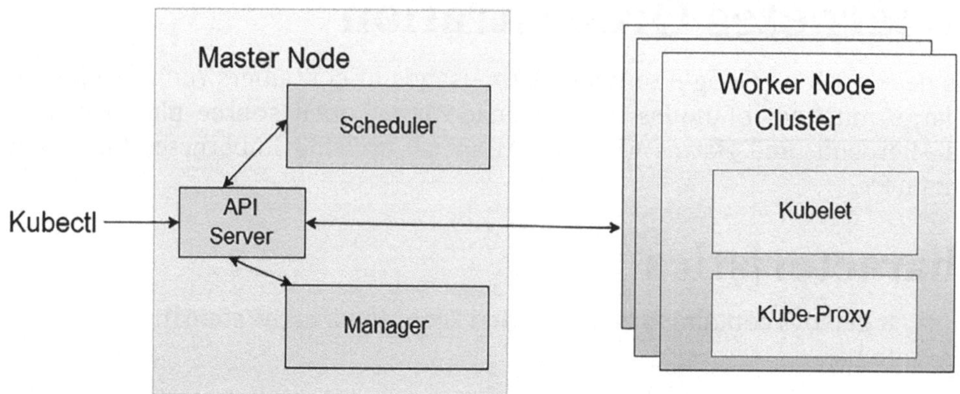

Figure 10.3: *Components of Kubernetes*

Control Plane Components

Cluster has a master node to control other nodes and thus, this master node has a control plane. The components in the control plane are:

- **Kube-apiserver**: It is an entry point to Kubernetes commands, and provides an interface to create clusters as well as configure them.
- **etcd**: It is a distributed key-value store that stores configuration of the cluster, metadata and the state data of the pods.
- **Kube-Scheduler**: It assigns nodes to newly created pods based on resource availability, hardware and software requirements.
- **Kube-controller Manager**: Collection of processes that continuously monitor the shared state of the cluster, and interact with API about it.
- **Cloud-controller Manager**: It manages the cluster's shared state, and communicates it with Cloud API.

Node Components

- **Kubelet**: It is a mediator between master nodes and managed pods in the nodes, using control plane instructions.
- **Kube-proxy**: It is a part of every node of the cluster, and is used to interact with the host machine as well as maintain network rules within the cluster.

Kubernetes for Edge

Kubernetes has proved to be a good solution for the Cloud environment, and it has been also very useful on the network edge too. However, original Kubernetes software has high complexity, and it requires a good number of resources for deployment as well as edge devices have limited resources. Lightweight Kubernetes distributions like K3s and Talos are utilized for edge deployments.

MicroK8 Kubernetes distribution is popular in making Raspberry Pi edge device clusters to utilize benefits of containerization technology. It can be installed on Raspberry Pi, using **`sudo snap install microk8s --classic command`**. To check running nodes in the microk8 cluster, run the command **`microk8s kubectl get nodes`**.

Container Scheduling

Scheduling is an optimization feature of containerization technology. When there is a cluster of edge devices and a container is created, the container has to be placed on edge devices such that the applications' performance is maintained and resource utilization of the cluster is efficiently managed. The placement decision of the container onto the edge device is made by a scheduler.

A schedule is created based on which the container is assigned an edge device. While scaling up, the replica is assigned a different edge device with the help of scheduler. Scheduling arranges edge devices as per current resources, assigns containers to specific edge devices based on load and executes the micro-service. The scheduler can also handle failures by automatically running containers on other edge devices instantly.

Scheduling in Docker Swarm

Docker swarm consists of a manager and multiple nodes connected to the manager, forming a swarm of nodes. The manager has a Swarm Scheduler that assigns images to the nodes and the nodes pull the images instructed by the scheduler and run them as containers. Three strategies are followed by a Swarm scheduler to select a node. Strategies are:

- **Strategy name**: Direct node name is assigned with the container.

- **Spread**: The node is selected that has the minimum containers running currently. This is the default strategy.
- **Binpack**: The node is selected whose resources are used the most.
- **Random**: Node is chosen randomly.

There are two filters provided to the user to filter a node selected from the scheduler. First filter is a constraint filter. This filter is in the form of a key value pair. When all the key value conditions are satisfied, the container runs. Second filter is a health filter that prevents the scheduler from selecting a node for a container that is unhealthy. Unhealthy means it is not behaving as expected due to some issues. There is a "**healthcheck**" option to check the health of the nodes.

Scheduling in Kubernetes

Kubernetes has an attribute named `PodSpec.NodeName` which allows developers to bypass scheduling. This attribute is assigned a node when running a pod. This keeps the pod running on the same node whenever it runs.

If scheduling is not manual, Kubernetes has its own scheduler. schedular of Kubernetes has two parameters: predicates and priorities, on the basis of which the pods are scheduled on nodes. There is a command line flag –policy-config-file which points to a JSON file having a list of predicates and priorities. The flag is used while starting the Kubernetes.

We will discuss the two parameters in detail as follows:

Predicates

- These are rules for scheduling a pod to a node. If any machine is not able to satisfy a pod's requirements, the machine or node will remain in a pending state. Therefore, predicates in simple terms are requirements of a pod for running onto a node.
- Some available predicates are: `PodFitPorts` (no port conflict), `PodFitResources` (resources should be sufficient), `NoDiskConflict` (has enough space), `MatchNodeSelector` (Query should be satisfied), `HostName` (node's name should match).

Priorities

- There is a chance that multiple nodes fulfil the predicates provided by the pod. In such a case, how does the scheduler handle the conflict? Priorities are the list of machines and their weight (key/value).
- Priorities available in the tool are `LeastRequestedPriority` (the node that has free CPU and memory resources as expected by pod), `BalancedResourceAllocation` (Same CPU and memory resources expected

by pod), **ServiceSpreadingPriority** (nodes that have spread of different running pods) and **EqualPriority** (Random selection).

Container Auto-scaling

As the number of **requests/data volume/load** on an application running on a cluster of edge devices increases, the application needs to scale dynamically. The application on the edge device is a collection of microservices running on a container.

One such container is edge intelligence that has to analyze data in real-time. With increasing load, the edge intelligence microservice needs to be scaled to be able to handle load in real-time and accurately. In containerization technology, scaling of containers is very easy. Scaling services on Docker containers are provided by Docker Swarm, Docker Compose and Kubernetes. Scaling provides high availability, and increases efficiency of the application, without being constrained by the hardware capabilities.

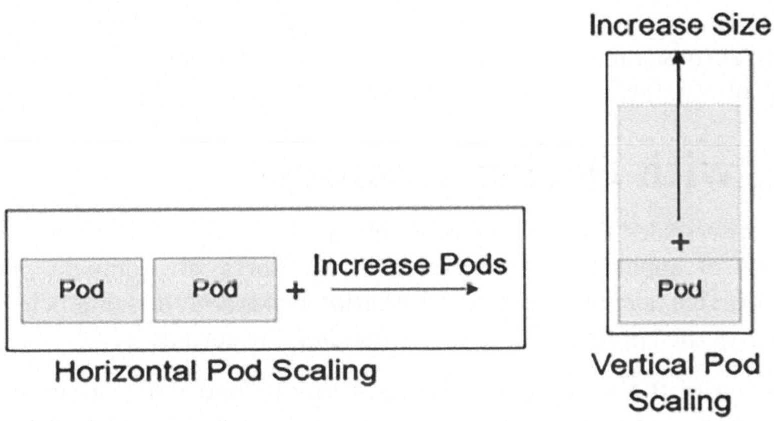

Figure 10.4: *Types of Auto-scaling in Containerization Technology*

There are two scaling methods in containerization as shown in *Figure* 10.4. They are explained as follows:

- **Vertical Scaling**: Suppose load increases at a given instance and resources of containers are not sufficient to handle the data. In such a situation, the CPU and memory of the running container is increased dynamically to handle the incoming load in real-time. Thus, the resource allocation of a container is optimized as per the current load. Dynamic scaling of the container's resources with respect to incoming data reduces resource wastage and optimizes resource utilization. It is suitable for consistent workloads where load hikes are predictable. Vertical scaling on edge devices is tricky and can lead to host edge device failure, if resources are scaled for specific containers. Once the device fails, the application can come down.

- **Horizontal Scaling**: For load that is unpredictable and with huge volume, one container is insufficient. In such a case, the running container is replicated and scaled horizontally to handle incoming data in parallel. This type of scaling increases the number of containers providing edge intelligence in parallel to streaming data.

Containerization technology providing auto-scaling. It means it scales the containers either horizontally or vertically depending on volume of input IoT data. Auto-scaling means upscaling as well as downscaling. Auto-scaling is a prominent feature of Cloud like AWS and Azure. In Cloud, vertical auto-scaling upgrades and downgrades resources of a single **instance/ container/server**. Horizontal auto-scaling increases or decreases replicas of the running container/server. Instance in Cloud is a virtual machine and both instances and containers in the cloud run as servers to handle data. Containers or instances required to run intelligence at Cloud are selected by the IoT application. However, in edge intelligence, containers are deployed to manage load. Auto-scaled on a single edge device using docker-compose and auto-scaling of containers on multiple edge devices is done by docker-swarm and Kubernetes.

Scaling with Docker Compose

Docker compose scales the containers within a single edge device. In a YAML file, configurations of application's services, network ports, environment and storage are specified. This single file defines relationships and dependencies between microservices of the application and corresponding docker image.

On the location of the YAML file, open the terminal and write command docker-compose up. This command runs the containers through a YAML file automatically preserving all dependencies, relationships, network, environment and storage. Docker-compose down command stops the YAML file, stopping all the containers.

To scale services in a YAML file, docker-compose has the command: `docker-compose up --scale` **`` ``service_name" = ``number_of_container". "service_name"``** is replaced by the service that needs to be scaled and "number of containers" is replaced by the value till which container of the service has to be replicated. Docker compose scales up as per the load, however, it does not remove containers until instructed. Docker compose does manual scaling of containers but has no auto-scaling feature.

Scaling with Docker Swarm

Vertical scaling can fail the system in edge devices and thus, horizontal scaling is more appropriate on edge device clusters. Docker swarm is an orchestrator tool having a manager and multiple nodes. Manager scales the containers and scaling is not only on a single device, but considering other nodes as well. Docker swarm effectively manages load by assigning appropriate nodes for replicating containers. Docker swarm master node is initiated using command "**`docker swarm init`**" and it advertises its IP address. The other nodes join the master node by using the command "docker swarm join -token" with a token number generated by the master node. "Docker node ls" command lists all the connected nodes to the master with their IP address. To scale docker service/ container the command is: docker service scale "**`service_name`**"="`scale count`". Docker swarm replicates the container on the nodes connected to the master node and can manage services of multiple IoT applications.

Major drawback of docker swarm is that the master node handles the cluster scaling, which is a single point of failure. Swarm does provide high availability, fault tolerance and optimized utilization of resources but if the master node fails for some reason, the whole application fails. Further, docker swarm also has manual scaling and cannot auto-scale dynamically.

Scaling with Kubernetes

In Kubernetes, the containers can be automatically scaled vertically or horizontally as per the load.

Manual scaling is also an option but auto-scaling is a bonus in Kubernetes which was not provided by Docker Swarm or Docker compose. For horizontal auto-scaling, Kubernetes has an API called **HorizontalPodAutoscalar** (HPA).

It deploys more pods on the cluster to deal with increasing data and scales the pods down automatically. "**`kubectl autoscale`**" command creates horizontal scaling pods with attributes as **`--min and -max`**. "**`min`**" tells minimum pods required for the micro-service and "**`max`**" tells maximum pods the microservice can scale to. To check the status of current auto-scaling, the command is "**`kubectl get horizotalpodautoscalar`**".

For vertical auto-scaling, API is **VerticalPodAutoscaler** (VPA), which is not a default API of Kubernetes. It is a separate GitHub project. It enables creation of **CustomResourceDefiations** (CRDs) for workload which defines conditions for scaling resources of all replicas. There are four different modes of VPA: recreate (resources are adjusted as per the current needs), initial (assigns resources on initial resource request), off (no change in resources).

Performance Optimization

Performance of the containers can be improved to have efficient resource usage, a faster build time and minimized overhead costs. Some popular technique for tuning and best practices are discussed as follows:

- **Container Resource Tuning for ARM Processors**
  - **Limit CPU and Memory Usage:** There is an option to set limit to CPU and memory usage during container runtime. With this limit, the container is unable to overuse the resources of the devices, reducing the burden over devices with limited capacity.

    The command is `docker run -d --memory="1g" --cpu="2" image_name`.
  - **Swap Memory Settings:** Swap memory setting is available to limit the container from using more memory than the available memory while running. It ensures that the memory usage is always within the limits of available memory of the device.

    The command is `docker run -d --memory="512m" -memory-swap="1g" image_name`.
  - **Adjust Container Restart Policies:** Containers are provided with restart option to optimize resources and u.
  - **ptime**: The container enabled with automatic restart under certain condition avoid utilizing unnecessary resources, and is faster compared to manual restart of the containers every time it fails.

    The command is `docker run -restart always image_name`.
- **Image Size Optimization Techniques**
  - **Use smaller base images:** Different base images have different files and thus, different size. For example, base image over an ubuntu OS takes more space and resources compared to smaller base images like alpine. Heavier the base image, it will take more time to push data over the base image and increase the build time. To optimize the image size, select appropriate base image that has only required files and nothing extra. Both, ubuntu and alpine are Linux distributions, however alpine is ideal for containers where resource efficiency is critical.
  - **Multi-stage builds:** Instead of building a single file of docker image in one build command, the image can be optimized by building it in stages. Multiple "`from`" command is used in dockerfile to build the complete image in each stage. For example, in first stage the image is built over a base image. In second stage, the image is built from specific file from the base image and all the relevant files are copied from previous stage to next stage using "`copy`" command in the dockerfile. All other files that are not

required in the final image are removed during copying of data as the build stages proceed. Further, with only single dockerfile and single docker build command, the image size is optimized using multiple stages to build the image. Another advantage is, every stage can be named uniquely and build can be done until a particular stage as per current requirement of the running container. This helps during debugging and testing of the images during production. The end result is tiny image with binary inside.

- **Cold Start Mitigation Strategies**

  Cold start time is the time when the container is started from scratch in case of inactivity or scaling. Cold start time includes time consumed to load the image, time taken in resource provisioning and then time taken to run the application code. Cold start increase latency, provide negative user experience and also consumes resources unnecessarily every time. There are multiple strategies to mitigate cold start discussed as follows:

  - Optimizing container image size.
  - Use local registries to store image file locally for faster download.
  - The containers can be configured as pre-warm to avoid chances of having cold starts.
  - Opting for containers running serverless functions and a serverless database for faster access, to handle workloads that have frequent cold starts. Serverless functions scale more efficiently but still suffer from cold starts but in lesser numbers.
  - There is a tool called liveliness probe that checks if the running container is healthy. The containers are killed if it fails the liveliness probe and declared unhealthy. By enabling custom liveliness probe, longer start time can be allowed to have reduced premature killing of the containers and thus, avoiding cold starts.
  - Application code can be optimized and fine-tuned to have reduced load time.

- **Network Performance in Multi-node Edge Clusters**

  Multi-node edge clusters reduce processing latency compared to Cloud, reduce data transmissions over the network, efficiently utilize bandwidth, performs real-time processing, increase scalability, and optimize costs. Network optimizations in the edge cluster of containers involves efficient communication between the containers and optimized utilization of network resources. Some techniques for optimizing network performance are as follows:

- **Network Policies:**

It is a set of rules that specify how the nodes would be communicating with each and in what conditions. For example, a network policy can be created to only allow traffic within same namespace. Network policies reduce attacks, provide security to network, and is capable of isolating sensitive content.

- **TCP/IP Stack Tuning:** This involves adjustments of various network stack parameters to have optimized performance in case of congested networks and long-distance communications. It is beneficial for workloads that require significant amount of network resources and have to process data in conditions of high network latency. Example of tuning of TCP/IP stack is increasing size of TCP send and receive buffers. This will allow more transmissions and improve network throughput. Another example of tuning is to allow fast open that reduce latency of establishing network connection. Fast open combines data with the first SYN packet.
- **Network Compression:** This technique is utilized in case of heavy bandwidth utilization. This technique reduces size of the data before transmission over the network. The application layer protocol can be configured with a built-in compression or we can use compressed protocols for communication between nodes.
- **Network Segmentation:** Dividing the network into smaller network segments to reduce network traffic for broadcasting as well as enhancing security.
- **Monitor Network Traffic:** By continuous monitoring the flow of network traffic means collecting, analyzing and visualizing communication of data between pods. The metrics that are administered are latency, throughput, error rates etc. with help of monitoring, we can identify network bottlenecks, and create network policies for optimization. Prometheus and Grafana are popular tools used for monitoring cluster network.
- **Connection Pooling:** This is a technique of creating and maintaining a cache of database connection objects with concurrent connections to the database server. The cache is reused with every new connection request rather than establishing new connection every time from scratch. This technique reduces latency and resource overhead in establishing connection to databases with new requests. This technique helps cluster of microservices that provide multiple services use connection pool in case of high-traffic requests to access same database and handle dynamic workloads efficiently. Connection pooling reduce load on the server and quickly scales the connections with the database as per the current number of requests.

Conclusion

This chapter discusses containerization technology and how it is different from virtualization. Virtualization creates virtual machines on the host OS and virtual machines have their own OS. Virtualization on edge devices having limited resources is not feasible. Thus, containerization that is popular in Cloud, is utilized on edge devices for providing services at the network edge. Containerization creates containers on host OS that are independent processes and have code, environment, libraries, dependencies, packaged together. Docker, Docker Swarm and Kubernetes are popular containerization technologies used worldwide. Docker is used to create containers and Docker, Swarm, Kubernetes manages clusters of machines running containers. Docker Swarm has a single point of failure, and therefore, Kubernetes is utilized more as an orchestrator tool. However, Kubernetes is very heavy for edge devices and thus, lighter versions of Kubernetes are used to deploy services on the edge device. Containers are scheduled on load to efficiently utilize resources, and have optimized load balancing. For scheduling containers on multiple nodes, there are various techniques that are different for Docker Swarm and Kubernetes. Auto-scaling is provided by containerization technology with dynamic horizontal as well as vertical scaling as per the incoming workload. Docker and Docker Swarm does manual scaling, whereas Kubernetes provides auto-scaling.

The next chapter discusses the security attacks and privacy threats faced by IoT applications, and respective counter-measures.

Points to Remember

- o Virtualization allows the user to partition the host machine into multiple machines, each running different applications on different environments.
- o Two popular virtualization technologies in IoT with edge devices are embedded virtualization and network virtualization.
- o Containerization is a type of virtualization technology that runs multiple applications packaged as a container on the host operating system.
- o Managing virtual machines is very complex and challenging, and requires great knowledge of hypervisors. In containerization, the containers are easy to manage and portable.
- o If the application can be divided into multiple independent services, each termed as micro-service, containerization is very beneficial.
- o Containers can be easily created, started, stopped, scaled and managed over a cluster of edge devices and thus, good for implementing edge intelligence.

- Docker is a building block of images and running containers and Kubernetes is a container orchestration tool.
- Docker is a platform to build images and run containers and deploy the running containers on the host machine.
- Docker Swarm is a pool of devices called nodes that consists of a manager node and multiple worker nodes. A running container is called a task.
- Kubernetes is a cluster of nodes and nodes are either physical machines or virtual machines. Each node consists of pods. Pods are a group of containers that share resources and are connected to a common network.
- The placement decision of the container onto the edge device is made by a scheduler. A schedule is created based on which the container is assigned an edge device.
- Vertical scaling can fail the system in edge devices and thus, horizontal scaling is more appropriate on edge device clusters.
- Major drawback of docker swarm is that the master node handles the cluster scaling which is a single point of failure.
- For horizontal auto-scaling, Kubernetes has an API called **HorizontalPodAutoscalar** (HPA). It deploys more pods on the cluster to deal with increasing data, and scales the pods down automatically.

Multiple Choice Questions

1. What is not virtualization?
   a. It runs multiple Virtual Machines on Host OS
   b. It has hypervisor to run Virtual Machine
   c. It follows micro-service architecture
   d. It provides hardware isolation
2. Which one of these is a hypervisor?
   a. Docker
   b. VirtualBox
   c. microK8
   d. Kubernetes

3. Where are docker images stored?
    a. Dockerfile
    b. Docker daemon
    c. Docker Container
    d. Docker Hub
4. Docker container is:
    a. Running docker image
    b. Micro-service
    c. Both
    d. None
5. Docker Kubernetes has:
    a. Pods
    b. Manager
    c. Swarm
    d. None of the above
6. What is defined in Predicate in Scheduling on Kubernetes?
    a. Priorities
    b. Node names
    c. Storage devices
    d. Rules
7. Which tool does manual as well as auto scaling?
    a. Docker
    b. Kubernetes
    c. Docker Swarm
    d. None of the above

8. What is vertical scaling?
    a. Increase number of hardware
    b. Increase number of containers
    c. Increase resources
    d. Increase battery capacity

Answers

1. c
2. b
3. d
4. c
5. a
6. d
7. b
8. c

Questions

1. Why is containerization better than virtualization?
2. Why cannot virtualization be implemented on edge devices?
3. What are the benefits of containerized edge intelligence?
4. What are popular tools of Docker?
5. What are the differences between monolithic, Service-Oriented Architecture and micro-service architecture?
6. What are the steps to deploy edge intelligence using Docker?
7. Explain the architecture of Kubernetes.
8. How does a scheduler of docker swarm and Kubernetes work?
9. What are the two types of scaling? Explain auto-scaling in Kubernetes.

CHAPTER 11
Data Security and Privacy

Introduction

A major drawback of Cloud is that the passwords, bank details, or any personal data stored in Cloud is susceptible to data breach. They can be easily accessed by unauthorized hackers. A well-known data breach where we get personalized recommendations through our data stored at Cloud is concerning. The social media data and what we search, type of access on google, and so on is already being stored at their respective Clouds (Facebook, Twitter, and Google Clouds). The data is shared by other websites for personalized recommendations to users, and we get related advertisements in our smartphones and YouTube videos. To protect data to be shared to the Cloud, Edge Computing does not share personal data to the Cloud through the network, and analyse it at edge itself. Example is federated learning. However, the data at edge is at high risk as it consists of highly sensitive information. The information at edge is more focused on specific users utilizing smart home application, smart grid application, smart health application, and security cameras.

However, data at the edge is not safe if someone tries to attack the specific data of a specific user or location. "Your personal data may be exposed" and edge devices require protection. In this chapter, we will study possible attacks on data at edge, and how to develop a privacy preserving and secured IoT edge application.

Structure

In this chapter, we will cover the following topics:

- Security Attacks
- Privacy Threats
- Security Countermeasures
- Blockchain
- Privacy-preserving AI

Security Attacks

Cybersecurity is a field that provides protection to the information in cyberspace. Attacking or breaching privacy of computers and user data is known as **cyber-attack**. Cloud has data security features, and attacking the data at the Cloud is less likely. However, Cloud can share the data with other Cloud and recommender systems to provide more personalized services. Further, even with security, if Cloud is attacked, the whole IoT application will fail. With edge computing, the data and services of Cloud are shared on multiple devices, making it a distributed architecture (no single point of failure) even for attackers. IoT edge devices are more prone to attacks because they are out of traditional security systems. They have a public IP, and collect data near the specific users. Further, they are located in the open, like on traffic lights, doors, and parking zones, that are not easy to be monitored physically. They can be stolen with all the data. Further, there are multiple edge devices giving more options to the attacks to attack on the data and application. If the edge is attacked, the service of the IoT application to that particular location will get blocked.

To provide cybersecurity to edge devices, there are three requirements, known as CIA Triad. CIA stands for Confidentiality, Integrity and Availability as shown in *Figure 11.1*.

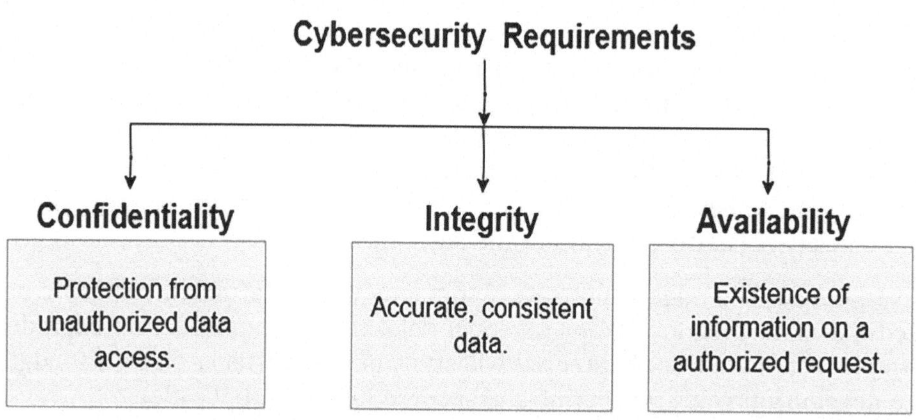

Figure 11.1: *The Three Utmost Requirements to Guarantee Cybersecurity*

- **Confidentiality:** This feature protects private information from unauthorized data access. To incorporate confidentiality in data, the account number is unique, and is required when doing any bank transfers. Username and passwords are another way to protect the data. Two-factor authentication with One-time Password (OTP) is a new and reliable way to access information as well as stop unauthorized access.
- **Integration:** The data should be accurate, consistent and trustworthy. It will only happen if the data is not altered by an unauthorized process or user. Only

authorized users and processes can take actions on the data. Rollbacks and previous versions can fix errors from authorized users. Backups are a form of recovery to keep the data integrated.

- **Availability:** The information should exist whenever asked by an authorized user. The data may be blocked or the system may be attacked, which prevents authorized users from accessing their data, hampering data availability. For safeguarding the information, the hardware of physical devices needs to be protected. To keep the hardware protected from natural disasters, the devices need to be waterproof and fireproof. Firewall also creates a barrier to keep devices protected from unauthorized network access.

If any of the CIA triad is compromised; it means the system is attacked. The attacking entity is known as a **hacker**. There are two types of attacks as shown in *Figure 11.2*: Active and Passive. Active Attack is when the hardware or software resources are impacted, and operations are hindered, and Passive Attack is when there is an extraction of sensitive information without affecting the resources.

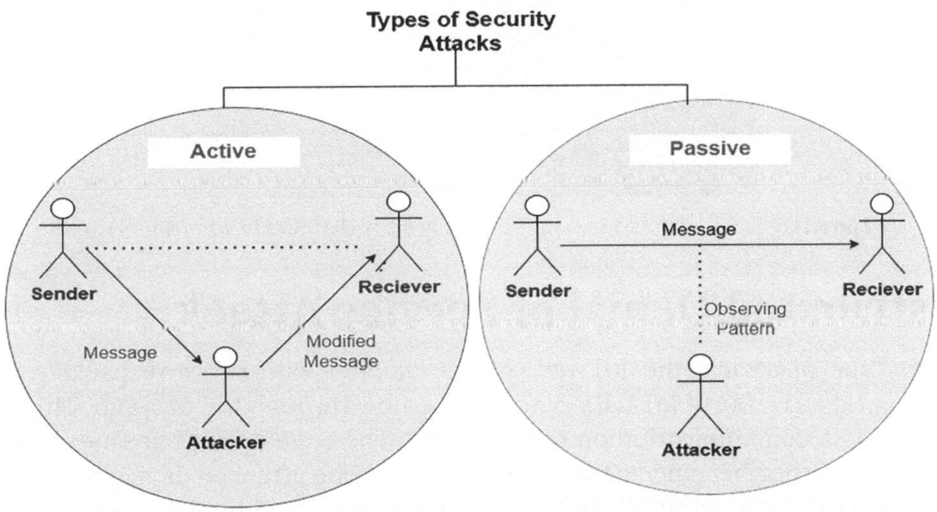

Figure 11.2: *Active Attack Where Attacker Modifies the Message, and Passive Attack Where Attacker Only Observes*

- **Active Attack:** When an attacker enters into a system and changes system state, alters data and aims to damage the application, then it is an active attack. Active attack is observable and action can be taken instantly. It is like attacking a king with an army where the attack is visible on the battlefield or a thief stealing a bank, altering the accounts by taking money with him.
- **Passive Attack:** It is a type of attack where the system is being attacked is not known at all. The data and operation are being continuously monitored through eavesdropping. It is continuously listening to data, and copying the data for personal use. This type of attack is hidden, and that is why it is more

dangerous. The attacker can read messages, and can detect who is the host OS taking services of the application.

Attacks that edge computing devices suffer shown in *Figure* 11.3 are discussed as follows.

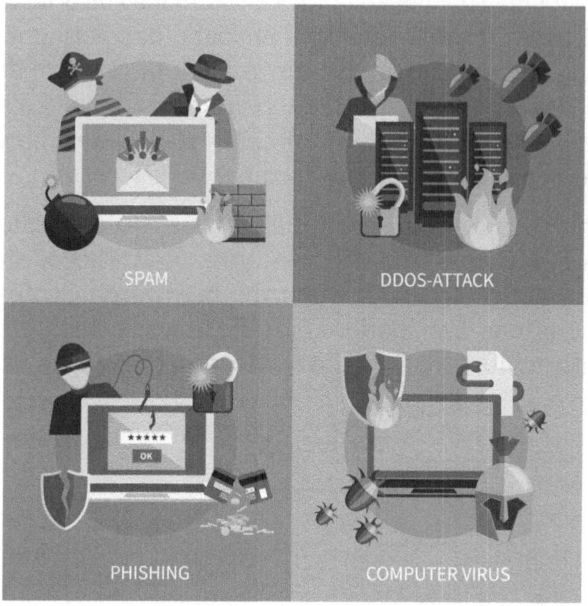

Figure 11.3: *Some of the Common Security Attacks that Steal Data from Systems*

Distributed Denial of Service Attack

In this type of attack, the IoT network is jammed with network packets. With jamming, usual traffic of IoT data is not able to flow through the network. This stack disrupts data communication on the network. The edge devices are injected with malware, and they become agents of the attacker. The attacked device is called bot and their group is a botnet. Each botnet is then instructed by the attacker to send network packets to a particular target machine.

Target machine can be a Cloud IP. With a huge number of packets on the network from distributed edge devices that form botnets, the network goes into denial of service. It is difficult to filter normal packets from packets sent by an attacker. If we press the refresh button, again and again, on the web browser, multiple HTTP requests are generated. These requests can cause the network to be congested, blocking network traffic. This attack is very similar to continuously refreshing the same website on different machines. Multiple packets from attacked edge devices block the normal operation of the network, causing system failure due to packet unreachability.

Side-Channel Attack

In this attack, the signals from electronic devices are captured to exploit hardware information and non-functional characteristics of the program. The data from signals can tell power consumption pattern, electromagnetic emissions, or sound. Through this data, the attacker can uncover cryptography keys and cryptic data.

It is a type of passive attack; it sneaks into the signal and the attack is unknown to the system. Hardware processors and memory are also prone to attack. Storage and processing instructions can also tell a lot about data. Through these signals, the system can be reconstructed at the attacker's end. After getting the private information like keys or passwords, the data may get leaked, and open the hardware to unauthorized access.

Malware Injection

In this attack, the attacker injects malware in the system. The malware then hinders the normal operation of the system. These attacks are very dangerous. The malware is a malicious code that can make the device perform unusual tasks. With the malware, it can steal the data, alter the processes, may send the data to different devices, and may hang the application. There are three types of injections:

- **SQL injection:** Through SQL queries, the database data can be altered. This affects data availability and integrity.
- **Command injection:** Through commands, the system is accessed and altered unauthorized. The command takes control of the device. Indirectly, with command, the attacker takes control of the device.
- **XML injection:** Processing of XML data or documents is hindered by attacking XML applications.
- **Cross-site Scripting Attack (XSS):** The malicious code is injected into the webpage, and the script runs when the user accesses the attacked webpage. There are three types of XSS attacks. First type is Stored XX where the script is stored at the webserver and is to the browser of the requesting user. Second type is reflected in XSS where the script is provided to the user upon request of something. It runs when the user clicks on or provides malicious content. Third type is DOM-based where the malware is present at the client-side web page, and not on the server. Through this attack, the user can steal cookies, passwords, or show fake logins.
- **Cross-site request forgery:** In this attack, the user is fooled to click on a malicious link during active sessions on a webpage. This malicious link executes actions on the browser without consent. Some malicious activities are fund transfer or passwords being updated.

- **LDAP injection:** Lightweight Directory Access Protocol (LDAP) is a protocol used for user authentications and sign-in systems. The attacker can construct LDAP statements based on user inputs to gain access to personalized information. After gaining access, the attacker can run the malicious code.

The data captured from this attack can be sold on the dark web, and can be used to access bank accounts as well as do bookings, or can be used for blackmailing.

Authentication and Authorization Attacks

To provide security to personal information, an application has to log in with a username and a password. The username and password must be unique for each of the users to access the application data having personal data. Further, the password is known by application as well as the user but no one else. The combination of usernames and passwords ensures authentication as well as authorization. A user is authentic if the username or password being provided matches the username and passwords stored in the application's database. Further, users that are provided access by the application are authorized to read and manipulate data. Thus, the user who is authorized will have a username and password, and the user is authenticated to access the application if he provides the correct username and password. Signing into the application is providing data security to the authentic users authorized to access the application data and services.

However, this security aspect is attacked by hackers in various ways. Data breach happens when the password is weak, or is being observed somehow.

Authentication Attacks

- Brute Force trials of password detection
- Weak Login Password
- Username enumerations like password incorrect/username incorrect messages
- Staying logged in
- Session management is poor
- Password recovery is insecure
- Human errors leaving devices behind or systems logged into accounts
- Two-factor login with number on stolen phone

Authorization Attacks

Authorization is when a user has privilege or rights to access data and application's services. Privilege escalation is an attack.

There are two types of privilege escalation: Vertical and horizontal. Vertical privilege escalation is when users get access to administrative services. Horizontal privilege escalation is when a user gets access to another user's data, and has all application's services normally from another user's account. These are unauthorized access, and thus categorized as an attack to security of the device and data.

Integrity Attacks Against Machine Learning

The ML/AI model for edge intelligence is being attacked, and the model's integrity is the prime target. IF the integrity of the ML model is not maintained, it will give erroneous decision-making, impacting the IoT services. This will undermine reliability on the Io/t application. Types of attacks on ML models that harm integrity are as follows:

- **Input Manipulation:** The attacker injects a malicious code that crafts different inputs which may force the system to provide erroneous results.
- **Denial of Service:** The ML/AI model is attacked with bursts of queries/ requests which cause the model to go into denial of service, and the model crashes.
- **Membership Interference:** ML model is attacked with undetectable input, thus, exploiting the unseen aspect of the ML model. This causes misclassification and model failing completely in understanding the input.
- **Infection Attacks:** The malware is embedded in the model by the attacker like a Trojan horse. Whenever the model runs, it attacks the integrity of the model from within by modifying the model. For instance, if the AI model of the cloud has malware, and is deployed on edge systems via network, the model will be damaged at all edge devices.
- **Model Poisoning:** The model is trained with tampered data, leading to inaccurate decision-making. Such AI models are dangerous for using IoT applications that are time-critical, for example, healthcare applications.
- **Model Inversion:** In this attack, reverse engineering is applied on the trained model, to capture the sensitive training data. This attack is possible in federated learning where the trained models are propagated to the Cloud for global trained models, hiding sensitive information into the trained models.

  There is a python library called "secml" that provide the testing of attacks on ML models for making it robust. The library requires Python version to be less than 3.11, and NumPy version to be less than 2. The code implements trained SVM model, and tests it on two popular attacks as follows:

```
from secml.adv.attacks import CAttackEvasionPGD
from secml.adv.attacks import CAttackPoisoningSVM
from secml.ml.classifiers import CClassifierSVM
```

```
from secml.data import CDataset
import pandas as pd
# Load a dataset
df = pd.read_csv("heart_failure_clinical_records_dataset.csv")
X = df.iloc[:,:-1].values
y = df.iloc[:,-1].values
dataset = CDataset(X, y)

# Train a simple SVM classifier
clf = CClassifierSVM(kernel='linear')
clf.fit(dataset.X,dataset.Y)
# Create an evasion attack
attack = CAttackEvasionPGD(classifier=clf, distance='l2')
# Perform the attack
x_adv = attack.run(dataset.X[0, :], dataset.Y[0])
print("Adversarial example:", x_adv)
attack = CAttackPoisoningSVM(classifier=clf, training_data=data-
set, val=dataset, solver_params={'eta': 0.1})
# Perform the poisoning attack
poisoned_data = attack.run(dataset.X[0, :], dataset.Y[0])
print(f"Poisoned Data: {poisoned_data}")
```

Privacy Threats

An "attack" is deliberate, intentional, and damages the device code. A threat is different from attack. It is a violation that can cause an attack later. Threats may be due to negligence, disaster, system failure, human error or accidental as shown in *Figure 11.4*. There are four types of threats to security: Unstructured threat, structured threat, external threat and internal threat.

Figure 11.4: A *Hacker Using Credit Card Details Shared Accidentally to Access an Account*

- **Unstructured threat** is when a non-hacker tries to guess the password or use shell scripts to hack the system.

- **Structured threat** is when a professional hacker deliberately does a privacy breech in an organization.
- **External threat** is when an outsider who does not have good terms with the organization, gets unauthorized access to the organization's data and devices.
- **Internal threat** is when someone within the organization who has authorized access to the data has ties with outsiders, and supplies them the data.

Some possible threats to IoT application with edge computing are:

- Smart Objects communicate with each other and have an IP address which is an open network for hackers.
- Outdated hardware and software, not complied with latest security updates.
- Complex structure of devices where faults created by hackers are hard to find.
- Weak username and passwords that are kept as default by developers.
- Data transfer is insecure with so many IoT devices over network.
- Continuous monitoring and tracking by IoT applications are an open threat for users, and threat for hackers.
- Each of the edge devices has heterogeneous security aspects, creating inconsistency for protection.
- Theft and tampering of the edge devices placed in remote areas is a possible threat, and security of these devices is overlooked.

These are threats that affect security as well as privacy of the data, device and users. There are privacy threats that are very crucial to know for edge computing, especially. Edge devices like smartphones have a lot of images, and many of the images are uploaded to the Cloud of Google or Dropbox or Apple. Billions of personal data is stolen from these Clouds by the hackers. So, we prefer keeping images in offline mode, and do not post it on social media Clouds, or store it to a third-party Cloud. Currently, the edge devices are being hacked, and the private information is being sent to unexpected locations. Therefore, anything that is connected to the Internet is a threat to privacy. A smart home camera can also be hacked, and an attacker can see the daily routine of the person, violating privacy.

There are multiple IoT applications that are for societal good, but compromising with the privacy of the people. And if the application is hacked, the private data can be misused for wrong intentions. Some of the IoT application use cases are:

Schools Aiding AI-powered Surveillance Camera

In this IoT application, the school is inbuilt with cameras on every corner that capture facial expressions of the students in real-time. With facial expressions, we can detect the mood of the student, and identify any harmful intentions. Further, it can also detect if the student has a weapon. This application is for U.S based schools where school shootings are increasing. The AI model can also detect unusual motion of a person within the school premises. If AI detects anyone, the security team will be alarmed immediately. The application's purpose is great, however, cameras are prone to hackers. The hackers can use the data to know about students and school premises. Thus, this application is good in providing real time security from harmful people, but it is very critical in providing safety from hackers and cyber-attacks.

Applications to Monitor Corona-spread in the People

The idea in this application is to monitor people having corona and alert people to corona possibilities in the neighbourhood. The application associates' people of a country with a centralized server using biometric to store all their information. The biometric devices are connected to the person, that are able to continuously monitor activity, temperature and heart rate of the person to detect Corona. Manual entry of the corona from the user is avoided as some people may choose not to provide information. This way, the spread of corona can be stopped in a particular location, making nearby users aware personally. Further, the corona-spread can be reduced by confining the people, monitoring them to get better and stay away from others. This application is for good cause, but it is a privacy threat to users who are being monitored all day. If the application is hacked, the private data of the users can be misused for different purposes.

Thus, before developing an application, the developer should also have counter measures to protect the data from cyber-attacks and privacy threats. IoT needs to be useful for society, making smart decisions, and in real-time. But these applications need to protect the data at edge or Cloud from attacks, and should have ways to handle/detect hacking beforehand. In the remaining sections, we will study how to protect edge devices from being hacked.

Security Countermeasures

There are effective countermeasures developed by researchers as defence to attacks, and privacy threats as shown in *Figure* 11.5. These are listed as follows:

- **Defence of Malicious Injections:** The injections can be detected by analysing side channels to detect a change in temperature, power consumption, or some unusual hardware activity. If there is a change in pattern, it means there is hardware trojan or malicious software inside the device.

  Trojan activation methods are used to create models of trojan injected, and trojan free devices as well as compare side-channel leakages, outputs and behaviour of the machine in both cases. When a real-attack happens on the device, it would be easy for the device to detect it when it sees a similar pattern as seen during comparison.

Another method is the device goes on self-destruction, and erases their data if an attack is happening. Mostly, the device tries to prevent an attack. Adding noise and delay to data during attack will prevent information from leakage. Basically, countermeasures are to prevent/hamper an attacker's software to function properly.

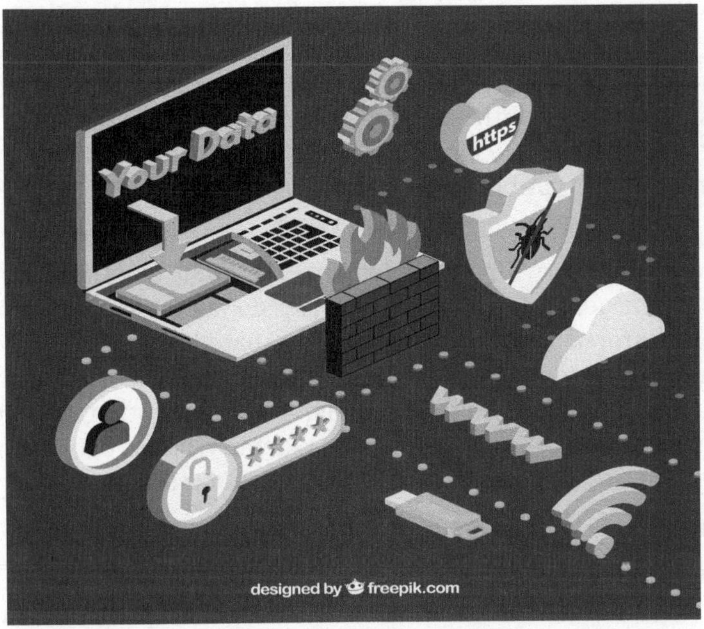

Figure 11.5: *Security Countermeasures such as Intrusion Detection System, Reliable Network Protocols and Authorization that Safeguard the Data from Attackers*

- **Policy-based:** Abnormal requests to the nodes are detected by the edge device and rejected. The requests are abnormal if they try to make the system sleep, or drain the battery, or make the system hang.
- **Firmware Security Updates:** Firmware is the software embedded in the hardware. For an IoT application, every IoT device needs to have updated firmware security, and they should keep a check on each other whether updates have happened or not. The update should maintain integrity of the device. The updates can be broadcasted on the network, or done via a remote connection.
- **Reliability of Network Protocols:** Routers and Switches have tables that consist of trusted IP addresses and Mac addresses, and if any request comes from outside the trusted IP address, it is immediately dropped.
- **Intrusion Detection System:** This is an application that monitors network traffic, and detects unusual activities over the network that are suspicious or a threat. Intrusion is when an attacker has unauthorized access into the system. It provides a second layer of security to the device over the network, keeping

a check on incoming network packets, and immediately generating alarms and reporting. The layer comes into action when the network packet somehow has managed to bypass the firewall, which is the first layer of security. This system is easily adaptable with new features to counter-attack new threats.

- **Cryptography:** It is a method that encrypts the data from the source node, and data is decrypted by the destination node. The key for encryption and decryption is only with the source node and destination node. No other device can understand the message sent by the source node without the key. The key is also secured with another key. Attacker is usually sniffing packets for the key so that it can decrypt the incoming message and do a privacy breach. Encryption/decryption method has increased data security and provides reliable communication over the network.

  Edge nodes are very tiny to implement encryption algorithms for every data it sends on the network. Thus, edge devices do not follow traditional algorithms. The data is stored in encrypted form over a shared network, and the devices need to search for the data on the shared network. Then the data can be decrypted with a key. There are multiple techniques of encryption/decryption that are light-weight on edge devices such as identity-based encryption, searchable encryption, attribute-based encryption, and homomorphic encryption.

- **Two-factor Authentication:**
  - **Biometric factor**: This uses physical attributes such as face, fingers, voice, and hand gestures to identify an authorized person. Every individual's biometric uniquely defines their physical trait, and helps in authentication. Biometric of two individuals cannot be the same.
  - **Location factor**: Logging into device is permitted only from a specific location, and the location is tracked whenever there is an access attempt on the device.
  - A **Single Factor Authentication (SFA)** is used to be a common approach to authenticate accessing user via one of these factors. However, only one factor could not stop attacks. Two-factor authentication is a two-way process, where user use first factor to access and system requires second factor to confirm the authentication of user. Second factor adds a new layer and also prevents attacker as it is hard to guess both the factors to gain access as shown in *Figure 11.6*. Second factor must be different from the first factor If two steps belong to same factor, the authentication is considered as SFA.

Steps in 2FA are as follows:

1. User enters username and password to login into a website, or a system application.

2. The server matches the username and password with the stored data.
3. If there is a match, the server generates prompt for second factor.
4. The second factor can be any of the factors above like one-time password, or a token key, or a specific location, or a biometric.
5. If second factor also matches with the stored data, the user is granted access.
6. If there is no match in any of the steps, the user is asked for other login attempts.
7. The login attempts are limited to prevent the hacker from trying with different patterns to access the data.

Figure 11.6: *Two-factor Authentication*

Most of the 2FA enabled system provide tokens to authorized users to access the data. These tokens can be software apps that generate one-time passwords (OTPs) or hardware devices such as smart cards or fobs. Hardware tokens are attached to the device, and it generates a unique key every time the user attempts to login. The company providing tokens to its employees need to deploy the security system to authenticate users with their tokens. The security system may be a hardware server, software server, or a third-party vendor.

2FA is also prone to attacks. There are multiple ways attackers bypass the 2FA system. The OTPs or passwords should not be communicated over internet or mobile network to be safe from unauthorized access. SMS-based

2FA is easy to implement however, it is very vulnerable as attacker on mobile phones can intercept the incoming messages and use the OTP after changing the password from temporary email. Thus, choosing a good combination of two factors is very much necessary step to provide authorized access to the personal information.

- **Secured Analysis of Data:** Partitioning of Cloud functions to multiple edge devices like training the model in distributed manner, and it may distribute the training data of AI model. This way the training data will not be accessed at one place. Example is federated learning.
- **Prior Testing:** The IoT network and devices are tested for all possible attacks to check if it can withstand it and secure data/hardware. If successful, the application is deployed, and runs on a public network.
- **Outlier Detection:** ML models are attacked by some unknown inputs that can provide erroneous results. These inputs can be detected as outlier during pre-processing of the data, and dropped.
- **Decentralization:** The sensitive information is not on one edge node but distributed among multiple edge nodes, such that the attacker has a hard time finding all information about the person at one place, cloud or edge.
- **Secure Data Aggregation:** All the devices in the IoT application follow a homomorphic encryption system. The data from edge devices is sent to the fog node in encrypted form, the fog node fuses the data in the encrypted form, and the Cloud decrypts the result as well as analyses it. The fusion is performed during data pre-processing.
- **Secure Removal of Duplicates:** Removal of duplicate data is performed at edge nodes during pre-processing for reducing network bandwidth consumption. This is a strategy of deduplication where if hackers get access to duplicate data, they will not get information through it.
- **Zero Trust Architecture:** It is a technical framework that implements zero trust principles in the IT infrastructure. The three principles of zero trust are as follows:
  - **Continuous monitoring and validation:** Usage of resources is monitored continuously to safeguard hardware from being attacked. The users are verified through Multi-Factor Authentication (MFA). Application whitelisting is done to ensure running of the pre-approved applications preventing any other application from running.
  - **Least privileged access enforced:** The users have access privilege to only the specific data, services or applications, where they are needed to perform operations. The enforcement safeguards the system from insider attack, and minimizes exposures of the application, data, and services to the compromised/hacked users.

- **Assumption of breach:** It assumes that the security/privacy breach is unavoidable and thus, it aims to reduce the impact of the breach. For avoiding or tackling breach, the architecture continuously monitors the user, device, software behavior, and has robust response to failures and a quick recovery process and implement an end-to-end encryption on sensitive resources through micro-segmentation.

To apply these principles, ZTA uses prominent security technologies that are micro-segmentation (divides the network into small segments for having control over resources), encryption, identity and access management, MFA and real-time monitoring.

The principles are applied to the systems, networks and the workflow to secure it from attackers. It replaces the implicit trust that applications or devices have while communicating data with each other over a network. This architecture provides security in IoT applications and multi-cloud applications that are directly accessed from anywhere, anytime. The key elements of the architecture are users, applications, and the infrastructure. Users and their device go through a strong authentication process. Applications are continuously monitored during runtime to validate their behavior. Infrastructure is also secured from routers, switches to Cloud, and IoT devices.

The architecture enhances security, provides protection against breach, increases visibility within the system and network, though logging can easily scale with the growing number of users and network devices, as well as allow secure remote work and authorized access to Cloud environments.

- **Regular Compliances:** It is a process to adhere to the laws, regulations and policies issued by government or regulatory bodies to protect sensitive data (financial and personal) and maintain business trust by ensuring legal standards are followed. Regulations vary depending on the scale of the organization. For example, organization spread in multiple countries need to comply with law and regulations of each of the country. The regulations increase in scale and volume, and thus, require right policies, measures and processes to ensure compliance. Regulatory compliance is important to protect data, organization from cybercrimes and hackers as well as intact integrity of the processes. The compliances increase trust in the clients and business partners and also the business operates in fair and ethnic manner. If any compliance is not followed, there is a lawful procedure for heavy penalties.

  Thus, to ensure data security from cyber-crimes, there are four popular and important laws: GDPR, CCPA, PCI-DSS and HIPAA. The key parameters in each law are discussed as follows:

  - **General Data Protection Regulation (GDPR):** It is law enforced in European countries that protects the personal information of European citizens. The organization having European clients is required to handle the data responsibly and provide more control to the people over their data. The law requires organizations to report any data breech within 72 Hrs. The law has heavy penalties in case a fraud activity with the data is detected.
  - **California Consumer Protection Act (CCPA):** This law requires organization to inform the California residents about their personal data collection, reason for collection and where it is being shared. It provides the consumer rights to get information on their data and also opt-out of the organization if they feel their data is not safe. This law increases the trust on the organization as well as provide business transparency to the California clients. If California clients find any breech, the client can lawfully sue the organization and organization has to go through heavy penalties.
  - **Payment Card Industry-Data Security Standard (PCI-DSS):** This law secures credit card transactions from breech and fraud. It also ensures that personal as well as card information of the client is protected. The transactions are required to be encrypted and only authorized personals are allowed to access and process the transactions. If found guilty, the organization pays fine or may have an increase in transaction fee.
  - **Health Insurance Portability and Accountability Act (HIPAA):** This law safeguards health information of the patients to protect against identity theft and frauds. The personal information, medical history and the health records of the patient needs to be provided only to the patient or the people the patient trusts and is not allowed to communicate all the information over phone calls, messages or emails.
- **Secure Boot and Attestation:** During boot of the system, there is an option of secure boot. The secure boot if enabled, checks all the components are not tampered before proceeding with the boot. Only trusted software is allowed to run when the system boots/starts up. It verifies digital signature of the operating system and the bootloader with stored keys in the system itself. Digital signature uses a digital certificate and cryptography tool to maintain integrity of a document. Digital certificate provides unique ID to the signer and it has public key for signature verification. The sign on the software is done by the developer and once signed, the document cannot be altered by the creator. If the software is tampered, the digital signature will change and will not match the original. If the digital signature is valid, then only boot proceeds. Secure boot is implemented as part of Unified Extensible Firmware Interface (UEFI).

The verification for all the components is done through attestation. Attestation is storing of measurements in current state of the software and hardware components during boot process in a Trusted Platform Module (TPM). The attestation provides assurance that the devices is currently in trusted state and no software is tampered. Attestation proves the trust over the software and software that is tampered is easily detected. Utilizing both the techniques provides more security to system components during boot process and checks for attacks before having a successful boot.

- **Edge Computing and Blockchain:** Blockchain is a security system that provides secure transactions of information in a distributed system. The edge devices perform transactions together with voting and consensus. There is no centralized system that is trusted for all the transactions within edge devices. Distributed and shared data schemes in cryptography can be easily implemented with blockchain technology. Blockchain preserves data privacy, and secure the data by distributing it, as well as performing secure transactions over it. We will study blockchain in the next section.

Blockchain

It is a database, but not the usual one we use. A database stores data in the form of attributes, and it is stored on some centralized server. Usually, databases have no chronological order of storage. Blockchain is a special database that stores data in a chronological order, distributed over devices. Further, blockchain restricts access to the data, and it is only for viewing.

Blockchain stores data as blocks and these blocks are in a chain like a linked list. Each block has transaction data, hash value of the block and hash value of previous block. Transaction data consist of sender, receiver and the value. For example, a **bitcoin block** has sender, receiver and bitcoin amount. **Hash value** is unique for each block and the act has a biometric of the block. It is calculated from the block header. The hash value changes when the data of the block is altered. The change in hash value is reflected in the next block as the next block has the hash value of the previous block. With this, the hash value of each block is updated in a chain manner.

When the attacker alters the data, it also needs to update the hash values of all the blocks in the chain which is not feasible. Thus, the attacked data is reverted back to its original value. The network on which blocks are stored is called **blockchain network**. Hashing is the most important part of blockchain that maintains security as well as the privacy of the data.

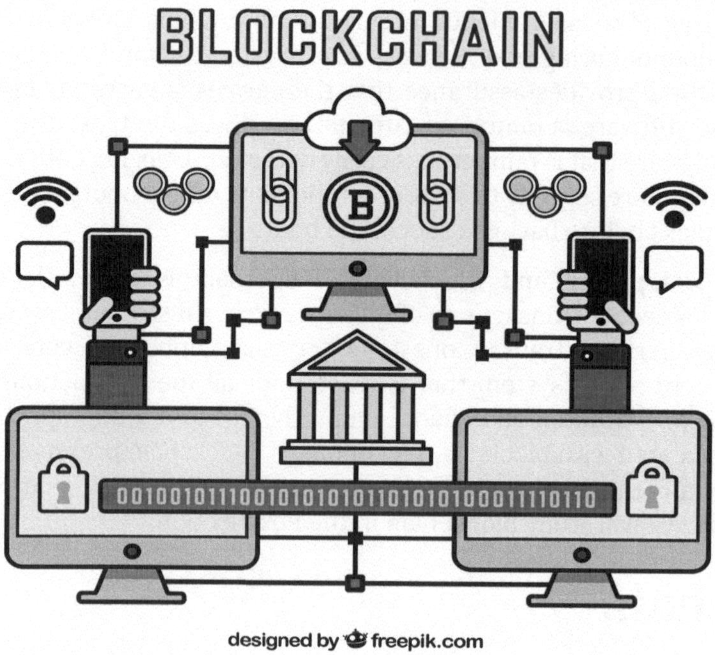

Figure 11.7: *Secured Transactions Being Carried Out between Two Mobile Devices Using Blockchain and Bitcoins*

Blockchain is a special database, popularly known as a **digital ledger of transactions**, and the ledger is distributed over the blockchain network. A ledger is a file that has records of all the successfully completed transactions, credits or debits, in a chronological manner.

Currently, blockchain is being implemented for bitcoin, a digital currency-based transaction as shown in *Figure 11.7*. The transactions do not require bank intermediates. Similarly, blockchain technology is being used to transfer intellectual properties and property titles, or digital information of the person.

Structure

Basically, the sender and the receiver can communicate securely without third party intervention in a blockchain technology. The core components of blockchain are:

- **Node:** They are network devices that keep track of the distributed ledger, and act as a communication hub.
- **Transactions:** It is a contract between the sender and the receiver to transfer assets. The blockchain stores the transactional data in a distributed ledger.

- **Block:** This is similar to nodes in a single linked list in which the next pointer points to the previous node. They store records of transactions. Multiple transactions happen every day, and so multiple blocks are required to store the transaction details.
- **Chain:** It is a link between blocks where the address of the previous block is linked with the address of the current block.
- **Miners:** This is a process to validate transaction steps, and is called blockchain mining. The people participating in the validation process are called miners.
- **Consensus:** It is a fault tolerant mechanism where the nodes agree on having a single state of the network when multiple transactions are going on simultaneously.

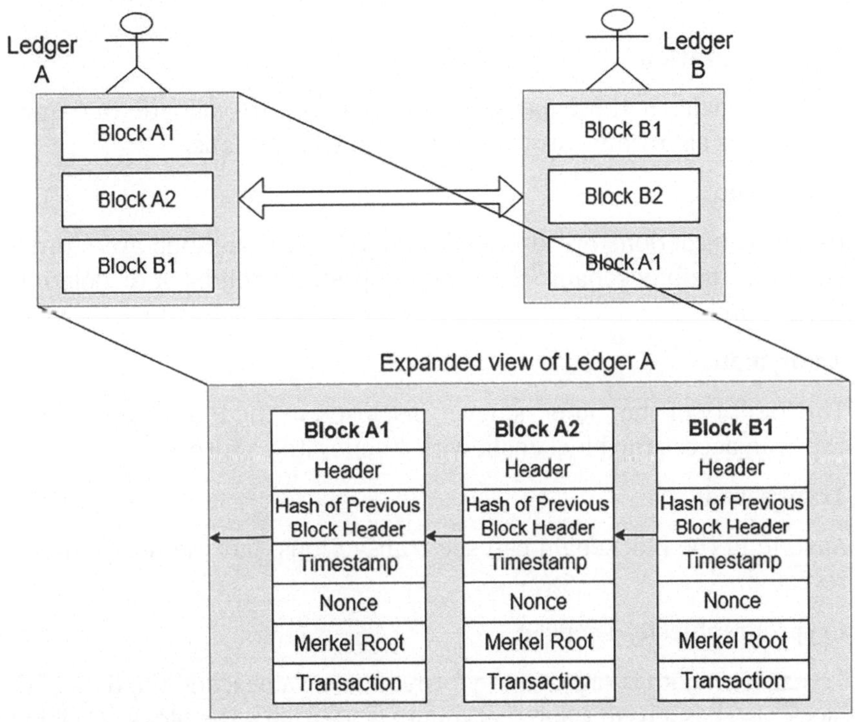

Figure 11.8: *Structure of Blockchain and Components of Block in a Blockchain*

Data Storage in a block have components as follows:

- **Header:** It uniquely identifies the block in the chain.
- **Previous block address:** The block is connected with the previous block using the hash value of the previous block.
- **Timestamp:** It verifies the block's freshness and assigns a time when the transaction data is created.

- **Nonce:** It is a counter that provides proof of work, and it is compared to a live target to check validation of mining. With nonce, we can vary the hash value of the block. The nonce value is initially 0 and it is incremented by 1, and hash values are generated continuously. The point where hash value varies dramatically from previous value, that value is the final nonce value.
- **Markel Root:** Root of Merkel tree that stores transactions in a block and a digital fingerprint is generated of the entire transaction. With digital fingerprint, a user can validate if a transaction can be included in a block or not. The tree leaves denote all transactions and nodes between root and leaves are hash values representing transactions.

  The structure and components of the Blockchain is depicted in *Figure 11.8*.

Features:

- **Decentralization**

  In blockchain, a third-party is not required to validate the transactions. Consensus algorithms provide stability in transactions.
- **Persistent**

  Invalid transactions are dropped, and valid transactions are stored as hash values in the blockchain. There is no option of roll back or deletion of valid transactions.
- **Anonymous**

  The identity of the miner is never disclosed in the blockchain network. Each user can access the blockchain with a generated address.
- **Transparent**

  Anyone in the blockchain can see transactions, but the user's identity is not revealed.
- **Cryptographically-secured**

  Transaction data is saved in the form of hash values, and the data of the whole block also has a hash value that uniquely identifies the block. Hashing is done using the SHA 256 algorithm.
- **Immutable Ledger**

  Once the valid transaction data is entered into the block, it cannot be modified even by the attacker.

Blockchain is a very useful technology, and is gaining popularity in recent times due to its vast applications. It has provided secure communication in edge computing, based on IoT applications. The features of blockchain keeps the IoT data secured during transmissions, and provide shared storage. Further, if one edge node fails, the network is not compromised. The data that is recorded cannot be modified or deleted, guaranteeing data integrity of the application. Most importantly, blockchain networks can only be accessed by authorized users/devices, and the data, once in the blockchain, is immutable, reducing chances of attack.

Privacy-preserving AI

To avoid privacy breach, there are some popular methods that can be implemented on edge AI applications. Preserving privacy provides data protection, customer trust, and maintaining the reputation of the application. We have studied about federated learning in *Chapter 8- Leveraging Edge Intelligence*, and it is a privacy preserving technique. Other techniques are as follows.

Data Anonymization

It is a process of hiding personal identification information (PII) from a dataset to protect the privacy of the user. With this technique, it is impossible to identify a person from the information provided. This process masks the data that is important to the user. PII data are phone numbers, social security numbers, Aadhaar details, photo, passport number etc. The anonymized data cannot completely guarantee privacy and there is a possibility of re-identification. Techniques in anonymization are:

- Masking replaces PII data with symbols, alphanumeric characters that are meaningless. The masking is done either by character substitution or data shuffling or truncation or synthetic data generation or data tokenization that substitute personal data with placeholders generated randomly.
- Pseudonymization replaces PII data with pseudonym. Pseudonym is a fictitious name to hide identity.
- Data aggregation combines collected data from different sources into a single view for decision-making, protecting individual data with combined representation.
- Data generalization replaces specific data with a generalized value, like a detailed address is replaced by only locality name.
- Data swapping replaces original value with fictitious values.

Data Perturbation

It is a process of adding noise into the data so that information is unreadable when breached. Authorized users have techniques to remove noise and get the original information. This technique is mostly used to preserve electronic health records of the patients. There are two methods to add noise: probability distribution and value distortion. In the probability distribution approach, the data is replaced with data within the same distribution sample.

For example, the patient names are scrambled by the sender and only the receiver knows the scramble pattern to convert it into original order. Value distortion approach uses decision trees to assign noise type to data if it matches a certain criterion. This way each data will have a different noise added. "Noise" in the context of privacy, is a random, controlled modification of data that hides personal details as well as provides trustworthy analysis of data.

Differential Privacy

It is a mathematical model that guarantees protection to the data. In this technique, the noise is added in the training process of AI. It is useful in protecting privacy during collaborative learning of AI models. The noise is added in the gradients calculated during training. The noise is determined by sensitivity of the model to the training data and privacy budget. Privacy budget determines the level of protection required. Added noise can increase privacy but also degrade the performance of the model. Larger the privacy budget means better accuracy but weak privacy. Thus, the privacy budget has a big role to play in determining noise value. More parameters mean more noise being added to the model, which degrades the application's performance. Further, models trained with smaller datasets are more sensitive to noise compared to trained models with large datasets.

Homomorphic Encryption

With this technique the data to be analysed is in cryptic form. The analysis is done on encrypted data, thus protecting original data. The result is decrypted and it is the same as the result from analysis of original data. The encryption is with public key and decryption is with private key, that only receiver and sender know. The data from the sender is shared on the network in encrypted form, and only authentic devices can decrypt the result. All computation, either centralized or disturbed, is performed on encrypted data and the result is shared with authorized devices or users. This protects data on the network, preserving privacy. The encrypted data can be shared with third parties to analyse and provide the result, without worrying of any privacy breach or information leak over the network and with third-party people. The following code applies homomorphic encryption on SVM model parameters and tests the model having encrypted parameters. "Tenseal" library is used in Python to implement homomorphic encryption. The code is as follows:

```
import tenseal as ts
import numpy as np
from sklearn.svm import SVC
import numpy as np
```

```
import pandas as pd
from sklearn.model_selection import train_test_split
#Split the dataset
df = pd.read_csv("heart_failure_clinical_records_dataset.csv")
X = df.iloc[:,:-1].values
y = df.iloc[:,-1].values
from sklearn.model_selection import train_test_split
X_train, X_test, y_train, y_test = train_test_split(X, y, test_
size=0.2, random_state=42)
#Tenseal Context
context = ts.context(
    ts.SCHEME_TYPE.CKKS,
    poly_modulus_degree=8192,
    coeff_mod_bit_sizes=[60, 40, 40, 60]
)
context.generate_galois_keys()
context.global_scale = 2**40

# Train the SVM model
svm_model = SVC(kernel='linear', C=1.0, random_state=42)
svm_model.fit(X_train, y_train)

# Extracting relevant parameters
weights = svm_model.coef_[0]
bias = svm_model.intercept_[0]

# Parameter Encryption
enc_weights = ts.ckks_vector(context, weights.tolist())
enc_bias = ts.ckks_vector(context, ⌊bias⌋) # Bias as a
single-element vector

# Data Encryption (for a single test example)
sample_x = X_test[0]
enc_sample_x = ts.ckks_vector(context, sample_x.tolist())

#Encrypted Inference
encrypted_prediction_result = enc_sample_x.dot(enc_weights) +
enc_bias

#  Decryption
decrypted_prediction_result = encrypted_prediction_result.
decrypt()
print(f"Original SVM prediction for sample_x: {svm_model.
predict(sample_x.reshape(1, -1))}")
print(f"Decrypted homomorphic prediction result: {decrypted_pre-
diction_result}")
```

Secure Multi-Party Computation (SMPC)

It is a cryptography-based approach. Multiple parties can compute data together without knowing the data from each other. Individual data is hidden, secured, and it cannot be seen but it is there to perform computations on. Data aggregation/fusion is performed using this technique to hide data from source devices from the network and other devices in the network who are performing fusion in collaboration. To understand the process, the data is shared in pieces, and one piece is with the sender itself. This way, even with all the pieces on the network, the original data cannot be generated. Each node fuses the data with the pieces it has from other nodes, and the piece it has from its own data. The fused data from all the fused is then fused for the final result.

One of the methods to divide numerical data for sharing is additive sharing. For example, if the data is 40, and there are 3 nodes in the network who are computing, then the number is divided into three parts such that the sum is 40. For example, (44 -11 + 7 sums up to 40). Keeping one part and sharing other two parts with other two nodes is termed as secret sharing, and the data shared is encrypted as from the data, the other node cannot guess the original.

When each node adds all the data, and then the added data from each node is added together, the result comes out to be the same. So, with privacy preservation, the computation is of three steps. The first step is data portioning and secret sharing, the second step is collaborative computation on data, and the third step is computing the final result from all the parallel computations. This technique is computational costly, but it increases the privacy of the data. The training data can also be secretly shared in similar ways, and AI models can be trained in a collaborative manner.

Conclusion

With IoT applications, there is a lot of data over the network including sensitive information. Cyber-attacks on hardware, applications and data are increasing as hackers are getting efficient. There is privacy-breach happening due to which personal information people are getting into wrong hands. For developing an IoT application, we need to know how to secure it from attacks and privacy breaches. Edge-based IoT applications are more prone to attacks.

In this chapter, we discussed popular security attacks and privacy threats that may harm the developed IoT application. To provide security to the hardware, software and data of the application, countermeasures are discussed. One of the counter-measures is blockchain, that is a very popular technology currently. The detailed study of blockchain is presented in detail. Lastly, we discussed privacy-preserving AI techniques to secure the training data of AI models from privacy breach. Thus, securing an AI model is very important in IoT applications that provide edge intelligence as IoT services are highly dependent on model's predictions.

The future scope of edge computing with advanced technologies in IoT applications is discussed in the next chapter.

Points to Remember

- Attacking or breaching privacy of computers and user data is known as cyber-attack.
- To provide cybersecurity to edge devices, there are three requirements, known as CIA Triad.
- IoT edge devices are more prone to attacks because they are out of traditional security systems. They have a public IP, and they collect data near the specific users.
- Any of the CIA triad is compromised; it means the system is attacked. The attacking entity is known as a hacker.
- Attacks on edge devices are distributed denial of service, side-channel attack, Malware injection, authentication and authorization attacks, as well as integrity attacks on ML.
- There are four types of privacy threats: Unstructured threat, Structured threat, External threat and Internal threat.
- There are multiple IoT applications that are for societal good, but compromising on the privacy of the people.
- The malicious injections can be detected by analysing side channels to detect a change in temperature, power consumption, or some unusual hardware activity.
- Intrusion detection system is an application that monitors network traffic, and detects unusual activities over the network which are suspicious, or a threat.
- Distributed and shared data schemes in cryptography on edge devices can be easily implemented with blockchain technology.
- Blockchain stores data as blocks, and these blocks are in a chain like a linked list.
- Blockchain networks can only be accessed by authorized users/devices and the data, and once in the blockchain, it is immutable, reducing chances of attack.
- Data anonymization is a process of hiding Personal Identification Information (PII) from a dataset to protect the privacy of the user.

- Noise is added to the data to secure it in data perturbation and differential privacy techniques.
- Computational analysis is done on the encrypted data in homomorphic encryption, and secures multi-party computation.

Multiple Choice Questions

1. What is the CIA triad?
    a. Compact, Inference, Adaptability
    b. Confidentiality, Inference, Availability
    c. Compact, Integrity, Adaptability
    d. Confidentiality, Integrity, Availability
2. When an attacker changes the state of the system, the attack is called:
    a. Passive
    b. Active
    c. Threat
    d. Not cyber
3. When a webpage is attacked with a script, it is known as:
    a. XML injection
    b. SQL injection
    c. XSS
    d. LDAP injection
4. Privilege escalation is:
    a. Authentication attack
    b. Authorization attack
    c. Side-channel attack
    d. Distributed Denial of Service attack
5. When an ML model is attacked with unknown input, it is called:
    a. Model poisoning
    b. Infection attack

   c. Input manipulation
   d. Membership Inference
6. When a threat is from a professional hacker, it is known as:
   a. Structured threat
   b. Unstructured threat
   c. Internal threat
   d. External threat
7. Which technique is not a countermeasure for an attack?
   a. Cryptography
   b. Reliable network protocol
   c. Model inversion
   d. Prior testing
8. What is a feature of blockchain?
   a. Immutable
   b. Transparent
   c. Secured
   d. All of the above
9. Which technique adds noise to the gradient of the model?
   a. Perturbation
   b. Differential privacy
   c. SMPC
   d. Anonymization

Answers

1. d
2. b
3. c
4. b

5. d
6. a
7. c
8. d
9. b

Questions

1. Why are edge devices prone to security attacks?
2. Explain cybersecurity requirements.
3. Discuss distributed denial of service attack.
4. What are authentication and authorization attacks?
5. Discuss attacks that harm integrity of the ML model.
6. What countermeasures secure data during pre-processing and model training?
7. How does a blockchain secure data in an edge computing model?
8. What are the components of a block for data storage?
9. Discuss methods for preserving privacy in AI models.

CHAPTER 12
Future Trends

Introduction

IoT applications using Cloud-edge architecture are here to stay, and are providing accurate services. They have shown promising results. Heavy analytical models are running on edge devices with limited capabilities using TensorFlow lite. Cloud services are deployed at the network edge using containerization. There are multiple edge platforms, tools and technologies available for successful implementation of a smart application. Further, continuous progress is happening in providing security to the application, and running a privacy-preserving AI. With IoT applications at boom, there are new trends in the parallel world. PyTorch library is getting popular for computations, and may be used more widely compared to the TensorFlow in the near future. The 5G network is being utilized for communication with very low latency. Every technology is being provided as a service to increase reusability. Edge devices are integrated with Real-Time OS that gives the highest priority to execution time, and use of digital twins are providing accurate predictions. Successful integration of edge computing with these technologies aims for more powerful, impactful, and scalable IoT edge applications. In this chapter, we will study these current trends integrated with edge computing.

Structure

In this chapter, we will cover the following topics:

- PyTorch at Edge
- 5G and IoT Use-cases
- Edge as a Service
- Real-Time OS
- Digital Twin

PyTorch at Edge

Python machine learning frameworks like TensorFlow and PyTorch have been developed to simplify creation of a neural network. They both have been widely utilized in deployment of deep learning models, including a new domain of deep learning, the Generative AI models. We already have seen the deployment of ANN, using TensorFlow in Chapter 8, *Leveraging Edge Intelligence*. In this chapter, we will see benefits of PyTorch that came later than TensorFlow, but has attracted people due to its ease-of-use and thus, it promises a good future to IoT and edge computing.

TensorFlow has Keras, a high-level API, that provides an interface to solve ML issues by utilizing modern deep learning models. TensorFlow has TensorFlow lite that is designed for edge computing. It optimizes the model to be lightweight for deployment on edge devices having resource constraints. To directly work on TensorFlow, its docker image exists, and so no need to install TensorFlow on the machine for deployment. TensorFlow will not be replaced from PyTorch, and it is still extensively used by Google search and Uber. PyTorch is a building block of ChatGPT and Tesla's autopilot that has gained a lot of attention these days. Every company has their preference of ML framework, and an ML engineer needs to know both of these frameworks to have more opportunities.

PyTorch is created by Facebook AI research lab, and it is simple as well as easy to use. PyTorch efficiently handles dynamic computational graphs. We should know dynamic computation graphs to know, why we need a framework that is efficient in it. Dynamic computational graph is a graph that is a visual representation of mathematical operations and relationships between them. Deep neural networks are dynamic computational graphs that have multiple nodes, multiple relationships and multiple computations, that dynamically change with every incoming training data. It helps users in straightforward-creation of deep learning models. For scaling and reliability with distributed training, TensorFlow is a better choice than PyTorch for deployment in the real-world. Because of simplicity, ease-of-use for development of any ML model for a beginner, with open scope of innovations, and flexible approach, PyTorch gets more attention.

Following is the PyTorch version of the TensorFlow code on CNN implemented in *Chapter 8, Leveraging Edge Intelligence*. The code is implemented on Google Collab, which is an online editor having most of the python libraries installed.

```
import torch
import torch.nn as nn
import torch.optim as optim
import torchvision
import torchvision.transforms as transforms
from torch.utils.data import DataLoader
import matplotlib.pyplot as plt
import numpy as np

# Import dataset and divide it into training and testing data

transform = transforms.Compose([
```

```
    transforms.ToTensor(),  # Convert images to PyTorch tensors
    transforms.Normalize((0.1307,), (0.3081,))  # Normalize with
MNIST mean and std
])
train_dataset = torchvision.datasets.MNIST(
    root='./data',  # Where to store the dataset
    train=True,     # This is training data
    download=True,  # Download if not present
    transform=transform  # Apply transformations
)
test_dataset = torchvision.datasets.MNIST(
    root='./data',
    train=False,
    download=True,
    transform=transform
)
train_loader = DataLoader(train_dataset, batch_size=64, shuffle=True)
test_loader = DataLoader(test_dataset, batch_size=64, shuffle=False)


#Create Neural Network Model
class SimpleNN(nn.Module):
    def __init__(self):
        super(SimpleNN, self).__init__()
        self.flatten = nn.Flatten()
        self.dropout = nn.Dropout(p=0.5)
        self.fc1 = nn.Linear(28*28, 120)
        self.relu = nn.ReLU()
        self.fc2 = nn.Linear(120, 10)
        self.softmax = nn.Softmax()

    def forward(self, x):
        x = self.flatten(x)
        x = self.dropout(x)
        x = self.fc1(x)
        x = self.relu(x)
        x = self.fc2(x)
        x = self.softmax(x)
        return x
model = SimpleNN()
print(model)
# Train the Model

criterion = nn.CrossEntropyLoss()
optimizer = optim.Adam(model.parameters(), lr=0.001)

# Check if GPU is available
```

```
device = torch.device("cuda:0" if torch.cuda.is_available() else
"cpu")
print(f"Using device: {device}")
model.to(device)
# Training loop
num_epochs = 50
train_losses = []
for epoch in range(num_epochs):
    running_loss = 0.0
for i, (inputs, labels) in enumerate(train_loader):
        # Move tensors to the configured device
        inputs, labels = inputs.to(device), labels.to(device)
        # Zero the parameter gradients
        optimizer.zero_grad()
        # Forward pass
        outputs = model(inputs)
        loss = criterion(outputs, labels)
        # Backward pass and optimize
        loss.backward()
        optimizer.step()
        running_loss += loss.item()
        if (i+1) % 100 == 0:
            print(f'Epoch [{epoch+1}/{num_epochs}], Step [{i+1}/
{len(train_loader)}], Loss: {running_loss/100:.4f}')
            train_losses.append(running_loss/100)
            running_loss = 0.0
plt.figure(figsize=(10, 5))
plt.plot(train_losses)
plt.title('Training Loss')
plt.xlabel('Training Steps')
plt.ylabel('Loss')
plt.grid(True)
plt.show()
model.eval()
correct = 0
total = 0
with torch.no_grad():
    for images, labels in test_loader:
        images, labels = images.to(device), labels.to(device)
        outputs = model(images)
        _, predicted = torch.max(outputs.data, 1)
        total += labels.size(0)
        correct += (predicted == labels).sum().item()
accuracy = 100 * correct / total
print(f'Accuracy on the test set: {accuracy:.2f}%')
```

```
#Test The results
from sklearn.metrics import confusion_matrix
cm = confusion_matrix(labels, predicted)
plt.imshow(cm, interpolation="nearest", cmap=plt.cm.Blues)
plt.colorbar()
plt.xlabel("Predicted class")
plt.ylabel("Actual class")
plt.show()
```

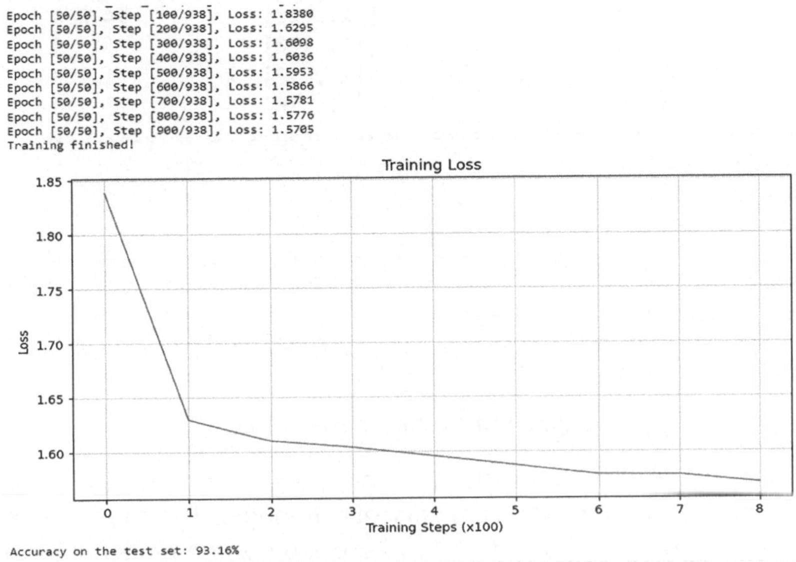

Figure 12.1: *Training of the Model*

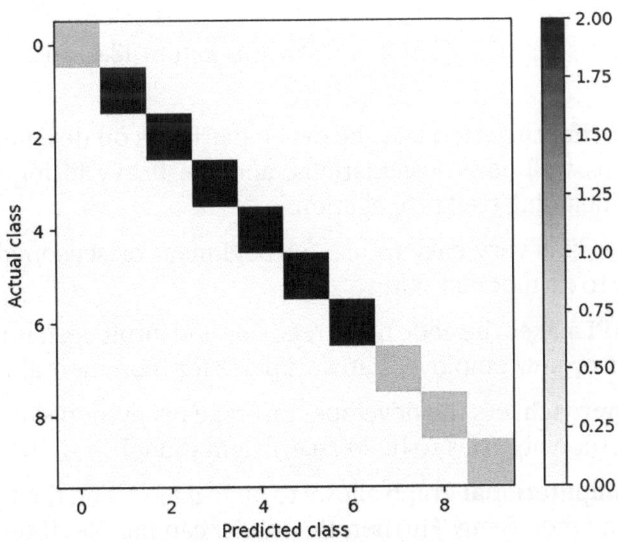

Figure 12.2: *Confusion Matrix*

#Summary of the Model

summary(model, (1, 28, 28))

```
----------------------------------------------------------------
        Layer (type)               Output Shape         Param #
================================================================
           Flatten-1                  [-1, 784]               0
           Dropout-2                  [-1, 784]               0
            Linear-3                  [-1, 120]          94,200
              ReLU-4                  [-1, 120]               0
            Linear-5                   [-1, 10]           1,210
           Softmax-6                   [-1, 10]               0
================================================================
Total params: 95,410
Trainable params: 95,410
Non-trainable params: 0
----------------------------------------------------------------
Input size (MB): 0.00
Forward/backward pass size (MB): 0.01
Params size (MB): 0.36
Estimated Total Size (MB): 0.38
```

Figure 12.3: *Summary of the Model*

Figure 12.1 and *Figure* 12.2 shows the loss, accuracy and confusion matrix of the model, and Figure 12.3 shows the summary of the model. The total size in PyTorch implementation of the model is 0.38 MB, whereas the same model implemented on TensorFlow is 1.85 MB.

Features

The salient characteristics of PyTorch is shown in *Figure* 12.4, and are discussed as follows:

- **Automatic Differentiation** lets the developer focus on designing and training the model, as well as all calculations, and the heavy lifting is done by the framework including backpropagation.
- This framework is very easy to use for beginners or seasoned deep learning experts due to its modular nature.
- **High level API** makes the code more readable and intuitive. It is understandable to beginners or new employees at workplace for incremental work.
- **Pythonic Approach** lets the developer leverage his python skills, and integrate the other python libraries to build an efficient model.
- **Dynamic computational graph** allows to build a model on the fly with dynamic reshaping and modifying. Further, the model can handle different input sizes due to its flexible nature.

- It provides **high performance** with fast training speeds, and optimizes the model during training to remove all possible delay causing elements.
- **Strong GPU support** to harness capabilities of parallel processing, and maximize GPU acceleration with optimized implementation of models.
- **Hybrid front-end support** like with ONNX platform and Tensorflow as well as the trained model can be seamlessly exported to the front-end systems.
- Support of a large community with a high number of research papers, pre-trained models, and tutorials to learn from to stay up to date with new innovations.
- Efficient production-deployment by converting the developed code into TorchScript or ONNX (Open Neural Network Exchange), and integrating into the deployment pipeline.
- Covers state-of-the-art in DL including deep learning, natural language processing, computer vision, and speech recognition.

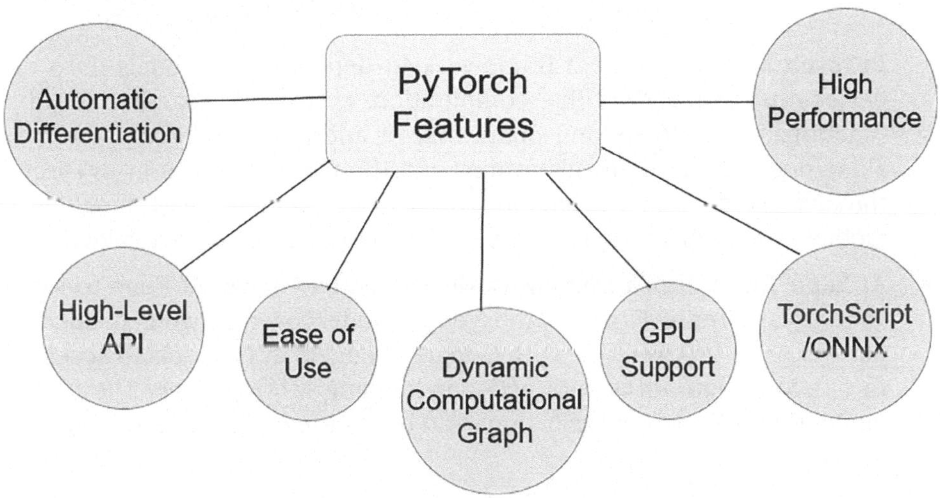

***Figure 12.4:** Features of PyTorch*

PyTorch Edge

PyTorch Edge supports seamless deployment of AI models on edge computing devices that include smartphones and embedded devices.

They have provided multiple solutions that enable on-device inferences across all types of edge devices. The following *Figure* 12.5 shows different frameworks on PyTorch Edge. These solution frameworks are discussed as follows.

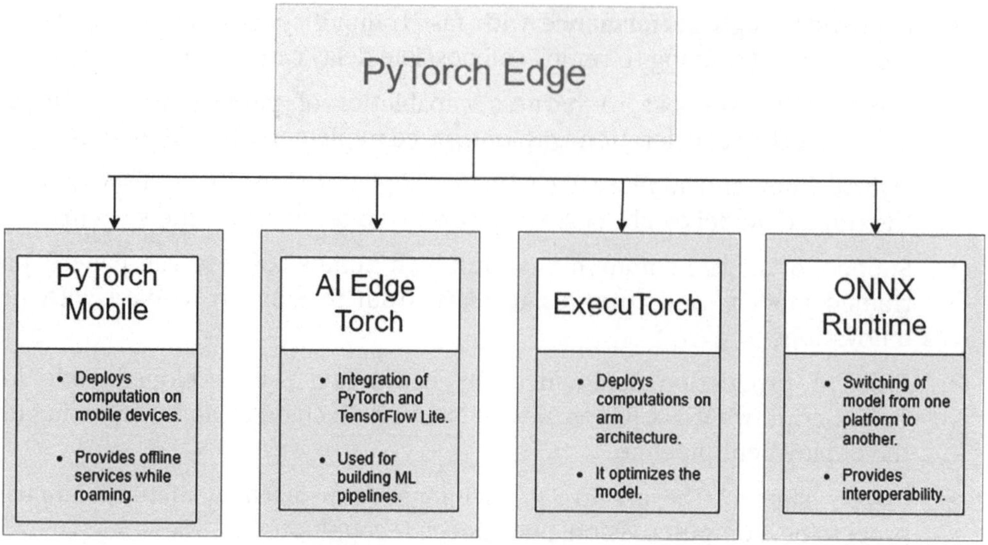

Figure 12.5: *Different Frameworks of PyTorch Edge*

- **PyTorch Mobile:** This is a framework to deploy torch models onto mobile devices to have 24/7 offline computation, even while roaming. It supports functionality (methods and operators) of android that PyTorch framework alone does not have. In this framework, the model is saved in PyTorch, and the saved model is converted into TorchScript. TorchScript of the model has a mobile-compatible format, and is deployed onto an android application.
- **AI Edge Torch:** It is a framework developed by Google AI Edge to integrate PyTorch and TensorFlow Lite for greater model coverage, and enhancing CPU performance. It is available with Google AI edge that has tools to access ready to use ML frameworks and tasks for building ML pipelines. The developed model through tools is easily deployed on multiple platforms with no change to code.
- **ExecuTorch:** This framework is designed specifically for arm architecture. It enables a smaller, optimized model, and use-case for which it is specifically built, that is generative AI. Generative AI models are trained on very large datasets and thus, are heavy to be implemented on edge devices. The framework optimizes the model, using quantization techniques and models like chatbots and AI assistants that have high performance and greater portability on a broader range of arm devices such as Jetson Nano and Raspberry PI.
- **ONNX Runtime:** It is an engine designed to provide speed up to ONNX models. It runs on Windows, Mac ad Linux and supports CPU, GPU. It supports models of PyTorch, TensorFlow, scikit-learn and thus, it is easy to move a model from one platform to another through this engine. ONNX runtime provides faster predictions on models that are exported into .onnx format. The major advantage of this engine is, it allows interoperability.

You can develop on one framework for training, and deploy on another framework for prediction.

Drawbacks of PyTorch

PyTorch do not have a visualization toolkit of its own. It needs to connect with python's visualization libraries or TensorBoard to visualize the data. Moreover, PyTorch is not as comprehensive as TensorFlow. The PyTorch code needs to be converted to application's framework for deployment as it has no one end-to-end solution for all real-time applications. The following *Figure* 12.6 shows comparison between PyTorch and TensorFLow in brief for the ease of understanding and use of both.

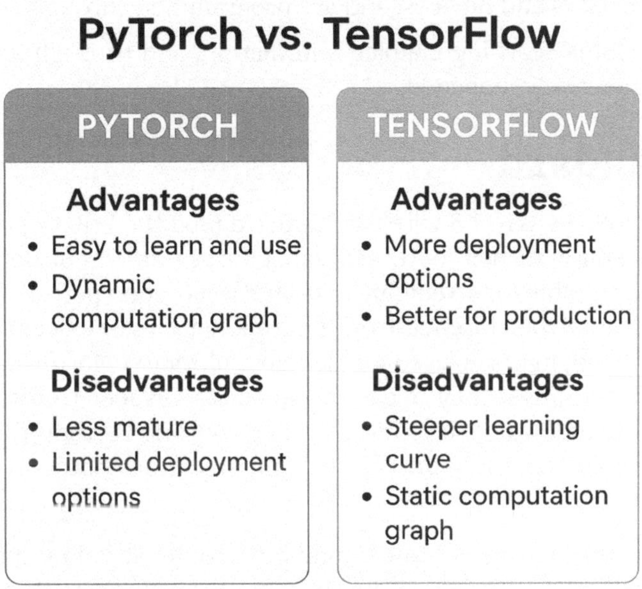

Figure 12.6: *Differences between PyTorch and TensorFlow*

5G and IoT Use Cases

We discussed 5G in brief, used in mobile edge computing in Chapter 4, *Integrating Edge with Cloud in IoT Infrastructure*. We will go deep into 5G by discussing its features, hardware requirements and benefits in the digital world. There are three types: Low-band that is 10 times faster than 4G network, mid-band 5G has higher bandwidth than low-band but cannot penetrate buildings, and high-band 5G use mmWave which have greater download speed and high-speed connectivity. However, it has line of sight travel, and cannot even sustain rains.

Salient Features

- It enables a new spectrum of Multiple Input, Multiple Output (MIMO) where more data can be transferred and received at the same time.
- A new spectrum is added known as millimetre wave (mmWave) for increased bandwidth.
- Faster Internet Speed of 20 Gbps, compared to 4G which has 1Gbps speed.
- It has a software-defined platform where the network can be programmed as per the requirements.
- It creates SDN subnets that are known as **network slices**. These slices function as per the users and devices, and are programmed through software.
- It has machine-learning enabled automation, and through its network traffic can be proactively managed.

Wi-Fi Standard

The 5G network follows Wi-Fi 6 wireless standard (802.11ax) that operates in 2.4 GHz and 5 GHz. This standard has increased capacity of number of devices connected, lower latency and suitable for streaming data, and it has good performance in crowded locations also without interference from multiple wireless devices. To have a 6GHz band, Wi-Fi 6E band may be used on wireless devices. However, 6Hz has more attenuation from buildings, they decay quicker with respect to distance. To have a network of 5G at home, we need to have Wi-Fi 6 routers. Further, the latest iPhones, smart TVs, laptops, and cars support WiFI 6 communication protocols and can connect to the 5G network.

However, 5G is good for long distance communications, it is not suitable for indoor communication with the outside world. People need to come out of the building to talk on mid-range and high range 5G as it is unable to penetrate walls and objects.

Low-range Wi-Fi is able to penetrate walls and objects but does not provide that much speed. If the devices are communicating with each other within walls, mid or high range 5G is the best option and if communicating outside long distance, low range 5G is suitable. So, this is the trade-off. IoT applications benefit from 5G communication by placing different types of 5G for different communications. For example, IoT devices communicating indoors may use high range 5G, IoT devices communicating to edge may use mid-range 5G and Edge devices communicating with the Cloud may go for low-range 5G. The following *Figure* 12.7 shows different bands of 5G with its vital characteristics.

Low Range 5G	Mid Range 5G	High Range 5G
• Easily penetrate walls. • Low speed. • Communicate over long distances.	• Cannot penetrate walls. • Medium Range of communication. • Medium Speed.	• Short distance communication. • Maximum Range of 1 mile. • Maximum Speed. • MmWave Spectrum. • Cannot Penetrate Walls.

***Figure* 12.7:** *Different Bands of 5G*

Benefits

- It provides support for heterogeneous networks consisting of licensed and unlicensed technologies.
- Ultra-low latency and faster response, suitable for real-time experience.
- No disconnections while on roaming and changing networks during travel.
- Increased capacity of simultaneous connections, serving crowded areas with ease.
- Allows network slicing where slice will be dedicated to highly critical applications.
- It is energy-efficient, ensuring longer battery life of devices.
- It provides home broadband services to areas that are unreachable to fixed line broadband.
- It incorporates authentication and advanced encryption methods for network security.

Use-case Applications

5G is a very powerful tool for new generation IoT use cases that are utilizing edge computing for real-time services which are provided near the location.

The edge computing devices are getting smarter in the present time. The applications are advancing, and the communication channel that is a backbone for reliable and fast data communication as well as decision-making have also advanced. Features of 5G take IoT applications to another level. The following *Figure* 12.8 shows abstract use-cases of 5G network. Some of the use-case applications where 5G's capabilities will provide important services are discussed as follows.

Figure 12.8: *Some Use-cases of 5G*

- **Augmented Reality (AR) Assistance:** AR remote assistance combines video and AR, and experts guide the technicians through it virtually as well as in real-time. The expert can view the video, and augment information using AR overlays like instructions or 3D models to solve challenges faced by technicians in real-time.

  For experts, it feels like being on the site even when they are remote and technicians view the site through AR smart glass and video from the smart glass is communicated from the field to the experts in real-time. Expert studies and augmentation is automatically seen by the technician through smart glass. This application is highly dependent on the network in between, and any delay will cause delay in the real-time field assistance. 5G with edge computing provides reliable communication, and also provides fast communication, due to which the on-site remote assistance seems as if the expert is standing just besides the technician during assistance, and it does not matter from how far the expert is guiding.

- **Remote Inspection:** IoT applications that monitor windmill or electric grid, require remote inspection. Normally, technicians are sent on-site for inspection of every equipment to identify problems visually. Regular inspection of this huge equipment on which the whole application is working, is very much required, to provide uninterrupted service. However, sending technicians is very expensive in terms of cost as well as resources. With 5G, drones and cameras can inspect these devices remotely, and send images to the Cloud for detecting problems.

Even drones can be utilized to find cracks, corrosion and rust to old structures to avoid collapse of these buildings. Drones can send continuous images or streaming video, using a 5G network and AI trained by experts, deployed on Cloud or Edge that can detect problems going through the videos/images.

- **Visual Inspection:** Edge devices in a manufacturing unit or factory with the help of 5G network may inspect the process flow from raw material to product. Edge devices capture images of the process until the product rolls out. The images are analysed by edge devices in real-time to inspect where the delay is happening or where there is a fault in the product. If a delay happens, the machine is inspected manually. If a fault happens, the machine is inspected and the product is also kept aside.

  There is another possibility by 5G that all units are maintained in real-time by Cloud. These devices are connected to the Cloud through a 5G network for real-time experience. This will ensure uptime as well as reduce maintenance cost.

- **Agriculture:** Drones, serve as edge devices, can continuously inspect crops and reduce farmer's workload with the help of 5G. 5G and Drones provide edge computing based visual analytics on the captured images to predict growth rate of the crops, pests in the crop, loss from pests in the crop, crop harvesting time etc. The farmer will get to know which location requires more attention and in what scenario in real-time. Drones integrated with 5G, will keep the farm healthy and crop productivity highest, reducing manual labour of checking each and every crop.
- **Facility Management:** 5G will enable smart monitoring of buildings, malls, stadiums, airports and provide energy efficient solutions, comfort to the people around by monitoring HVAC, maintaining lifts and escalators in real-time, detecting suspicious activity and managing occupancy to avoid rush.
- **Connecting Vehicles:** In the internet of vehicles, vehicles are integrated with multiple sensors and it is attached to the internet to communicate with traffic lights, lamp posts which are edge computing devices. With 5G, the vehicles may bi-directionally communicate with each other, to keep them collision free, and also tell all of them about congestion or accidents directly, rather than through Cloud. With 5G, vehicles not only senses but also see through other vehicles and make decisions. This will make self-driving more trustworthy.

Edge as a Service

Edge computing provides multiple advantages to IoT applications and therefore, many applications that are being developed on a daily basis, utilize edge-cloud architecture. In edge-cloud architecture, Cloud considered is mostly third-party and it is shared by multiple IoT applications that work on large-scale data. For edge, every application has its own edge device and a network for connecting edge devices to IoT and Cloud.

With multiple applications being deployed every day, multiple edge devices are also being integrated to the network, increasing hardware. When a large-scale IoT application is to be deployed by an enterprise, a lot of new edge devices are required, and their setup costs a lot. Further, creating edge computing models, maintaining security, deploying edge intelligence using containerization, will take a lot of time if done separately for every edge device in the large-scale application.

To reduce the introduction of more edge devices on the network, and to support ease of deployment on edge, a concept is introduced called the **Edge as a service**. In this concept, the edge architecture, consisting of device, software and network, is provided as a service to the enterprises. With this, the applications need no edge device, no maintenance, no deployment of its own device and network. The applications use edge as a service for deployment of edge computing and just pay for the services. NTT Ltd. announced edge as a service concept which is globally available and manageable edge with private 5G network in 2022. It is provided by VMWARE's edge compute stack and will enable industries to analyse, monitor and make decisions at the location where the data is collected. Currently, NTT developed private 5G for securing their edge devices and AI. They collaborated with Schneider Electric to build one for a smart factory.

The edge as a service provides all capabilities similar to building our own edge device. It has the following features:

- Delivers operational efficiency
- Speeds up the profits
- Secured
- Real-time decision-making
- Provides greater insights in data
- Digitizing business capabilities
- Adapts to the modern era
- Easy deployment with use-case applications
- Accessible to IoT applications from anywhere
- Shifts focus on business logic

- Faster deployment of applications
- Cost-effective

With great advantages, IoT will be easy to deploy, using edge as a service without bothering about hardware deployment and hardware costs. The concept of edge as a service is similar to public Cloud, and NTT, ARISTA Networks provides these services. The following *Figure* 12.9 demonstrates the use of Edge as a Service for multiple IoT application domains.

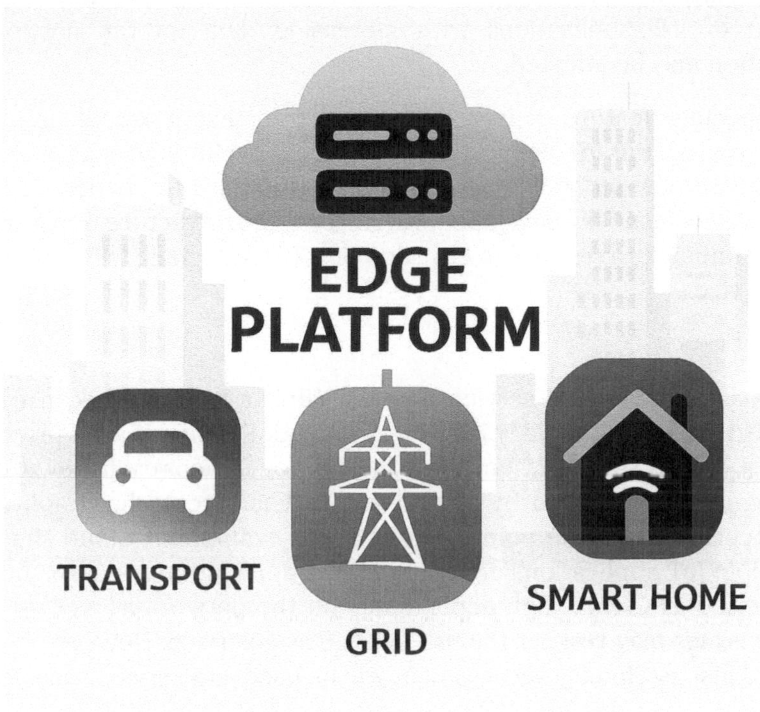

***Figure* 12.9:** *Edge Platform Used as a Service by IoT Applications*

In edge as a service, the company provides all the hardware, network, and resources to deploy the edge model. It provides faster response on a network of limited computational devices. It also provides infrastructure as a software, platform as a service, and software as a service. It allows scaling of applications, and also routes network traffic appropriately. The only thing required from the client side is the sensor data, and its modelling, everything else is taken care of by the edge as a service.

Features

Edge as a service provides hardware to deploy the model, provides a private network to collect data, and communicate data to Cloud, as well as manages the application's load balancing, security, scalability, and resource utilization.

In simple terms, it is a ready-made edge cloud architecture, and the enterprise has to plug and play with sensor data as well as model design and pay only for whatever is being used as a service. No cost of deployment, no network cost, no hardware cost, and no tedious task of deploying the model on hardware from scratch! Thus, the edge as service guarantees performance similar to manual edge deployment for an IoT application.

A very important feature of edge as a service is **ultra-low latency** and **ultra-high bandwidth network** capabilities for the delivery of data. This feature is the future requirement of IoT applications with increasing data on the network, reliable communication may be affected.

Another important feature of edge as a service is that it would be easy for the developers to align the IoT application with recent technologies as the edge would be updated with new technology continuously. It is hard to change an existing IoT application that is manually developed with its own infrastructure, software, network, and already running in a real-world environment. The switching will get very easy with edge as a service.

Drawbacks

The drawbacks of edge as a service are very similar to Cloud because the data is going to third-party, and privacy is not guaranteed. Further, if a 5G private network breaks down due to some reason, the edge service is not reachable at all, and the network service is controlled by a third-party. It is a centralized approach which creates concerns of a single point of failure. For example, if Cloud shuts down on which multiple IoT applications are running, the application will also shut down for the same period as Cloud. High dependency on the network as well as third-party and privacy issues may restrict the use of edge as a service. However, it has a lot of benefits, and just as Cloud is successful, it will be used as a service successfully in the near future.

Real-Time OS

Our desktop and laptops have popular operating systems such as Windows, Unix and Mac. These OS seems to respond in real-time on a web browser or opening an application, or working with a bunch of applications and web pages. However, these OS are not really real-time. For large scale web requests or running applications, it will hang or delay response. This is because these OS do context switching between processes to provide real-time response. But it is a near-real-time.

If there are a lot of requests, more than the capacity of the laptop, the requests will be responded with delay even with context switching. The reason being the scheduler of these OS treats all the tasks equally, maintaining overall performance. These OS have limited capabilities in guaranteeing timeliness when most of the requests are time-critical.

Real-time operating systems are popular for a long time but not used by normal users in industry or research. That is why the capabilities are unknown to us. Real-time OS also does context switching like any OS; however, the major difference is, it will execute requests based on priority as shown in *Figure 12.10*. For example, high priority tasks will definitely be responded to in real-time and least will be context switched until all higher priority requests are not responded to. This ensures timeliness to at least the processes that are highly time-critical irrespective of the number of incoming requests.

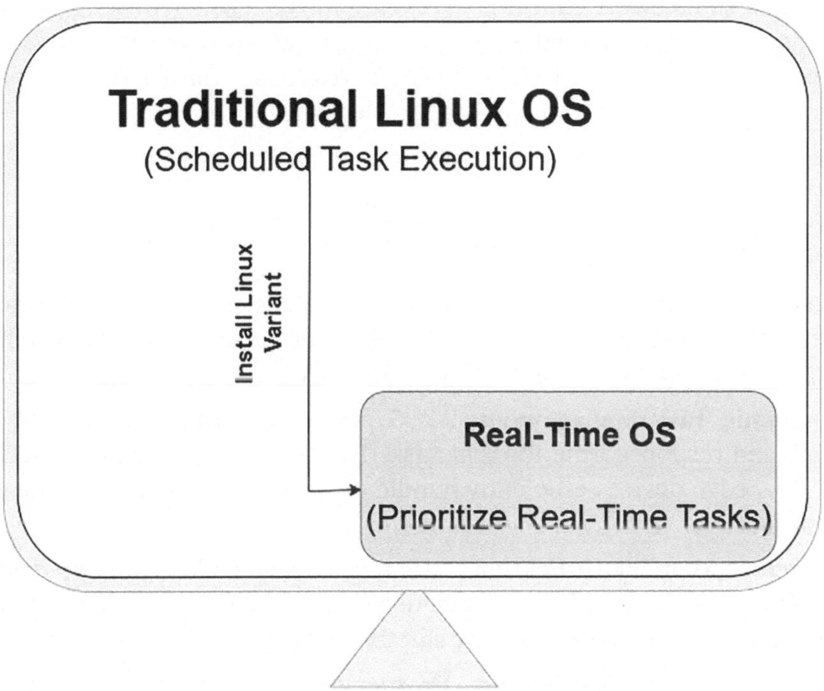

Figure 12.10: *Importance of RTOS over Traditional OS*

Real-time OS is not a new operating system; it is just a version. Already used OS on our desktop and laptops can be made real-time OS. In Linux-based OS, Linux kernel can be replaced with real-time kernel and the Linux OS behaves like a real-time OS. Most of the Linux vendors provide real-time OS that are variants of the original OS. Real-time kernels can also be constructed manually. Real-time OS is very useful for time-critical applications such as self-driving cars, manufacturing processes or heart attack monitoring systems.

In an IoT application, edge devices compute real-time data for time-critical decision-making. If an edge device gets multiple requests that are highly time-critical, it will naturally respond to requests as they come, rather than handling critical requests before. Thus, RTOS is highly beneficial for edge computing in an IoT application that deals with time-critical events. Thus, edge intelligence with RTOS will provide faster response in future. RTOS needs to be updated as per requirements of new, more powerful edge devices for easy integration.

There are two types of RTOS: Soft time RTOS and Hard time RTOS. Soft time RTOS works on large data and it may have some delay for time-critical applications but tries its best to provide real-time response to most time-critical tasks. If an error occurs in soft RTOS, it rolls back to the previous point and continues running. Hard time RTOS needs to strictly provide real-time response to critical tasks. It has small data files to compute. If hard RTOS is not able to provide real-time performance due to some reason, it shuts down. Soft time RTOS are mostly used in desktop, smartphone, cameras that are performing edge computing for detecting events in real-time, but there is not much impact in case of delay in response. Hard RTOS is deployed in autopilot systems, aircrafts, and life-support devices.

Benefits

RTOS provides multiple advantages that make it a good candidate to enhance performance of edge computing in IOT.

- **Real-time Response:** It will make edge devices capable of responding time-critical requests in real-time, and avoid emergency situations, which will add trust to the application and mitigate failures.
- **Dynamic Task Management:** RTOS prioritizes critical tasks, and provides reduced response time for that task. The scheduling is done by RTOS. With RTOS, edge devices efficiently handle critical tasks, and deliver the expected services.
- **Efficient Memory Utilization:** Memory is very limited in edge devices, and RTOS dynamically allocates and deallocates memory to manage resources efficiently. Thus, RTOS is highly suitable for edge devices.
- **Support Most Application Protocols:** RTOS provide communication functionality to edge devices, and supports essential protocols for communication.
- **Modularity:** RTOS has a task-based architecture where each task is an independent unit that can be developed, maintained and tested separately. Thus, it provides modularity to edge devices to manage tasks as per priority, and execution of each task is separate. There is no shared data or conflicts.
- **Scalability:** RTOS supports multi-core processors, and provides efficient resource management, and thus, has capability to increase scalability of edge devices as well as it can also scale on multiple edge devices for edge computing in collaboration.

Challenges

RTOS has benefits for edge computing, but also has some issues which need to be tackled by edge devices on its own.

- **Distributed Computing:** It does not guarantee data consistency in a distributed architecture. In addition to RTOS, synchronization techniques are required to maintain data consistency.
- **Limited Resources:** Resource utilization is not efficiently managed by RTOS. The edge device needs to schedule resources as per the scheduled task, with resources provided to the highest priority task first.
- **Security:** RTOS does not provide security to devices or networks. The device needs to be secured for maintaining data integrity in-device, and during data communication explicitly.
- **Real-time Data Communication:** Edge devices need to connect to real-time communication protocol to get the most benefit from real-time OS, and deliver decisions in time.

Digital Twin

Digital twin is a technology that replicates a physical object virtually. The replication is updated with real-time data, and it produces results similar to physical objects. The digital twin has a life span similar to the actual device. Digital twin use machine learning models to respond similar to actual devices responding to the real environment. The sensors are attached to the physical object, and the data from the sensors is provided to the digital twin of the physical device continuously.

Based on data, the digital twin produces output similar to physical objects. Once the digital twin functions similar to a physical object, it can be used to improve performance of a physical object. Creating a digital twin from a physical object is a challenging task. What sensors are required to replicate exact functioning is critical. Further, the digital twin continuously gathers real data from the physical object to function similar to the physical object. This technology is very beneficial in IoT applications. We can virtually represent smart objects and improve their performance. After working with the digital twin of the smart object, the smart object can be implemented in a real environment.

How is it Different from Simulation?

People confuse digital twin with simulation. Although they are similar in terms of virtual representation of the physical entity, they vary in features. Simulation is a method to test a system. It represents a process or product, and conducts multiple tests, to check its performance and efficiency. However, the test is done in a static environment with fixed environment variables at a given instance.

On the other hand, a digital twin is a complex concept. It represents physical objects virtually by gathering real-time data from physical objects continuously. This way the digital twin replicates the physical object with respect to time. For example, if a physical object is working, digital twin works, if it stops, digital twin stops. Thus, a digital twin is an exact replica of an actual physical object and the environment variables are updated in real-time. Further, data from digital twin is also processed by physical objects to have better performance. Thus, the digital twin has two-way information flow. Simulation assumes virtual representation is similar to actual object but digital twin is an active replication of physical object due to two-way information.

Integration with Edge Computing

Edge devices monitor multiple smart objects, and digital twin of multiple IoT devices can be created by communicating with edge devices only, rather than monitored smart objects.

IoT devices are replicated in a digital twin and they both communicate with each other through edge computing. Edge devices monitor the IoT devices that can be accessed to make digital twin. Edge devices transfer data in real-time and response from digital twin will help edge devices monitor the IoT device efficiently as well as have better analytical models. This analytical model can make more efficient decision-making in complex scenarios.

Use-Case Applications

Multiple IoT applications can benefit from digital twin because of three reasons:

- It makes the smart objects more efficient
- Analytical model more trustworthy
- Provide prior testing and performance enhancement of IoT applications.

Once the digital twin approves the IoT application, each IoT device and analytical model, the application is deployed for actual work in a real environment. We will now discuss some use-case applications that may be benefited from digital twin technology in future.

Renewable Energy Sector

IoT enables the monitoring of windmills remotely and the application checks on their health and energy production. The sensors used on wind mills are wind speed, temperature, vibration, oil level, humidity and additional as per service requirements of the application. From sensor data, the application can predict maintenance before time to avoid failures as well as reduce operational cost. Further, the windmill operation can be adjusted as per current demand. Further, the storage of energy can be monitored. The decision of when to store energy and when to use it is very crucial. The stored energy then helps during peak hours of demand.

Figure 12.11: *Digital Twin of a Windmill*

A digital twin is created of a wind farm representing the physical environment in current conditions. The digital twin of a windmill is shown in *Figure 12.11*. The data from the sensors attached to the windmill is used to create the perfect digital twin. Digital twin identifies issues, monitors performance, and makes decisions in real-time.

Edge device monitoring wind farms acquire data from each windmill, and then analyze it to provide decisions in real-time. The edge device can work as an intermediary between the actual windmill and its digital twin. Digital twin of the farm is created by capturing real-time data from edge devices, and then updating the analytical model of edge devices in real-time to have optimized performance.

Once the performance of the application is optimized, the edge analytical model is deployed in the real-environment, ensuring efficient predictions.

Internet of Vehicles

The Internet of Vehicles (IoVs) consists of a network of vehicles, traffic lights, roadside units, buildings, and other entities in the environment. It enables efficient traffic management, self-driving vehicles, providing safety to individuals by real-time decision-making, as well as providing faster routes.

With digital twin, vehicles and other entities are represented virtually for experimental purposes. Using digital twin, the developer gets a sense of requirements in the analytical model. The application can be simulated, and tested in real-time environment before even actually implementing the physical object in real-time environment.

Digital twin is very helpful in determining scenarios in self-driving cars. Digital twin of vehicle may provide real-time feedback to the drivers, based on current conditions around the car ensuring safety. With digital twin, self-driving cars may be a reality ensuring maximum trust over the vehicle. Self-driving cars are automated; hence, it can provide efficient driving, safe driving, reduced emissions, and help incapable people in driving. Human errors cause accidents and the main causes of accidents are mobile phones while driving or not knowing the rules or being late. Accidents cause roadblocks. To avoid accidents, human errors, self-driving cars if designed may malfunction but will behave as per instructions.

Moreover, the road network can be virtually represented using digital twin. On road network digital twin, current traffic flow is generated with real-time data from the physical environment (sensors, camera, GPS). The traffic is modelled and visualized in real-time with the help of digital twin. This generates efficient analytical models that handle all possible scenarios and manage traffic congestion in real-time. The analytical model is capable of managing traffic signals, controlling speed of self-driving cars, changing routes of some traffic, all in real-time. With digital twin, the accuracy of decision-making increases, ensuring trust in the application.

Industry 4.0

Manufacturing devices are getting digital. They operate autonomously with the help of the Internet of Things. The machines are made smart with sensors and internet connectivity. The smart machines can now collaborate, and work efficiently as well as their work is monitored remotely, using Cloud or edge devices. The analytical model provides predictive maintenance, and optimizes the manufacturing process in terms of energy consumption and heat emissions.

Digital twin of these machines will help to observe the functioning of machines in real-time, and determine issues causing deteriorations. Further, creating digital twin of the whole manufacturing process consisting of digital twin of all machines and the network exchanging data, can help in providing more efficient data flow between processes, reduced cost and optimal usage of all machines. IF there is a change in the optimal environment, Digital twin detects it, takes a decision, generates an action as per its current decision and the action optimizes the manufacturing process and machines and the data flow in real time.

Basically, automating any physical object is robotics and digital twin is reliable as it provides visual representations of the real environment covering all conditions that a physical object may face in its life span. **Thus, digital twin is the future of IoT and edge computing covering many more IoT domains.**

Benefits

- Reduces downtime.
- Reduces operational costs.
- Provides remote access to physical objects.
- Requires real-time data to build and model, and provide real-time visualization as well as decision-making.
- Accurate analytical model.
- Provide faster deployments in the market.
- Easily detects complex problems.
- Ensures trust.
- Optimizes resource utilization.
- Energy-efficient.
- Ensures a safe environment.

Conclusion

Edge computing is evolving, and it is very beneficial for IoT applications that provide services in real time. Timeliness of the service makes the application trustworthy and increases user experience. In this chapter, we discussed PyTorch, 5G, Edge as a service, Real-time OS and Digital Twin. PyTorch is a python framework that provides tools for easy building of AI models. IT also has multiple frameworks for different types of edge computing requirements like PyTorch Mobile, AI Edge Torch, ExecuTorch and ONNX runtime. These frameworks optimize the model to speed up inference on edge devices like android-based smartphone and arm architecture-based embedded devices.

5G is a new generation of mobile communication that provides high speed and reliable communication. It supports edge computing by fast, and multi-way data communication. 5G and edge computing will open opportunities for drones and connected vehicles, to communicate large amounts of data with ultra-low latency and respond in real-time. Edge as a service is an opportunity for developers and enterprises to directly utilize hardware and software as a service from Edge Devices provided by third parties. This way the enterprise will be able to have fast deployment of the IoT application in the market with lower cost of development and maximized profits. Real-time OS provides special scheduling to latency sensitive tasks and prioritizes the tasks that are time-critical. Digital twin replicates actual physical objects from real-time data acquired from sensors attached to physical objects, and this is useful to make the application robust during development to have efficient performance after deployment.

Points to Remember

- PyTorch is a building block of ChatGPT that has gained a lot of attention these days, and Tesla's autopilot.
- PyTorch is created by Facebook AI research lab, and it is simple and easy to use. PyTorch efficiently handles dynamic computational graphs.
- The four PyTorch edge frameworks to deploy AI on edge devices are PyTorch Mobile, AI Edge Torch, ExecuTorch, and ONNX runtime.
- Strong GPU support to harness capabilities of parallel processing, and maximize GPU acceleration with optimized implementation of models.
- 5G has faster Internet Speed of 20 Gbps, compared to 4G which has 1Gbps speed.
- The 5G network follows Wi-Fi 6 wireless standard (802.11ax) that operates in 2.4 GHz and 5 GHz.
- 5G are of three types: Low-band that is 10 times faster than 4G network, mid-band 5G, and high-band 5G.
- Low-range Wi-Fi is able to penetrate walls and objects, but does not provide that much speed.
- If the devices are communicating with each other within walls, mid or high range 5G is the best option, and if communicating outside long distance, low range 5G is suitable.
- IoT will be easy to deploy using edge as a service without bothering about hardware deployment and hardware costs.
- Edge as a service is a ready-made edge cloud architecture, and the enterprise has to plug and play with sensor data and model design as well as pay only for whatever is being used as a service.
- A very important feature of edge as a service is ultra-low latency and ultra-high bandwidth network capabilities for delivery of data using 5G.
- Real-time OS (RTOS) also does context switching like any OS; however, the major difference is, it will execute requests based on priority.
- RTOS is highly beneficial for edge computing in an IoT application that deals with time-critical events.

- Digital twin represents physical objects virtually by gathering real-time data from physical objects continuously.
- Digital twin identifies issues, monitors performance, and makes decisions in real-time.
- Once the performance of the application is optimized using digital twin, the edge analytical model is deployed in the real-environment ensuring efficient predictions.

Multiple Choice Questions

1. PyTorch is:
   a. Easy to use for beginners
   b. Efficiently handles dynamic computational graphs
   c. Both a and b
   d. None of the above
2. A PyTorch edge framework that integrates PyTorch and TensorFlow:
   a. AI Edge Torch
   b. ExecuTorch
   c. PyTorch Mobile
   d. None of the Above
3. What does the ONNX runtime provide?
   a. Support to Windows only
   b. Interoperability
   c. Android-support
   d. Support only for arm architecture
4. Which of the 5G bands has mmWave?
   a. Low-band
   b. Mid-band
   c. High-band
   d. None of the above

5. Which wireless standard does 5G follow?
    a. Wi-Fi 7
    b. Wi-Fi 5
    c. Wi-Fi 6E
    d. Wi-Fi 6
6. Drones can be used to continuously and remotely inspect crops with the help of:
    a. Edge Computing
    b. 5G
    c. Edge Computing and 5G
    d. Edge Computing and 4G
7. Edge as a Service is:
    a. Edge-Cloud infrastructure as service
    b. Edge devices as services
    c. Cloud services at Edge
    d. Edge infrastructure with 5G as service
8. Real-time OS is:
    a. OS
    b. Version
    c. Kernel
    d. Thread
9. Digital twin is:
    a. Replica of physical object using real-time data
    b. Blueprint of physical object
    c. Static visualization
    d. Simulation

Answers

1. c
2. a
3. b
4. c
5. d
6. c
7. d
8. b
9. a

Questions

1. What is the difference between TensorFlow and PyTorch?
2. Discuss different frameworks of PyTorch Edge.
3. How does Edge Computing get efficient with 5G?
4. How augmented reality assistance will get efficient using 5G?
5. What is the need of Edge as a Service?
6. How edge as a service will benefit enterprises?
7. Why is Real-Time OS (RTOS) different from popular OS ? What are the different types of RTOS?
8. Discuss the benefits and challenges of RTOS.
9. How is a digital twin created? Explain with a use-case IoT application example.
10. How is digital twin different from simulation?
11. How will digital twin support the Internet of Vehicles?

Index

Symbols

A

B

C

D